THE KING'S BODY

The King's Body

Burial and Succession in Late Anglo-Saxon England

NICOLE MARAFIOTI

UNIVERSITY OF TORONTO PRESS
Toronto Buffalo London

Toronto Buffalo London
www.utppublishing.com
ISBN 978-1-4426-4758-9

Library and Archives Canada Cataloguing in Publication

Marafioti, Nicole, 1978-, author
The king's body : burial and succession in late Anglo-Saxon England/Nicole Marafioti.

(Toronto Anglo-Saxon series)
Includes bibliographical references and index.
ISBN 978-1-4426-4758-9 (bound)

1. Anglo-Saxons – Kings and rulers – Death and burial – Political aspects. 2. Anglo-Saxons – Politics and government. 3. Great Britain – Politics and government – 449-1066. 4. Great Britain – History – Anglo Saxon period, 449-1066. I. Title. II. Series: Toronto Anglo-Saxon series

DA152.M37 2014 942.01'7 C2014-900822-8

University of Toronto Press gratefully acknowledges the financial assistance of the Centre for Medieval Studies, University of Toronto, in the publication of this book.

University of Toronto Press acknowledges the financial assistance to its publishing program of the Canada Council for the Arts and the Ontario Arts Council.

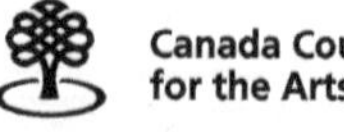

University of Toronto Press acknowledges the financial support of the Government of Canada through the Canada Book Fund for its publishing activities.

For my parents

Contents

Tables and Figures

Tables

Figures

Acknowledgments

This book could not have been begun or completed without the generous help of many colleagues and friends. Paul R. Hyams, Oren Falk, Thomas D. Hill, and Samantha Zacher offered prodigious insight and encouragement as I untangled the intricacies of medieval death and politics. Christopher Bailey, Cynthia Turner Camp, and Ionuţ Epurescu-Pascovici provided extensive, thought-provoking critiques of early drafts; and discussions with Andrew Galloway, Carol Kaske, Masha Raskolnikov, and Carin Ruff invariably inspired new avenues for exploration. The faculty and students at Trinity University have shown unwavering enthusiasm for my work, and Trinity's faculty research grants were vital to this project. My colleagues in the History Department have been especially helpful: John McCusker, Kenneth Loiselle, Aaron Navarro, and Joy Rohde offered valuable advice on my work in progress; and Don Clark, Anene Ejikeme, Alan Kownslar, Carey Latimore, David Lesch, and Linda Salvucci have been unfailingly supportive. I am indebted to Jeremy Donald, Amy Roberson, Tony Infante, and Eunice Herrington for their assistance in navigating maps, books, and all things administrative. I have also benefited enormously from the feedback I received from participants at conferences where I presented preliminary work, notably the International Society of Anglo-Saxonists, the Charles Homer Haskins Society, the International Medieval Congresses at Kalamazoo and at Leeds, the Fiske Conference on Medieval Icelandic Studies, and Cornell University's European History Colloquium. Conversations with Helen Foxhall-Forbes, Stefan Jurasinski, Dan O'Gorman, Lisi Oliver, Andy Rabin, and Elaine Treharne have been particularly stimulating, and Jay Paul Gates's expertise has been indispensable. It has been a genuine pleasure to work with Suzanne Rancourt at the University of Toronto Press, whose enthusiasm and professionalism have helped bring this project to fruition. Barb Porter saw the book safely through production, and the copy-editing skills of James Leahy and Bridget Cooley were most welcome as I prepared the final manuscript. Heartfelt thanks are also due to Dianne Ferriss, Tricia Har, Sarah Harlan-Haughey, Leigh Harrison, Curtis Jirsa, Johanna Kramer, Jessica Metzler, Jimmy Schryver, Colleen Slater, Misty Urban, Jennifer Watkins, and Sarah and James Disley. Finally, I am immeasurably grateful to Marcia and Robert Marafioti, Elise and Paul Yanon, Bea Fogelman, and Michael Paul Simons, who have endured more than their fair share of medieval exhumation, mutilation, and corpses. Their constant support and encouragement have made this book possible.

Abbreviations

Ælfric, CH I	Ælfric of Eynsham, *Catholic Homilies: First Series*, cited by homily and line
Ælfric, LS I and LS II	Ælfric of Eynsham, *Lives of Saints*, cited by volume, homily, and line
Alfred 5, VIII Æthelred 1.1, etc.	Anglo-Saxon laws: Liebermann, *Die Gesetze der Angelsachsen*, vol. 1, cited by code and chapter
ASC A	Bately, *Anglo-Saxon Chronicle: MS A*, cited by annal year
ASC B	Taylor, *Anglo-Saxon Chronicle: MS B*, cited by annal year
ASC C	O'Brien O'Keeffe, *Anglo-Saxon Chronicle: MS C*, cited by annal year
ASC D	Cubbin, *Anglo-Saxon Chronicle: MS D*, cited by annal year
ASC E	Irvine, *Anglo-Saxon Chronicle: MS E*, cited by annal year
ASC F	Baker, *Anglo-Saxon Chronicle: MS F*, cited by annal year
B., *Vita Dunstani*	Winterbottom and Lapidge, *Early Lives of St Dunstan*, cited by page
Bede, *HE*	*Ecclesiastical History of the English People*, cited by book and chapter
Bosworth-Toller	Toller, *An Anglo-Saxon Dictionary Based on the Manuscript Collections of the Late Joseph Bosworth*, cited by page

Byrhtferth, *Vita Oswaldi*	Lapidge, *Byrhtferth of Ramsey*, cited by page
De Antiquitate	Scott, *Early History of Glastonbury*, cited by page
De Miraculis Sancti Eadmundi	Thomas, *Memorials of St. Edmund's*, vol. 1, cited by page
EETS	Early English Text Society
Encomium	Campbell, *Encomium Emmae Reginae*, cited by page
JW	John of Worcester, *Chronicle*, vol. 2, cited by page
MS	manuscript
MR	Mercian Register, cited by ASC manuscript and annal year
PL	Migne, *Patrologia Latina*, cited by volume and column
S	Sawyer, *Anglo-Saxon Charters*, cited by charter number
Vita Ædwardi	Barlow, *The Life of King Edward*, cited by page
Whitelock, *EHD* I	Whitelock, *English Historical Documents*, cited by page and item number
William of Malmesbury, *GP*	*Gesta Pontificum Anglorum*, vol. 1, cited by book, chapter, and section
William of Malmesbury, *GR*	*Gesta Regum Anglorum*, vol. 1, cited by book, chapter, and section
William of Malmesbury, *Vita Dunstani*	*Saints' Lives*, cited by book, chapter, and section
William of Poitiers, *GG*	*Gesta Guillelmi*, cited by page

Table 1. Kings of England, 871–1087

King	Regnal dates	Royal dynasty/ Lineage	Son of	Kinship to previous king	Burial place
Alfred	871–899	West Saxon	Æthelwulf	Brother	Old Minster, Winchester Translated to New Minster, Winchester
Edward the Elder	899–924	West Saxon	Alfred	Son	New Minster, Winchester
Ælfweard	924	West Saxon	Edward	Son	New Minster, Winchester
Æthelstan	924–939	West Saxon	Edward	Half-brother	Malmesbury
Edmund of Wessex	939–946	West Saxon	Edward	Half-brother	Glastonbury
Eadred	946–955	West Saxon	Edward	Brother	Old Minster, Winchester
Eadwig	955–959	West Saxon	Edmund	Nephew	New Minster, Winchester
Edgar	959–975	West Saxon	Edmund	Brother	Glastonbury
Edward the Martyr	975–978	West Saxon	Edgar	Son	Wareham Translated to Shaftesbury
Æthelred II	978–1013 1014–1016	West Saxon	Edgar	Half-brother	St Paul's, London
Swein Forkbeard	1013–1014	Danish	Harald Gormsson	N/A	York Translated to Roskilde, Denmark
Edmund Ironside	1016	West Saxon	Æthelred II	Son	Glastonbury
Cnut	1016–1035	Danish	Swein Forkbeard	N/A	Old Minster, Winchester
Harold Harefoot	1035–1040	Anglo-Danish	Cnut	Son	Westminster Monastery Translated to St Clemens, London
Harthacnut	1040–1042	Danish/Norman	Cnut	Half-brother	Old Minster, Winchester
Edward the Confessor	1042–1066	West Saxon/Norman	Æthelred II	Half-brother	Westminster Abbey
Harold Godwineson	1066	N/A	Godwine	Brother-in-law	Unknown
William of Normandy	1066–1087	Norman	Robert II	Cousin (once removed)	Caen, Normandy

Table 2. Notices of kings' deaths and burial places in the Anglo-Saxon Chronicle

King	Alfred r. 871–899						Edward Elder r. 899–924						Æthelstan† r. 924–939						Edmund r. 939–946					
ASC manuscript	A	B	C	D	E	F	A	B*	C*	D*	E	F	A	B	C	D	E	F	A	B	C	D	E	F
Death place								x	x	x						x						x		
Burial place								x	x	x														
King	Eadred r. 946–955						Eadwig r. 955–959						Edgar r. 959–975						Edward Martyr r. 975–978					
ASC manuscript	A	B	C	D	E	F	A	B	C	D	E	F	A	B	C	D	E	F	A	B	C	D	E	F
Death place	x					x																x	x	x
Burial place				x		x																x	x	x
King	Æthelred II r. 978–1016						Swein Forkbeard r. 1013–1014						Edmund Ironside r. 1016						Cnut r. 1016–1035					
ASC manuscript	A	B	C	D	E	F	A	B	C	D	E	F	A	B	C	D	E	F	A	B	C	D	E	F
Death place			x	x	x	x															x	x	x	x
Burial place															x	x	x	x			x	x	x	x
King	Harold Harefoot r. 1035–1040						Harthacnut r. 1040–1042						Edward the Confessor r. 1042–1066						Harold Godwineson r. 1066					
ASC manuscript	A	B	C	D	E	F	A	B	C	D	E	F	A	B	C	D	E	F	A	B	C	D	E	F
Death place					x						x	x			x	x	x					x	x	
Burial place					x	x					x	x			x	x	x							

x = Death and/or burial place noted in the Anglo-Saxon Chronicle.

[shaded] = No annals for the king's reign or manuscript cuts off before the king's death.

* = Death and burial place noted only in the Mercian Register.

† = Ælfweard (r. 924) was not identified as a king in the Anglo-Saxon Chronicle and is omitted from this table.

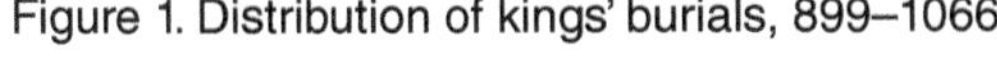

Figure 1. Distribution of kings' burials, 899–1066

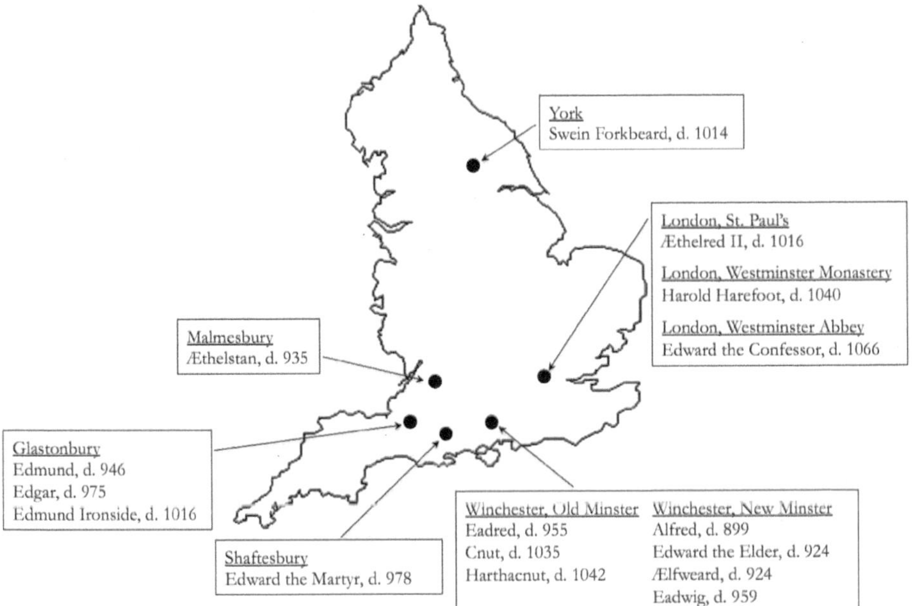

Figure 2. West Saxon dynasty, 865–1016

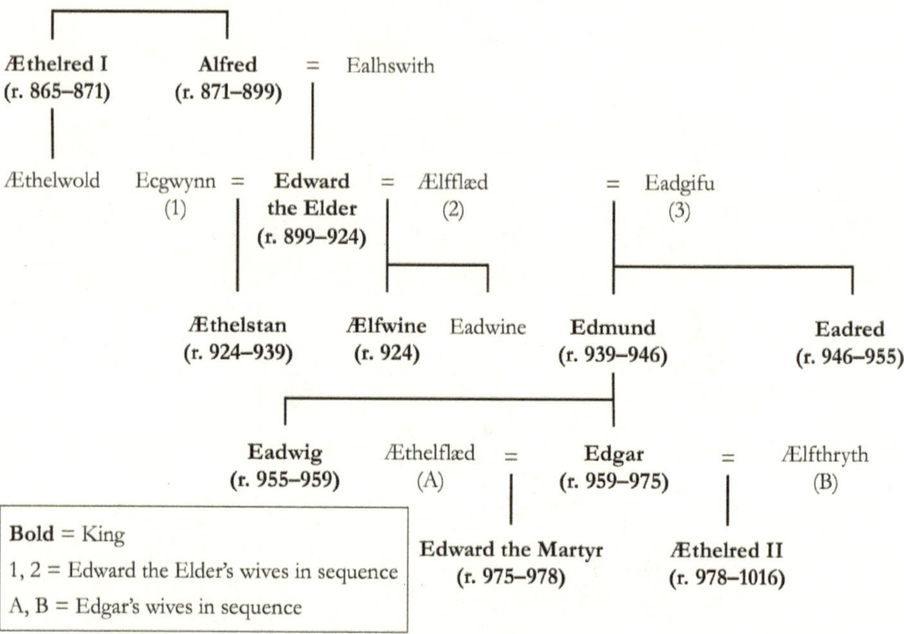

Figure 3. Kings of England, 978–1066

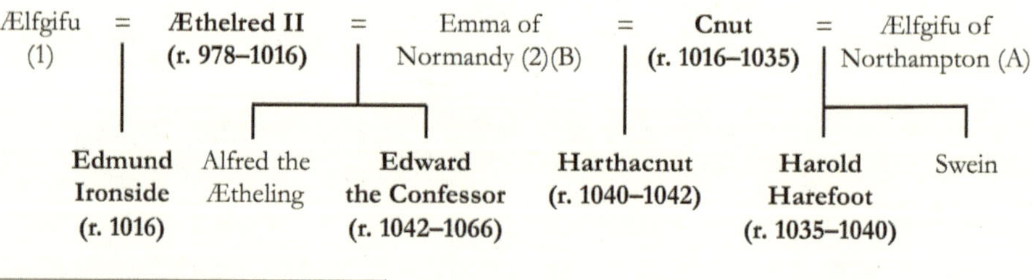

Bold = King of England
1, 2 = Æthelred's wives in sequence
A, B = Cnut's wives in sequence

THE KING'S BODY

Introduction: The Politics of Royal Burial in Late Anglo-Saxon England

On 5 January 1066, Edward the Confessor died in his palace at Westminster. A few years later, the king's anonymous biographer produced the following account of his burial:

> The funeral rites were arranged with royal expense and honour, as was fitting, and with the infinite mourning of all. They carried his blessed remains from his palace home into the church of God, and offered prayers and sighs along with the psalms, all that day and the following night. Meanwhile, when the day of the mournful celebration dawned, they blessed the funeral office they were to conduct with the singing of masses and relief of the poor. And so, the body was buried before the altar of St Peter the Apostle, washed in the nation's tears, in the sight of God.[1]

The author's foremost purpose in this passage was to illustrate the country's grief at the loss of its beloved king, but he incidentally provided one of the few existing descriptions of an Anglo-Saxon royal funeral. We learn from this passage that Edward's body was publicly carried into its burial

All Old English translations are my own, except where noted. Latin translations have been adapted from printed editions, where these exist; otherwise, translations are my own.

1 "Parantur ergo illa funebria regio, ut decebat, sumptu et honore, et cum omnium infinito merore. Deferunt eius felices exequias a domo palatii in aulam dei, precesque et gemitus cum psalmodiis celebrant tota illa die cum nocte succedenti. Orta interim die funeste celebritatis, decantatione missarum et recreatione pauperum officium beatificant perficiendi funeris, sicque coram altare beati Petri apostoli conditur corpus patrię lacrimis lotum ante conspectum dei"; *Vita Ædwardi*, 80–1. The *Vita* was composed in 1066 and 1067 by a monk of St Bertin: *Vita Ædwardi*, xiv–xxx and xliv–lix.

church, where mourners kept vigil until it was interred before the high altar the next day. We are told that the funeral office was accompanied by masses and the distribution of alms, all conducted with the honour – and expense – worthy of a king. We may also assume that a considerable number of mourners were present, including prominent laypeople who accompanied the body from the palace and clergymen who prayed and kept vigil over the royal remains. Yet while this excerpt provides an exceptionally detailed account of the burial of an eleventh-century English king, there were still aspects of the funeral that the author did not address. Who exactly was present? How was the body displayed? What sort of memorialization did the king receive afterwards? Although Edward's biographer showed considerable interest in the liturgical and processional aspects of the king's funeral, he found few of its mundane elements worth relating.

This silence is emblematic of most depictions of Anglo-Saxon royal death. Unlike Continental chroniclers, who regularly provided detailed accounts of rulers' funerals, tombs, and bodies, Insular authors shied away from explicit descriptions of their dead kings. Most pre-Conquest English texts offered few details about royal burial and memorialization, simply noting where a monarch died and where his grave was. However, despite their cursory treatment in contemporary writings, kings' funerals and tombs were not modest or obscure. As royalty, kings received privileged burial inside churches alongside abbots, bishops, and saints; as influential and wealthy Christians, they benefited from memorial masses and inclusion in monastic *libri vitae*; and as prominent political figures, they were provided tombs that advertised their exceptional earthly status.[2]

Although the details of individual royal funerals in tenth- and eleventh-century England must be pieced together from casual textual references, monastic records, and archaeological remains, this evidence indicates that kings' bodies and tombs were important political objects which were systematically evoked during periods of crisis and interregnum. At a time when hereditary succession was not guaranteed and few accessions went unchallenged, control of the royal corpse and its legacy offered potential successors a considerable strategic advantage. Rival political factions vied to dictate and deploy the memory of the last regime; aspiring rulers offered competing identities for the dead monarch and strengthened their own status by defining themselves in relation to the previous king. Some

2 Deliyannis, "Church Burial"; Brown, "Burying and Unburying," 242; Wright, "Royal Tomb Program," 229; Keynes, "*Liber Vitae*," 151–3; Gerchow, "Prayers for Cnut."

royal candidates portrayed their predecessor as a legitimizing ancestor, forging a close relationship with his remains by appearing prominently at his funeral and staging public rituals, such as acclamations and consecrations, in close proximity to his tomb. Those who had problematic relationships with the most recent ruler – illegitimate sons, for instance, or individuals who had contested the king's authority during his lifetime – displayed respect for the established royal dynasty by providing an honourable tomb but distanced themselves from the remains, burying the body outside of major political centres and holding their accession ceremonies far away from the grave. Conquerors and usurpers, by contrast, validated the displacement of existing regimes by depicting their predecessors as rightly deposed tyrants. In such cases, allegations of unlawful rule might be accompanied by the dishonourable or secret interment of the royal body, with the dead king's shameful burial confirming that he had not been a legitimate ruler.

These patterns of interaction were consistent through the tenth and eleventh centuries, indicating that royal remains – whether they were glorified, minimized, desecrated, or obliterated – could not simply be ignored. A ruler's corpse was a volatile symbolic object which needed to be carefully defined and controlled during moments of political crisis: just as a king's reign would be framed and interpreted by contemporary chroniclers, his body would be ascribed a particular identity in the days following his death and burial. Yet most written accounts were recorded in hindsight, after a new ruler had assumed power, and consequently give the deceptive impression that their assessments of recent kings were objective and universal. In the immediate aftermath of a monarch's death, by contrast, a number of competing identities for the dead king might emerge, each offering a different interpretation of his reign. A distant kinsman, for example, might portray the dead king as a legitimizing ancestor; a member of a rival dynasty might label him a tyrant; a widowed queen promoting her son's accession might remember him as a doting father or even a saint. Despite the cohesive retrospectives of contemporary narrative sources, the scattered evidence for kings' funerals and succession debates indicates that aspiring rulers fought to manipulate the royal legacy to their own advantage, using a particular interpretation of the body to buttress their claims to the throne. The royal corpse offered contenders a concrete connection with the previous regime – a connection which could provide an ideological justification for their accession and authority.

This book examines the ways in which the bodies, tombs, and memories of dead monarchs were used to advance the political interests of the living.

Focusing on the period between the death of Alfred the Great in 899 and the accession of William the Conqueror in 1066, the following chapters reconstruct what happened after a king's death and assess the political significance of the display, disposal, and memorialization of royal bodies. By investigating the ceremonial activity that accompanied royal death – or, in some cases, its conspicuous absence – this study aims to illuminate aspects of Anglo-Saxon political and mortuary ritual that are not immediately apparent in our extant sources and that have received little attention from modern scholars.

The starting point for this analysis is the corpus of contemporary and near-contemporary writings that cited royal deaths and burials. The various recensions of the Anglo-Saxon Chronicle often provide the earliest records of when kings died and where they were buried.[3] Their annals offer predominantly logistical information about royal death, however, and more extensive accounts can be found in contemporary prose – royal panegyrics, hagiography, and the occasional narrative passage in a charter or *liber vitae*.[4] Twelfth-century chronicles complement these pre-Conquest sources, and the works of John of Worcester and William of Malmesbury have proved especially valuable, as they were based in part on earlier writings that have not survived independently.[5] As vital as these sources are in illuminating political transitions, they present an uneven picture of royal death and burial in the later Anglo-Saxon period. Some rulers' deaths receive considerable attention while others' are treated briefly and superficially; many individuals are portrayed in a subjective or even propagandistic light, informed by the authors' biases and interests; and where some accounts provide complementary evidence, some contradict each other

3 I have relied primarily upon the Collaborative Edition of the ASC, under the general editorship of David Dumville and Simon Keynes, from which quotations are drawn (unless otherwise noted). I have also consulted the following editions and translations: Plummer, *Two Saxon Chronicles*; Whitelock, *EHD* I, 145–261 no. 1; Swanton, *Anglo-Saxon Chronicles*.

4 For example: the *Vita Ædwardi*; the *Encomium Emmae Reginae*; Byrhtferth of Ramsey's *Vita Oswaldi*; Abbo of Fleury's *Life of St Edmund*; the New Minster *Liber Vitae*. These texts are discussed at length in the following chapters.

5 For the Chronicle of John of Worcester, see: JW xvii–xx; Darlington and McGurk, "'Chronicon' of 'Florence,'" 185–96, especially 192–4; Gransden, *Historical Writing*, 143–8; Brett, "John of Worcester and His Contemporaries." For William of Malmesbury, see: William of Malmesbury, *GR* II, xvii–xlvi; William of Malmesbury, *GP* II, xix–liii; Southern, "European Tradition of Historical Writing," 253–6; Farmer, "William of Malmesbury's Life and Works"; Gransden, *Historical Writing*, 166–85.

outright. Accordingly, in addition to using medieval texts to reconstruct the circumstances surrounding royal burial, this book seeks to understand why contemporary authors represented and interpreted kings' deaths as they did.

Alongside the textual accounts of royal death and burial, this study draws upon material evidence from late Anglo-Saxon England and archaeological analyses of medieval burial practices. Although the tombs and physical remains of most pre-Conquest kings can no longer be identified with certainty, other English graves of the tenth and eleventh centuries offer templates for burial in this period.[6] Scholars such as Victoria Thompson, Dawn Hadley, and Jo Buckberry have examined the variety of burial practices used in later Anglo-Saxon England, assessing the wide range of acceptable funeral rites that are evident in the archaeological record and outlining the components of honourable Christian burial.[7] Andrew Reynolds's work on execution cemeteries, by contrast, has identified signifying components of deviant burial – such as physical desecration and interment in unconsecrated ground – which firmly distinguished condemned bodies from the remains of ordinary Christians.[8] These models of normative and deviant burial practices contextualize the royal burials I investigate in this project: the extravagance of kings' funerals is measured against the more modest graves of most Christian laypeople, while the occasional desecration of royal remains is comparable to the humiliating punishments inflicted on the bodies of condemned offenders.

As well as establishing a context for royal funerals and tombs, interpretations of the archaeological record have provided a broader framework for this analysis. Recent scholarship on early medieval burial practices has shown that the living created new identities for the dead through mortuary ritual, with funerals and graves offering survivors a precisely constructed memory of the deceased. Scholars including Guy Halsall, Martin Carver, Heinrich Härke, and Howard Williams have construed early medieval graves as "texts," through which the deceased were inscribed with

6 The notable exception is Edward the Confessor, whose tomb has been prominent at Westminster since his body was elevated in the mid-twelfth century.

7 Thompson, *Dying and Death*, especially 102–31; Hadley, "Burial Practices in Northern England"; Hadley, "Burial Practices in the Northern Danelaw"; Hadley and Buckberry, "Caring for the Dead"; Hadley, "Socially and Physically Distinctive."

8 Reynolds, *Deviant Burial Customs*; Reynolds, "Definition and Ideology." See also recent excavation reports for execution cemeteries: Hayman and Reynolds, "42–54 London Road, Staines"; Buckberry and Hadley, "Walkington Wold."

posthumous identities that could be "read" by living observers.[9] Prestigious graves represent the most conspicuous examples: Halsall, in his analysis of Merovingian royal burials, and Carver, in his work on the Sutton Hoo mounds, offer parallel models in which monumental tombs projected political authority and religious legitimacy at times of crisis.[10] This sort of interpretation is not restricted to elite burials, however. Even modest assemblages of grave goods could proclaim particular identities for the dead in pre-Christian and conversion-era burials, as Härke has shown, and the wide range of burial practices within superficially uniform churchyard cemeteries of tenth- and eleventh-century England likewise conveyed deliberate information about the deceased.[11]

Furthermore, as Howard Williams has noted, mortuary practices were part of a larger strategy of "selective remembering and ... active forgetting" in the early Middle Ages.[12] Williams regards ceremonial funerals and the composition of individual graves as mnemonic devices that instilled an identity for the deceased in the minds of observers – a model which, I suggest, pertains to the funerals and tombs of later Anglo-Saxon kings as well as to the graves of pre-Christian individuals. Like the remains of Edward the Confessor, the bodies of most tenth- and eleventh-century English kings were carried in funeral processions and displayed before their entombment in monumental churches and monasteries. Royal burials constructed a final image of the dead to be instilled in the memory of his subjects and survivors, confirming the dignity of the monarchy through a ritualized celebration of the dead king. This study contends that attempts to create and deploy royal memory were analogous to the process of ascribing identities to other categories of dead through mortuary ritual. In the immediate aftermath of his death, a king's legacy was anchored to the final treatment of his mortal remains.[13]

---

9 For instance: Halsall, "Burial, Ritual, and Merovingian Society"; Carver, "Early Medieval Monumentality"; Härke, "Cemeteries as Places of Power"; Williams, *Death and Memory.*

10 Halsall, "Burial, Ritual, and Merovingian Society"; Halsall, "Social Change around A.D. 600"; Halsall, "Childeric's Grave"; Carver, "Early Medieval Monumentality"; Carver, *Sutton Hoo.* Compare also: Effros, "Monuments and Memory"; Williams, "Prehistoric and Roman Monuments."

11 Härke, "Warrior Graves." For the variety of burial practices in Christian cemeteries, see: Thompson, *Dying and Death*, 102–31; Hadley and Buckberry, "Caring for the Dead"; Hadley, "Burial Practices in the Northern Danelaw."

12 Williams, *Death and Memory*, 2.

13 Compare Thompson, *Dying and Death*, 118.

Although royal funerals and graves drew on technologies of remembrance attested in the archaeology of conversion-era interments and churchyard cemeteries, the tombs of late Anglo-Saxon kings bore little resemblance to these types of burials. Both before and after the adoption of Christianity, kings were interred in extraordinary ways. The bodies of pagan rulers were often installed amid monumental earthworks, which distinguished their remains from those of the population at large.[14] From the earliest days of Christianity, Anglo-Saxon kings were buried inside churches, a prerogative denied to most of their subjects; and from the tenth century, when English Christians began systematically to seek consecrated churchyard burial, intramural tombs distinguished royalty from the ordinary laymen whose graves were exposed to the elements.[15] The situation of royal tombs in privileged intramural space associated dead kings with saints and ecclesiastics, the only other figures in England who were regularly interred inside church buildings.

Given the posthumous proximity of royal bodies and the remains of the spiritual elite, it is natural that these two groups came to share an aesthetic. As royal graves proliferated in churches and monasteries, kings' funerals and graves appropriated the visual vocabulary of saints' cults. Rulers' tombs, like saints' shrines, became prominent features of churches: they were coveted by ecclesiastical communities, became objects of popular reverence, and attracted the patronage of living royalty.[16] This is not to suggest that all tenth- and eleventh-century kings aspired to sanctity or were regularly identified as saints. Rather, saints' shrines and ecclesiastical graves provided archetypes for prestigious burial at a moment when an ideology of Christian kingship permeated English political thought. The tenth century saw a rise in royal anointing, the proliferation of spiritual

14 Effros, "Monuments and Memory"; Williams, "Cemeteries as Central Places"; Williams, "Prehistoric and Roman Monuments"; and above, n. 10. Compare also the monumental eighth- and ninth-century royal tombs at Repton: Biddle, "Cult of Saints," 18–22.

15 Intramural burial among Anglo-Saxon royalty is examined by Deliyannis, "Church Burial"; and compare Frankish churches crowded with graves of non-royal laymen despite ecclesiastical prohibitions: Effros, *Merovingian Mortuary Archaeology*, 201–12; James, "Merovingian Cemetery Studies," 43; Sapin, "Architecture and Funerary Space," 40. For the emergence of consecrated churchyards in tenth-century England, see: Gittos, "Anglo-Saxon Rites"; Hadley and Buckberry, "Caring for the Dead," 126–7; and compare the Continental developments outlined by Zadora-Rio, "Making of Churchyards," 12–13; Rosenwein, *Negotiating Space*, 178–81.

16 Below, chapter 1.

regulations in royal law, royal endorsement of monastic reforms, and the revival of cults of seventh- and eighth-century royal saints. It was in this context that kings adopted the funerary trappings of the most revered category of Christian dead.

The association between royal burials and saints' shrines went beyond superficial similarities. Patrick Geary has remarked that "relics were actually the saints themselves, continuing to live among men"; their bodies remained the locus of their miraculous and intercessory power.[17] The present study contends that an analogous phenomenon is evident in the earthly afterlives of rulers in the later Anglo-Saxon period, for like saintly relics, kings' corpses were invested with meaning and continued to exert influence among the living. Reverential activity provides one point of comparison between royal and saintly bodies. Like saints' shrines, kings' tombs attracted visitors and became destinations for seekers of sanctuary, and churches that housed a king's grave often benefited financially from this attention. In addition, the public reburial of royal corpses capitalized on the impact of spectacular display. Just as saintly translations highlighted the authority of the presiding bishop and exhibited the spiritual resources of the Church, the ceremonial relocation of kings' bodies emphasized the unique status of Christian rulers and the exceptional prestige of the monarchy.[18]

Still, it is the political functions of Anglo-Saxon saints' cults which are most useful in framing this study, for in addition to advancing the spiritual interests of the faithful, relics were frequently manipulated for mundane purposes. Alan Thacker, David Rollason, and Susan Ridyard have illuminated how relics were used to promote regional and national identity, how ecclesiastical communities benefited from their relationships with patron saints, and how royal saints in particular were used to enhance the monarchy's claims to divinely sanctioned authority on earth.[19] Other scholars, including Christine Fell and Catherine Cubitt, have examined the cults of royal saints who suffered violent deaths, noting how allegations of martyrdom

17 Geary, *Furta Sacra*, 124.

18 For the significance of early medieval saints' translations, see Thacker, "Making of a Local Saint."

19 Thacker, "Dynastic Monasteries"; Thacker, "*Peculiaris Patronus Noster*"; Thacker, "Chester and Gloucester"; Thacker, "*Membra Disjecta*"; Thacker, "Oswald and His Communities"; Thacker, "Making of a Local Saint"; Rollason, *Saints and Relics*; Rollason, "Relic-cults as Royal Policy"; Rollason, "Murdered Royal Saints"; Ridyard, *Royal Saints*.

might be used as a political weapon against a saint's living enemies.[20] In any of these scenarios, the saints' spiritual authority was paramount. Their connection with the divine made their memories and relics political commodities; when effectively manipulated by the living, they could be understood to reflect God's approval or displeasure. The removal of relics from a conquered territory, for instance, could signal a shift in divine favour; the ceremonial elevation of a royal saint might remind detractors that God had endorsed a reigning king; and ostensible responsibility for a martyrdom might cast a powerful magnate as the enemy of Christ.[21]

As will be demonstrated below, there are significant correlations between the political uses of saints' cults and the posthumous treatment of kings' bodies and legacies. Just as religious supplicants sought spiritual benefits by interacting with saintly relics, political figures advanced their secular ambitions by forging relationships with royal corpses.[22] Based on trends in royal burial practice during the tenth and eleventh centuries, the following chapters argue that kings' remains were regarded as embodiments of royal legitimacy and authority, much as relics were seen as manifestations of spiritual power and divine endorsement. Yet the manipulation of royal remains did not simply imitate the activity associated with saints' cults. Rather, the honourable treatment of royal and saintly bodies engaged a common discourse: once a corpse was invested with spiritual or political meaning, it would be treated in a particular, recognizable way. High-status lay corpses in pre-Christian and conversion-era England were disposed of with distinctive and politically significant sets of ritual practices – graveside feasting, interment with rich grave goods, cremation, or mound burial.[23] By the tenth and eleventh centuries, when demonstrative Christian behaviour was a component of royal authority and an indicator of social prestige, kings adopted the sensory and ritual aspects of saintly and ecclesiastical burial, identifying themselves in death with the Christian elite.[24]

---

20 Fell, "Anglo-Saxon Hagiographic Tradition"; Cubitt, "Murdered and Martyred Saints." See also Rollason, "Murdered Royal Saints."

21 Examples are provided in the sources listed above, nn. 19 and 20, and are discussed in the chapters that follow.

22 On cultivating relationships with saints, see Brown, *Cult of the Saints*.

23 Williams, *Death and Memory*; Williams, "Cemeteries as Central Places"; Lee, *Feasting the Dead*, 2–7.

24 For an overview of the shift between pagan and Christian modes of burial, see especially Boddington, "Final Phase Reviewed."

Nevertheless, however greatly the treatment of royal bodies might have resembled the superficial aspects of saintly relic cults, a ruler's death had predominantly secular rather than spiritual consequences. Interregnums could last months or even years, as rival candidates competed for the throne. Royal funerals provided an opportunity to ease the transition between regimes, offering a public forum for ritualized negotiation and consensus.[25] By staging ceremonial activity by the body or tomb of their predecessor, new and aspiring kings forged a symbolic link with their dynastic past. Whether their hereditary claims were real or imagined, candidates regularly construed themselves as the legitimate successor of a dead ruler by publicly demonstrating their reverence for his earthly remains. To some extent, this anticipates the political theory of "the king's two bodies," which Ernst Kantorowicz has identified in the funerary rituals of later medieval monarchs. This model distinguished between a mortal ruler and the transcendent body politic, which was assumed by a successor upon the death of a king.[26]

While Kantorowicz sees this theory epitomized by the lavish royal funerals that flourished in the early modern period, it is clear that kings' funerals were vital transitional moments during the early Middle Ages as well. The political considerations that informed the location and practical components of kings' burials have been illuminated in Janet Nelson's work on Carolingian royal funerals, which shows that burial was integrally connected with the process of succession and the assertion of royal authority.[27] Nelson notes that individuals who controlled a royal funeral gained a distinct political advantage in the ensuing succession debate, particularly at the expense of contenders who were relegated to a lesser role in the proceedings or excluded from the event altogether. Charlemagne's funeral, for instance, was overseen by his daughters while their brother was abroad; in the absence of their father's heir apparent, the princesses had their own royal candidate crowned.[28] A similar pattern is evident in the Ottonian Empire some two centuries later, when the funeral procession of

25 Below, chapters 2 and 3.

26 By Kantorowicz's reckoning, the earliest version of this theory in the Middle Ages appeared ca 1100: Kantorowicz, *King's Two Bodies*, especially 42–8.

27 Nelson, "Carolingian Royal Funerals," which assesses royal funerals from 741 through 888.

28 The brother was Louis the Pious, who reclaimed the throne once he returned to the kingdom: Nelson, "Carolingian Royal Funerals," 147–9.

Otto III was commandeered by Henry of Bavaria, Otto's kinsman and one of three competitors for his throne. Henry's impromptu participation in the funeral – he seized the royal regalia, carried the king's casket on his shoulders, oversaw the burial of his entrails, and made a generous donation to the burial church – highlighted his kinship with Otto and helped him overcome opposition to his accession.[29]

In England, descriptions of this sort of activity were minimal, and it is unclear why Anglo-Saxon authors were more reticent than their Continental counterparts when it came to chronicling royal death. One explanation may be that royal funerals were dominated by secular concerns and therefore of relatively little interest to the clerical authors committing recent events to parchment.[30] However, even ecclesiastical ritual got short shrift in English accounts when compared to Continental texts. Alternatively, chroniclers who wrote in retrospect, after the accession of a new ruler, may have been reluctant to draw attention to the succession debates that accompanied the previous monarch's burial, preferring to gloss over any political wrangling that might suggest a lack of consensus at the new king's election.[31] Or perhaps this silence should be attributed to the narrative style of the extant sources. The Anglo-Saxon Chronicle, which provides the greatest amount of contemporary information concerning kings' deaths and burials, is notoriously pithy, and it may be simply that texts which provided more elaborate accounts have not survived. Still, even twelfth-century chroniclers, who worked from a wider range of pre-Conquest source material, found little to embellish when it came to tenth- and eleventh-century royal funerals.

While any of these factors may have contributed to the lack of written evidence for royal death in Anglo-Saxon England, it is also possible that this textual silence derived from a sense of propriety, which discouraged contemporary authors from emphasizing royal mortality.[32] Once anointing

29 The episode is detailed in the *Chronicon* of Thietmar of Merseburg, book IV, chapters 50–3: Thietmar, *Chronik*, 166–70; Warner, *Ottonian Germany*, 187–90. For commentary, see: Bernhardt, "Henry II of Germany," 44–6; Buc, *Dangers of Ritual*, 83–4.

30 Nelson, "Carolingian Royal Funerals," 135.

31 For a comparable phenomenon in textual accounts of the Norman Conquest, see Otter, "1066."

32 It is telling that the only full description of an Anglo-Saxon king's funeral was written by a Continental author, who cast Edward the Confessor's death in strictly hagiographical terms: *Vita Ædwardi*, xliv–lix and above, n. 1.

had become an integral part of royal inaugurations, the king's body was recognized as God's instrument and the earthly manifestation of the body politic, invested with the authority to govern a Christian nation.[33] There was little doubt that all but the most saintly royal bodies would eventually be subject to decay, but kings were usually safely entombed by the time decomposition set in, sparing their subjects the spectacle of a vulnerable, mortal royal corpse.[34] This ideal may well have been reflected in the texts produced during this period, which described living kings and mentioned buried bodies, but rarely referred to anything in between.

Despite this silence, contemporary texts do offer some insight into royal death in tenth- and eleventh-century England. From the end of the ninth century, the Anglo-Saxon Chronicle provided a consistent, formulaic record of rulers' deaths. The annalists typically offered logistical information – the date of the king's death, the extent of his empire, or the length of his reign – and concluded by identifying the successor to the realm. The template for this formula appears in the obit for King Alfred, who died in 899:

> In this year, Alfred, Æthelwulf's son, died six days before All Saints' Day. He was king over all the English except for the part that was under Danish rule, and he held that kingdom a half a year less than thirty winters. Then his son Edward ascended to the kingdom.[35]

Conspicuously, there is no mention of Alfred's funeral or burial place. From 978, however, the entries began to list the location of the king's death and his grave with greater regularity.[36] Of the forty-two annals that

33 As articulated in VIII Æthelred 2.1. On royal anointing in the early Middle Ages, see the works of Janet Nelson: "National Synods," "Symbols in Context," "Inauguration Rituals," "Ritual and Reality," "Earliest Royal *Ordo*," and "Second English *Ordo*." See also Kantorowicz, *King's Two Bodies*, especially 13–14 and 42–8.

34 A comparable evasiveness about physicality is evident in a general reluctance among Anglo-Saxon authors to depict acts of eating and drinking: Magennis, *Anglo-Saxon Appetites*, especially 58–9. For descriptions of mutilated or decomposed bodies as shocking, see: O'Brien O'Keeffe, "Body and Law"; and below, chapter 4.

35 "Her gefor Ælfred Aþulfing, syx nihtum ær ealra haligra mæssan, se wæs cyning ofer eall Ongelcyn butan ðæm dæle þe under Dena onwalde wæs, 7 he heold þæt rice oþrum healfum læs þe .xxx. wintra; 7 þa feng Eadweard his sunu to rice"; ASC A 900 (*recte* 899). The obit also appears in BC 901, with an abbreviated version in DEF 901 (all *recte* 899).

36 The provision of this information was not limited to this period or to royal deaths, but it had now become a consistent feature of royal obits in the ASC. For an earlier example, see for instance ASC A 962.

describe rulers' deaths between 899 and 977, only seven entries (17 per cent) note where the king died and only five (12 per cent) mention where he was buried. Of the thirty entries from 978 to 1066, by contrast, nineteen (51 per cent) provide the place where the king died and eighteen (49 per cent) cite his place of burial.[37]

This textual attention indicates that the transportation and resting places of kings' corpses had become points of historical interest from the later tenth century. Although the movement of royal bodies to particular burial sites was surely not a new development, the chroniclers' increased focus on rulers' remains implies that funerals and funeral processions had begun to hold greater significance. Some of these journeys were in fact quite short: Æthelred II and Edward the Confessor were each buried in the church next door to the palace where they died.[38] Yet the Bayeux Tapestry's depiction of the Confessor's funeral suggests that even brief processions merited considerable ritual display, and the chroniclers' increasingly prominent references to sites of kings' death and burial may reflect a change in the degree or type of ceremonial activity that preceded royal interment.[39] Longer processions to more distant mausolea certainly allowed ample opportunity for funerary spectacle. Edward the Elder's corpse was carried approximately two hundred miles from Farndon to Winchester; Edmund Ironside's was carried over one hundred miles from London to Glastonbury; Harthacnut's was carried more than sixty miles from Lambeth to Winchester; and Harold Harefoot's was carried some sixty miles from Oxford to Westminster.[40] These journeys would have taken days or even weeks to complete, and an increase in ritual activity during the processions might explain the shifting focus of the Anglo-Saxon Chronicle entries. Perhaps royal burials generated broader public interest once autonomous Anglo-Saxon kingdoms were more firmly consolidated under a single English king,

37 See table 2.
38 Below, chapters 1 and 3.
39 Wilson, *Bayeux Tapestry*, 29–30.
40 The distribution of kings' graves is illustrated in figure 1. Shorter funeral processions included: Swein Forkbeard's fifty-mile journey from Gainsborough to York; Edmund's thirty-five mile journey from Pucklechurch to Glastonbury; Æthelstan's thirty-mile journey from Gloucester to Malmesbury; Cnut's thirty-mile journey from Shaftesbury to Winchester; Eadred's twenty-mile journey from Frome to Glastonbury; and Edward the Martyr's twenty-mile journey from Wareham to Shaftesbury. For maps and royal itineraries, see Hill, *Atlas of Anglo-Saxon England*.

whose death would have had greater consequences than the passing of a regional leader; perhaps ecclesiastical involvement in the funerals had escalated, sparking the interest of clerical chroniclers; or perhaps royal remains were now taken on lengthier tours around the kingdom before burial, a practice attested among Carolingian and Ottonian rulers, rather than delivered immediately to their grave.[41] In any case, a spectacular procession would have fixed a final, deliberate image of the dead ruler in the public memory.[42]

Where such recognizable elements of royal burial reinforced the dignity of the monarchy and emphasized the prestige of the individual king, there were also established ways to divest royal bodies of legitimacy, and a handful of late Anglo-Saxon rulers were purposely denied the rites and graves that their status should have merited. Rather, their bodies were desecrated, obliterated, or refused public burial by political opponents who appropriated the familiar symbolic vocabulary of criminal executions in their treatment of royal corpses. From the tenth century, there was an increasing emphasis on consecrated burial for Christians in good standing with the Church, while excommunicants and criminals were conspicuously excluded from hallowed ground: they were interred at execution sites and borderlands, well away from consecrated churchyards and the prayers of the pious.[43] Remains of the condemned might be crammed into

41 The body of Emperor Otto III (d. 1002), for instance, made at least nine ceremonial stops on the way to its resting place at Aachen; it is not impossible that the bodies of English kings were taken on similar tours of the realm. For Otto's funeral, see: Thietmar, *Chronik*, 166–70; Warner, *Ottonian Germany*, 187–90; Bernhardt, "Henry II of Germany," 44–6.

42 It is unclear how royal corpses were displayed before burial. Embalming, as attested on the Continent at this time, usually had the short-term objective of preventing decomposition before burial; similar efforts at preservation may have been employed in England. If so, embalming could have prolonged the illusion that a king's body was extraordinary, as Janet Nelson notes; "Carolingian Royal Funerals," 165. See also: Camp, "Incorruptibility of Cuthbert"; Thompson, *Dying and Death*, 21.

43 The exclusion of condemned bodies from consecrated burial was first decreed in II Æthelstan 26 in the mid-tenth century. For exclusion and other deviant burial practices, see: Reynolds, *Deviant Burial Customs*, especially the handlists of deviant burials in the appendices; Reynolds, "Definition and Ideology"; Reynolds, "Burials, Boundaries and Charters"; Effros, "Beyond Cemetery Walls"; Thompson, *Dying and Death*, 170–80. On consecrated burial, see: Bullough, "Burial, Community and Belief"; Gittos, "Anglo-Saxon Rites"; Hadley, "Burial Practices in Northern England"; Hadley and Buckberry, "Caring for the Dead"; Blair, *Church in Anglo-Saxon Society*, 463–7.

shallow or short grave-cuts, buried face down, interred together with other executed corpses, or mutilated before burial; in some cases, the body or body parts might be exposed, with hanged corpses left suspended on gallows and decapitated heads displayed on stakes.[44] Such posthumous treatment clearly differentiated the condemned from the rest of Christian society and may have been thought to impact the fate of the executed in the afterlife.[45] Moreover, these modes of burial affected how offenders were remembered by the living. Because their bodies were publicly desecrated, the condemned were indelibly identified as deviants who had been unworthy of honourable burial; they were cast out of the Christian community, deprived of intercessory prayer and pious memorialization.[46] Like executions themselves, deviant burials were demonstrative acts that were meant to be witnessed and interpreted.[47]

This penal context provides a backdrop for the exceptional fates of a number of usurped, conquered, or assassinated rulers of the tenth and eleventh centuries.[48] Instead of receiving royal funerals and prestigious graves, their bodies were mutilated, exposed, interred in unconsecrated ground, or even buried without memorialization by political enemies who aimed to recast their royal antagonists as sinful criminals. These rulers were not simply deprived of the royal tombs to which they were entitled; they were denied Christian burial altogether. This inversion of normative burial practice retrospectively cast aspersions on the legitimacy of the deceased, for by contemporary reasoning, a true king would never be equated in death with social and religious deviants. For the rulers who oversaw these acts of desecration and obliteration, the abuse of their predecessors' bodies was deliberate, spectacular propaganda: if their rivals

---

44 On execution cemeteries, see especially Reynolds, *Deviant Burial Customs*. See also: Reynolds, "Definition and Ideology"; Hadley and Buckberry, "Caring for the Dead," 128–30; Owen-Crocker, "Mutilation, Decapitation, and Unburied Dead"; Hayman and Reynolds, "42–54 London Road, Staines"; Buckberry and Hadley, "Walkington Wold."

45 Thompson, *Dying and Death*, 170–80; Effros, "Beyond Cemetery Walls"; Marafioti, "Punishing Bodies."

46 For excommunication as an implicit component of death sentences, see Treharne, "Unique Old English Formula," 195–7. The effects of excommunication on the survivors of the condemned are also discussed by Vodola, *Excommunication in the Middle Ages*, 8 and 20–4; Little, *Benedictine Maledictions*, 31.

47 For public execution as a signifying spectacle, see: Foucault, *Discipline and Punish*, 3–69; O'Brien O'Keefe, "Body and Law"; Richards, "Body as Text."

48 These are detailed below, in chapters 4 through 7.

were remembered as criminals, then their own accession could be portrayed as the righteous restoration of royal dignity rather than an illicit act of usurpation.

Significantly, however, these instances of desecration and obliteration appear to have backfired on their instigators. Medieval chroniclers denounced the abuse of royal bodies, concluding that they were anomalous manifestations of cruelty or barbarism. This study proposes the opposite: that this sort of dishonourable treatment deliberately engaged a familiar mode of physical discourse. The denigration of royal bodies drew on the symbolic vocabulary of criminal punishment, just as prestigious royal tombs adopted the outward signs of saintly or ecclesiastical burial. In itself, the shameful treatment of bodies must not have been exceptionally shocking, given the legislative concern with corporal penalties in the later Anglo-Saxon period.[49] Rather, it was the application of these punishments to royal bodies that inspired outrage. At a time when kings' bodies were transformed by consecration and interred after death with extraordinary funeral rites, the subjugation of a royal corpse to physical humiliation was enough to provoke outcry among contemporary authors. Because there was such a pervasive understanding of how a royal corpse ought to be treated, deviation from the norm met with controversy.

This book examines how modes of honourable and dishonourable burial were deployed in England from the death of Alfred the Great in 899 through the early years of the Norman regime, ca 1070. For much of this period, power was held by kings of the West Saxon dynasty, who claimed sole rulership over formerly independent Anglo-Saxon kingdoms and their subjects – variously labelled the *Angli Saxones*, the *gens Anglorum*, the *Angelcynn*, or the *Englisc*. However, the unity implied by such rhetoric often reflected aspirational ideals more than practical reality. Scandinavian settlement in the British Isles, royal intermarriage with foreign powers, and close contact with Continental kingdoms made for a more complex demography than self-proclaimed *Englisc* identity might suggest. Moreover, the West Saxon dynasty was frequently troubled by factional conflict, with nearly every royal succession in this period accompanied by a power struggle between competing heirs to the throne. While the Danish

49 Reynolds, *Deviant Burial Customs*, 1–33; Gates and Marafioti, *Capital and Corporal Punishment*.

conquest of 1016 and the Norman Conquest of 1066 loom large in the historiography of eleventh-century England, political crises spurred by contested succession were by no means exceptional.

Modes of royal burial varied with the political needs of each generation. The tenth century was characterized by intradynastic, West Saxon succession. From 899 through 1013, every ruler of England was a patrilineal descendent of Alfred the Great, with each king succeeded by his brother, son, or nephew. Although conflicts routinely emerged between members of the West Saxon royal family, power was concentrated exclusively within this lineage for more than a century. Between 1013 and 1066, by contrast, every royal succession was accompanied by a struggle between members of competing dynasties, as claimants with West Saxon, Danish, Anglo-Scandinavian, and Norman ties asserted their right to the kingdom.[50] Where members of a dead king's own dynasty typically sought to stress familial continuity in their bids for power in order to prove themselves more throne-worthy than any other kinsman, outsiders generally emphasized their break from the previous regime, sometimes going so far as to question the legitimacy of the displaced dynasty and its members. Significantly, however, a royal candidate's family heritage or national identity rarely proved an obstacle to accession. Danish and Norman rulers were accepted as lawful kings of England, regardless of their background. Although lineage and ethnicity were sometimes cited by English authors seeking to praise or critique a reigning king, these factors seem not to have influenced royal burial practice. Honourable funerals of eleventh-century rulers conformed to the norms established in the tenth century, whatever the ancestry of the deceased. Conversely, there is no indication that the desecration of royal bodies was motivated by ethnic prejudice or informed by foreign custom. In every case study presented below, the treatment of the royal body would have been familiar to each ruler's English subjects and within the scope of acceptable practice.

The following chapters reconstruct the political contexts of royal burial in late Anglo-Saxon England. The approach is thematic rather than chronological, and the book is divided into two parts. The first three chapters establish patterns for honourable burial in the tenth and eleventh centuries, tracing the rise of royal mausolea and examining how kings' bodies, funerals, and graves contributed to the political process of succession. The

50 See table 1 and figures 2 and 3.

remaining four chapters consider exceptions to these trends, with case studies that investigate the handful of instances in which royal bodies were desecrated, mutilated, obliterated, or minimized. Taken together, the evidence examined in both parts of the book indicates that royal burial practices did not develop linearly or adhere strictly to earlier exempla. Rather, kings and their survivors drew from a range of burial options and adapted existing practices as they addressed each new set of political circumstances. As a public spectacle which signalled the transition from one regime to the next, royal burial was a potent mode of political discourse at times of crisis and transformation.

1 Royal Tombs and Political Performance: New Minster and Westminster

The starting point for this study is the piece of information supplied most consistently in later Anglo-Saxon texts: the locations of kings' graves. The most prominent of these sites was Winchester's Old Minster. As a favoured mausoleum of the West Saxon dynasty, Old Minster had a sizeable collection of royal graves by the mid-eighth century and became an increasingly important ritual centre as its royal patrons emerged as England's dominant ruling family.[1] Located at the heart of Wessex, Winchester thrived as a royal and episcopal hub in the ninth century, and by the tenth century it was operating as the capital of the realm.[2] The ancient royal mausoleum at Old Minster thus allowed the city's cathedral church to double as a repository for dynastic memory, with its collection of prestigious tombs reinforcing the legitimacy and continuity of the West Saxon line.

It is remarkable, given this context, that royal burial shifted away from Old Minster in the tenth century. This move was initiated by Edward the Elder (r. 899–924), who opened his reign by building a large new church, known as New Minster, next door to Winchester's mother church. The king intended his foundation to supersede Old Minster as the kingdom's premier royal burial place, but the mausoleum faltered after Edward's own death;

1 The earliest Winchester burials cited in the Anglo-Saxon Chronicle belonged to Cynewulf (d. 786) and Æthelwulf (d. 858). The twelfth-century Winchester Annals listed other early kings buried at Old Minster: Cerdic (d. 534), Cenwalh (d. 672), Æscwine (d. 676), and Centwine (d. ca 686). In addition, the inscription on a sixteenth-century mortuary chest stated that the bones of Cynegils (d. 643) were contained inside. ASC ABCDE 755, ADE 855 and BCF 856; Luard, *Annales Monasterii de Wintonia*, 3–5; Yorke, "Foundation of Old Minster," 80; Biddle, "Development of an Early Capital," 246.

2 Biddle, "Development of an Early Capital."

only one later Anglo-Saxon ruler, Eadwig (d. 959), would be entombed there.[3] But neither did Edward's successors return to Old Minster for interment. In 955, Eadred was the last West Saxon monarch to be installed in the dynasty's ancestral mausoleum, and just two other pre-Conquest kings would be buried at Old Minster: the Danish conqueror Cnut in 1035 and his son Harthacnut in 1042. Other tenth- and eleventh-century rulers were interred in various and often unprecedented locations: Æthelstan (d. 939) at Malmesbury; Edward the Martyr (d. 978) at Shaftesbury; Swein Forkbeard (d. 1014) at York; Æthelred II (d. 1016) at St Paul's, London; Harold Harefoot (d. 1040) at the early monastery at Westminster; and Edward the Confessor (d. 1066) at his newly built Westminster Abbey. A small West Saxon mausoleum also emerged at Glastonbury, housing the tombs of Edmund (d. 946), his son Edgar (d. 975), and his great-grandson Edmund Ironside (d. 1016).[4]

These foundations all benefited from royal patronage, and some rulers likely designated them as burial churches during their lifetimes. The fact that their corpses were often transported a considerable distance for burial, carried to diverse locations rather than interred in the nearest church or well-established mausoleum, suggests a high degree of intentionality. The geographical dispersion of their graves indicates that kings and their survivors made deliberate decisions concerning location. The collective move away from Winchester's established necropolis seems to reflect a desire to differentiate the recent dead from their predecessors; the new mausolea of the tenth century firmly distanced their royal tombs from Old Minster's collection of prestigious graves. The shift may also have been guided by spiritual calculations, for if there were only a few royal tombs at a particular church, its inhabitants would be more prominent in the intercessory prayers of the resident religious community. A king entombed amid generations of his royal predecessors, by contrast, could claim only a fraction of the community's attention.[5]

Whether motivated by religious considerations or more mundane concerns, these changing burial patterns offer insight into the political afterlives of English rulers. While posthumous prestige had previously been generated in part by a body's proximity to established and successful ancestors, tenth- and eleventh-century royal tombs now projected status and

3 Edward's son Ælfweard was also buried at New Minster in 924 after a reign of just a few weeks: n. 19 and chapter 2, below.

4 See figure 1 for the distribution of these burials.

5 Hallam, "Royal Burial," 367–9.

legitimacy in their own right (no doubt assisted by the promotional efforts of religious communities eager to attract continued royal patronage). Conspicuously, this shift coincided with an increasing interest in royal sanctity. The Anglo-Saxons' predilection for posthumously sainting their rulers was especially pronounced from the tenth century, when cults emerged around the tombs of newly martyred or especially pious members of various royal dynasties.[6] The development of such cults was usually a matter of local concern in this period, as there was not yet an official process of canonization which required saints to be recognized by the pope.[7] This is not to say that claims of sanctity were treated lightly or casually. In addition to their value as spiritual intercessors, relics were lucrative business for churches and monasteries, and religious communities went to great lengths to increase the public profiles of their resident saints and to defend their own rights as custodians. Ruling monarchs appealed to public sentiment by cultivating relationships with their saintly predecessors, overtly demonstrating their piety while emphasizing that their ancestral line had attracted divine favour.

Although the number of royal saints in pre-Conquest England was unparalleled in Western Europe, only a small minority of later Anglo-Saxon kings attained this status. While individuals of royal blood had a better chance at sainthood than most laypeople, sanctity was never guaranteed. The pantheon of English royal saints consisted predominantly of nuns and widows, conversion-era monarchs, and the occasional martyred prince or king; very few acting rulers of the later Anglo-Saxon period were venerated as saints after their deaths.[8] Nevertheless, tenth- and eleventh-century documentary sources indicate that the remains of many contemporary, non-saintly kings were treated in much the same ways as saints' relics. Even if a ruler was never recognized as extraordinarily pious or posthumously identified as a holy intercessor, his corpse still might serve as a church's focal point, be translated and reburied in a public ceremony, become the object of exonerating or reverential pilgrimage, and generate revenue and status for the religious institution that housed it. Some kings may well have become objects of undocumented, localized, or short-lived

6 Ridyard, *Royal Saints*; Cubitt, "Murdered and Martyred Saints," 67.

7 Edward the Confessor was the first English saint to be canonized, in 1161. Before this, elevation and translation were the most effective ways for ecclesiastical authorities to demonstrate their endorsement of a cult: Scholz, "Canonization of Edward," 57; Thacker, "Making of a Local Saint"; Kleinberg, *Prophets in Their Own Country*, 26–31.

8 Ridyard, *Royal Saints*, 107; Cubitt, "Murdered and Martyred Saints," 67.

saints' cults, but the overall lack of evidence for spiritual devotion suggests that the above-mentioned practices were not straightforward manifestations of religious piety.[9] Instead, they reflect a broader understanding of how prestigious corpses were supposed to be treated. Although kings were almost invariably interred in churches, reverence was usually initiated by secular figures and attested only in incidental remarks; the lack of fuller accounts implies that such activity did not merit full documentation by clerical authors. However, by adopting the superficial indicators of sanctity – replicating the religious environment of saints' shrines and the ceremonial aspects of their cults – kings, their followers, and their heirs appropriated a familiar symbolic vocabulary to advance their own political ends, highlighting the extraordinary status of the monarchy by forcing a comparison between the treatment of royal remains and holy relics.

This chapter considers how these cult-like practices developed in two major religious foundations, each commissioned as a burial church by a king of the West Saxon dynasty. The first is Winchester's New Minster, built by Edward the Elder ca 901 as a mausoleum for his father Alfred and the rest of his immediate family. The second is Westminster Abbey, which Edward the Confessor commissioned in the 1050s to replace a more modest monastic complex. Both foundations were large, costly, and prominent in the landscape, and both were expressly constructed to house the remains of kings who, at the time of their death and burial, were not considered saints.[10] These building projects should be understood as sound spiritual investments in their own right, for the lavish patronage of a church might offset the inevitable sins of ruling a kingdom and improve a monarch's chance of salvation in the afterlife. It is significant, in this context, that the clergy began to regulate and standardize Christian burial in the tenth century, dictating for the first time where graves should be located and establishing the prerequisites that entitled a person to last rites and interment in consecrated ground.[11] By sponsoring new churches designed to serve the royal dynasty and its subjects in life and death, Edward the Elder and Edward the Confessor each signalled their endorsement of this expanding ecclesiastical monopoly over the physical remains of the Christian dead.

9 There might have been a saint's cult at the grave of King Edgar at Glastonbury, for example, but there is no pre-Conquest evidence for his sanctity: William of Malmesbury, *GR* ii.160.2–3; *De Antiquitate*, 134–5; and further below, chapter 2.

10 Edward the Confessor's survivors would identify him as saintly, but it is unlikely that he was making a case for his own sanctity when he began building, approximately fifteen years before he died.

11 See above, Introduction.

Yet the two Edwards' construction of large and expensive new mausolea suggests that they tailored church burial to suit their own needs, dictating how they would be interred and adopting the pervasive material and ritual vocabulary of saints' cults to convey a more worldly message. Whereas ordinary churches were provided with the relics of a saintly patron at the time of their foundation, theirs were designed to house not saints but kings. The centrepiece of each establishment in its first generation was the grave of a decidedly secular magnate, conspicuous in a setting that contemporaries would normally associate with high-ranking ecclesiastical tombs or saintly relics. This chapter contends that despite their surroundings and prominent placement, these royal bodies were not meant to draw religious veneration. On the contrary, the kings' documented requests for intercessory prayer confirm that they considered their souls to be vulnerable; New Minster and Westminster served to counteract that vulnerability. From an earthly perspective, however, these new establishments conveyed deliberate political messages about their patrons. By appropriating the trappings of sanctity and having their (and their families') remains installed in unambiguously Christian spaces, these kings used royal graves to reinforce the idea that they had been selected by God to rule. Each church was designed to inspire reverence for the king entombed inside, but this reverence was merited by his earthly status as a secular leader – not the extraordinary spiritual accomplishments that made a saint.

New Minster, Winchester in the Reign of Edward the Elder: 901–924

Winchester's Old Minster was founded ca 648 by King Cenwalh of Wessex.[12] Although the minster may have been established to serve an adjacent royal residence, there is little evidence that Winchester had much clout before the reign of Alfred (871–899), when it was developed into an administrative and defensive centre.[13] Old Minster, the city's mother church and episcopal see, benefited from the city's transformation: it held a near monopoly on Christian burial, housed the tombs of numerous West

12 Bede, *HE* III.7; ASC F 648. Burial around the church also began around this time: Kjølbye-Biddle, "Disposal of the Winchester Dead," 22; Kjølbye-Biddle, "Problems in Excavation and Interpretation," 101 and 105.

13 Winchester's history and its development under Alfred are discussed by: Biddle, "*Felix Urbs Winthonia*," 289–93; Biddle, "Development of an Early Capital," 237–52; Biddle, *Winchester*, 290–2 and 305–6; Yorke, "Bishops of Winchester," 108–14; Yorke, "Foundation of Old Minster"; Kjølbye-Biddle, "Disposal of the Winchester Dead," 224; Blair, "Minster Churches in the Landscape," 40–50.

Saxon kings, possessed a noteworthy collection of relics, and attracted frequent displays of royal munificence. Alfred himself was buried there in 899. Yet Old Minster had not been significantly renovated or expanded since its foundation, and it lacked the resources to fulfil the spiritual needs of a growing urban population.[14] By the first decade of the tenth century, two new religious houses had joined Winchester's mother church: Nunnaminster, founded by Alfred's widow, Ealhswith; and New Minster, built by Alfred's son, Edward the Elder. Nunnaminster originated as a small women's community with a modest endowment, but New Minster was built to rival Winchester's cathedral as the favoured church and mausoleum of the West Saxon dynasty.[15] Situated just north of Old Minster, Edward's foundation was an enormous, modern structure that dwarfed its older neighbour.[16]

Despite its grand scale, the details of New Minster's foundation remain sketchy. Later tenth-century accounts credited the project to Alfred, claiming that he intended to build a monastery for a favoured adviser, Grimbald of St Bertin, but died before construction had begun.[17] Alfred's involvement seems to be a product of later legend, however. The earliest grants to New Minster date to 901, two years after Alfred's death, and stated that Edward commissioned the church "for the salvation of my soul and for that of my honourable father, King Alfred."[18] Shortly thereafter,

14 Old Minster underwent substantial renovation in the later tenth century; before that, the only changes to the original building were a remodelled apse and the construction of an adjacent tower: Kjølbye-Biddle, "St Swithun's Day, 1093"; Sheerin, "Dedication of Old Minster."

15 For Nunnaminster, see Foot, *Veiled Women* II, 243–52.

16 Kjølbye-Biddle, "St Swithun's Day, 1093"; Kjølbye-Biddle, "7th Century Minster." Architectural parallels with seventh-century Anglo-Saxon and Continental churches are discussed by Gem, "Anglo-Saxon Buildings," 278–9; Pickles, *Texts and Monuments*, 141–2.

17 Quirk, "Winchester New Minster," 17–18; Grierson, "Grimbald of St. Bertin's."

18 "For mine saule hælo 7 mines ðæs arwyrðan fader Ælfredes cyninges"; S 1443. Compare also S 365 and S 366; and see Miller, *Charters of the New Minster*, xxvi. By the later tenth century, the date of New Minster's foundation was erroneously held to be 903: this was the date provided in New Minster's spurious dedication charter (S 370) and in ASC F, which recorded its foundation in the same year as Grimbald's death. Yorke, "Bishops of Winchester," 114–15; Biddle, "*Felix Urbs Winthonia*," 295–7; Biddle, *Winchester*, 313; Miller, *Charters of the New Minster*, xxv; Grierson, "Grimbald of St. Bertin's," 554–7. The precise dates of New Minster's foundation and Alfred's translation are uncertain; I consider the evidence for dating more thoroughly in a forthcoming article, "Seeking Alfred's Body."

Edward had Alfred's body exhumed from its original grave in Old Minster and reburied in New Minster. At least four more members of Alfred's immediate family would be interred there in the following decade, along with Grimbald, who died before the church was completed and was posthumously recognized as a saint.[19] New Minster also acquired the relics of St Iudoc, a seventh-century royal Breton saint whose community fled to Winchester from Ponthieu in 901 to escape Viking raids.[20]

It is not impossible that Edward was fulfilling an unrealized goal of his father's when he built New Minster; certainly, there is no reason to doubt that Edward sought the spiritual benefits of ecclesiastical patronage.[21] The rationale behind the placement of New Minster is less apparent, however. Why did Edward build his foundation on the very doorstep of Winchester's ancient mother church? Perhaps he intended to evoke Continental monastic complexes, which often consisted of multiple churches in close proximity, or perhaps the arrangement was meant to resemble the double minsters attested elsewhere in Anglo-Saxon England.[22] It is likely that Edward intended his minster as a gathering place or *burh* church, with its spacious interior designed to serve a growing congregation that Old Minster could no longer fully support.[23] Yet the lack of space between Old and New Minsters – the two were separated by mere feet – eventually caused problems. Later inhabitants of New Minster recalled that the walls were so close together that "there was scarcely a passage for one man between their foundations," and by the end of the tenth century, property disputes between

19 Royal burials continued at New Minster until shortly after Edward's death and included: Edward's mother, Ealhswith (d. 902); his brother, Æthelweard (d. 920 or 922); his son, Ælfweard (d. 924); and Edward himself. Miller, *Charters of the New Minster*, xxvi–xxvii; Biddle, *Winchester*, 314–15; Yorke, "Bishops of Winchester," 115. For Grimbald's death, see: ASC F 903 (*recte* 901); Grierson, "Grimbald of St. Bertin's," 554–7.

20 ASC F 903 (*recte* 901); and above, n. 18, for the dating of this annal.

21 Three early charters refer explicitly to Edward and Alfred's souls: S 365, S 366, and S 1443.

22 Quirk, "Winchester New Minster," 18; Blair, "Anglo-Saxon Minsters," 246–58. The concentration of ecclesiastical buildings in the south-east sector could also have been an attempt to create a spiritual enclave in an urban landscape, anticipating later tenth-century developments in the city: S 807, S 1376, and S 1449; Rumble, *Property and Piety*, 137; Biddle, "*Felix Urbs Winthonia*," 298 and 301; Quirk, "Winchester New Minster," 18.

23 New Minster covered more than twice the area of Old Minster, and its open nave contrasted with Old Minster's labyrinthine interior: Biddle, *Winchester*, 314; Biddle, "*Felix Urbs Winthonia*," 295–7 and 304; Kjølbye-Biddle, "St Swithun's Day, 1093"; Lapidge, *Swithun*, 336 and 374–6; Quirk, "Winchester Cathedral," 44–8.

Winchester's minsters required royal intervention.[24] Tensions may have been exacerbated by the fact that Edward appropriated Old Minster's lands to build his foundation.[25] The placement of New Minster may well have been perceived as an encroachment upon Winchester's bishops, for Old Minster's community remembered Edward as a "greedy king."[26]

Nevertheless, Edward's building program should not be interpreted as an act of royal hostility. Despite the architectural intrusion, both minsters remained favoured foundations and benefited from royal patronage.[27] Rather, Edward's establishment of New Minster may have been motivated by the changing nature of West Saxon kingship. Beginning with Alfred, the rulers of Wessex claimed authority over all the English, and this change in status was reflected in Winchester's ecclesiastical landscape. While Old Minster was the favoured foundation of the kings of Wessex, New Minster was designed to serve the kings of the entire Anglo-Saxon people.[28] Accordingly, instead of being entombed at Old Minster, among kings who had defended a relatively small kingdom from neighbouring rulers and hostile factions of their own family, the new *reges Anglorum Saxorum* would be interred in New Minster, a burial church created expressly for the new

24 "Vix unius hominis transitus inter ipsorum fundamenta haberetur." This complaint was recorded shortly after 1110, when New Minster relocated outside Winchester's city walls: Biddle and Quirk, "Excavations Near Winchester Cathedral," with text and commentary at 179–82. See also: William of Malmesbury, *GR* ii.124.1 and *GP* ii.78.2; Biddle, *Winchester*, 317. Edgar's intervention in a dispute between the Old and New Minsters is recorded in S 1449: Rumble, *Property and Piety*, 141; Quirk, "Winchester Cathedral," 64. Over the following two centuries, rivalry between the two foundations was expressed through competitive expansion and renovation of buildings, the increasing volume of their chanting and bell ringing, and the slighting of one another's saints: Biddle, "*Felix Urbs Winthonia*," 303; Quirk, "Winchester New Minster," 21 and 35; Biddle, *Winchester*, 317; Kjølbye-Biddle, "St Swithun's Day, 1093," 16–19; Lapidge, *Swithun*, 278–83; and further below.

25 S 1443 recorded Edward's acquisition of the site for New Minster, and additional grants are detailed in S 365 and S 366; other purportedly early grants are suspect: Miller, *Charters of the New Minster*, 12–17 and 26–34; Rumble, *Property and Piety*, 50–6; Rumble, "Edward the Elder," 231–4; Keynes, "West Saxon Charters," 1141–3.

26 "Rex avidus"; S 814. See also: Rumble, *Property and Piety*, 118; Rumble, "Edward the Elder," 244. For tensions between Winchester's bishops and the West Saxon kings ca 900, see: Rumble, "Edward the Elder"; Yorke, "Bishops of Winchester," 115–16; Yorke, "Foundation of Old Minster"; Thacker, "Dynastic Monasteries," 251.

27 Significantly, Winchester's tenth-century palace was located just forty metres west of Old Minster: Biddle, *Winchester*, 289–92; Biddle, "Development of an Early Capital," 237–48; Yorke, "Foundation of Old Minster."

28 Yorke, "Bishops of Winchester," 116.

dynastic order.[29] Winchester was already a regular stop on the royal itinerary, and Edward's prompt translation of his father's remains from Old Minster – the first step in the creation of the mausoleum – confirmed New Minster's status as a premier church of the kingdom, where festivals were celebrated, court was held, and the bodies of kings entombed.[30]

Given New Minster's prestigious origins, it is remarkable that there were initially so few well-known saints who might attract pilgrims. The foreign St Iudoc eventually generated a significant cult, but at the time of his serendipitous arrival in Winchester ca 901 – a result of Viking attack rather than English initiative – it is unclear whether his relics inspired much veneration.[31] Likewise, it was probably Grimbald's favoured status as Alfred's mass-priest, and perhaps his reputed involvement in the minster's foundation, that ensured his privileged burial place inside.[32] In neither case is there evidence for cultic activity at New Minster during Edward's reign.[33] A lack of cultic focus is likewise apparent in New Minster's dedication, which was attributed variously to the Holy Trinity, the Virgin Mary, St Peter, and the Holy Saviour in different tenth-century documents.[34] Although the

---

29 Thacker, "Dynastic Monasteries," 253. Under Alfred, the title "king of the West Saxons" was first changed to "king of the Anglo-Saxons," a trend which continued under Edward: he was styled *Anglorum Saxonum rex* in his 901 charter to New Minster, S 366. Keynes, "Edward, King of the Anglo-Saxons," 57–62; Keynes, "West Saxon Charters," 1147–9; Miller, *Charters of the New Minster*, xxvii. The prologue to New Minster's *Liber Vitae*, composed in the 980s, maintained that Edward founded the church "for royal purposes" [regalibus usibus]: Keynes, *Liber Vitae*, 31–2 and fol. 9r; Birch, *Liber Vitae*, 4; Wormald, *Making of English Law*, 170–1.

30 Biddle, "Seasonal Festivals"; Keynes, "West Saxon Charters," 1133. New Minster's ceremonial functions are discussed by Brooke, "Bishop Walkelin," 9.

31 On Iudoc's cult, see: Lapidge, "*Vita S. Iudoci*," 261–4; Quirk, "Winchester New Minster," 19. Iudoc's relics remained at Winchester, although the community at his home foundation of Saint-Josse claimed to have discovered them on the Continent in 977: Orderic Vitalis, *Ecclesiastical History* II, 158–9 and 366–7; Lapidge, "*Vita S. Iudoci*," 267–8.

32 Grimbald was cited as Alfred's mass-priest in the Old English preface to Gregory's *Cura Pastoralis*. Schreiber, *Regula Pastoralis*, 14–15 and 195.

33 Grimbald was translated in the 930s and again between 1057 and 1063; each saint had a Latin *vita* composed in his honour in the second half of the tenth century; and both were included in the Old English list of saints' resting places compiled in the early eleventh century: Grierson, "Grimbald of St. Bertin's," 539–40 and 558–9; Lapidge, "*Vita S. Iudoci*," 265–6; Liebermann, *Heiligen Englands*, 15; Rollason, "Lists of Saints' Resting-Places"; Rollason, "Shrines of Saints," 36; Biddle, "Cult of Saints," 11.

34 Biddle, *Winchester*, 313.

community would claim the relics of nearly one hundred saints by the eleventh century, it seems that saints' cults were not Edward's priority.[35]

The situation at New Minster may have been a deliberate departure from that at Old Minster, where saints were actively promoted and conspicuously enshrined.[36] If relics were intentionally downplayed at Edward's foundation in its first generation, Alfred's grave would have been better accentuated. In light of this prominent positioning and the general interest in royal saints in England at the turn of the tenth century, it is significant that neither Alfred nor other members of his family buried at New Minster were considered saintly: they were never identified as spiritual intercessors and did not become objects of religious devotion.[37] However, the treatment of Alfred's body during his son's reign mirrored the treatment of saints' relics, with its translation from Old Minster providing one point of comparison. As described in New Minster's *Liber Vitae*:

> After the completion of his monastic foundation, the most powerful king Edward, striving, for just reasons, to accomplish what he had long planned to do, wished to translate with worthy splendour the remains of his father Alfred, who had been committed to burial in Old Minster, to a shrine in his own building.[38]

The *Liber Vitae* indicated that Edward had been dissatisfied with his father's first burial at Old Minster because it lacked the grandeur that a ruler of his magnitude deserved; by contrast, Alfred's new grave in its new

35 For New Minster's relic collection, see: Birch, *Liber Vitae*, 159–63; Keynes, *Liber Vitae*, 105. Edward's apparent disinterest in saints' cults at New Minster distinguishes him from other Anglo-Saxon royalty, including his sister, Æthelflæd of Mercia, and his son, Æthelstan, who were both avid relic collectors: Thacker, "Dynastic Monasteries," 252–4 and 255–7; Rollason, "Shrines of Saints," 36; Rollason, "Relic-Cults as Royal Policy"; Yorke, "Bishops of Winchester," 116; Heighway et al., *Golden Minster*, 35–6; Thacker, "*Membra Disjecta*," 119–23; Thompson, *Dying and Death*, 15–18; Rollason, *Saints and Relics*, 153–4; Geary, *Furta Sacra*, 49–52; and further below, chapter 2.

36 For the placement of the reliquaries inside Old Minster, see: Biddle, "Cult of Saints," 11; Quirk, "Winchester Cathedral," 58.

37 Ridyard, *Royal Saints*, 116–21; Thacker, "*Peculiaris Patronus Noster*," 20–2; Thacker, "Dynastic Monasteries."

38 "Prepollentissimus denique rex . EADUUARDUS . post monasterialis suę fundationis perfectionem ... diu quod mente conceperat iustis quidem ex causis exequi moliens cineres sui patris . ALFREDI qui sepulturae mancipatus fuerat in ueteri coenobio . dignis cum apparatibus transferri uoluit in propriae ędificationis sacello"; Keynes, *Liber Vitae*, fol. 9r, and 31–2 and 81 for commentary.

foundation provided an appropriate degree of splendour. The Annals of St Neots noted that the king's tomb was made of the "most precious purple marble," and such a monument would have clearly reflected the prestige of its inhabitant.[39] A public translation with appropriate ceremony (*dignis apparatibus*) into this new, magnificent shrine would elevate Alfred to his rightful place of honour, ensuring that his remains could not be lost among the many tombs of saints, bishops, and earlier West Saxon kings.[40]

The language of the *Liber Vitae* implies that Alfred's translation to New Minster was no casual affair. Like other royal rituals, this was presumably a high-profile ceremonial event attended by secular magnates and clergy and witnessed by a broad segment of the local population.[41] Comparison may be made with descriptions of another near-contemporary royal translation. King Edmund of East Anglia, killed by Vikings in 869 and buried hastily during the ensuing chaos, was translated ca 915, when the local population – "not just the common people but the nobles as well" – built a new church for him "on a royal estate, to which they translated him with great glory, as was fitting."[42] Although Alfred's translation preceded Edmund's and the earliest written accounts of both events were composed decades after the fact, the parallels between the two events are informative: both kings were interred unworthily soon after their deaths, only to be translated later into newly built churches in royal centres. The greatest difference was that Edmund's translation was inspired by the miraculous

39 "Marmore porfiro pretiosissimo"; Dumville and Lapidge, *Annals of St Neots,* 99; and see also Stevenson, *Asser's Life of Alfred*, 143. This description surely refers to the tomb at New Minster, with which the twelfth-century author would have been familiar.

40 William of Malmesbury, who credited Alfred with the foundation of New Minster, offered a different perspective on the king's translation: according to the "nonsense of the canons" [deliramento canonicorum], Old Minster was haunted by Alfred's ghost until Edward put his remains to rest in the new church; *GR* ii.124.2.

41 Compare the crowd at New Minster's 966 refoundation, as tabulated by Rumble, *Property and Piety*, 65; and see also Biddle, "Seasonal Festivals," 57–63.

42 "Non solum uulgi sed etiam nobilium"; "in uilla regia ad quam eum ut decebat transtulit cum magna gloria"; Abbo, "Life of Edmund," 84. Abbo composed his *vita* ca 987. Ælfric of Eynsham produced an Old English rendition a few years later and offered a similar account of the translation. Edmund had first been buried "in great haste" [in swylcere hrædinge], but once peace was restored, "that suffering people then came together and honourably built a church for the saint. They then wanted to bear the holy body with the people's veneration and lay it inside the church" [þam geswenctan folce, þa fengon hi togædere / and worhton ane cyrcan wurðlice þan halgan … Hi woldon þa ferian mid folclicum wurðmynte / þone halgan lichaman, and læcgan innan þære cyrcan]; Ælfric LS II, 326.166–75.

revelation of his sanctity, whereas Alfred's was not. However, it is significant that neither king's translation was said to be initiated by ecclesiastical figures.[43] In Edmund's *vita*, the *uulgi* and *nobiles* came together to translate their long-dead ruler, building a church on their own initiative.[44] Even if this popular enthusiasm represents a hagiographical trope, it nevertheless implies that it was acceptable – even admirable – for a translation to be initiated by laymen.

Edward's removal of his father's body from Winchester's mother church may have been intended to tap a comparable degree of public enthusiasm, especially given his new foundation's emerging role as a *burh* church and local burial place. New Minster was exempt from Old Minster's near monopoly on Christian burial, meaning that Winchester's inhabitants might choose to be interred beside Edward's foundation rather than in the ancient churchyard next door; Alfred's translation would have solidified New Minster's credibility as a prestigious cemetery.[45] Yet the translation may have also helped assert royal influence in a city dominated by an increasingly powerful bishop.[46] By moving Alfred's remains out of Winchester's cathedral church and into his own foundation, Edward proclaimed royal ownership of the body – essentially liberating it from episcopal control.[47] In addition to serving Edward's political interests, the move had economic consequences as well. Alfred's will, preserved in New Minster's *Liber Vitae*, earmarked a sum of fifty pounds "to the church in which I shall rest"; his bequest may have followed his body out of Old Minster.[48]

---

43 For lay involvement in Edmund's early cult, see Cubitt, "Murdered and Martyred Saints," 63–5.

44 Abbo, "Life of Edmund," 84.

45 The earliest reference to this right dates to 1110, but Martin Biddle regards burial rights as an early and well-established privilege: Biddle, *Winchester*, 314; Biddle, "*Felix Urbs Winthonia*," 297 and 311n38.

46 The political use of royal burials by bishops is evident in later medieval examples: Wright, "Royal Tomb Program," 224–39; Spiegel, "Cult of Saint Denis," 53–8; Hallam, "Royal Burial," 363–4. Compare also Archbishop Dunstan's efforts to create a royal mausoleum at Glastonbury, examined in chapter 2.

47 It is relevant that Edward radically redrew the episcopal boundaries of Wessex early in his reign, creating new dioceses that reduced the jurisdiction of Winchester's bishops: Rumble, "Edward the Elder," 238–44. For relations between bishops and kings in this period, see: Giandrea, *Episcopal Culture*, 35–69; Yorke, "Bishops of Winchester"; Yorke, "Foundation of Old Minster."

48 "To þære cyrican þe ic æt reste"; S 1507, and see Keynes and Lapidge, *Alfred the Great*, 173–8 and 313. Different opinions on the value of this bequest are offered by: Smyth, *King Alfred*, 512; Thacker, "Dynastic Monasteries," 252.

Given Edward's infringement upon the cathedral's lands and revenues when he built New Minster, it is not surprising that he wished to install his father's body in a foundation that prioritized royal interests instead of leaving the remains of his predecessor in the power of a disenfranchised community. It is remarkable, however, that he imitated a well-established episcopal ritual in order to do so. Before the rise of papal canonization in the twelfth century, the process of elevation and translation – exhuming a body from its grave and placing it in a more prominent tomb or shrine, so that it was easily accessible for veneration – was the principal means of making a saint and establishing ecclesiastical control of his cult.[49] In addition to validating the sanctity of the person being translated, the public ceremony, often performed together with a church dedication, reinforced the authority of its episcopal officiant.[50] From an observer's standpoint, it was the presiding bishop who determined whether an individual was worthy of formal reverence by installing his relics in a new shrine. Yet at Alfred's translation, it seems that Edward was the one in charge, having ordered the ceremonial relocation of his father's remains, possibly in conjunction with the dedication of his new church.[51]

The ramifications of this event may be clarified by comparison with another, later royal translation: that of Edward the Confessor in 1163. Although the Confessor was the first English saint to be canonized by the pope, his translation was dominated by the king, Henry II, who physically lifted and moved the corpse with the help of his nobles while the archbishop and clergy stood by.[52] Leaving aside the Confessor's sanctity, the parallels with Alfred's translation are striking: both Henry and Edward the Elder arranged the public translation of a prominent predecessor, both presided over what would normally be an ecclesiastical ceremony, and both overshadowed the bishop's role in the proceedings. Edward adopted the superficial aspects of relic translations without ever identifying his

49 Thacker, "Making of a Local Saint," 72; Rollason, "Relic-Cults as Royal Policy," 100–1; Ridyard, *Royal Saints*, 110.

50 Thacker, "Making of a Local Saint," 65–9, and compare Alfred 5 for the bishop's role in church consecrations.

51 The cartulary of Hyde Abbey indicated that Alfred was translated as part of New Minster's dedication: Edwards, *Liber Monasterii de Hyda*, 83.

52 The translation took place in the midst of Henry's conflict with Thomas Becket, placing tensions between crown and mitre into high relief: Barlow, *Edward the Confessor*, 283–4; Barlow, *Thomas Becket*, 85, 95, and 296n14; Scholz, "Canonization of Edward," 56–7; Bozoky, "Sanctity and Canonisation," 182–4.

father as a saint, capitalizing upon the symbolic and sensory impact of ecclesiastical ritual to emphasize the unique status of this *rex Anglorum Saxorum*.

Perhaps the most politically significant element of this spectacle, however, is the fact that Alfred's translation coincided with a serious challenge to Edward's accession. In 899 or 900, shortly after Alfred's death, the Anglo-Saxon Chronicle recorded an uprising by Edward's first cousin, the ætheling Æthelwold:

> Then Edward, Alfred's son, acceded to the kingdom. And then Æthelwold, Edward's father's brother's son, seized the residence at Wimborne and at Twinham, against the will of the king and his councillors. Then the king rode with the army until he camped at Badbury near Wimborne. And Æthelwold remained inside the residence with the men who were loyal to him. And he had all the gates barricaded against him and said that he would either live there or die there. Then meanwhile Æthelwold stole away in the night and sought the Viking army in Northumbria.[53]

Æthelwold was the son of Æthelred, Alfred's brother, with whom Alfred had ruled jointly until Æthelred's death in 871.[54] Edward's military successes, along with his close kinship with Alfred, made him a leading candidate for the throne and allowed him to assert authority in Wessex from the time his father died. However, it would have been reasonable for Æthelwold, himself a king's son, to make a competing bid for the kingdom which might legitimately attract popular support.[55] He was confident enough to make a

53 "Þa feng Eadweard his sunu to rice. Þa gerad Æðelwald his fædran sunu þone ham æt Winburnan 7 æt Tweoxneam, butan þæs cynges leafe 7 his witena. Þa rad se cyning mid firde þæt he gewicode æt Baddanbyrig wið Winburnan; 7 Aðelwald sæt binnan þam ham mid þam monnum þe him to gebugon 7 hæfde ealle þa geatu forworht in to him 7 sæde þæt he wolde oðer oððe ðær libban oððe þær licgan. Þa under þam þa bestæl he hine on niht onweg 7 gesohte þone here on Norðhymbrum"; ASC A 900. ASC A provides the earliest version of this episode, as the annal was probably written between ca 915 and ca 930: Bately, *MS A*, xxxvi. The version found in ASC BCD 901 (*recte* 900) gave somewhat more credence to Æthelwold's claim: he was identified twice as *ætheling*, which emphasized his throne-worthiness, and the entry concluded with the Danish army in Northumbria submitting to him and receiving him as king. For ASC A's connection with the West Saxon house and the implications of these variants, see Whitelock, *EHD* I, 207 no. 1. For Æthelwold's uprising, see: Stafford, *Unification and Conquest*, 24; Keynes and Lapidge, *Alfred the Great*, 173.

54 See figure 2 for the West Saxon genealogy.

55 Æthelwold's seniority over Edward and the validity of his claim to the throne are discussed by Yorke, "Edward as Ætheling," 29–31. On the political tensions among

stand at Wimborne, which seems to have been home territory for his branch of the family; his ability to give Edward's army the slip there may attest to his strength in the region. But Wimborne was also distinguished by the fact that Æthelwold's father Æthelred was buried there, a point not mentioned in any of the Chronicle descriptions of the uprising.[56] It seems that Æthelwold considered the site of Æthelred's grave a position of particular strength from which to press his claim to the kingdom. Accounts of succession disputes on the Continent attest that royal candidates gained a distinct advantage when they could take control of their predecessor's corpse, and Æthelwold's actions indicate that this was the case in tenth-century England as well.[57] Even though Æthelwold was defeated and killed the following year, this early threat to Edward's authority provides an additional context for his prompt translation of Alfred's corpse. By claiming and celebrating his father's remains, Edward countered a challenger who used his own dead father as political capital. Funerary ritual was not Edward's only political tactic, of course. He continued his military efforts against his cousin until the latter's death in 903. He also married Æthelwold's niece, Ælfflæd, during the conflict, anointing her queen in a gesture meant to reconcile the warring branches of the West Saxon family.[58] Taken together, the marriage and the translation seem to have been carefully arranged to prove

Edward, his brothers, and his cousins in the final years of Alfred's reign, as well as the possibility that Edward was not Alfred's preferred heir, see Nelson, "Reconstructing a Royal Family," 62–6; but compare Yorke, "Edward as Ætheling," for an investigation of Alfred's efforts to ensure that Edward was his heir. Edward's own military initiative and accomplishments during Alfred's reign are described in the Latin Chronicle of ealdorman Æthelweard, a layman writing in the third quarter of the tenth century: Campbell, *Chronicle of Æthelweard*, 49.

56 Asser reported that Æthelred was buried at Wimborne Minster, as did ASC ADE 871 and B 872; ASC C 872 said that he was buried at Sherborne Minster, but no other sources made this claim. See also: Stevenson, *Asser's Life of Alfred*, 31–2; Keynes and Lapidge, *Alfred the Great*, 80; Whitelock, *EHD* I, 207 no. 1; Nelson, "Carolingian Royal Funerals," 133; Thacker, "Dynastic Monasteries," 250.

57 Nelson, "Carolingian Royal Funerals"; Halsall, "Childeric's Grave"; Buc, *Dangers of Ritual*, 83–4. This point is pursued further below, chapter 3.

58 The marriage probably took place in 900 or 901. Before this, Edward was joined with – though perhaps not married to – Ecgwyna, the mother of his eldest son and eventual successor Æthelstan. Despite Ælfflæd's probable consecration, her union with Edward appears to have ended before her death, allowing the king to enter into another politically advantageous union; it is possible that their marriage was dissolved on the basis of consanguinity, as the two were second cousins. Sharpe, "Dynastic Marriage," 81–2; Stafford, *Unification and Conquest*, 41–2; Nelson, "Second English *Ordo*," 367. Ælfflæd's identity as Æthelwold's niece is questioned by Yorke, "Æthelwold and the Politics of the Tenth Century," 70.

the legitimacy of Edward's rule, mitigating tensions within the royal family while reinforcing Edward's own position as the rightful heir to Alfred's undisputed authority.

A final event should be included in this discussion of Edward's use of Alfred's body: an exonerating pilgrimage to the king's tomb, undertaken by an outlawed thief in order to secure his pardon. The episode is related in the Fonthill Letter, a unique Old English document which detailed two thefts committed by a thegn named Helmstan and the ensuing fate of his property at Fonthill.[59] Addressed to Edward, the letter was composed by ealdorman Ordlaf, Helmstan's sponsor at confirmation and his chief advocate in a case that spanned more than two decades.[60] It opened by recounting the circumstances of the first theft, detailing Ordlaf's own successful appeal to Alfred on Helmstan's behalf, some twenty years earlier. Ordlaf then reviewed the particulars of his godson's second offence, committed early in Edward's reign, in an attempt to ascertain Helmstan's legal standing and confirm the status of his land at Fonthill. We are told that after his second theft, Helmstan was declared an outlaw by the king and had his property confiscated by a royal reeve. At this point in the narrative, Ordlaf recalled an earlier exchange with Edward:

> Then Helmstan sought your father's body (*lic*) and brought a seal (*insigle*) to me, and I was with you [Edward] at Chippenham. Then I gave the seal to you, and you removed his outlawry and gave him the estate to which he has withdrawn.[61]

No further context is provided for this episode, but there was evidently a direct correlation between Helmstan's visit to Alfred's body and Edward's

59 The Fonthill Letter is S 1445 and listed as items 23–6 in Wormald, "Handlist of Anglo-Saxon Lawsuits," 247–81; I have used the edition included in Brooks, "Fonthill Letter," 302–6. I follow the chronology proposed by Simon Keynes, who places the letter's composition ca 920, some two decades after the events it described; the events themselves spanned the reigns of Alfred and Edward and probably occurred over an eighteen-month or two-year period between 897 and 901: Keynes, "Fonthill Letter," 56 and 94–5.

60 I follow Keynes and Brooks in accepting Ordlaf as the author: Keynes, "Fonthill Letter," 55–6; Brooks, "Fonthill Letter," 313–14. For the possibility that a third party was involved in its composition, see: Boynton and Reynolds, "Author of the Fonthill Letter," 91–5; Gretsch, "Fonthill Letter: Language, Law," 668–89.

61 "Ða gesahte he ðines fæder lic 7 brohte insigle to me, 7 ic wæs æt Cippanhomme mit te. Ða ageaf ic ðæt insigle ðe. 7 ðu him forgeafe his eard 7 ða are ðe he got on gebogen hæfð"; Brooks, "Fonthill Letter," 305. See also Marafioti, "Seeking Alfred's Body."

reversal of his sentence. An interpretation of this exchange requires some explanation of what the *insigle*, or seal, actually was. Although the word sometimes referred to a wax seal, the Old English *insigle* could also indicate a sealed document, perhaps one which confirmed Helmstan's visit or attested that he had sworn an oath at Alfred's tomb.[62] Helmstan's actions may have been analogous to the legal practice of vouching a dead man to warranty, that is, testifying that a transaction was legitimate after one of its participants had died.[63] Yet as a repeat offender, Helmstan would not normally have been trustworthy enough to clear his name with an oath.[64] Alternatively, the presentation of a royal writ or seal could have been an ordinary way to initiate pleas or judgments, for a similar action is attested in a handful of other Anglo-Saxon lawsuits.[65] However, Helmstan's case is unique in two ways. First, the seal was acquired at the body of a dead ruler; and second, its presentation prompted an immediate judgment by the king rather than further legal action by royal subordinates.

A less troublesome explanation for Helmstan's visit to Winchester is that he was seeking sanctuary. Under Alfred's law, an offender could be granted a period of respite if he took refuge from his pursuers in any "church which the bishop consecrated," with the peace (*frið*) extended to the church's outlying buildings.[66] The Fonthill Letter made no explicit mention of a church or consecrated ground, but this episode is centred around Alfred's remains, which were undoubtedly inside one of Winchester's minsters at the time.[67] The direct mention of the body (*lic*) is significant in this context, for instead of referring euphemistically to the king's tomb or to his burial church, Ordlaf unambiguously cited a corpse as Helmstan's objective. This choice of vocabulary forces a comparison with saintly relics – dead bodies or body parts which could provide

62 The earliest English sealed writs date from Edward the Confessor's reign, but a similar format may have been used earlier: Harmer, *Writs*, 12–13 and 92–3; Roberts, "Anglo-Saxon Seals," 134–5; Bosworth-Toller, 596.

63 This possibility is presented by Simon Keynes, with the process of vouching a dead man to warranty cited in Ine 53 and II Æthelred 9.2: Keynes, "Fonthill Letter," 88–9.

64 Furthermore, Ordlaf was not available to vouch for him after the second theft, as he had been after the first: Keynes, "Fonthill Letter," 65, 76, 80, and 84–5.

65 Wormald, *Making of English Law*, 157–8.

66 "Cirican, ðe biscep gehalgode"; Alfred 5. See also Alfred 2; Ine 5–5.1; Wormald, *Making of English Law*, 280.

67 It is unclear whether these events occurred before or after Alfred's translation to New Minster: Keynes, "Fonthill Letter," 78 and 88n143. Neither scenario is incompatible with my argument here.

an effective refuge for asylum seekers.[68] Given the ever-increasing royal interest in sanctuary rights during the tenth century and Edward's cultivation of his father's tomb around the year 900, it is conceivable that the king had declared Alfred's body a site of sanctuary.[69]

This possibility becomes more compelling when Helmstan's case is set beside a series of eleventh- and early twelfth-century writs requesting pardon for offenders who sought the tomb of Edward the Confessor.[70] In the earliest of these documents, Westminster's abbot and monks requested that the sheriff "have mercy on and forgive" an offender who "sought out Christ and St Peter and the grave of King Edward."[71] The earliest Latin writ, composed in the first quarter of the twelfth century, reveals even closer parallels with the Fonthill account:

> Abbot Gilbert and the community of Westminster greet all the faithful of the king of the English. Know that this Jordanus has sought the altar of St Peter and the body (*corpus*) of King Edward, and therefore we pray that he receive liberty of his body and the king's peace.[72]

This formula mirrors Ordlaf's reference to Alfred's *lic*, expressly stating that the offender sought Edward's *corpus*.[73] It is not impossible that Helmstan's *insigle* was attached to a writ with a comparable Latin formula, which Ordlaf rendered into Old English with the phrase *gesahte he ðines fæder lic*, "he sought your father's body."[74] In any case, these writs reveal a

68 Hall, "Sanctuary of St Cuthbert," 425; Hyams, *Rancor and Reconciliation*, 94–5.

69 Anglo-Saxon sanctuary practices are discussed by: Hurnard, *King's Pardon for Homicide*, 3–4; Hyams, *Rancor and Reconciliation*, 95–6; Hall, "Sanctuary of St Cuthbert," 431.

70 Most of these writs predate the Confessor's 1161 canonization. In addition to those quoted below, the relevant texts are: Mason, *Westminster Abbey Charters*, nos. 239 (English, 1085 x 1117), 248 (Latin, 1121 x 1136), 272 (Latin, 1138 x 1154), 274 (Latin, 1138 x 1157), and 279 (Latin, 1158 x 1174).

71 "Gemiltsie and forgif"; "gesoht to Criste and Sancte Petre and Eadwardes Kynges rste [*sic*]"; Mason, *Westminster Abbey Charters*, no. 238 (1086 x ca 1104).

72 "Gilbertus abbas et conventus Westmonasterii omnibus fidelibus Regis Anglie salutem. Sciatis quod iste Jordanus altare Sancti Petri et corpus [*sic*] Regis Edwardi requisivit, et ideo precamur ut libertatem sui corporis et pacem regis habeat"; Mason, *Westminster Abbey Charters*, no. 240 (1105 x 1117).

73 By contrast, examples dating from the 1130s onward cite Edward's grave (*sepulcrum Regis Edwardi*) as the outlaws' destination.

74 On the Fonthill Letter as evidence for lay literacy, see: Gretsch, "Language of 'the Fonthill Letter'"; Gretsch, "Fonthill Letter: Language, Law."

process of sanctuary and pardon analogous to Helmstan's case some two centuries earlier: after his outlawry, an offender sought the grave of a non-saintly king; he received a seal or sealed document confirming that he had visited the body; and the appropriate authorities consequently rescinded his punishment.

Ordlaf's casual reference to the *insigle* and its presentation to the king hints that this was not a singular event that required further explanation, even though the exchange may have occurred as much as twenty years earlier. Furthermore, Edward's quick pardon of a repeat offender – reversing his reeve's judgment, annulling his own pronouncement of outlawry, and forgiving Helmstan's apparent violation of his requisite loyalty oath – suggests that his decision was based on a policy of conditional forgiveness.[75] This implies that a procedure for confirming visits to Alfred's tomb had been established in the opening years of Edward's reign and that outlawed offenders were one group who might benefit from this system.[76]

Whether or not comparable policies had been in place before 899, it is clear that Alfred's body was invested with an array of symbolic meanings in the wake of his son's accession. Edward's decision to make his father's remains a focal point in his new foundation, removing Alfred's corpse simultaneously from episcopal control and from the traditional burial place of West Saxon rulers, demonstrates how completely a king might dictate the conditions of royal burial. Without declaring his father a saint – even implicitly acknowledging in his charters that Alfred's soul needed whatever help it could get – Edward made his tomb a centrepiece of New Minster, a founder's grave around which a mausoleum for the kings of a new, united Anglo-Saxon kingdom might emerge. Moreover, the unrestricted burial rights granted by New Minster to the inhabitants of Winchester allowed them to choose burial around the city's royal minster instead of its episcopal church – *ad potentes* as well as *ad sanctos*.[77]

75 This anticipates VIII Æthelred 1.1, which allowed an offender the opportunity to redeem a *botleas* offense – i.e., an offense that cannot be remedied with compensation – if he "should seek so great a sanctuary that the king grant him life on account of it" [swa deope friðsocne gesece þæt se cyningc him þurh þæt feores geunne]. If, as Keynes suggests, Helmstan's greatest offence was violating his oath to the king (which may have included a promise not to commit theft), the *botleas* offence of treachery was in fact pardoned after his visit to Alfred's tomb: Keynes, "Fonthill Letter," 81–4 and 87–8; Wormald, "Charters, Law," 165; Hurnard, *King's Pardon for Homicide*, 1–5.

76 I pursue this argument elsewhere: Marafioti, "Seeking Alfred's Body."

77 Compare Effros, *Merovingian Mortuary Archaeology*, 211.

Despite Edward's efforts and intentions, New Minster's royal necropolis did not endure. Ælfweard, Edward's son, was buried in New Minster less than a month after his father in 924, but the only other king to be buried there was Edward's grandson Eadwig, in 959. Although it failed to attract new royal burials in the interim, it is clear that Edward's mausoleum remained a recognizable source of political legitimacy some sixty years after its foundation. Even without professions of sanctity, Edward's careful positioning of Alfred's tomb made New Minster a witness to the prestige and endurance of the West Saxon line of English kings.

Westminster in the Reign of Edward the Confessor: ca 1050–1066

The *Vita Ædwardi*, the earliest account of the life and death of Edward the Confessor (r. 1042–1066), was effusive in its praise of the king's construction of Westminster Abbey during the 1050s and 1060s.[78] The anonymous author provided a detailed account of the monastery's lavish refoundation under Edward's patronage, including an extensive description of the new Romanesque building. Writing shortly before the king's death, he attributed Edward's efforts to an exceptional devotion to St Peter: "especially because of his love of the Prince of the Apostles, whom he revered with unique and special affection, he chose to have his burial place there."[79] Such a sentiment is characteristic of the *Vita*, which was commissioned by Edward's queen and intended in part as a tribute to her husband's piety, but other near-contemporary sources also ascribed the king's interest in Westminster to religious motives.[80] So generous a gift might improve one's chances of salvation in the next life, and there is no reason to doubt that Edward anticipated a spiritual reward for his endowment of the monastery.[81]

---

78 On the dating of the work, see *Vita Ædwardi*, xiv–xxx; and above, Introduction.

79 "Potissimum autem ob amorem principalis apostoli, quem affectu colebat unico et speciali, eligit ibi habere sibi locum sepulchri"; *Vita Ædwardi*, 44–5.

80 ASC CD 1065 praised Edward's patronage of Westminster, "which he himself built out of love for God and St Peter and all God's saints" [þe he sylf getimbrode Gode to lofe 7 Sancte Petre 7 eallum Godes halgum]. The Westminster monk Sulcard provided a more elaborate account of Edward's motivations in his *Prologus de construccione Westmonasterii*, a history of the foundation composed between ca 1076 and ca 1085: Edward had planned to undertake a pilgrimage to Rome but was dissuaded by his subjects, who feared chaos in his absence; the king honoured St Peter with a new church at Westminster instead. Scholz, "Sulcard," 68–9 and 90–1.

81 This logic is implicit in the bequests to churches which appear regularly in Anglo-Saxon wills; and see also Bethurum, *Homilies of Wulfstan*, 248.

Yet mundane concerns are also evident in the king's enthusiastic patronage of Westminster, and its refoundation is tellingly similar to Edward the Elder's commission of New Minster a century and a half earlier. Like its Winchester counterpart, the Confessor's Westminster was designed from the outset as a royal foundation that would house a new mausoleum, with its patron's tomb as a focal point. Furthermore, it quickly became a locus for political activity and popular worship within the emerging economic and administrative capital of the kingdom, and its large size and sophisticated architecture meant that it would soon overshadow London's episcopal centre at St Paul's.[82] Edward the Confessor, like Edward the Elder, wanted his new church to proclaim the authority, wealth, and prestige of the monarchy, even as it advertised his personal piety.

Unlike his namesake, however, Edward the Confessor did not establish an entirely new foundation for his burial church. Westminster was a working monastery with an illustrious history before it attracted the Confessor's attention.[83] According to the abbey's later tradition, the first church on the site was established in the early seventh century at the request of King Æthelberht of Kent, who wished to complement his London see of St Paul's with a foundation dedicated to St Peter.[84] Westminster enjoyed the intermittent patronage of Anglo-Saxon rulers thereafter, and King Edgar granted the foundation in the tenth century to Archbishop Dunstan, who installed monks in place of its community of regular clergy.[85] Despite this

82 For Westminster's size, see Fernie, *Architecture*, 154–6.

83 Accounts of its earlier history were first produced at the abbey in the late eleventh century: Harvey, *Westminster and Its Estates*, 20–2 and 372; Mason, *Westminster and Its People*, 2–3; Scholz, "Sulcard," 65.

84 This story was first attested by Sulcard, who claimed that the original church had been miraculously consecrated by St Peter. Bede claimed that the church was conceived by Æthelberht but endowed by the East Saxon king Sæberht and his wife, who were later thought to be buried there. On Westminster's foundation legends, see: Bede, *HE* II.3; Scholz, "Sulcard," 64–6 and 72–4; Harvey, *Westminster and Its Estates*, 20–1; Mason, *Westminster and Its People*, 1–3.

85 Earlier royal patrons included Offa of Essex (r. 694–709), Offa of Mercia (r. 757–796), Edgar (r. 957–975), Æthelred II (r. 978–1016), Cnut (r. 1016–1035), and Harold Harefoot (r. 1035–1040). The earliest foundation housed a community of secular clerics, and there is no evidence of a monastery before Archbishop Dunstan obtained the church and some of its estates from Edgar. The community later dated its establishment as a monastery to 958, while Dunstan was bishop of London; but the refoundation may be more accurately dated to 970, when he was reforming other houses as archbishop of Canterbury. Mason, *Westminster Abbey Charters*, 1; Mason, *Westminster and Its People*, 4–17; Harvey, *Westminster and Its Estates*, 20 and 22–3; Scholz, "Sulcard," 66–8; Rosser, *Medieval Westminster*, 13.

royal and episcopal attention, Westminster supported only a modest community of a dozen monks by the mid-eleventh century.[86] Although the monastery had a comfortable endowment, Edward's biographer lamented that its residents could only just feed themselves when the king began his patronage.[87] It was from this purported poverty that the king rescued St Peter's, according to the *Vita Ædwardi*:

> The king, therefore, being devoted to God, gave his attention to that place, for it neighboured the famous and rich city and was also a sufficiently sunny spot, surrounded with fertile lands and green fields and near the channel of the principal river, which bore abundant merchandise of wares of every kind for sale from the whole world to the town on its banks ... Accordingly he ordered that out of the tithes of all his revenues, the building of a noble edifice should be started, worthy of the Prince of the Apostles, so that he would make God well-disposed towards him after the transitory course of this life, both for the sake of his piety and for the gift of lands and ornaments with which he intended to ennoble that place ... There was no weighing of the costs, past or future, so long as it proved worthy of, and acceptable to, God and St Peter.[88]

Although the author emphasized Edward's love of God and St Peter in this passage, Westminster's proximity to a thriving economic hub – the "famous and rich city" of London – was also listed as an advantage, and the king's burial church quickly became a prominent landmark in a highly trafficked area.[89] The building lived up to the promise of this location, for

86 Mason, *Westminster and Its People*, 9; William of Malmesbury, *GP* ii.81.1.

87 *Vita Ædwardi*, 44. Barbara Harvey calculates that in 1042, Westminster was worth about £80 annually: "In comparison with other English monasteries of this period, it was in fact neither poor nor rich"; *Westminster and Its Estates*, 24.

88 "Intendit ergo deo deuotus rex locum illum, tum uicinum famose et opulente urbi, tum satis apricum ex circumiacentibus fecundis terris et uiridantibus prediis atque proximo decursu principalis fluuii, a toto orbe ferentis uniuersarum uenalium rerum copiosas merces subiecte ciuitati ... Precipit deinde ex decimis omnium redituum suorum initiari opus nobilis edificii, quod deceret apostolorum principem, quatinus propitium sibi pararet deum post huius uitę cursum labilem, et pro gratia pietatis suę, et pro oblatione prediorum et ornamentorum quibus eundem locum disponit nobilitare ... Nec impensa siui impendenda pensantur, dummodo deo et beato Petro dignum et acceptum probetur"; *Vita Ædwardi*, 44–5. On Edward's endowment of Westminster, see: Harvey, *Westminster and Its Estates*, 24–5; Mason, *Westminster and Its People*, 16–17.

89 Mason, *Westminster and Its People*, 9–10; Mason, "Site of King-Making," 57; Rosser, *Medieval Westminster*, 14–16.

the new Westminster became the largest and most architecturally ambitious foundation in the British Isles, on par with the greatest Continental churches of its day.[90] Like Edward the Elder's enormous and modern New Minster, Edward the Confessor's Westminster was unparalleled by local churches and would have stood out among the nearby urban structures.[91]

Although the Confessor chose to patronize an established monastery instead of creating a separate foundation, he did not simply expand or renovate the existing monastic complex. Rather, he commissioned a completely new building for the monks of St Peter's and arranged for the old monastery to be demolished.[92] The *Vita Ædwardi* attributed this decision to Edward's desire not to disturb the prayers of the monks with construction, but this does not sufficiently explain why the king sought out a seventh-century foundation only to abandon its existing buildings.[93] It is likely that he had a twofold intention for the site. On the one hand, cultivation of Westminster wrote Edward into the history of a prestigious foundation with conversion-era royal roots. On the other, a new architectural monument distinguished him from his ancestors. Just as Edward the Elder maintained his dynasty's presence in Winchester while removing his immediate family from the ranks of West Saxon rulers, Edward the Confessor, in adopting Westminster, participated in a tradition of patronage that linked him to the earliest Anglo-Saxon kings while singling himself out among his predecessors as the most extravagantly generous of St Peter's benefactors.

90 Westminster's dimensions were comparable to those of the imperial cathedrals of Mainz and Speyer, and its architecture closely resembled the abbey of Jumièges, whose Norman abbot was involved in Westminster's construction: Fernie, *Architecture*, 154–6; Fernie, "Edward the Confessor's Westminster," 143–4 and 150; Gem, "Romanesque Rebuilding," 45–55; Mason, *Westminster and Its People*, 13–14; Mason, "Site of King-Making," 59–60; Brooke, "Princes and Kings as Patrons," 130–2; Barlow, *Edward the Confessor*, 230–2; *Vita Ædwardi*, 45–6.

91 William of Malmesbury reported that Westminster was "built using for the first time in England the style which almost everyone now tries to imitate at great expense" [illo compositionis genere primus in Anglia edificauerat quod nunc pene cuncti sumptuosis emulantur expensis]; *GR* ii.228.6. For the novelty of Westminster's Romanesque architecture in England and its influence on later buildings, see: Gem, "Resistance to Romanesque Architecture"; Gem, "Romanesque Architecture of St Paul's"; Mason, *Westminster and Its People*, 13.

92 Gem, "Resistance to Romanesque Architecture," 133–4; Gem, "Romanesque Rebuilding," 37–8 and 46.

93 *Vita Ædwardi*, 46.

Where Westminster's monastic community thrived as a result of Edward's initiative, the new house posed a threat to the heretofore premier church of London: St Paul's cathedral. Another conversion-era foundation, with a bishop's seat and a community of regular clergy, St Paul's boasted popular saints' cults and lay adjacent to London's royal palace.[94] Edward shifted his activity away from the city's cathedral, establishing a residence next door to Westminster and adopting the complex as his preferred royal centre.[95] Perhaps this move was motivated by a desire for distance from London's episcopal see; or perhaps an association with the reformed monks of St Peter's may have brought the monarchy more spiritual prestige than a relationship with the secular clergy of St Paul's.[96] It is significant, however, that Edward's father, Æthelred II, was buried at St Paul's, which had served as his chief administrative centre in the final years of his reign.[97] Whereas earlier kings – including Edward's half-brother Harthacnut, his grandfather Edgar, and Edward the Elder – reinforced the solidarity of their dynastic lines by having themselves buried near their fathers, the Confessor chose to distance himself from his own father's tomb.[98] Æthelred's legacy was troubled by usurpation and invasion, and Edward perhaps believed that burial at St Paul's would have associated him with a reign that had been widely, if retrospectively, condemned.[99]

Still, Edward did not opt to be buried with his immediate predecessor either.[100] His half-brother Harthacnut (r. 1040–1042) was interred at Old Minster, and although Edward had reigned jointly with Harthacnut and been crowned in close proximity to his remains, he was not interested in a Winchester burial of his own. It is possible that by the 1050s, Edward sought to distance himself from the Anglo-Danish branch of his family.[101]

---

94 As at Winchester, competition between the two establishments soon emerged. The greatest point of contention was Westminster's claim to be independent of St Paul's episcopal authority: Mason, *Westminster and Its People*, 9 and 260–2.

95 This shift to Westminster as a royal centre had begun earlier in the eleventh century: Mason, *Westminster and Its People*, 11–12 and 14.

96 For monastic and regular clergy, see: Cubitt, "Images of St. Peter"; Foot, *Veiled Women* I, 96–104.

97 Below, chapter 3. Edward's genealogy is illustrated in figure 3.

98 Compare Karkov, *Ruler Portraits*, 164.

99 For Æthelred's decreasing popularity, see Keynes, "Declining Reputation." His reputation may have been rehabilitated somewhat during Edward's reign: Keynes and Love, "Earl Godwine's Ship"; and below, chapter 3.

100 Harthacnut's grave is discussed at length below, chapter 3.

101 Mason, "Site of King-Making," 59; and below, chapter 3.

It seems more likely, however, that Edward saw little practical advantage in associating himself with his father or brother. Because he was a member of the West Saxon dynasty, the Confessor's royal credentials were not in doubt, and by the time he began work at Westminster, his authority was well established; he was able to advertise the exceptional status of the monarchy with a pious display of wealth rather than by association with a dead predecessor. This message would have been particularly important in the early 1050s, when the most substantial threat to the king's authority came not from a royal rival but from Godwine, the earl of Wessex. Godwine had risen to power under Cnut, and by Edward's reign, his family controlled an enormous amount of land and wealth; his daughter, Edith, married the king in 1045, and his son Harold would assume the kingdom in 1066. Despite these promising connections with the royal house, Godwine rebelled against Edward in 1051 and was exiled with his sons. He reclaimed his family's English holdings and re-established their authority the following year.[102]

Given Godwine's extensive influence in Wessex and his munificent patronage of Winchester's minsters, it seems no coincidence that Edward's investment in Westminster coincided with Godwine's revolt and subsequent return to England.[103] A handful of authentic writs attest that royal endowment had begun by 1051, and construction probably commenced around the same time.[104] Unlike the Winchester minsters, which had profited substantially from Godwine's generosity, Westminster, under Edward's sole sponsorship, would exclusively support royal interests. Edward's ostentatious expenditure, which simultaneously demonstrated his devotion to God and his vast disposable wealth, should be understood as an attempt to reassert his royal status in the face of an increasingly powerful aristocratic family.[105] The foundation of Westminster also coincided

102 This conflict was triggered by Edward's appointment of Robert Champart as archbishop of Canterbury, which the Godwines opposed: Mortimer, "Edward the Confessor," 8–12. Edward repudiated Edith during this period, but she was reinstated as queen the following year when her father returned to power: Stafford, *Emma and Edith*, 262–6.

103 The Godwines patronized Old and New Minsters during and after the earl's lifetime, while Edward's interest in the Winchester minsters was concentrated toward the early years of his reign: Karkov, *Ruler Portraits*, 163–4.

104 No contemporary sources specify when building began, but a series of writs issued ca 1051 seem to be the earliest authentic grants to St Peter's: Gem, "Romanesque Rebuilding," 33–4; Mason, *Westminster and Its People*, 13; Harmer, *Writs*, 294, nos. 71–9.

105 Edward's lavish ornamentation of Westminster is described in the *Vita Ædwardi*, 114–15.

with the Confessor's cultivation of imperial imagery, which increased after 1053.[106] Representations of Edward on coins and seals, modelled on Continental and Byzantine imperial portraits, diverged markedly from earlier depictions of English rulers and accentuated the king's authority.[107] This reconception of traditional royal iconography complemented Edward's departure from recent trends in royal burial and his construction of an imperial-style church on a Continental scale, located at the new economic and administrative heart of his kingdom.

If Edward's construction of Westminster was part of a broader program to emphasize the uniqueness of royal authority, however, it is remarkable that the new foundation was not designed as a more extensive royal necropolis. Unlike Continental royal mausolea such as Speyer and Saint-Denis, or the minsters of Winchester, Westminster was intended to house Edward's tomb alone. No royal predecessors were translated there, and he had no children who might eventually join him; even his wife, Edith, was endowing her own burial church at Wilton while her husband was rebuilding St Peter's.[108] Edward evidently planned to be interred by himself, surrounded by the community's saints.[109] Nevertheless, when he died, Westminster did not yet house any other graves or full-body relics to

106 It is perhaps significant that this change followed the deaths of Edward's mother Emma in 1052 and Godwine in 1053: Jones, "*Anglorum Basileus*," 103 and 105; Mason, *Westminster and Its People*, 15–16; Mason, "Site of King-Making," 58; Stafford, *Emma and Edith*, 268.

107 Karkov, *Ruler Portraits*, 157–60; Jones, "*Anglorum Basileus*," 99–105.

108 Edward's solitary entombment anticipates twelfth-century royal foundations on the Continent and in England. However, Edward would later be joined by two royal women: Edith was buried there by William the Conqueror in 1075, despite her intention to be buried at Wilton; and Matilda, the wife of Henry I, was buried near the Confessor in 1118, likely in order to emphasize her kinship with Edward. It was only after Henry III's burial at Westminster in 1272 that the church became the premier necropolis of English kings. Mason, "Westminster and the Monarchy," 270–1; Mason, "Site of King-Making," 61; Barlow, *Edward the Confessor*, 267; Hallam, "Royal Burial," 372; and below, n. 117.

109 St Peter was Westminster's most prominent saint, but the abbey also fostered cults of Sts Paul, Agnes, Katherine, and Margaret, as well as the Virgin. Westminster's oldest relics were remembered as gifts by seventh-century kings, and these were supplemented with Edward's own gifts of fragmentary and secondary relics. *Vita Ædwardi*, 46n1 and 113; Flete, *History of Westminster*, 68–73; Mason, *Westminster and Its People*, 262–4; Jones, "*Anglorum Basileus*," 113.

distract attention from the king's remains.[110] His was the only complete corpse on the premises.

If Edward envisioned his tomb as his abbey's centrepiece, it did not remain so. By the 1080s, the precise location of the king's body seems to have been in doubt.[111] Although he was unquestionably buried near the high altar, his exhumation in 1102 was reportedly motivated by a desire to confirm his exact resting place.[112] The discovery that his body was incorrupt, a widely recognized indicator of saintly chastity, sparked rumours at Westminster of the king's holiness.[113] Yet the purported need to pinpoint the exact site of his grave suggests that there was persistent fascination with the dead king. The last Anglo-Saxon abbot of Westminster paid daily visits to Edward's grave, and Bishop Wulfstan of Worcester was remembered as having evoked the king's body as he argued a legal case before William the Conqueror.[114] I have already discussed the explicit mentions of Edward's body in early Westminster writs of sanctuary, which attest to laymen's contact with the remains and the Norman abbot's endorsement of this practice.[115] Late-eleventh-century accounts confirm that Westminster had become a popular site of pilgrimage. Writing before ca 1085, the monk Sulcard described the crowds that assembled on St Peter's feast days, and his contemporary, Goscelin of St Bertin, cited Westminster as a destination for people in search

110 At its refoundation, Westminster's relics were all fragmentary or secondary: *Vita Ædwardi*, 46n1 and 113. For parallels with Norman churches, see Brooke, "Princes and Kings as Patrons," 132–3.

111 Barlow, *Edward the Confessor*, 263–4; and below, chapter 7.

112 Barlow, *Edward the Confessor*, 263–4; but compare Mortimer, "Edward the Confessor," 35. For the possible site of Edward's original grave, see Rodwell, "Edward the Confessor's Abbey," 154–5.

113 *Vita Ædwardi*, 113–15. An account of the 1102 exhumation was provided by Osbert of Clare in 1138, as part of his attempt to secure Edward's canonization. For Edward's exhumation and canonization, see: Barlow, *Edward the Confessor*, 267–9; Scholz, "Canonization of Edward." On Westminster's general indifference to Edward's sanctity, see: *Vita Ædwardi*, 13–14; Barlow, *Edward the Confessor*, 266–7; Scholz, "Sulcard," 71–2; Mason, "Site of King-Making," 63–4

114 For Abbot Edwin, who died ca 1068, see: Flete, *History of Westminster*, 83–4. For Wulfstan, see: Bloch, "Vie de Édouard," 116–20; Mason, "Wulfstan's Staff," 159–63.

115 The earliest of these writs date from the abbacy of Gilbert Crispin (ca 1085–1117x18), who witnessed the 1102 exhumation and may have encouraged reverence for Edward; this increasing attention may have inspired Henry I to invoke the laws of Edward after his coronation at Westminster in 1100. Mason, "Site of King-Making," 65; Mason, "Westminster and the Monarchy," 272–3. For the possibility that the sanctuary formulas were written after the discovery of the incorrupt body, see Mason, *Westminster and Its People*, 264.

of healing.[116] Although these descriptions focused on the cult of the apostle, Edward's grave must also have been an attraction. Edith's burial at Westminster in 1075, "with her lord, King Edward," and Queen Matilda's interment there in 1118 would have provided further reminders of the Confessor's presence.[117] In light of the hagiographical depiction of the king in the *Vita Ædwardi*, it is possible that some people sought to express religious devotion at his tomb soon after his death.[118] Perhaps this type of activity inspired the designer of the Bayeux Tapestry to depict the hand of God extended over Westminster as Edward's shrouded corpse was carried inside.[119]

Still, it is telling that there was virtually no ecclesiastical acknowledgment of a cult of Edward before the twelfth century. Westminster's monastic community seems to have discouraged claims of sanctity in the late eleventh century, recognizing that the cultivation of a West Saxon king might invite Norman displeasure in the generation after the Conquest.[120] Sulcard described Edward with respect but not religious veneration, and the Westminster sanctuary writs were careful to call the dead man a king rather than a saint. Before Osbert of Clare began advocating his canonization in the 1130s, allusions to Edward's sanctity were limited to works that were more political than devotional: the *Vita Ædwardi* was commissioned by Edith in defence of her husband and brothers, while the Bayeux Tapestry illustrated the events surrounding the Norman Conquest. A handful of twelfth-century Westminster charters likewise implied that Edward, while remembered and revered, did not initially receive saintly honours: in these documents, grants were given "for the soul of our king Edward," implying that his salvation was not a foregone conclusion.[121]

---

116 Goscelin twice depicted St Peter steering pilgrims away from Westminster, directing them instead to Canterbury or Thanet – whichever monastery Goscelin happened to be extolling at the time: Scholz, "Sulcard," 73–4. The revival of St Earconwald's cult at St Paul's in the 1130s may have similarly been characterized by an effort to draw pilgrims from Westminster: Scholz, "Canonization of Edward," 40–1.

117 "Wið Eadward kyng hire hlaforde"; ASC D 1076 (*recte* 1075) and E 1075. Edith was interred at Westminster despite her intention to be buried at Wilton: above, n. 108.

118 *Vita Ædwardi*, lxxiii–lxxiv; and compare Bloch, *Royal Touch*, 43–8.

119 In addition, the funeral bier resembles reliquaries depicted elsewhere in the Tapestry: Karkov, *Ruler Portraits*, 169.

120 Mason, "Site of King-Making," 63–4; Mason, "Westminster and the Monarchy," 278–87; and below, chapter 7. Compare also Mortimer, "Edward the Confessor," 33.

121 "Pro anima regis nostri Edwardi"; Mason, *Westminster Abbey Charters*, no. 250. See also Mason, *Westminster Abbey Charters*, nos. 244, 264, and 265, all issued between ca 1121 and ca 1157. For commentary: Mason, "Westminster and the Monarchy," 272–3.

Even at the time of his canonization in 1161, Edward could be remembered as an object of non-saintly veneration. Ailred of Rievaulx, who composed Edward's official hagiography, recalled the dead king's popularity among the laity.[122] Drawing upon an anecdote first related by Osbert in the 1130s, Ailred depicted a woman who was unable to decide whether to continue with her work or to go celebrate the feast of St Edward the Martyr.[123] She consulted her servant, who, mistaking Edward the Martyr for Edward the Confessor, asked, "Is this not the Edward whom the crowd of rustics venerates as king (*ut regem*) at Westminster? Let others find the time and mourn or honour that dead man with their songs."[124] That the servant would describe the population mourning (*plangant*) for Edward is noteworthy, for saints were not to be mourned; unlike ordinary Christians, whose fate would be determined on the Day of Judgment, the saints had already earned their salvation and entered God's company immediately after their earthly deaths. Undoubtedly, the purpose of Ailred's *vita* was to confirm Edward's sanctity, revealed here when the irreverent servant came down with a sudden bout of paralysis that could only be cured at the Confessor's tomb. Nonetheless, Ailred had the servant depict Edward being venerated *ut regem*, as a king, rather than as a saint. Although the author took for granted that the anniversary of Edward's death was being celebrated annually, the reverence displayed at the tomb should not automatically be categorized as a saint's cult. Even for the king's official hagiographer, popular reverence for Edward could be couched in terms of his royal status rather than his saintly abilities.[125]

Edward's reputation during the late eleventh and early twelfth centuries is largely obscured by later hagiographical rhetoric, which maintained that his sanctity was continuously acknowledged from the time he died. This was not in fact the case, for even Osbert was hard pressed to come up with miracles that had occurred at the king's tomb after the composition of the

---

122 PL 195 col.783D.

123 This story was recorded by Osbert but does not survive in the extant versions of his *life*: *Vita Ædwardi*, 121–5. Edward the Martyr began to be revered as a saint soon after his regicide in 978, and his cult remained popular through the Norman Conquest; below, chapter 5.

124 "Istene est Edwardus quem apud Westmonasterium haec rustica multitudo veneratur ut regem? … Vacent alii et suis cantibus vel plangant mortuum vel honorent"; PL 195 col.783D.

125 William of Malmesbury condemned this type of reverence, dismissing claims that the Confessor effected cures "from hereditary virtue in the royal blood" [ex regalis prosapiae hereditate fluxisse]; *GR* ii.222.

Vita Ædwardi.[126] Yet despite the absence of early evidence for saintly behaviour, and despite the monastic community's delayed promotion of his sanctity, Edward's corpse soon became the subject of an exhumation, a destination for seekers of sanctuary, and the object of prayer, song, and mourning by clergy and laymen. In the century before his canonization, the Confessor was undoubtedly recognized as a king worthy of posthumous honours.

Conclusions

The two kings discussed in this chapter advertised the extraordinary status of the monarchy by arranging prestigious burials in magnificent churches built expressly for the purpose. The fact that cult-like activity was generated at the foundations' royal tombs suggests that their patrons' efforts to promote their royal line with funerary display successfully attracted public interest and sympathy. To some degree, these burial churches resemble much earlier examples of elite memorialization. While comparisons with pre-Christian or conversion-era royal interments should be drawn with caution, New Minster and Westminster – imposing monuments designed to project royal authority and presence in the surrounding area – recall the seventh-century mounds at Sutton Hoo or even the barrow of Beowulf.[127] Like earlier spectacular burials, the graves of Alfred, Edward the Elder, and Edward the Confessor were placed within ostentatious structures and surrounded by immense material display, all intended to sustain the memories of their entombed inhabitants. By constructing a royal burial church that would dominate the urban landscape, each ruler cemented his own legacy as a local patron while providing his successors with the potential support of a major religious foundation in a leading economic centre.

The two Edwards' newly constructed churches are the most dramatic examples of this thinking, but parallels may be found in the burial choices of other Anglo-Saxon kings. The royal tombs placed in monasteries during the tenth and eleventh centuries would have been surrounded by monastic, episcopal, and saintly burials, and this proximity to the bodies of spiritually prestigious figures would have highlighted the kings' unique status as laymen. Monastic houses likewise benefited from the presence of royal

126 *Vita Ædwardi*, lxxii–lxxiv and 127–8.

127 Fulk et al., *Beowulf*, ll.3156–68; Carver, *Sutton Hoo*. Compare Christian-era parallels, attested at Repton: Biddle, "Cult of Saints," 22.

remains: kings' bodies evidently attracted enough attention to inspire English monasteries to revive the cults of ancient royal saints as well as promoting the tombs of more recent rulers.[128] Given the intrusion of these select secular bodies into patently religious environments, it is not impossible that the distinction between revering a saint and honouring a king became increasingly unclear. It might be argued that without firm differentiation between relics and other prestigious bodies, there would have been no way to effectively prevent high-status lay burials from drawing religious devotion.[129]

I contend, however, that this was not the case. Rather, it appears that two distinct traditions of reverential activity were at work in later Anglo-Saxon England. The more prominent tradition consisted of ecclesiastically sanctioned saints' cults, promoted by churches and monasteries to increase their prestige, attract revenue, and inspire piety among the local population. This category might include cults of sainted royalty, which were often patronized by reigning rulers seeking to enhance their authority through association with a saintly predecessor. Nevertheless, such cults were fundamentally controlled by clergy, who regulated access to the relics and oversaw other forms of veneration.

A parallel but less well-attested brand of reverence was developed by the rulers themselves, who initiated and encouraged the veneration of dead kings in order to further their own political interests. Such activity might appropriate the symbolic vocabulary of saints' cults, reproducing their ceremonial displays and worldly benefits – translation, elevation, pilgrimage, sanctuary – but without their spiritual implications. Edward the Elder's celebration of his father's corpse is the archetype for this model: although he never portrayed Alfred as saintly, Edward's spectacular treatment of the body sharply differentiated this corpse from the remains of other Christian laymen and unsainted clergy. Even without extraordinary piety or intercessory abilities, kings constructed their own recognizable category of "very special dead."[130]

This is not to suggest that these two modes of reverence were mutually exclusive. The immediate impulse among the Confessor's survivors to describe their king in hagiographical terms suggests that tributes devoid of saintly implications were less palatable or effective in the mid eleventh

128 Below, chapter 3.
129 For example: Rollason, "Relic-Cults as Royal Policy," 99–100.
130 The term is Peter Brown's: *Cult of the Saints*, 69–85.

century than they seem to have been in Edward the Elder's day. Yet although there is early evidence of interest in the Confessor's tomb and memory, it is only in the anonymous *Vita Ædwardi* that we find any reference to miracles, which were a standard element of popular saints' cults. Furthermore, the fact that it took over sixty years for Westminster to capitalize on claims of their founder's sanctity suggests that there was little external pressure to recognize Edward as a saint. I propose that the interest in Edward's remains between 1066 and the 1130s resembled the activity at Alfred's tomb more closely than the religious veneration that characterized the Confessor's own later saint's cult. Despite the scarcity of documentation in both instances, the reverence attested at the tombs of Alfred and Edward the Confessor demonstrates that even non-saintly kings' bodies had the potential to attract substantial popular attention. Perhaps this interest emerged organically among populations mourning a beloved leader.[131] Indeed, it is unlikely that such sentiment was applied indiscriminately to all dead kings.[132] However, it is clear that living rulers made concerted efforts to harness the symbolic power of royal tombs for their own ends, making them integral elements of Anglo-Saxon political performance.

131 Cubitt, "Murdered and Martyred Saints," 54; Ridyard, *Royal Saints*, 120.
132 Below, chapter 4.

2 Tenth-Century Royal Mausolea and the Power of Place

The burials of Alfred and Edward the Elder at Winchester and Edward the Confessor at Westminster were consistent with the political landscapes of their respective reigns. Winchester boasted conversion-era roots and a history of collaboration with the rulers of Wessex, but its emergence as a royal administrative centre dates to the reign of Alfred, when the town was refounded as a *burh* that would serve as the effective capital of England for much of the tenth century.[1] Winchester's importance persisted through the following centuries, with Old Minster rejoining New Minster as a favourite site of royal ritual: Cnut (r. 1016–1035) and his son Harthacnut (r. 1040–1042) were both buried there, and Edward the Confessor was consecrated there in 1043. However, Winchester's economic role was surpassed in the eleventh century by London's, whose commercial growth was accompanied by increasing political clout. In the 1010s, the city was a bastion of military and political support for Æthelred II (r. 978–1016) and Edmund Ironside (r. 1016) as they fought off Scandinavian invaders; by the 1040s, its citizens claimed a vital role in acclaiming new kings.[2] Edward the Confessor's choice of London, rather than Winchester, as the site of his

1 Most early administrative activity took place nearby at Southampton until Viking attacks forced a relocation to Winchester in the later ninth century: Biddle, "*Felix Urbs Winthonia*," 289–93; Biddle, "Development of an Early Capital," 237–52; Biddle, *Winchester*, 290–2 and 305–6; Yorke, "Bishops of Winchester," 113–14; Yorke, "Foundation of Old Minster." Winchester's influence was already growing in the ninth century, as building works, saints' cults, foreign visitors, and a regular royal presence signalled the city's prominence: S 307; Yorke, "Bishops of Winchester," 108–12.

2 Brooke, "Central Middle Ages"; Biddle, "City in Transition"; Nightingale, "Origin of the Court of Husting," 566 and 577–8; Mason, *Westminster and Its People*, 9–10.

burial church speaks to the city's rising prominence as a royal centre.[3] The evolving economic and political roles of these two sites make it clear that kings' burial places were not chosen arbitrarily but were informed by a shifting geography of royal power.

Yet for most of the tenth century, royal burial was dispersed across areas of varying political influence. Although Edward the Elder's son Ælfweard (r. 924) was interred at New Minster just a few weeks after his father, other royal burials of this period follow no clear pattern. Æthelstan (r. 924–939) was buried at Malmesbury; Edmund (r. 935–946) and Edgar (r. 959–975) at Glastonbury; Eadred (r. 946–955) at Old Minster; Eadwig (r. 955–959) at New Minster; and Edward the Martyr (r. 975–978) at Shaftesbury. This general move away from Edward's dynastic mausoleum initially appears incongruous, particularly in light of Winchester's increasing importance as a hub for royal, economic, and ecclesiastical activity. However, the new range of royal burial sites is not at odds with the political priorities of tenth-century rulers. Æthelstan was responsible for the first enduring unification of Mercia and Wessex under a single king, and his patronage of Malmesbury – a foundation nearer the border of these two territories than Winchester was – signalled his authority and investment in both regions. A different ideology underpinned Edmund and Edgar's burials: the monastic reforms that spanned the mid-tenth century originated at Glastonbury, and the royal burials there commemorated these kings' endorsement of the movement and affirmed their spiritual prestige.[4] There is evidence that Eadred also intended to be interred in a reformed monastery instead of Old Minster, but he had nonetheless been an active benefactor of Winchester's cathedral in his lifetime, and his burial there confirmed his role as a royal patron. Edward the Martyr's grave at Shaftesbury defies the trend of royal burials being inspired by the dead king's own interests, as the teenaged Edward showed little interest in the nunnery before his reign was cut short by regicide.[5] Still, the fact that Edward was not brought to an established royal mausoleum – to Glastonbury with his father and grandfather, or to Winchester with one of his uncles – suggests that those in charge of his body saw the burial as an opportunity to make their own statement about the king's identity and status.

---

3 *Vita Ædwardi*, 44–5, quoted above, chapter 1.

4 Whitelock, *EHD* I, 921 no. 238; Wulfstan of Winchester, *Life of Æthelwold*, 32–3; and further below.

5 The burial of Edward the Martyr at Shaftesbury, where he was translated in 979 after his initial burial at Wareham in 978, is discussed at length below, chapter 5.

The burial of Edward the Martyr seems at first glance to be quite different from those of other tenth-century kings: they were interred at favoured foundations and established royal mausolea, while he was deposited in a nunnery which he had not actively patronized during his lifetime. The early sources affirm that Edward's burial was arranged by others, and this is logical in the case of political assassination. However, his was not the only premature royal death in the tenth century. Of the seven kings who ruled between the death of Edward the Elder in 924 and the accession of Æthelred II in 978, six died young or unexpectedly, and the logistics of their burials were probably determined by the most influential individuals on hand.[6] The closest parallel to Edward the Martyr's assassination was the lethal stabbing of Edmund in a brawl, when he was in his twenties; the body was quickly claimed by the abbot of nearby Glastonbury, but it is unclear what the king's own wishes were. Other tenth-century royal deaths were evidently less dramatic. No contemporary chroniclers provided explanations for the deaths of Ælfweard and Eadwig, both in their twenties, or of Eadred and Edgar, both in their early thirties – although later authors noted that Eadred had been ill, and his will suggests that he had time enough to prepare for his death and funeral.[7] The other kings left no known wills, and while they were each buried in honourable locations, there is no indication of whether their last wishes were articulated or obeyed. The only apparent exception to this pattern was Æthelstan, who oversaw the transformation of Malmesbury into a royal mausoleum during his lifetime and almost certainly expressed a desire to be interred there himself.[8]

Nevertheless, rather than building a monumental burial church *ex novo*, like Edward the Elder and Edward the Confessor, Æthelstan adopted a seventh-century monastery whose patron saint he regarded as an ancestor.[9] While his extravagant generosity towards Malmesbury ensured that it would be deemed a worthy place for a king's body to lie, the foundation evoked the West Saxon past as much as it did a unified English future. The same was true at Glastonbury: notwithstanding the tenth-century additions to its fabric and its community's involvement in forward-looking

6 Æthelred II is not counted among this group: he died in 1016 and will be considered in the next chapter.

7 Eadred's will is S 1515.

8 The circumstances of Æthelstan's death are unknown, but he was in his mid-forties when he died.

9 This was St Aldhelm: William of Malmesbury, *GP* v.246.1.

monastic reforms, the foundation's conversion-era roots associated its tenth-century royal graves with more ancient kings of Wessex. Such connections with West Saxon dynastic history may have appealed to this generation of rulers as they sought support and legitimization for increasingly ambitious programs of rulership. Still, the overall move away from New Minster by three of Edward the Elder's sons and two of his grandsons is significant, given the resources invested in the foundation and the ideological motivations behind its construction. Accordingly, this chapter investigates the considerations that informed kings' burials in the tenth century, examining the political motivations behind the choices of royal mausolea from the death of Edward the Elder through the accession of his great-grandson, Edward the Martyr.[10] The following discussion demonstrates that a king's agency over his own remains was limited; burial places were determined by the political interests of the living, which only sometimes corresponded with the wishes of the dead. It is significant, in this context, that the individuals who took control of rulers' funerals from 924 through 975 consistently buried the remains respectfully, in prestigious locations appropriate to the royal dignity. Despite the geographical dispersal of kings' graves in this period, their burials conformed to contemporary expectations about how royal bodies ought to be treated in death.

Royal Burial in Wessex and Mercia in the Reign of Æthelstan: 924–939

Edward the Elder died at Farndon, in northern Mercia, on 17 July 924, while suppressing a revolt in Chester.[11] Æthelstan, the king's eldest son by his first marriage, was probably present when he died, and later sources claimed that Edward bequeathed him the kingdom on his deathbed.[12] However, Edward was not interred nearby in Mercia, where Æthelstan

10 See figure 2 for the genealogy of tenth-century kings of England.

11 ASC BCD [MR] 924; JW 384–5; William of Malmesbury, *GR* ii.133.1. The ASC in the period 896–924 includes annals of the Mercian Register [MR], which focus on the activities of Edward's sister Æthelflæd: Stafford, "Annals of Æthelflæd"; Wainwright, "Mercian Register"; Smith, *Land and Book*, 167–73; Cubbin, *MS D*, xxx–xxxi.

12 Æthelstan's Mercian support would have been essential to Edward's military efforts in the region, making it likely that he was with his father at Chester: Foot, *Æthelstan*, 17 and 38–9. John of Worcester reported: "departing from this life, Edward bequeathed the governance of the kingdom to his son Æthelstan" [ex hac uita transiens, Athelstano filio regni gubernacula reliquit]; JW 384–5. William of Malmesbury stated that Æthelstan was acclaimed king "by his father's command and his will" [iussu patris et testamento], implying that this occurred directly after Edward's burial at Winchester; *GR* ii.133.1.

held power under his father's authority, but was carried some two hundred miles to Winchester and buried at New Minster. This arrangement surely conformed to Edward's own wishes, given his long-standing patronage of the foundation and his creation of a dynastic mausoleum there. Yet the king's posthumous journey from the edge of Mercia to the heart of Wessex foregrounds the regional division that would persist through Æthelstan's consecration at Kingston more than a year later, on 4 September 925. In the interim, the sons of Edward's second marriage gained support in Wessex and asserted their own claims to the kingdom. The elder, Ælfweard, may have been acclaimed at Winchester shortly after his father's funeral; when he died, just a few weeks later, his younger brother Eadwine likely made his own bid for power.[13] Æthelstan retained practical control of Mercia during this period, and his support in the region proved a sufficient counterweight to his half-brothers' strength in Wessex, ultimately allowing him to accede to the entire kingdom.[14]

These regional tensions led to a shift in patronage away from Winchester during Æthelstan's reign, particularly from New Minster, whose community cultivated ties with Edward's second wife and her children.[15] Edward's remarriage around the year 900 seems to have provided the impetus for Æthelstan's connection with Mercia: as the child of the king's first union, he was reportedly removed from the court at Winchester and placed in the care of his paternal aunt Æthelflæd and her husband Æthelred, who held Mercia under Edward's authority.[16] In addition to establishing military credentials in the region, the young Æthelstan would have witnessed and

13 ASC BCD [MR] 924; JW 384–5; Keynes, *Liber Vitae*, fol. 9v. ASC D was the only recension to note that Ælfweard died sixteen days after his father, which would place his death on 2 August. One version of the West Saxon regnal list preserved in the twelfth-century Textus Roffensis attributes to Ælfweard a four-week reign after his father's death: Dumville, "West Saxon Genealogical Regnal List," 29; Foot, *Æthelstan*, 39. Both dates were recorded well after the fact, but it is reasonable to place Ælfweard's death between 2 and 17 August.

14 For the succession debate of 924–925, see: Foot, *Æthelstan*, 17–18 and 37–40; Yorke, "Æthelwold and the Politics of the Tenth Century," 71–3; and further below.

15 Keynes, *Liber Vitae*, 19–20.

16 William of Malmesbury noted that Æthelstan was fostered by his aunt and uncle in Mercia but attributes his placement there to Alfred's initiative: *GR* ii.133.2; Foot, *Æthelstan*, 33–6; Thacker, "Dynastic Monasteries," 254–5; but compare Dumville, *Wessex and England*, 146. Claims concerning Æthelstan's illegitimate birth may date to this period, although they are only preserved in post-Conquest sources: William of Malmesbury, *GR* ii.131.2 and ii.139.2. For Æthelstan's stepmothers and early medieval queens in general, see Stafford, "King's Wife in Wessex," 9–13 and 25–6.

participated in a mode of ecclesiastical patronage in Mercia that paralleled Edward's activity in Winchester.[17] Æthelflæd and Æthelred were avid benefactors of Mercian religious houses, including a new foundation in Gloucester which they built alongside the *burh*'s existing minster and endowed as their burial church.[18] Unlike Edward, who focused his attention at New Minster on non-saintly royal bodies, his sister and brother-in-law made their foundation the focus of a major relic cult.[19] In 909, the miracle-working remains of the Northumbrian saint-king Oswald (d. 642) were taken from Bardney and translated to Gloucester by the Mercian royal family after a military victory in the area.[20] The appropriation of such a prominent conversion-era royal saint had important political implications at a moment when Mercian and West Saxon forces were initiating collaborative military efforts in the Danelaw, with the objective of unifying these regions under Edward's rule.[21] Oswald, memorialized by Bede as the Northumbrian overking of all the Anglo-Saxon kingdoms, offered a historical precedent for the type of wide-ranging rulership pursued by Alfred's children, and by the time Æthelred and Æthelflæd were buried in their minster, Gloucester's collection of royal bodies emblematized Anglo-Saxon cohesion across regions and generations.[22] The ideological power of such a mausoleum would surely have been evident to Æthelstan, with the

17 Thacker, "Dynastic Monasteries," 255–6; Thacker, "Kings, Saints, and Monasteries," 18–20.

18 Gloucester's layout in the early tenth century was consistent with the layout of Alfred's *burhs* in Wessex, and the town became an increasingly important administrative centre under Æthelred and Æthelflæd: Heighway, "Gloucester"; Heighway et al., *Golden Minster*, 5–12 and 33–6; Thacker, "Chester and Gloucester," 208–9; Thompson, *Dying and Death*, 12–15.

19 Thacker, "Dynastic Monasteries," 255–6; and above, chapter 1.

20 The translation is recorded in ASC BC [MR] 909; JW 362–3; William of Malmesbury, *GR* ii.125.5. See also: Heighway et al., *Golden Minster*, 10–11 and 35–6; Heighway, "Gloucester," 108; Thacker, "Dynastic Monasteries," 255–6; Rollason, *Saints and Relics*, 153–4; Thompson, *Dying and Death*, 15–18. The association of Oswald with Mercia dates from the late seventh century: Thacker, "Kings, Saints, and Monasteries," 2–4; Thacker, "*Membra Disjecta*," 104–7. Æthelred and Æthelflæd patronized and translated other Anglo-Saxon saints in other Mercian foundations: Heighway et al., *Golden Minster*, 36; Thacker, "Kings, Saints, and Monasteries," 18–19.

21 Thacker, "Chester and Gloucester," 212.

22 For Oswald, see: Bede, *HE* II.5; Thacker, "*Membra Disjecta*," 113; Wormald, "*Gens Anglorum*." Æthelred died in 911 and Æthelflæd in 918: ASC BC [MR] 911, ASC D 912 (*recte* 911), ASC BCD [MR] 918; Campbell, *Chronicle of Æthelweard*, 53–4; JW 380–1; William of Malmesbury, *GR* ii.126.4–5.

political potential of a royal funeral becoming particularly apparent at his aunt's death in 918. When Æthelflæd died at Tamworth, a major Mercian political centre, Edward quickly made his way there: he "immediately hastened to Tamworth and subjected it to his rule."[23] The chronology of these events is vague, but Edward's earlier celebration of his father's body and memory at a time of political crisis suggests that he would have taken a comparable course of action at his sister's death.[24] If the king arrived at Tamworth as Æthelflæd was dying or before her remains had been moved, he would have had the opportunity to secure the allegiance of the Mercian magnates without the delay of an interregnum. His presence at the funeral in Gloucester would have further confirmed the transfer of royal authority.[25] The burial of the West Saxon princess with her Mercian husband in their newly founded *burh* minster reiterated the consolidation of the two regions – and helped legitimize claims of West Saxon overlordship in the wake of Æthelflæd's death.[26]

Edward's own funeral, just a few years later, was followed by similar bids for power. Events moved quickly in the summer of 924. The king died on 17 July and his body was brought to Winchester's New Minster; his son Ælfweard died at Oxford at the beginning of August and was also interred at New Minster.[27] The sources indicate that Edward was already buried when his son died, so the king's funeral must have taken place in late July or early August, leaving Ælfweard enough time to travel to Oxford before his own death. Æthelstan's activity during this period is unclear. If he had accompanied Edward's body from Mercia to Wessex or overseen a ceremonial entrance into Winchester, he would have been well positioned as his father's heir – particularly if he could claim to be the beneficiary of a deathbed bequest.[28] However, Ælfweard's branch of the

23 "Tomwurðigene mox properauit, eamque suo dominio subiugauit"; JW 380–1. It is implied in the following sentence that Edward's army (*exercitum*) was with him. This episode is discussed by: Foot, *Æthelstan*, 14; Thompson, *Dying and Death*, 23–5; Smith, *Land and Book*, 171–2.

24 Edward's use of Alfred's body is discussed above, chapter 1.

25 Compare this hypothesis with the case studies in chapter 3, below. For the chronology of Edward's movements before Æthelflæd's death, see Wainwright, "Mercian Register," 387–8.

26 For the construction of Edward's legitimacy in Mercia, see Stafford, "Annals of Æthelflæd," 110–13.

27 ASC BCD [MR] 924; JW 384–5; William of Malmesbury, *GR* ii.133.1. The dating of Ælfweard's death is discussed above, n. 13.

28 Above, n. 12.

family enjoyed significant political support in Wessex, where the ætheling held authority during Edward's lifetime comparable to Æthelstan's in Mercia.[29] If the succession was debated or determined in Winchester in the days following the king's funeral, Ælfweard likely benefited from local political support.[30] Although there is no definitive evidence that he was ever formally elected or consecrated king, Ælfweard was remembered at New Minster "crowned with royal insignia" and was included in a recension of the West Saxon regnal list; William of Malmesbury also referred to Ælfweard as his father's chosen heir.[31] It may be that royal power was split between the half-brothers at this time, with Ælfweard acceding to Wessex and Æthelstan to Mercia.[32] Alternatively, the decision could have been deferred to a later date but pre-empted by Ælfweard's death. Reports of a Winchester plot to blind Æthelstan and place Ælfweard's younger brother Eadwine on the throne were recorded in the twelfth century, and while there is no contemporary notice of this conspiracy, the long period between Edward's death and Æthelstan's consecration indicates a protracted and possibly violent succession debate.[33] The new *ordo* used at Æthelstan's coronation in 925 stressed that two populations were uniting under a single king, perhaps in response to such divisiveness.[34] Nevertheless, the Anglo-Saxon Chronicle's assertion that Æthelstan was "chosen as king by the Mercians and consecrated at Kingston" hints that his accession won comparatively little initial support in Wessex.[35]

---

29 Foot, *Æthelstan*, 15–17.

30 A Winchester election is implied by William of Malmesbury, *GR* ii.133.1.

31 "Regalibus infulis redimitus"; Keynes, *Liber Vitae*, 81 and fol. 9v. The author used this phrase to distinguish Ælfweard from another member of the royal family buried at New Minster, who was simply identified as an ætheling (*clito*). For the regnal list, see Dumville, "West Saxon Genealogical Regnal List," 29. William of Malmesbury implied that Ælfweard was Edward's intended heir in a discussion of Æthelstan's reputed illegitimacy, but elsewhere he asserted that Edward bequeathed Æthelstan the kingdom: *GR* ii.133.1 and ii.139.2; and compare above, n. 12.

32 Foot, *Æthelstan*, 38–40; Yorke, "Æthelwold and the Politics of the Tenth Century," 71.

33 *GR* ii.131.1, ii.137.1, and ii.139.3–5. Eadwine may have remained a threat to Æthelstan until the former's death in 933, in which Æthelstan was reputedly complicit: William of Malmesbury, *GR* ii.137.1 and ii.139.3–5; Yorke, "Æthelwold and the Politics of the Tenth Century," 70–3; Foot, *Æthelstan*, 40–3; Miller, *Charters of the New Minster*, xxviii–xxx and 54.

34 Nelson, "First Use of the Second *Ordo*," 124.

35 "Of Myrcum gecoren to cinge 7 æt Cingestune gehalgod"; ASC BCD [MR] 924. The selection of Kingston as a coronation place may have been significant in this respect, as it was close to the Wessex-Mercia border: Foot, *Æthelstan*, 17–18. If Edward had also

In this context, it is unsurprising that Æthelstan maintained cool relations with Winchester during his early reign, and his omission from New Minster's *Liber Vitae* indicates that he never became a beloved patron of his father's foundation.[36] On the contrary, a charter issued toward the beginning of his reign alienated one of its core estates: twenty hides at Chisledon, which had been granted to the community by Edward the Elder in 901, were leased to one of the king's thegns "with the consent and devotion of Æthelstan, the most glorious king of the Anglo-Saxons and the Danes."[37] The charter's description of New Minster as the place "where the entombed bodies of the glorious kings Alfred and Edward rest" underlined the king's dynastic connection with the foundation while depriving the community of revenue – a simultaneous reminder of Æthelstan's ancestral authority and the importance of royal favour to the house's fortunes.[38]

---

been crowned at Kingston, as indicated in a post-Conquest source, this location and the *ordo*'s reference to the new king's hereditary right to the kingdom might also reflect an attempt by Æthelstan to capitalize on his father's legacy. For the location of Edward's coronation, see: Stubbs, *Ralph de Diceto*, 140; Keynes, *Diplomas*, 270. For references to paternal rights in the ordo, see: Nelson, "First Use of the Second *Ordo*," 124; Nelson, "Second English *Ordo*," 365.

36 Keynes, *Liber Vitae*, 20–1 and 81; Miller, *Charters of the New Minster*, xxx. Bishop Frithestan of Winchester (r. 909–931) was conspicuously absent from royal councils in 925 and 926, likely reflecting continued tensions with Æthelstan, but the subsequent two bishops of Winchester had been members of Æthesltan's household, leading to improved relations with the diocese: Keynes, *Liber Vitae*, 20–1; Foot, *Æthelstan*, 97–8; Wood, "Æthelstan's Empire," 253–8. It may also be relevant that St Grimbald was translated at New Minster in the 930s, although it is unclear whether the king collaborated with the community: the translation is noted by Grierson, "Grimbald of St. Bertin's," 559.

37 "Cum consensu ac deuotione Æðelstani Angelsaxonum Denorumque gloriosissimi regi": S 1417, edited with commentary by Miller, *Charters of the New Minster*, 49–54. The original grant to New Minster for fifty hides at Chisledon (which had previously been held by Old Minster) is recorded in S 366: Miller, *Charters of New Minster*, 30–4 and 54. For Æthelstan's initiative in this matter, and for a dating to the king's early reign (925x7), see Keynes, *Liber Vitae*, 20–1. This is only one of two extant charters issued in connection with New Minster during Æthelstan's reign; the other, S 418, is a land grant to a thegn, issued at New Minster, who later bequeathed the lands back to the foundation: Miller, *Charters of New Minster*, 54–9.

38 "Ubi corpora gloriosorum regum Ælfredi et Eadweardi sepulta quiescunt"; Miller, *Charters of the New Minster*, 50. Alternatively, the references to Edward could be an attempt by the community to capitalize upon its status as a royal mausoleum: it may be significant that the lease also required a payment to New Minster "every year on the death-day of the most glorious King Edward" [omni anno die obitus Eadweardi gloriosissimi regis]. For the possibility that S 1417 was a local rather than royal production, see Miller, *Charters of the New Minster*, 52.

His lack of generosity to New Minster is all the more conspicuous in light of his extensive patronage elsewhere. Æthelstan was widely remembered as a donor of relics and privileges, who cultivated ties with prominent saints.[39] In addition to establishing two new minsters during his reign, the king was a celebrated benefactor of Malmesbury, where he would eventually be buried.[40] Founded in the seventh century and entrusted to St Aldhelm at the turn of the eighth, Malmesbury enjoyed the consistent patronage of Mercian and West Saxon kings through the early tenth century.[41] During the reigns of Alfred and Edward, however, the foundation suffered two severe fires.[42] If Malmesbury's original fabric was damaged or destroyed, Æthelstan may have rebuilt some or all of its buildings according to his own specifications, possibly with the addition of a crypt like the one his aunt and uncle commissioned for themselves at Gloucester.[43] In doing so, however, he would have departed from the examples set by Æthelflæd and Æthelred at Gloucester and by Edward at Winchester: rather than creating a new minster to complement or compete with the *burh*'s established ecclesiastical centre, Æthelstan enriched and enhanced the existing foundation, thereby associating himself with the community's prestigious roster of earlier royal patrons. With Edward's legacy proving complicated, Æthelstan linked his reign with a more distant West Saxon and Mercian past by adopting a foundation near the border of these territories, with historical ties to kings of both regions.

The timeline for Malmesbury's rise as a favoured foundation is unclear. It was the beneficiary of royal grants from at least the time of St Aldhelm, and Alfred's father Æthelwulf (r. 839–858) was remembered as a particular friend of the community.[44] By the end of the ninth century, the surrounding town had been replanned as part of Alfred's network of *burhs*, and

39 Foot, *Æthelstan*, 17–26; Rollason, *Saints and Relics*, 144–63; Keynes, "Athelstan's Books"; Dumville, *Wessex and England*, 163–4; Lambert, "Sanctuary and Legal Privilege"; Wilson, "King Athelstan and St John of Beverly"; Wilson, *St John of Beverly*, 14–16. Æthelstan also continued the tradition of royal patronage at St Oswald's minster at Gloucester: Heighway, "Gloucester," 103 and 110.

40 The two new foundations were Milton Abbas and Muchelney: Foot, *Æthelstan*, 125.

41 Kelly, *Charters of Malmesbury*, 1–22.

42 Ibid., 15–16. The fires were noted by William of Malmesbury, who said they "consumed the entire monastery" [totum cenobium ... consumpserunt]; *GP* v.216.3.

43 Kelly, *Charters of Malmesbury*, 22.

44 Ibid., 10–13.

both Alfred and Edward attested the occasional charter there.[45] Praise poetry for Æthelstan was composed at the foundation as early as 925, suggesting that he had already established himself as a benefactor before his coronation, and William of Malmesbury commemorated the king as an exceptionally magnanimous patron in his later years.[46] It was only toward the end of his reign, however, that there is evidence that Æthelstan intended Malmesbury to become a royal mausoleum. After two of his cousins were killed in the 937 Battle of Brunanburh, Æthelstan had their remains brought to Malmesbury, where they were buried "to the right and left of the altar in the church of the blessed Mother of God."[47] William asserted that the king designated the church as his own burial place at the same time, "announcing that his own body should likewise rest there."[48] When Æthelstan died at Gloucester, just two years later, his corpse was carried approximately thirty miles to Malmesbury and interred in the tower, beneath the high altar.[49] The remains were accompanied by lavish treasure: "many gifts of silver and gold were carried before the body, as well as relics of saints."[50] It is telling that Æthelstan was not buried in Gloucester's new minster alongside his aunt and uncle, despite his history of patronage there; his funeral arrangements seem not to have been driven by convenience.[51] Rather, it appears that the king was interred at Malmesbury in accordance with his own wishes.

At Malmesbury, Æthelstan was able to differentiate himself in death from recent Mercian and West Saxon rulers. While tensions with his

45 Malmesbury was listed in the Burghal Hidage: Keynes and Lapidge, *Alfred the Great*, 193; Kelly, *Charters of Malmesbury*, 18–19; Haslam, "Towns of Wilstshire," 115–17. The charters of Alfred and Edward are edited by Kelly, *Charters of Malmesbury*, 194–211.

46 Lapidge, "Some Latin Poems," 72–83; Foot, *Æthelstan*, 32–3 and 110–12; Kelly, *Charters of Malmesbury*, 20; Wood, "Aethelstan's Empire," 261–2. See also William of Malmesbury, *GP* v.246–250; *GR* ii.131.2, ii.135.6, and ii.140.

47 "Dextra leuaque altaris in ecclesia sancte Matris Dei"; William of Malmesbury, *GP* v.246.2. The cousins were Ælfwine and Æthelwine. William indicated that the king's patronage dated to the period after the Battle of Brunanburh, at which he called on St Aldhelm for assistance: *GP* v.246.2.

48 "Sui quoque corporis requiem ibidem futuram denuntians"; *GR* ii.135.6.

49 *GR* ii.140; *GP* v.246.3–4.

50 "Portata ante corpus multa in argento et auro donaria, simul et sanctorum reliquiae"; *GR* ii.140.

51 For Æthelstan's patronage at Gloucester, see Heighway, "Gloucester," 103 and 110. A close connection between Malmesbury and Gloucester was noted by William of Malmesbury: *GP* iv.155.3; Kelly, *Charters of Malmesbury*, 22.

half-brothers by Edward's second marriage may have made the mausoleum at New Minster unappealing, it is significant that Æthelstan chose a foundation with no claims to the bodies of earlier kings. Certainly, he was not alone at Malmesbury: his body was placed between his cousins' and beside the shrine of St Aldhelm, whom he reportedly considered a kinsman (*cognato*).[52] Nevertheless, his choice of an ancient, respected foundation which had limited ties to the immediate royal past implies that he sought to distinguish his reign from his predecessors'. In some respects, his efforts at Malmesbury resemble Edward the Elder's attempt to create a new dynastic legacy at Winchester. Yet where his father built New Minster in a city already known for its royal necropolis, Æthelstan significantly altered the landscape of royal burial by creating a new mausoleum at Malmesbury. This shift anticipates, to some extent, Edward the Confessor's construction of a new burial church at Westminster, which housed no royal graves when the king began building there.[53] Like Æthelstan, the Confessor declined to be entombed with his father or with the half-brother who preceded him as king.[54] Both rulers broke away from established West Saxon mausolea while appropriating foundations associated with the conversion-era past.

In contrast to Westminster, however, Malmesbury attracted no additional kings' burials. After Æthelstan's death, royal donations to the foundation became uneven, and the next generation of rulers focused their patronage on Glastonbury and other houses at the forefront of monastic reform.[55] The fact that Æthelstan was succeeded by half-brothers rather than sons may have made him less sought after as a legitimizing predecessor. Alternatively, he may have been regarded by later kings as a problematic figure, despite his military and administrative accomplishments; perhaps his successors sought to distance themselves from his political legacy. Whatever his posthumous reputation, Æthelstan's interment at Malmesbury set a precedent for burial outside of Winchester. Although later kings directed considerable attention and patronage to the city, it was no longer the default burial place for Edward the Elder's dynasty. The geography of royal burial had begun to shift to the west.

52 William of Malmesbury, *GP* v.246.1.

53 Harold Harefoot had been buried there for a few months, but his body had been exhumed and moved by the time construction started at Edward's new Westminster Abbey in the 1050s. Harold's burial is examined below, chapter 4.

54 Above, chapter 1.

55 Malmesbury was not reformed until the reign of Edgar: Kelly, *Charters of Malmesbury*, 24.

Royal Burial at Glastonbury: 946–975

Three West Saxon kings of England were buried at Glastonbury: Edmund in 946, Edgar in 975, and Edmund Ironside in 1016. There is a good possibility that a fourth, Eadred, planned to be entombed there, despite his eventual interment at Winchester in 955 under the auspices of his successor.[56] Like Malmesbury, Glastonbury offered a prestigious alternative to Winchester's West Saxon mausolea. The earliest evidence for the Anglo-Saxon minster dates from the seventh century, and its foundation was attributed variously to the West Saxon kings Cenwealh (r. 642–672), Centwine (r. 676–685), and Ine (r. 688–726).[57] There is little surviving documentation of the community's activities in the eighth and ninth centuries, but it emerged from obscurity in the early tenth century, when the young St Dunstan, future archbishop of Canterbury, was educated and tonsured there.[58] The foundation was already favoured during the reign of Æthelstan, who was remembered for his gifts of relics; in addition, he issued more than a dozen grants there, and the abbot appeared regularly on the witness lists of royal charters.[59] Early tenth-century Glastonbury was identified by later authors as a royal possession, perhaps signalling that the foundation's core estates had passed into the king's hands at some point in the preceding centuries.[60] If so, it seems that much of this property was later restored. Edmund was the first

56 Keynes, "'Dunstan B' Charters," 188–9. The seventh-century king Centwine was also reportedly buried at Glastonbury; see further below.

57 Overviews of the excavation of the Anglo-Saxon buildings are provided by Radford, "Glastonbury Abbey"; Taylor and Taylor, *Anglo-Saxon Architecture* I, 250–7. For the minster's seventh-century history and charter evidence that indicates the minster was already founded by the reign of Ine, see: Abrams, *Anglo-Saxon Glastonbury*, 124–6; Abrams, "Diploma of King Ine," 97–8; Blows, "Pre-Conquest History of Glastonbury," 109–37. There is no persuasive evidence for later medieval claims for Glastonbury's connections with early Christian history or pre-Saxon ecclesiastical foundations: Abrams, *Anglo-Saxon Glastonbury*, 1–9.

58 The earliest extant life of St Dunstan was composed in the 990s by a cleric who identified himself as "B." and was well acquainted with Dunstan's youth at Glastonbury: B., *Vita Dunstani*, 12–21. Dunstan's career and influence are discussed by Winterbottom and Lapidge, *Lives of Dunstan*, xxiii–lxiii; Brooks, "Career of Dunstan," 5–6; Foot, "Glastonbury's Early Abbots," 186–7; Orme, "Glastonbury Abbey and Education," 286; Abrams, *Anglo-Saxon Glastonbury*, 267–8 and 337–41. On Latin learning and composition at Glastonbury, see Lapidge, "Hermeneutic Style," 95–7 and 108–11.

59 Abrams, *Anglo-Saxon Glastonbury*, 311–2.

60 Ibid., 7 and 340–1.

tenth-century king to make direct grants to the foundation, a gesture that was replicated by his successors Eadred and Edgar.[61] The fact that Glastonbury came to function as a royal chancery, as well as a repository for the king's charters and occasional home to his treasury, likewise reflects its importance as a tenth-century political and administrative centre.[62]

Glastonbury also became a spiritual landmark during the tenth-century monastic reforms. It was celebrated as the first community in England to adopt the Benedictine Rule and ordain monks alongside its resident clerics.[63] Dunstan was appointed abbot by Edmund in the early 940s, and his tenure was marked by the cultivation and dissemination of Benedictine ideals, as new generations of reformers were trained under his supervision.[64] Just as importantly for the reformers, Dunstan's working relationship with Edmund laid the groundwork for Glastonbury to increase its wealth and status over the following decades.[65] Notwithstanding early conflicts which nearly resulted in Dunstan's exile, Edmund granted significantly more lands to the community than any of his predecessors had, and it appears that the nobility were encouraged to imitate the king's generosity.[66] It is in the context of this patronage that the twelfth-century *De*

61 Until Edmund, Edward the Elder was the only king after 860 to make a direct grant of land to Glastonbury, and he made just one: Abrams, *Anglo-Saxon Glastonbury*, 337–43.

62 Keynes, "'Dunstan B' Charters," 180–6; Keynes, *Diplomas*, 147–8 and 151–2.

63 Glastonbury's primacy is noted in an Old English account of Edgar's establishment of monasteries, probably composed by Bishop Æthelwold in the 970s or 980s: Whitelock, *EHD* I, 921 no. 238; and compare also Wulfstan of Winchester, *Life of Æthelwold*, 32–3. For the likelihood that Glastonbury retained a community of clerics after the introduction of the Benedictine Rule, see: Brooks, "Career of Dunstan," 12–13; Robertson, "Dunstan and Monastic Reform," 154–9.

64 Dunstan was appointed abbot by Edmund in 940 or 943; it is unclear when (or whether) he relinquished the position: "Edgar's Establishment of Monasteries," in Whitelock, *EHD* I, 921–2, no. 238; Brooks, "Career of Dunstan," 10–14; Foot, "Glastonbury's Early Abbots," 179–80. His protégés are listed by William of Malmesbury, *Vita Dunstani*, ii.12.13.

65 Winterbottom and Lapidge, *Lives of Dunstan*, xxiv–xxix. Glastonbury's material success was manifested in part by the substantial expansion of the church and monastic buildings during Dunstan's abbacy: Radford, "Glastonbury Abbey," 118–25; Taylor and Taylor, *Anglo-Saxon Architecture* I, 252–5.

66 For donations from the nobility inspired by the king, see: Abrams, *Anglo-Saxon Glastonbury*, 344; *De Antiquitate*, 114–19. Burials of tenth-century lay benefactors at Glastonbury are examined by Blows, "Glastonbury Obit–List"; Abrams, *Anglo-Saxon Glastonbury*, 344–5. The burial and commemoration of lay patrons before the tenth century are discussed by Dodwell, *Anglo-Saxon Art*, 113–15; Radford, "Glastonbury Abbey," 123–4. For Dunstan's early tensions with Edmund, see: B., *Vita Dunstani*, 44–51; Brooks, "Career of Dunstan," 10–11.

Antiquitate Glastonie Ecclesie noted Edmund's gift of relics to the abbey and the bequest of his remains: "he even promised his own body to the place after his death, where it rests up to the present day."[67] The post-Conquest community remembered Edmund designating Glastonbury a worthy resting place for nobles, saints, and kings.[68]

Although there is little doubt that Edmund was in fact interred at Glastonbury, the circumstances surrounding his death and burial were less straightforward than the *De Antiquitate* implied. In 946, the king was fatally stabbed at Pucklechurch, a royal estate approximately thirty-five miles from Glastonbury.[69] Edmund's unexpected death meant that funeral plans had to be made on the spot, and there must have been debate over where to place the body. Glastonbury was not an automatic choice of burial place at this time. Winchester's New Minster, which had benefited in the past from Edmund's generosity, offered a prestigious dynastic mausoleum where the king could be laid to rest with his father and grandfather.[70] Malmesbury would have been another option: ten miles closer to Pucklechurch than Glastonbury was, the foundation had hosted Æthelstan's funeral just seven years earlier and would have been a convenient, respectable choice at a time of political upset.[71] It may be that Glastonbury, as a reformed community, would have been seen to offer greater spiritual benefits than the other two foundations – perhaps an important consideration among his survivors, since the king's sudden death left him little time to prepare his soul.[72] Alternatively, it is possible that Edmund had expressed a wish to be buried there, choosing a favoured location just as Edward and Æthelstan had done. Yet there is no contemporary suggestion that Edmund had designated Glastonbury his burial church, and his interment there should almost

67 "Cui eciam corpus proprium post decessum suum … deuouit, ubi et requiescit usque in hodiernum diem"; *De Antiquitate*, 116–17, and compare also William of Malmesbury, *Vita Dunstani*, i.21.5. The *De Antiquitate* was composed by William of Malmesbury but survives only in a heavily interpolated revision of the late twelfth century: *De Antiquitate*, 27–33; Abrams, *Anglo-Saxon Glastonbury*, 21–7.

68 *De Antiquitate*, 116–19.

69 ASC D 946, E 948 (*recte* 946); JW 398–9; William of Malmesbury, *GR* ii.144.

70 S 470, dated 940, is a grant of thirty hides to New Minster "for the redemption of the sins of my father, King Edward" [pro redemptione piaculorum patris mei . Eadweardi regis]; the charter is edited by Miller, *Charters of the New Minster*, 60–7 no. 12.

71 Malmesbury evidently fell out of favour under Æthelstan's immediate successors, as Edmund and Eadred made no known grants to the foundation. Royal attention seems to have revived under Eadwig, and Edgar may have become a patron once Malmesbury was refounded as a reformed monastery ca 974: Kelly, *Charters of Malmesbury Abbey*, 23–4.

72 Later tenth-century accounts of the monastic reforms noted that Glastonbury was reformed during Edmund's reign: Whitelock, *EHD* I, 921 no. 238.

certainly be attributed to Dunstan's efforts. The saint was remembered as the driving force behind Edmund's funeral, responsible for consigning the body "to mother earth at Glastonbury."[73] If the burial place was in fact chosen by "common council," as one chronicler indicated, Dunstan's voice was probably the most influential.[74] By claiming the king's remains, he reinforced his foundation's royal connections, thereby ensuring that the patronage Glastonbury had enjoyed during Edmund's lifetime would persist beyond his death.[75] Dunstan's efforts were justified, for after the king's burial, the nobility's generosity towards the foundation continued, sustaining the community through the tenth century.[76] Indeed, Pucklechurch itself soon entered Glastonbury's possession by royal grant, and later authors imagined the estate as a gift made on behalf of Edmund's soul.[77]

The trend of royal patronage continued under Edmund's brother and successor Eadred, who was reported to have "preferred almost none of his nobles to Dunstan" and granted the abbot a more prominent position at court than he had previously enjoyed.[78] During Eadred's reign, Glastonbury emerged as a royal chancery, with the abbey's scriptorium issuing a high volume of charters for the king in its own diplomatic styles.[79] It is significant that a number of authentic charters produced at Glastonbury in Eadred's name were issued without the king in attendance: this arrangement, perhaps a result of Eadred's inability to travel due to poor health, reflects the king's confidence in Dunstan to conduct royal business in his name and in Glastonbury's ability to meet an increasing demand for royal document

73 "Funerauit et Glestoniae matri terrae commendauit": this account is from Adelard of Ghent's *Lectiones in depositione S. Dunstani*, composed between 1006 and 1012; Winterbottom and Lapidge, *Lives of Dunstan*, cxxv and 124–5.

74 "Communi ... consilio"; William of Malmesbury, *GR* ii.144.3. John of Worcester likewise noted that Edmund "was brought to Glastonbury, and buried by St Dunstan, the abbot" [Glæstoniam delatus, a beato Dunstano abbate sepelitur]; JW 398–9.

75 For Dunstan's initiative, see: Yorke, "Royal Burial," 41–2; Yorke, *Nunneries*, 114–15.

76 Abrams, *Anglo-Saxon Glastonbury*, 344–5.

77 S 553, a twelfth-century creation ostensibly issued by Eadred in 950, granted Pucklechurch to Glastonbury "for the soul of my brother, King Edmund" [pro animæ ... fratris mei Eadmundi regis]. Three other charters for Pucklechurch (S 1724 by Edmund, S 1744 by Eadred, and S 1777 by Æthelred) are of questionable authenticity, but the estate was in Glastonbury's possession in 1066 and 1086; the acquisition may be best datable to Æthelred's reign: Abrams, *Anglo-Saxon Glastonbury*, 211–14; Abrams, "Lucid Intervals."

78 "Nullum poene ex primatu sibi pretulisset"; B., *Vita Dunstani*, 60–1. See also Brooks, "Career of Dunstan," 13.

79 Hart, *Danelaw*, 431–45; Keynes, "'Dunstan B' Charters"; Abrams, *Anglo-Saxon Glastonbury*, 328; Winterbottom and Lapidge, *Lives of Dunstan*, xx–xxiii.

production.[80] In addition to his grants and gifts to the abbey, Eadred entrusted part of his own treasury to Dunstan's care, and his earliest hagiographer noted that when the king died, the saint was en route to his deathbed with all the royal treasure which was kept at Glastonbury.[81] Yet although Eadred died at Frome, a royal estate just twenty miles from Glastonbury, his body was carried nearly sixty miles to Winchester and interred at Old Minster.[82] There is little indication that Eadred had made these arrangements himself. Although he willed a generous bequest to "the place where he wishes his body to rest," his final donation to Old Minster is inconsistent with an intent to be buried there.[83] Some sources credited Dunstan with overseeing the funeral, but it is unlikely that the abbot of Glastonbury would have relinquished the opportunity to expand his foundation's royal mausoleum by burying the body so far away.[84]

A more convincing possibility is that Eadred's burial at Old Minster was overseen by Bishop Ælfsige of Winchester, under the direction of the king's nephew and successor Eadwig.[85] Ælfsige was a notable figure at Eadwig's court, as he had been at Eadred's, but he was not part of Dunstan's reforming circle; rather, he was remembered as overtly hostile to monastic ideals and to the reformers themselves.[86] Whereas Dunstan quarrelled with

80 Keynes, "'Dunstan B' Charters," 185–6; Abrams, *Anglo-Saxon Glastonbury*, 345. Glastonbury reportedly remained a royal scriptorium through the Norman Conquest: Keynes, *Diplomas*, 152.

81 B., *Vita Dunstani*, 60–1 and 64–5; Keynes, *Diplomas*, 147–8; Brooks, "Career of Dunstan," 14.

82 ASC A 955; Swanton, *Chronicles*, 112n3.

83 "Þære stowe þær he wile þæt his lic reste"; S 1515. For Eadred's will and burial, see: Miller, *Charters of the New Minster*, 79; Keynes, "'Dunstan B' Charters," 188–9. Eadred was nevertheless remembered at Winchester as a "lover and defender" [amator et defensor] of Old Minster: Wulfstan of Winchester, *Life of Æthelwold*, 18–19.

84 JW 404–5; William of Malmesbury, *Vita Dunstani*, i.25; Adelard's *Lectiones*, in Winterbottom and Lapidge, *Lives of Dunstan*, 124–5; and above, n. 73.

85 The involvement of Ælfsige (r. 951–958) is suggested by Winterbottom and Lapidge, *Lives of Dunstan*, 124n45; and see also: Yorke, "Ælfsige"; Miller, *Charters of the New Minster*, 82–3. His prominence at Eadwig's court is discussed by Jayakumar, "Eadwig and Edgar," 85–6.

86 Ælfsige was regularly named first among bishops in lists of charter witness during the reigns of both Eadred and Eadwig: Keynes, *Diplomas*, 53–5; Brooks, *Early History of Canterbury*, 237–8 and 375. At the turn of the twelfth century, Eadmer described Ælfsige gloating over the tomb of the reforming archbishop Oda: Eadmer, *Lives*, 30–5, with dating at xxxv–xxxvi. While his hostility cannot be corroborated, it is clear that Ælfsige was not a reformed monk; on the contrary, he was evidently married with at least one son: Yorke, "Ælfsige"; Miller, *Charters of the New Minster*, 83.

Eadwig and was forced into exile shortly after Eadred's death, Ælfsige retained his place of prominence and was elevated by Eadwig to the archbishopric of Canterbury in 958.[87] The rift with Dunstan soon became part of a broader political conflict, however. The king's brother Edgar, seeking to expand his own influence, gained control of Mercia in 957 and recalled Dunstan from exile, making him a key adviser.[88] The final two years of Eadwig's reign were marked by the brothers' competing alliances with leading ecclesiastics: Edgar's devotion to Dunstan was paralleled by Eadwig's attachment to Ælfsige, making the clergymen's divergent attitudes toward religious life a point of political and ideological contention.[89] Although Eadwig's antagonism towards Dunstan was deemed un-Christian and even anti-monastic by later authors, his apparent prejudice must be understood in its political context.[90] During his four-year reign, Eadwig sought to differentiate himself from his predecessors. He replaced the advisers and administrators his father and uncle had favoured, and he diverted his patronage from the religious houses they had supported, including Glastonbury.[91] In some cases, Eadwig may have deliberately reversed recent trends in royal giving: where Eadred and Edmund had done little for Malmesbury, Eadwig apparently patronized Æthelstan's mausoleum and its cult of St Aldhelm.[92] He also fostered a close relationship with New Minster. His burial there in 959 alongside Edward the Elder and Alfred associated his reign with theirs – a connection echoed in the foundation's *Liber Vitae*, which commemorated Eadwig, like his grandfather Edward, as the imperial ruler of the English, the 957 division

87 Dunstan was reportedly driven from court after pulling Eadwig away from a sexual liaison on his coronation night: the earliest account of this is provided by B., *Vita Dunstani*, 66–71; and see also Brooks, "Career of Dunstan," 14–18. For Ælfsige's promotion, see B., *Vita Dunstani*, 78–81.

88 B., *Vita Dunstani*, 74–7; ASC BC 957, and compare ASC D 955, which has the brothers splitting the kingdom at Eadred's death. See also: Stafford, *Unification and Conquest*, 47–50; Brooks, "Career of Dunstan," 18–19.

89 Brooks, "Career of Dunstan," 18.

90 For example: B., *Vita Dunstani*, 76–7; William of Malmesbury, *GR* ii.147.2–3; *De Antiquitate*, 120–1; and see also Jayakumar, "Eadwig and Edgar," 84–90.

91 The *De Antiquitate* condemned Eadwig's installation of a false abbot (*pseudo-abbati*) at Glastonbury after Dunstan's expulsion but acknowledged that the king issued him two grants: *De Antiquitate*, 57–8; Kelly, *Charters of Glastonbury*, 71–8. For the change in advisers, see: Yorke, "Æthelwold and the Politics of the Tenth Century," 75–7; Jayakumar, "Eadwig and Edgar," 84–90; Fleming, *Kings and Lords*, 37–9.

92 Kelly, *Charters of Malmesbury*, 23; William of Malmesbury, *GR* ii.147.3.

of his kingdom notwithstanding.[93] By looking to earlier examples of West Saxon patronage, Eadwig may have intended to reinforce his authority against a younger brother who had just come of age and who cultivated relations with prominent monastic reformers.[94] If Eadwig had anticipated conflict with Edgar and his partisans as early as 955, it is logical that he would decline to have his uncle buried at Glastonbury or another reformed monastery, whatever Eadred's own intentions may have been.[95] By having him interred at Winchester's cathedral, under the auspices of a friendly bishop, Eadwig ensured that the king's body would not become political leverage for his opponents.

Under Edgar, Glastonbury's fortunes revived. Royal gifts to the foundation resumed, and it once again served as a royal chancery, with diplomatic styles associated with Dunstan coming back into fashion after Eadwig's death.[96] Edgar's connection with monastic reform was highly praised by the movement's apologists, and the appointments of Dunstan as bishop of Worcester and London ca 958 and as archbishop of Canterbury in 959 confirm that his circle's reforming efforts had earned royal support.[97] The king was buried at Glastonbury when he died in 975. It is possible that he specifically designated the foundation as his final resting place, although there is no extant evidence to that effect.[98] His burial there was not inevitable, however, especially since his focus had rested less on Glastonbury than on Winchester in his final years. Edgar's celebrated collaboration with St Æthelwold, his erstwhile tutor whom he made bishop of Winchester in 963, helped the city re-emerge as a centre for royal

93 "Angligeni imperii adeptus diadema"; Edward was the only previous king to be associated with an *imperiuum* in the text: Keynes, *Liber Vitae*, fols. 8r–10r, with quotation at 10r. Eadwig's imperial-style titles in the diplomas of his reign offer a parallel to this language: Keynes, "Edgar, *Rex Admirabilis*," 6–7. For Eadwig's relations with New Minster, see Miller, *Charters of the New Minster*, xxxi and 93.

94 Brooks, "Career of Dunstan," 20–1; and below, n. 99.

95 Simon Keynes suggests that Eadred intended to be buried at Glastonbury or Abingdon: "'Dunstan B' Charters," 188. Eadwig appears to have disregarded other stipulations of Eadred's will: Miller, *Charters of the New Minster*, 79; Keynes, "'Dunstan B' Charters," 188–9.

96 Abrams, *Anglo-Saxon Glastonbury*, 346; Keynes, "'Dunstan B' Charters," 190–1.

97 B., *Vita Dunstani*, 76–81 credits Edgar with Dunstan's various elevations. See also: Brooks, "Career of Dunstan," 20–1; Brooks, *Early History of Canterbury*, 243–4. Dunstan's involvement in reforms of the later tenth century may have been more limited than generally assumed, however: Robertson, "Dunstan and Monastic Reform"; Winterbottom and Lapidge, *Lives of Dunstan*, xliii–li.

98 Abrams, *Anglo-Saxon Glastonbury*, 346.

ceremonial.[99] The king was remembered as an important benefactor of Old Minster, who authorized the expulsion of secular canons in 964 and supervised Æthelwold's translation of St Swithun in 971, an event which he may have observed from a new western addition to the cathedral designed to accommodate its royal patron.[100] Edgar was also committed to revitalizing New Minster, and its refoundation as a reformed monastery in 966 was commemorated with a lavish illustration of the king on the frontispiece of the community's *Liber Vitae*, along with a narrative paean to his piety.[101] Just a few years later, in 972, he oversaw the foundation's rededication.[102] The 970s were also marked by a revival of iconography from the reigns of Alfred and Edward, and Edgar's activity at New Minster had the additional benefit of accentuating the continuity of his dynastic line, represented by the graves of his grandfather and great-grandfather as well as that of his brother Eadwig.[103] An evocation of the West Saxon royal past at New Minster would have been a fitting prelude to Edgar's coronation at Bath in May 973, an event designed to highlight the king's imperial authority in Britain.[104]

99 Wulfstan of Winchester, *Life of Æthelwold*, 28–31; Symons, *Regularis Concordia*, 1–9. For Æthelwold, rather than Dunstan, as the chief agent of monastic reform in the reign of Edgar, see Robertson, "Dunstan and Monastic Reform," 159–60.

100 Wulfstan of Winchester, *Life of Æthelwold*, 28–31 and 42–3; Lapidge, *Swithun*. For the westwork, begun in Edgar's reign and dedicated under Æthelred in 980, see: Biddle, "*Felix Urbs Winthonia*," 305–7; Biddle, "Development of an Early Capital," 255–6; Biddle, *Winchester*, 307; Kjølbye-Biddle, "St Swithun's Day, 1093," 16–18; Quirk, "Winchester Cathedral," 48–56; Karkov, *Ruler Portraits*, 97; Nelson, "Inauguration Rituals," 303.

101 Secular canons were expelled from New Minster and replaced with monks in 964, but its refoundation charter, S 745, was produced two years later, in 966: Miller, *Charters of the New Minster*, xxxi–xxxii and 95–111; Rumble, *Property and Piety*, 65–97. For the frontispiece: Karkov, "Frontispiece to the New Minster Charter"; Karkov, *Ruler Portraits*, 85–93. See also Wulfstan of Winchester, *Life of Æthelwold*, 36–7. For the prose account of Edgar's patronage, which notes his burial at Glastonbury, see Keynes, *Liber Vitae*, 81–2 and fol. 10.

102 This event was recorded exclusively by John of Worcester: JW 420–1. See also: Miller, *Charters of the New Minster*, xxxi–xxxii; Karkov, "Frontispiece to the New Minster Charter," 225.

103 Karkov, *Ruler Portraits*, 102–6; Karkov, "Frontispiece to the New Minster Charter," 236–7.

104 ASC A 973, BC 974, DE 972 (all *recte* 973); JW 422–5; William of Malmesbury, *GR* ii.160–1. The event's imperial overtones are discussed by Nelson, "Inauguration Rituals," 296–303.

In light of his increasing interest in imperial ideology and his ceremonial focus on Winchester in the 970s, Glastonbury does not seem an obvious place for Edgar's burial, its prestige as a royal centre notwithstanding. Winchester's re-emergence as a locus for royal and ecclesiastical activity would have made one of its established mausolea an appealing choice for a ruler who associated himself with a religious reform movement now based at the city's cathedral. Even though his own father Edmund was interred at Glastonbury, that grave alone was not enough to ensure Edgar's burial there by default. Two sets of circumstances may explain why the king's body was brought to Glastonbury. First, Dunstan maintained his ties to the community well into his career as archbishop and may have kept his abbacy as late as 974.[105] When Edgar died in 975, it is a fair assumption that he made a bid for the body, as he had when Edmund died nearly thirty years earlier. After the premature and possibly unexpected death of another young king, Dunstan once again faced an opportunity to enhance his home foundation by doubling the size of its royal mausoleum.

Second, Edgar was buried at the outset of a heated political conflict over the succession. In 975, there were two contenders for the throne: Edward, Edgar's eldest son from his first marriage, who was approximately eleven years old when his father died; and Æthelred, Edgar's younger son by his consecrated queen, who was perhaps nine years old. Edgar may have intended the younger Æthelred to be his heir, but there was nevertheless a tendentious succession dispute, in which Dunstan advocated for Edward and Æthelwold for Æthelred.[106] In light of this conflict, it is revealing that Edgar was buried at Dunstan's home foundation of Glastonbury rather than at Æthelwold's Winchester see.[107] If Edward's supporters were able to gain possession of the body and dispose of it as they saw fit, then Edgar's burial – conducted with "worthy rites" in a "kingly manner" – was surely choreographed to highlight the primacy of his eldest son.[108] It is clear that Edward's faction gained enough support to have their candidate crowned

105 Foot, "Glastonbury's Early Abbots," 179–83; Brooks, "Career of Dunstan," 22; Lapidge, "Dunstan."

106 See especially: Keynes, *Diplomas*, 163–6; Yorke, "Æthelwold and the Politics of the Tenth Century," 82–5. This dispute is treated at length in chapter 5.

107 Dunstan's involvement is highlighted in post-Conquest sources, including the *Passio S. Eadwardi* (discussed below, chapter 5) and the *vitae* of Dunstan by Osbern, Eadmer, and William of Malmesbury: Winterbottom and Lapidge, *Lives of Dunstan*, xl–xli. See also Karkov, "Frontispiece to the New Minster Charter," 236–7n64.

108 "Congruis exequiis"; Keynes, *Liber Vitae*, fol. 11r. "Regio more"; JW 424–5.

shortly after Edgar's death on 8 July, for the Anglo-Saxon Chronicle implies that the consecration took place before autumn.[109] Edward's election was not uncontested, however. Twelfth-century accounts indicate that Dunstan lobbied aggressively for his candidate's coronation but was not concerned with winning unanimous consent. John of Worcester stated that the full *witan* was not assembled for the consecration; rather, Dunstan's party "convened together as many of their fellow bishops, abbots, and nobles as possible and elected Edward as his father had ordered; once elected, they consecrated him and anointed him king."[110] William of Malmesbury specified that this was done "against the will" of many of the kingdom's magnates.[111] In spite of this opposition and an election which may have been irregular, Edward's cause had evidently gained enough momentum in summer 975 for Dunstan to propel him through a royal consecration. In this context, Edgar's Glastonbury funeral is significant. It is conceivable that Edward and his allies buried the body and then travelled directly to Kingston, soliciting support along the hundred-mile journey.[112] In this scenario, the incomplete *witan* could have acclaimed and crowned the ætheling within just a few weeks of his father's death, without giving his detractors an opportunity to formally object.[113] Dunstan's control of Edgar's remains at the beginning of the succession dispute may well have been instrumental to Edward's accession.

Dunstan's personal relationships with tenth-century rulers were essential to Glastonbury's emergence as a royal mausoleum, but Edgar's burial there was the last he lived to see. It would be forty years before another

---

109 ASC DE 975: "In this year, Edward, Edgar's son, ascended to the kingdom. And immediately in autumn in that same year, the star 'comet' appeared" [Her Eadweard, Eadgares sunu, feng to rice. 7 sona on þam ilcan geare on hærfest æteowde cometa se steorra].

110 "Cum coepiscopis, abbatibus, ducibusque quamplurimis in unum conuenerunt et Eaduuardum, ut pater suus preceperat, elegerunt, electum consecrauerunt, et in regem unxerunt"; JW 426–7. Compare also the *Passio Eadwardi*, which reported that the king was chosen "by St Dunstan and certain nobles" [a sancto Dunstano et quibusdam principibus]; Fell, *Edward, King and Martyr*, 2. See also Winterbottom and Lapidge, *Lives of Dunstan*, xl–xli.

111 "Contra uoluntatem"; *GR* ii.161.1. For Edward's election, see also: Keynes, *Diplomas*, 166; Yorke, "Æthelwold and the Politics of the Tenth Century," 84–5.

112 For Edward's consecration at Kingston, see Keynes, *Diplomas*, 271.

113 In this context, the ASC comment that Edward's killers "did not want to bow to his living body" [noldon ... to his libbendan lichaman onbugan] may reflect their refusal to acknowledge his election or consecration as legitimate: ASC D 979 (*recte* 978); and below, chapter 5.

king was interred at the monastery.[114] In 1016, the body of Edmund Ironside was brought to Glastonbury for burial, marking the conclusion of the Danish conquest begun by Swein Forkbeard and completed by his son Cnut. The circumstances and political implications of his burial will be examined in greater detail in the next chapter. However, a few points are pertinent to the present discussion. One is that Glastonbury was still deemed an appropriate place to bury a king, nearly half a century after its last royal burial. Although the foundation suffered financially during the reign of Æthelred II and was overshadowed by other houses as an object of royal patronage, it retained much of its wealth and did not see an abrupt decline in status during this period.[115] In addition, Edmund Ironside's burial reiterated Glastonbury's connection with the West Saxon dynasty, which the abbey sought to accentuate in the decades after Edgar's death. By the later tenth century, the foundation was documenting its conversion-era past and compiling charters purportedly granted in the seventh century by the West Saxon kings Cenwealh, Centwine, and Ine.[116] Twelfth-century reports that Centwine had been interred at Glastonbury may reflect an older tradition, as the stone monument marking his grave was noted for its "great age" by William of Malmesbury.[117] If such an early

114 Edward was buried at Wareham in 978 and translated to Shaftesbury in 979; Swein Forkbeard was buried at York and then translated to Roskilde, Denmark in 1014; and Æthelred II was buried at St Paul's, London, in 1016. These burials are discussed in detail in later chapters.

115 Abrams, *Anglo-Saxon Glastonbury*, 347–8; Keynes, *Diplomas*, 180.

116 These charters (several of which are no longer extant) were enumerated in the *Liber Terrarum*, a list of charters produced at Glastonbury, likely in the late tenth century: Abrams, *Anglo-Saxon Glastonbury*, 14–18, 31–4, and 124–30. See also Abrams, "Diploma of King Ine," 132.

117 "Nimia uetustate"; *De Antiquitate*, 84–5. According to this account, Centwine was buried in Glastonbury's monastic cemetery, inside one of its two "pyramid" monuments: "The remains of this king rest in the monks' cemetery, in a pyramid that was once nobly carved" [Huius regis exuuie in cimiterio monachorum in piramide quondam nobiliter exculpta requiescunt]; 90–1, and see also 82–3. The *De Antiquitate* also reports that Glastonbury's two pyramids – which could be dated as early as the eighth century – were inscribed with names of early abbots and bishops, leading the author to posit that the bones of those named were preserved inside: *De Antiquitate*, 84–5; and compare also William of Malmesbury, *GR* i.21.3; Dodwell, *Anglo-Saxon Art*, 115. The pyramids are discussed by Dodwell, *Anglo-Saxon Art*, 113–18; Taylor and Taylor, *Anglo-Saxon Architecture* I, 255–6. For Centwine as an early ecclesiastical patron, see: Abrams, *Anglo-Saxon Glastonbury*, 125; Blows, "Pre-Conquest History of Glastonbury," 109–37. However, the twelfth-century Winchester Annals claim that Centwine was buried at Old Minster: Luard, *Annals Monastici de Wintonia*, 5; Yorke, "Foundation of Old Minster," 80; Blows, "Pre-Conquest History of Glastonbury," 130–1 and 146n101.

West Saxon patron was already memorialized there in the pre-Conquest period, the foundation could have asserted ancient royal connections to rival those of other religious houses – perhaps a relevant concern as royal activity increasingly shifted back to Winchester and then to London in the tenth and eleventh centuries.[118] Such a message would certainly have been implicit in 1052, when Abbot Æthelweard translated Edgar's remains into a reliquary by Glastonbury's altar – an event that coincided with Edward the Confessor's building project at Westminster and may have been choreographed to reassert Glastonbury's prominence as a royal centre.[119] Allegations of Edgar's sanctity were confirmed by the discovery that his body was incorrupt, but rumours of his saintliness must have emerged earlier in Æthelweard's abbacy, which spanned the reigns of Cnut, Harold Harefoot, Harthacnut, and Edward the Confessor.[120] A nascent royal saint's cult offers a compelling context for a story that was circulating by the 1060s: during the reign of Cnut, Bishop Brihtwold of Ramsbury saw a prophetic vision of St Peter crowning Edward the Confessor during a vigil near Glastonbury's high altar, where both Edgar and Edmund Ironside were buried.[121] Regardless of whether Edgar's sanctity was widely acknowledged, Glastonbury continued to be recognized as a repository for West Saxon dynastic memory and legitimacy.

Although Glastonbury's collection of kings' graves was more a product of chance and opportunity than an active rejection of established royal burial sites, the foundation's mausoleum – like those at Malmesbury and

---

118 For tensions with Westminster around the year 1000, see Brooks, "Career of Dunstan," 3. For competition between the foundations in the early twelfth century, see Radford, "Glastonbury Abbey," 110.

119 The reliquary was placed in a shrine which also contained relics of St Vincent, but the translation ended in disaster for Æthelweard, who reportedly went mad after mishandling Edgar's body. The episode is dated to 1052 by William of Malmesbury: *GR* ii.160; *Vita Dunstani*, ii.18.1; *De Antiquitate*, 84–5 and 134–5.

120 Æthelweard was abbot from ca 1024 through 1053: Knowles, *Heads of Religious Houses*, 51; Blows, "Glastonbury Obit-List," 267. It may be relevant that Æthelweard had reportedly prepared the reliquary in advance, suggesting that the exhumation of Edgar's body had been carefully planned: William of Malmesbury, *GR* ii.160; *De Antiquitate*, 134–5. For the local nature of Edgar's cult, see Rollason, *Saints and Relics*, 140–1.

121 *Vita Ædwardi*, 8–9 and 85–7; *De Antiquitate* 84–5 and 140–1; William of Malmesbury, *GR* ii.221; William of Malmesbury, *GP* ii.83.4–5; Abrams, *Anglo-Saxon Glastonbury*, 348. Brihtwold was a patron of Glastonbury and had been a monk there before his elevation to Ramsbury, sometime between 995 and 1005; he died in 1045. For Brihtwold's career, see Stephens, "Brihtwold."

New Minster – maintained a clear sense of continuity with earlier generations of West Saxon royalty. Yet the kings who were buried there also gained a connection with religious reforms which looked to the future and linked England with its Continental neighbours. When the senior Edmund was buried at Glastonbury in 946, he was interred in an eastern tower that Dunstan had recently built – an early manifestation of the foundation's revitalization.[122] A decade later, Eadred apparently intended to replicate his brother's move away from Winchester, perhaps to benefit from the spiritual purity of a reformed monastery. If so, it is likely that the king was following Dunstan's advice in this matter, just as the organizers of Edgar's funeral seem to have done in 975, when they brought the king's body to Glastonbury and placed it "in a column before the entrance to the church."[123] By 1016, when Edmund Ironside's remains were brought there, Glastonbury's credentials as a royal burial site were well established: the honourable placement of his body before the high altar would have reinforced his identity as a legitimate king at a time when most surviving members of the West Saxon dynasty had been driven out of Danish-ruled England. With Edgar's translation in 1052, the bodies of all three kings would have been grouped towards the east end of the church in close proximity to the altar, much like the royal graves at New Minster.[124] If Edward the Confessor's accession in 1042 was understood as a restoration of the West Saxon house, the royal mausoleum at Glastonbury would have become increasingly relevant as a monument to the dynasty's past.[125]

Conclusions

As the preceding discussion demonstrates, royal grave sites were not chosen arbitrarily in the tenth century but conformed to a shifting political geography. While Malmesbury and Glastonbury were not urban centres on the scale of Winchester and London, their distance from these areas may have contributed to their appeal. A king's burial in a major city might soon be overshadowed by surrounding attractions and activity; a less

122 *De Antiquitate*, 84–5 and 118–19; William of Malmesbury, *GR*, ii.144.3. The tower is described by Radford, "Glastonbury Abbey," 120–1.

123 "In capitulo ante introitum ecclesie"; *De Antiquitate*, 84–5, and compare also 130–1.

124 The proximity of the bodies of Edgar and Edmund Ironside are noted by JW 492–3; William of Malmesbury, *GR* ii.180.9.

125 For the restoration of West Saxon rule, see *Vita Ædwardi*, 9.

trafficked location would ensure it greater reverence from visitors and attention from its ecclesiastical custodians. The adoption of mausolea in western Wessex also reflected territorial expansion, as Mercia and Wessex became better integrated as a political unit over the course of the tenth century. When Edward the Elder came to power, Mercia was held by his sister and brother-in-law under his nominal lordship, which he solidified at their deaths; but the regions were poised to split under Æthelstan and Ælfweard in 924, had the latter not died so quickly, and they were divided between Eadwig and Edgar from 957 through 959.[126] Malmesbury and Glastonbury, both located on the Roman Fosse Road, were more convenient to western Mercia than Winchester was, and it is probable that they became more regular stops on the royal itinerary in this period.[127] The burials at these foundations would have been familiar to the political elites of both populations as they met or travelled with the king, providing material reminders of the ascendency and continuity of the West Saxon dynasty.

Nevertheless, with few exceptions, these burial sites were determined by the kings' survivors rather than the kings themselves. Certainly, the foundations were all prestigious enough to house royal graves, and it is difficult to imagine objections being raised about their propriety. However, in deciding where to bury their rulers, the individuals who took charge of the bodies and funerals used the placement of remains to create specific legacies for the dead. Edmund and Edgar's interment at Glastonbury retroactively confirmed their support of Dunstan and his allies, whereas Eadred's burial at Old Minster limited his posthumous association with monastic reform. Ælfweard and Eadwig were celebrated at New Minster, where the royal bodies could be used to remind these kings' successors – both of whom were based in Mercia – of their dynasty's connections and obligations to the foundation. It is also significant that the mothers and widows of these kings patronized the houses in which their kinsmen were buried. Ælfweard's mother Ælfflæd and Eadwig's wife Ælfgifu remained benefactors of New Minster; Edmund's widow Æthelflæd shared in her husband's generosity towards Glastonbury in life and listed the foundation as the first beneficiary of her will; and Edmund and Eadred's mother Eadgifu was

126 ASC D 955 stated that the kingdom was split between the brothers as soon as Eadred died; above, n. 88. The regions would be divided again by Cnut and Edmund Ironside in 1016 and held as separate regencies by Emma and Harold Harefoot from 1035 through 1037; see chapter 3 below.

127 Hill, *Atlas of Anglo-Saxon England*, 87–90 and 135–9; Stenton, "Road System," 3–4.

remembered as a champion of St Dunstan during his tenure as abbot.[128] Although it is impossible to pinpoint their exact roles in royal burials, these women were undoubtedly involved in the funerals and may have had considerable influence over where the graves would be located.[129]

The question, then, is how much agency kings had over their own burials. In some cases, it seems clear that the deceased's intentions were respected. Malmesbury, which housed no royal graves before the 930s, was remembered as Æthelstan's designated mausoleum, and the treasure which accompanied his body was likely a bequest to his burial church.[130] The fact that his intentions were followed confirms the stability of his kingdom in 939; there were apparently no political drawbacks to fulfilling his wishes. Eadred's burial at Old Minster, by contrast, served the interests of his successor at the expense of the deceased's own wishes. Although it is difficult to believe that Eadred's remains were abandoned and neglected, as one later author asserted, it is certainly possible that his burial lacked the ceremony which normally characterized royal funerals.[131] Perhaps there was a dispute over the fate of Eadred's remains: it may be that Dunstan and Eadgifu sought possession of the body but were thwarted by Eadwig, who took control of the corpse and buried it as quickly as possible at Old Minster, whose clergy were more amenable to the new regime than the community at Glastonbury was. Eadwig's critics could not fault the king for burying his predecessor at Winchester's most venerable royal mausoleum, yet this move prevented Eadred's partisans from using his body and legacy as ideological leverage against his nephew. Under such circumstances, fulfilling or neglecting the king's intentions was a political strategy in its own right.

128 None of these women is mentioned in accounts of royal funerals, which is why their roles are not treated in greater depth above. For patronage by Ælfflæd, Ælfweard's mother, see: Keynes, *Liber Vitae*, 19–20; Thacker, "Dynastic Monasteries," 253–4. Ælfgifu, Eadwig's wife, bequeathed an estate and a hundred gold mancuses to New Minster (although she designated Old Minster as her burial place): S 1484. Æthelflæd, Edmund's wife, bequeathed an estate to Glastonbury "for King Edmund's soul, and for King Edgar's, and for my soul" [for Ædmundes cinges sawle . 7 for Eadgares cinges . 7 for mire sawle]: S 1494; edited in Whitelock, *Anglo-Saxon Wills*, 34 no. 14. Eadgifu, mother of Edmund and Eadred, was praised as a supporter of Dunstan and other reformers: B., *Vita Dunstani*, 62–3; Wulfstan of Winchester, *Life of Æthelwold*, 18–21.

129 Compare Nelson, "Carolingian Royal Funerals," 147–9.

130 William of Malmesbury, *GR* ii.140.

131 Adelard reported that everyone but Dunstan deserted the body, "disdaining the royal funeral rites" [exequias regias fastidientibus]: Winterbottom and Lapidge, *Lives of Dunstan*, 124–5.

Similarly forceful claims to royal corpses were likely made at the deaths of Edmund and Edgar. While neither king's burial at Glastonbury was objectionable, their interment there dramatically enhanced the status of the foundation and furthered the political aims of its abbot. In Edmund's case, there is no indication of conflict, yet the king was credited with planning building works at New Minster and was remembered fondly by the community; his burial at Glastonbury may have been regarded as a loss.[132] Where the transfer of power proceeded smoothly after Edmund's death, Edgar's burial was almost certainly part of a protracted struggle for succession. The fact that Dunstan's party crowned its candidate so soon afterwards suggests that the funeral was one component of a broader effort to promote Edgar's elder son. While these circumstances do not preclude concern for the souls of the dead, it appears that Dunstan – like Edward the Elder – recognized the value of a royal body in building the prestige of a religious foundation and enhancing the legitimacy of an aspiring king.

Still, despite the best efforts of the living, it is unlikely that Malmesbury and Glastonbury would have become royal burial sites had they been peripheral outposts on the edge of the kingdom. Dunstan's creation of a royal mausoleum at Glastonbury coincided with the beginnings of the monastic reform movement and a political shift to western Wessex which had begun in the reign of Edward the Elder. Likewise, it was Malmesbury's strategic importance in the reign of Æthelstan that made the *burh* a viable alternative to Winchester.[133] Yet the converse is also true: the promise or presence of kings' graves likely helped bolster these centres as they assumed a more prominent role in tenth-century political culture. The fortunes of Malmesbury and Glastonbury fluctuated in the century before the Norman Conquest, but their royal graves remained a point of pride and authority for the communities which housed them. As monuments to the West Saxon past, the royal graves kept these foundations relevant under the Danish and Norman regimes, just as they had under tenth-century English kings.

132 The foundation's *Liber Vitae* indicated that Edmund's plan to enhance New Minster "out of reverence for Christ and the memories of his kinsmen" [ob Christi uenerationem propinquorumque memorias] was preempted by his death: Keynes, *Liber Vitae*, fol. 9v and 81; and see also: Miller, *Charters of the New Minster*, xxxi; JW 420–1. A thirty-hide grant by Edmund to New Minster (S 470) is cited above, n. 70.

133 Haslam, "Towns of Wiltshire," 117.

3 Funeral, Coronation, and Continuity: Political Corpses in the Eleventh Century

At the end of the ninth century, Alfred the Great identified himself as *rex Anglorum Saxonum*, king of the Anglo-Saxons.[1] Having gained nominal rule over Wessex, Mercia, and Northumbria, he envisioned a unified English kingdom led by a single Christian ruler.[2] It would be decades before these claims were realized, for it was the military and administrative advances of the tenth century that finally enabled a meaningful consolidation of these territories. Nevertheless, Alfred's heirs continued to employ his aspirational rhetoric, depicting England's semi-autonomous regions as parts of a cohesive realm with a West Saxon king at its head. The result was an increasingly well-defined ideology of Christian rulership which identified the king as an exceptional individual, uniquely qualified to undertake the combination of spiritual and earthly responsibilities needed to rule a Christian nation. Ecclesiastical endorsement was vital to the cultivation and dissemination of this ideology. By the turn of the millennium, clerical authors had begun to identify the king as God's vicar on earth; kings presided over Christian festivals and other religious events, like church dedications and saints' translations; and the ritual of royal anointing, by which an episcopal blessing transformed an earthly leader into a divinely recognized king, became an integral component of a ruler's accession. Lavish patronage of burial churches also identified kings as extraordinary, ensuring that their exceptional status would continue to be recognized beyond their physical deaths.

1 Keynes, "Edward, King of the Anglo-Saxons," 57–62; and above, chapter 1.
2 Keynes, "Edward, King of the Anglo Saxons," 60–2; Wormald, "*Lex Scripta*," 132; Wormald, "*Gens Anglorum*."

Although kings' burial places were designed to advertise this singularity, however, accounts of royal funerals are largely absent from the documentary record; Edward the Confessor was the only pre-Conquest ruler to have his burial recorded in detail by a contemporary author. Still, it is clear that funerals were part of a cycle of royal ceremonial which helped distinguish kings from the rest of the population. Accordingly, decisions about royal burials were not made casually or arbitrarily, regardless of whether or not the dead king's wishes were respected. If his preferences were flagrantly neglected, attention would be drawn to his mortality and lack of enduring authority – a poor legacy for the deceased, whatever his accomplishments in life.[3] By contrast, a burial which celebrated a king by fulfilling or exceeding his expectations would have confirmed his exceptionality and relevance. Ideally, a ruler's funeral would provide an opportunity for his subjects to acknowledge his death, mourn his passing, and pray for his soul. Yet funerals also served the living in more mundane matters. In addition to providing a king's reign with ceremonial closure, a royal funeral allowed potential successors to associate themselves with the memory of an established monarch. In the eleventh century, when royal succession was rarely certain or secure, an aspiring ruler's high-profile interaction with the remains of his predecessor could generate a sense of continuity and stability, thereby strengthening his bid for the kingdom. A candidate's prolonged contact with his predecessor's earthly remains and his continued evocation of his memory could be construed as a commitment to govern in the same way as the dead king had, to preserve his administrative structure, and to perpetuate his political ideals. By ostensibly adopting the previous reign as a model for his own, an aspiring successor might secure the endorsement of those who had benefited under the dead ruler – especially the powerful magnates whose support was vital and whose interests were most vulnerable during a change of regime. Whether a candidate's relationship with the dead king was genuine, exaggerated, or altogether fabricated, a prominent appearance at the funeral or grave could lend weight to his claims of legitimacy.

Interaction with a royal corpse was not enough to make a king, of course. A contender with enough military strength and political support to gain practical power would still need to undergo a process of election

3 Eadred's intentions were evidently disregarded after his death: above, chapter 2. Compare also Edith, Edward the Confessor's widow, whom William the Conqueror buried at Westminster despite her intention to be entombed at Wilton.

and consecration, for even if a candidate already exercised some degree of de facto control, it was his recognition by the kingdom's lay and ecclesiastical elites that confirmed his royal status and his authority over the realm. Royal elections, in which a new king was acclaimed by the realm's leading magnates, were usually held soon after the death of the previous monarch. Though mentioned regularly in the documentary record, elections were rarely described in depth, suggesting that these were events spearheaded by laymen rather than by the clergy.[4] Consecration, by contrast, was an ecclesiastical ritual in which a new king was anointed and granted an episcopal blessing; he would swear to uphold the tenets of Christian rulership, which were explicated in detail by the officiant.[5] According to tenth- and eleventh-century political theory, it was this latter rite of anointing that qualified a candidate to rule a Christian nation, making him God's instrument on earth.[6]

Through the tenth century, consecrations were often performed at the royal centre of Kingston-on-Thames, Surrey, usually after an election had been conducted at a different locale.[7] Between 1016 and 1066, however, there is little indication that any ruler received or was even interested in a Kingston consecration. Instead, six of the seven kings who reigned in the half-century leading up to the Norman Conquest – Edmund Ironside, Cnut, Harold Harefoot, Edward the Confessor, Harold Godwineson, and William of Normandy – were elected in the immediate aftermath of their predecessor's funeral or consecrated at the site of his tomb.[8] Whereas a

---

4 Brooke, *Saxon and Norman Kings*, 29–31; Nelson, "Inauguration Rituals," 287.

5 Royal anointing has been discussed extensively by Janet Nelson: "National Synods," "Symbols in Context," "Inauguration Rituals," "Ritual and Reality," "Earliest Royal *Ordo*," and "Second English *Ordo*."

6 Nelson, "Symbols in Context," 270; Nelson, "Inauguration Rituals," 288–9. The distinction was also articulated by Ælfric of Eynsham at the turn of the first millennium: see CH I.14.111–15; Godden, "Ælfric and Anglo-Saxon Kingship."

7 According to pre-Conquest sources, Æthelstan (925), Eadred (946), and Æthelred II (979) were all consecrated at Kingston; according to sources from the twelfth century and later, Edward the Elder (900), Edmund (939), Eadwig (956), Edgar (960), and Edward the Martyr (975) were consecrated there as well. Keynes, "Kingston-Upon Thames," 272; Keynes, *Diplomas*, 270–1, Keynes, "Burial of King Æthelred," 112–1; Swanton, *Chronicles*, 104n10. There was typically a delay between a king's election and anointing: this time could be used to prepare an appropriate ceremony or to have the consecration coincide with a particular feast day. Alternatively, anointing might be postponed if a king was still establishing his power or fighting off rivals for the throne.

8 The seventh, Harthacnut, was out of the country when his predecessor died but still interacted with the corpse upon his return; see below.

Kingston consecration had provided a sense of continuity for earlier generations of kings, it appears that by the eleventh century, it was a new ruler's public association with his predecessor's remains that counterbalanced the political uncertainty of an interregnum. The most significant change in this period involved shifts in England's ruling families: while tenth-century kings were all patrilineal descendants of Alfred, the eleventh century saw the introduction of competing foreign dynasties. The reign of Æthelred II was marked by escalating Viking invasions and the eventual conquest of England by Danish kings. From Æthelred's death through the accession of William of Normandy in 1066, power fluctuated between kings of West Saxon, Danish, Anglo-Scandinavian, and Norman backgrounds. This dynastic instability meant that each new king struggled to prove his legitimacy, and royal funerals became prime occasions for new kings to establish their credentials. This chapter investigates the convergence of royal funerals, elections, and consecrations in the fifty years before the Norman Conquest, assessing how aspiring kings used the bodies and legacies of their predecessors to advance their own claims to authority at times of political crisis and interregnum.

Æthelred II, Edmund Ironside, and Cnut: 1016–1017

> Then it happened that King Æthelred died. He ended his days on St George's mass-day, and he held his kingdom with great effort and hardship as long as his life lasted.[9]

The Anglo-Saxon Chronicle's pithy account of the death of Æthelred II appears in the midst of a long entry detailing the military and political crisis of 1016, the culmination of the disastrous final decade of his reign. After years of Viking incursions, Æthelred was driven into exile in 1013 by the Danish king Swein Forkbeard, who promptly claimed the English throne. When Swein died in February 1014, Æthelred returned home after promising his subjects to be a better king than he had before. He spent his final two years resisting the advances of Cnut, Swein's son, and died in

9 "Þa gelamp hit þæt se cyning Æþelred forðferde ... he geendode his dagas on Sancte Georgius mæssedæig, 7 he geheold his rice mid myclum geswince 7 earfoðnessum þa hwile ðe his lif wæs"; ASC CDEF 1016. St George's day was 23 April.

London shortly before Cnut launched an attack on the city. He was buried at St Paul's Cathedral as the citizens prepared for a siege.[10]

There were now two contenders for the English throne, each of whom claimed the kingdom as his paternal inheritance. Swein's supporters considered Cnut the rightful heir to his father's conquered kingdom, and in the spring of 1016, he pressed his claim by heading an assault on London. Æthelred's son, Edmund Ironside, was the senior member of the West Saxon royal dynasty and was regarded by his partisans as the natural successor to the realm; he was leading London's defence when his father died. Although control of the kingdom ultimately depended on a military victory, Æthelred's memory was integral to both candidates' claims of legitimacy. For Cnut, Æthelred was remembered as a conquered king who submitted to Swein and forfeited his family's right to rule.[11] For Edmund, Æthelred was a lawful ruler with an ancient pedigree, who, despite his oppression by foreign invaders, had not abdicated his throne and had been welcomed back from exile by his subjects.[12] The candidates' evocation of their shared predecessor was not limited to recollections of kinship and conquest, however, for they each laid claim to Æthelred's administrative landscape as well. Both men angled for control of Wessex, the home territory of West Saxon kings, but the most important prize was London. As Æthelred's chief administrative centre, his primary residence, and the place where he had died and been buried, London had become an established staging point for royal ceremonial, as well as a repository for the memory of Æthelred's thirty-eight-year reign.[13] Accordingly, Edmund and Cnut each recognized that possession of the city's royal centre – in addition to providing considerable military and economic advantages – would help bestow legitimacy on their claims to the kingdom.

---

10 ASC CDEF 1016 noted that Æthelred died in London. John of Worcester added: "His body was honourably buried in the church of St Paul the Apostle" [Corpus autem illius in ecclesia sancti Pauli apostoli honorifice sepultum est]; JW 484–5.

11 This idea was articulated in the Old Norse poetry produced at Cnut's court: Whitelock, *EHD* I, 334–41 nos. 14–19; Frank, "King Cnut in the Verse of His Skalds"; Townend, "Contextualizing the *Knútsdrápur*"; and below, chapter 6.

12 ASC CDE 1014; Wormald, "Æthelred the Lawmaker," 59; Stafford, "Royal Promises," 181.

13 London had been in the possession of West Saxon kings since Edward the Elder annexed the city in 911, upon the death of his brother-in-law, Æthelred of Mercia: ASC A 911, BCD 912, E 910 (all *recte* 911); and see above, chapter 2. London's importance in the reign of Æthelred II is discussed by Keynes, "Burial of King Æthelred," 137–44.

Early in 1016, Æthelred and Edmund held London as Cnut planned a siege; by the end of the year, Æthelred and Edmund were both dead and Cnut had been recognized in London as England's sole king. The earliest discrete descriptions of these events appear in the Anglo-Saxon Chronicle, the *Encomium Emmae Reginae*, and the Chronicle of John of Worcester, but there are substantial discrepancies between these three texts. The Anglo-Saxon Chronicle annals for this period were composed shortly after Cnut's accession, probably by a Londoner who had supported Edmund's candidacy and encountered the siege and its aftermath first-hand.[14] He wrote that "after Æthelred's end, all the *witan* who were in London and the *burh*-guard elected Edmund as king."[15] Cnut's fleet, which had been heading toward London, arrived a few weeks later, but Edmund had left the city before the siege began and "rode into Wessex, and all the people submitted to him."[16] He then engaged in a series of battles with the Danes, reclaiming London but suffering a major defeat in October at the battle of Assandun, in Essex. Afterwards, the two claimants agreed to divide the kingdom, with Cnut ruling the north and Edmund ruling Wessex; they exchanged hostages, the English army paid a tribute, and the Danish fleet retired to London.[17] The arrangement did not last, however. Edmund died on St Andrew's day, 30 November, and was buried at Glastonbury.[18] In 1017, the Chronicle continued, "Cnut acceded to the entire kingdom of the English," dividing the realm into four earldoms and exiling or killing a number of his English opponents.[19] The annal concluded by noting Cnut's marriage to Emma, Æthelred's Norman-born widow.

---

14 These annals, which are common to ASC CDEF, were part of a self-contained account of the years 983 through 1022, probably composed retrospectively by a single author writing in London between 1016 and 1023: Keynes, "Declining Reputation," 229–32. Compare also O'Brien O'Keeffe, *MS C*, lxviii.

15 "Þa æfter his ende ealle ða witan þa on Lundene wæron 7 seo burhwaru gecuron Eadmund to cyninge"; ASC CDEF 1016.

16 "Gerad þa Westsexon, 7 him beah eal folc to"; ASC CDE 1016. Æthelred died on 23 April. Cnut's ships assembled after Easter, 1 April, and arrived in London after stopping in Greenwich during the Rogation Days, 7–9 May. For these dates, see Swanton, *Chronicles*, 148–9.

17 ASC CDEF 1016.

18 Some post-Conquest authors, including William of Malmesbury and Henry of Huntingdon, claimed that Edmund was murdered, but there is no indication of foul play in the earliest accounts of his death: William of Malmesbury, *GR* ii.180.9; Henry of Huntingdon, *Historia Anglorum*, vi.14; Gates, "Eadric *Streona*'s Execution."

19 "Feng Cnut kyning to eallon Angelcynnes ryce"; ASC CDEF 1017.

Emma would be responsible for a second interpretation of these events when she commissioned the *Encomium Emmae Reginae* some twenty-five years later.[20] The work was composed soon after Harthacnut, her son by Cnut, became king in 1040, and its anonymous author had the dual task of glorifying Emma and emphasizing the righteous inevitability of her son's accession. The *Encomium*'s account of the 1016 succession accordingly stressed the legitimacy and primacy of Cnut's claim to the kingdom, minimizing any references to Emma's first marriage to Æthelred and depicting Edmund as a factional leader who unknowingly violated God's will by pursuing his claim to the throne.[21] After the death of Æthelred (who went unnamed in the text), the citizens of London provided him an honourable burial and immediately sent messengers to Cnut, asking him to be their king and take charge of the city. Yet some of London's garrison opposed this action, according to the Encomiast, and smuggled Edmund out so that he could gather an army in Wessex. Meanwhile, "Cnut entered the city and sat on the throne of the kingdom," but, suspicious of the Londoners' intentions, he quickly left again.[22] Edmund had amassed a large force by this time and re-entered London, where the citizens and the crowd which had followed him from Wessex declared their allegiance to him and repudiated Cnut. After a series of battles, the two men agreed to share power, but God was unwilling to see the kingdom divided and caused Edmund to die; "he was buried in a kingly tomb" and mourned by his subjects.[23] Cnut was now the sole king, and the entire population voluntarily submitted to him and recognized him as their ruler.

A third variation was composed in the twelfth century by John of Worcester, who drew on pre-Conquest sources for his information.[24] His first major diversion from the other early accounts of 1016 is the assertion that Edmund and Cnut were both elected king, each by a different faction:

20 The *Encomium* was composed between 1041 and 1042 by a monk of Flanders who may have been part of Emma's household. On the authorship, date, manuscript, style, and purpose of the *Encomium*, see: Keynes, "Introduction to the Reprint," xxxix–liii and lxvi–lxxi; Campbell, "Introduction," xi–xl [xciii–cxxii], Stafford, *Emma and Edith*, 28–40; Tyler, "Treasure and Artifice", John, *Reassessing*, 151–3.

21 An alternative ending to the *Encomium* has recently been discovered in which Æthelred is explicitly named and celebrated; it was presumably composed after the accession of Edward the Confessor, Æthelred's son, in 1042: Keynes and Love, "Earl Godwine's Ship."

22 "Cnuto autem ciuitatem intrauit, et in solio regni resedit"; *Encomium*, 22–3.

23 "Regio tumulatur sepulchro"; *Encomium*, 30–1.

24 See Introduction above for John of Worcester's use of source materials.

> After [Æthelred's] death, the bishops, abbots, ealdormen, and all the nobles of England, assembled together and, by general agreement, elected Cnut as their lord and king, and, coming to him at Southampton, renounced and repudiated in his presence all the descendants of King Æthelred and made peace with him and swore fidelity to him, and he swore to them that he would be a faithful lord to them, both before God and before the world. But the London citizens and those nobles who were at that time at London by unanimous agreement raised the ætheling Edmund to the kingdom. And he, raised to the height of the royal throne, undauntedly approached Wessex without delay and was received with great joy by the whole population, whom he very swiftly subjected to his rule. When they heard this, many of the English hastily committed themselves to him.[25]

John then expanded on the Anglo-Saxon Chronicle's version of the ensuing events, providing detailed descriptions of Edmund's journey into Wessex, Cnut's siege of London, the clashes between the two armies, the truce after the battle of Assandun, and the division of the kingdom.[26] He then departed again from the Chronicle and *Encomium*: soon after Edmund's death, Cnut ordered all the English magnates to gather in London, where they falsely attested that Edmund had wanted Cnut to rule the kingdom instead of his own brothers and sons; they then swore their loyalty to Cnut and repudiated Edmund's kin. For his account of the events of 1017, John returned to the Chronicle's narrative and reported that Cnut "undertook the government of the whole of England," divided the realm into four earldoms, and exiled Edmund's kinsmen; he also "concluded a treaty with the magnates and the whole people, and they with him, and they confirmed a firm friendship between them with oaths, and

---

25 "Cuius post mortem episcopi, abbates, duces et quique nobiliores Anglie in unum congregati, pari consensu, in dominum et regem sibi Canutum elegere, et, ad eum in Suthamtoniam uenientes, omnemque progeniem regis Agelredi coram illo abnegando repudiantes, pacem cum eo composuere, et fidelitatem illi iurauere, quibus et ille iurauit quod et secondum Deum et secundum seculum fidelis esse uellet eis dominus. At ciues Lundonienses et pars nobilium qui eo tempore consistebant Lundonie clitonem Eadmundum unanimi consensu in regem leuauere. Qui solii regalis sullimatus culmine intrepidus Westsaxoniam adiit sine cunctatione, et ab omni populo magna susceptus gratulatione, sue ditioni subegit eam citissime. Quibus auditis, multi Anglorum populi magna cum festinatione illi se dederunt uoluntarie"; JW 484–5.

26 Unlike the ASC, John maintained that Cnut took control of Wessex, East Anglia, Essex, and London, while "to Edmund remained the realm" [regni Eadmundo remansit]. The discrepancy seems to stem from a corrupt source; JW 492–3n9.

laid aside and set at rest all their old animosities."[27] John concluded with Cnut's marriage to Emma in July and the execution in London of a handful of English nobles at Christmas.

In all three texts, Æthelred's death served as the catalyst for Cnut and Edmund's succession dispute, and the descriptions of the candidates' acclamations were consistently conflated with references to the dead king. Each author introduced his description of the royal election by noting that the assembly took place after Æthelred had died, giving the impression that the magnates who gathered to choose a new ruler had also witnessed the funeral of his predecessor.[28] The scale and status of these king-making assemblies varied from source to source, however. John described two comparably prestigious companies; the *Encomium* depicted the most impressive magnates electing Cnut and dismissed Edmund's partisans as a minority faction of soldiers; and the Anglo-Saxon Chronicle did not mention Cnut's acclamation at all.[29] Yet these accounts reflect their authors' certainty that a legitimate royal election ought to be attended by the realm's most important individuals, including the citizens of London, and all three descriptions imply that Æthelred's funeral at St Paul's and at least one of the subsequent elections formed a single continuous event.

London's importance in the election dispute is another consistent element of these three accounts. In later centuries, Londoners played a prominent role in royal elections, and the fact that the citizens' involvement was emphasized in the sources for 1016 suggests that the city's endorsement

---

27 "Totius Anglie suscepit imperium"; "Foedus etiam cum principibus et omni populo ipse et illi cum ipso percusserunt, et amicitiam firmam inter se iuramentis stabilierunt, omnesque ueteres inimicitias postponentes sedauerunt"; JW 502–3.

28 In ASC CDEF 1016, the English magnates designated Edmund their king "then, after Æthelred's end" [Þa æfter his ende]. In the *Encomium*, the London citizens made peace with Cnut "after having given their prince an honorable burial" [suo honorifice sepulto principe]; *Encomium*, 22–3. John of Worcester reported that succession councils were held "after Æthelred's death" [cuius post mortem]; JW 484–5.

29 John of Worcester maintained that Cnut was chosen by "the bishops, abbots, ealdormen and all the nobles of England" [episcopi, abbates, duces et quique nobiliores Anglie] and that Edmund was declared king by "the London citizens and those of the nobles who were at that time at London" [ciues Lundonienses et pars nobilium qui eo tempore consistebant Lundonie]; JW 484–5. The Encomiast stated that London's "citizens" [ciues] elected Cnut and that only "part of the garrison" [pars interioris exercitus] supported Edmund; *Encomium*, 22–3. ASC CDE 1016 reported that Edmund was chosen by "all the *witan* who were in London and the *burh*-guard" [ealle ða witan þa on Lundene wæron 7 seo burhwaru]; ASC F 1016 stated that he was chosen by "all the *witan* of the English" [ealle Angelcynnes witan].

was already considered essential by the beginning of the eleventh century.[30] However, the *Encomium*'s claim that the citizens chose Cnut as their king is problematic, given the political climate at the time of Æthelred's death. The city had been a particular target for Scandinavian attacks since the ninth century, and it had been Æthelred's most reliable source of political and military support in his later years. Would London have submitted so easily to a Danish invader in the aftermath of their own king's funeral, especially when there was a West Saxon candidate standing by? John's statement that Cnut and Edmund were elected by two different factions seems a more plausible explanation. His language indicates that one party, consisting of London's citizens and some of the nobility, crowned Edmund inside the city, while a second party, made up of the remaining English magnates, pledged their allegiance to Cnut at Southampton.[31] This explanation could clarify the *Encomium*'s unique claim that all but a few of the London *ciues* supported Cnut: it is logical that the author rendered a divided election as a near-unanimous acclamation to serve his patroness's political purposes.

If the Encomiast's narrative reflects the perceived importance of London in royal elections in the 1040s, Cnut's delayed attack on the city confirms that the citizens' endorsement was also considered crucial in 1016. The Danish ships had assembled after Easter, which fell on 1 April, and were en route to London when Æthelred died on 23 April; but the fleet arrived more than a fortnight later – after Æthelred's funeral and the royal elections had taken place.[32] John of Worcester took for granted that some sort of ceasefire had been called, allowing the kingdom's magnates to assemble and decide the fate of the realm, and another twelfth-century account stated that "Æthelred's death forestalled Cnut's attempt" to attack London, implying that the king's death was important enough to delay even the battle plans of a foreign invader.[33] If Cnut in fact suspended his army's advance to allow a royal funeral to take place, he must have expected his

30 1016 was the first time that London was recorded as having such a significant impact on royal elections: Nightingale, "Origin of the Court of Husting," 566. For the city's role during the final years of Æthelred's reign, see: Hill, "Development of Towns," 217; Hill, "Urban Policy," 103; Brooke and Keir, *London*, 21–3; Keynes, "Burial of King Æthelred," 137–44.

31 Above, n. 25.

32 These dates are provided above, n. 16.

33 "Preuenit conatum eius mors Egelredi"; William of Malmesbury, *GR* ii.180.3. See also JW 484–5.

partisans to use the opportunity to advocate his claim and obviate the need for further fighting. Unlike his father Swein, who had been content to seize control in a military coup d'état, it seems that Cnut sought to be legitimately elected, like earlier Anglo-Saxon monarchs.[34] Thanks to his military success and his status as Swein's son, he commanded considerable support in England when Æthelred died.[35] He also benefited politically from marrying into an influential English family: perhaps as early as 1013, he wed Ælfgifu of Northampton, an English noblewoman of Scandinavian descent, whose brothers and father had been blinded and killed under Æthelred.[36] By integrating himself into a network of Æthelred's Anglo-Scandinavian opponents, Cnut would have been well situated to win the allegiance of other magnates who might support his candidacy and advise him on the political procedure that would follow the death of a king.[37]

While it is perfectly credible that Cnut was elected by some of the English population, the Anglo-Saxon Chronicle made no reference to Cnut's election in 1016, stating only that Edmund was chosen king in London after his father died. This omission made Edmund's election seem unanimous and inevitable, but his political position may in fact have been tenuous.[38] Although he was recognized as an effective war leader, Edmund had moved against his father in 1014, attempting to unseat his chief adviser and possibly making a bid for the crown after Swein Forkbeard died.[39] By the time Edmund reconciled with Æthelred in 1015, he may have damaged his relations with some of his father's nobles, whose endorsement would be indispensible in a contested royal election. Moreover, his support in the north, where his power had been concentrated in 1014 and 1015, was

34 The language of the ASC implies that Swein took control of England without a ceremonial inauguration: Campbell, "Introduction," liii [cxxxv] and lxiii [cxlv]; and see below.

35 Howard, *Swein Forkbeard's Invasions*, 106.

36 ASC CDEF 1006; Stafford, "Royal Policy and Action," 35–7; Keynes, "Alfred and Æthelred," 214–15.

37 Cnut had already participated in an English royal succession when his father died in 1014: below, chapter 6.

38 Stafford, "Royal Policy and Action," 35–7.

39 For Edmund's military successes, see Keynes, "Alfred and Æthelred," 216. The adviser was Eadric Streona, Æthelred's son-in-law and foremost councillor in the final decade of his reign; he was blamed for the death of the Northumbrian ealdormen Sigeferth and Morcar in 1015, after which Edmund took over their territory: Stafford, "Royal Policy and Action," 35–7; Stafford, *Emma and Edith*, 225; Keynes, *Diplomas*, 211–14; Keynes, "Alfred and Æthelred," 213–17; Stenton, *Anglo-Saxon England*, 388.

diminished with Cnut's military success in the region, and the Danish conquest of Wessex in 1015 would have further reduced Edmund's resources.[40] Cnut's legitimate election by members of the English nobility was a real possibility in early 1016.

Consequently, during the final months of Æthelred's life, Edmund and his supporters would have had considerable incentive to promote the primacy of the West Saxon dynasty and emphasize their candidate's close kinship to a lawfully consecrated Anglo-Saxon king. In 1016 "the ætheling Edmund went to London, to his father" as he was suffering his last illness, and Edmund was likely on the premises when he died.[41] Æthelred may have willed his son the kingdom in his final days or otherwise designated him his successor.[42] However, it was at the funeral that Edmund's status as heir could be most clearly expressed. Æthelred was buried at St Paul's cathedral, next door to London's royal residence where he had died.[43] In Cnut's absence, attention would have focused on Edmund.[44] As the king's eldest living son, his presence at his father's burial would have made it all but impossible for the assembled company to deny his hereditary claim to the kingdom. With the Danish fleet threatening London, it was practical to acclaim the new king shortly after his predecessor's funeral, as all three early sources imply. Just as importantly, a ceremonial funeral would have reaffirmed Æthelred's own royal status among detractors who might have recalled his temporary forfeiture of the throne in 1013. Buried in a preeminent cathedral founded by conversion-era kings, there could be no doubt that he and his dynasty retained their royal dignity and authority. It was not simply control of Æthelred's body and funeral that validated Edmund's hereditary right to the kingdom but also the promulgation of a legitimizing interpretation of his father's reign and legacy.

---

40 ASC CDE 1015; Stafford, *Unification and Conquest*, 71.

41 "Se æþeling Eadmund gewende to Lundene to his fæder"; ASC CDE 1016. On Æthelred's illness, see: ASC CDE 1015; Keynes, "Alfred and Æthelred," 216.

42 Deathbed bequests were not uncommon: Hazeltine, "General Preface," viii–xiii. Compare Edward the Confessor granting the kingdom to Harold Godwineson shortly before he died and Edward the Elder's alleged bequset to Æthelstan: see chapters 2 and 3.

43 For St Paul's and London's royal palace, see: Bede, *HE* II.3; Taylor, "Foundation and Endowment"; Kelly, *Charters of St Paul's*, 1–46; Keene, "Conquest to Capital," 18–20; Biddle, "City in Transition," 22–3 and 28; Brooke, "The Earliest Times," 2–15; Keynes, "Burial of King Æthelred." In its logistics, Æthelred's funeral was quite similar to Edward the Confessor's, in which the king's body was carried from his Westminster palace to the adjacent abbey: Wilson, *Bayeux Tapestry*, 29–30; *Vita Ædwardi*, 81.

44 John of Worcester and the Encomiast both noted that Cnut's partisans pledged him their allegiance outside of the city; see above.

Nevertheless, despite the posthumous legitimacy that accompanied a funeral at St Paul's, Æthelred may not have intended to be buried in London at all. No king had been interred there in over three centuries, and he may have planned to be entombed at Old Minster with his eldest son, who had died in 1014.[45] The military circumstances of 1016 and Cnut's control of Wessex would have made a funeral procession to Winchester risky; a journey to Kingston, to crown Edmund Ironside where his father and grandfather had been consecrated, would also have been dangerous.[46] Locating the funeral and acclamation in London may have been a logistical necessity, but it was fortuitous for the city, as the citizens, hosting their king's election for the first time, established a precedent for future accessions to take place there.[47] The bishop and clergy of St Paul's would have benefited from the prestige of a royal tomb, and they likely lobbied to keep Æthelred's body in the cathedral.[48] Installed beside the grave of the East Saxon king Sæbbi (d. 694), Æthelred doubled the size of St Paul's royal mausoleum and helped reinforce its position as the premier church in London.[49] The king's body may also have held ideological value for St Paul's, which had become something of a cult centre for victims of Viking violence. In 1016, its most popular shrine belonged to St Ælfheah, the archbishop of Canterbury who had been killed in London by Vikings in 1012.[50] Just a few years earlier, St Paul's had temporarily housed the relics of St Edmund, the East Anglian king martyred by Vikings in 869: the relics were brought to London when his church at Bury was threatened by Swein Forkbeard in 1009, and they were returned to their home in 1012.[51] By the time Æthelred died, he too may

45 This was the ætheling Æthelstan: Keynes, "Introduction to the Reprint," xx–xxi.

46 Kingston is discussed above, n. 7.

47 Above, n. 30.

48 For parallels, see: Yorke, "Royal Burial," 41–2; William of Malmesbury, *GR* ii.144.2–3; and above, chapter 2.

49 On royal and saintly burials at St Paul's, see: Thacker, "Cult of the Saints," 113–16; Taylor, "Foundation and Endowment," 8–9; Cragoe, "Fabric, Tombs, and Precinct," 132.

50 Cnut translated Ælfheah's relics to Canterbury in 1023; see below, chapter 6. For Ælfheah's death and sanctity, see: ASC DEF 1012 and 1023; Rumble and Morris, "*Translatio Sancti Ælfegi*," 283–8 and 291–315; Thacker, "Cult of the Saints," 115; Lawson, *Cnut*, 181–3; Nightingale, "Origin of the Court of Husting," 566–7.

51 Edmund's relics were placed in the church of St Gregory, which adjoined St Paul's; the body was returned to Bury in 1012, despite the efforts of London's bishop to keep the saint permanently in the city: Thacker, "Cult of the Saints," 115. The account of the relics' sojourn in London appears in the *De Miraculis Sancti Eadmundi*, a late eleventh-century text derived from a source (now lost) composed late in Æthelred's reign: Arnold, *Memorials of St. Edmund's Abbey*, 26–92; Gransden, "Composition and Authorship," 26–9. For the church of St Gregory and its relation to St Paul's, see Brooke, "Central Middle Ages," 35.

have been regarded locally as a victim of Scandinavian aggression, since his reign had been plagued by attacks and invasions which culminated in his exile, just a year after Ælfheah's martyrdom. The proximity of the king's grave to Ælfheah's shrine would have commemorated these Viking outrages along with Æthelred's memory. Four years after Ælfheah's death and the departure of St Edmund's relics, the king's funeral recalled once again the offences committed by Cnut and his ancestors.[52]

Such a message would no doubt have resonated among Londoners who had supported Æthelred in his later years, had borne the brunt of the Scandinavian attacks, and would soon endure another siege. When Cnut finally relaunched his assault on the city in May 1016, the attack may have been reconceived as a response to the citizens' support of Edmund Ironside. Still, London was a valuable conquest in its own right, for in addition to the city's strategic and material resources, it had now become a staging point for royal ritual.[53] Cnut evidently recognized the city's ceremonial potential and sought to confirm his authority there shortly after Æthelred's funeral, while Edmund was rallying support in Wessex. According to the *Encomium*, the magnates who had pledged their allegiance to Cnut arranged for his entrance into London and his enthronement there:[54]

> Cnut entered the city and sat on the throne of the kingdom (*in solio regni*). Nevertheless, he did not believe that the Londoners were loyal to him yet. Accordingly, he had the equipment of his ships renewed that summer, so that if the army of his enemies happened to besiege the city, he should not be delivered by the enemies within to the enemies without and perish. Guarding against this, he withdrew again for the moment like a wise man, and having boarded the ships and left the city, he went to the island called Sheppey with his followers.[55]

52 On St Paul's resistance to Scandinavian rule, see: Lawson, *Cnut*, 181–2. For Viking attacks on London and St Paul's, see: Taylor, "Foundation and Endowment," 11–12; Kelly, *Charters of St Paul's*, 24–6 and 35–7; Stafford, "Royal Policy and Action," 35.

53 On London's wealth and population in the Anglo-Saxon period, see: Brooke, "Central Middle Ages"; Biddle, "City in Transition"; Nightingale, "Origin of the Court of Husting," 577–8.

54 "A treaty was made, with a day set for his entry" [faedus firmatum est, ingressui eius die constituto]; *Encomium*, 22–3.

55 "Cnuto autem ciuitatem intrauit, et in solio regni resedit. Sed tamen Londonienses non sibi adhuc esse fideles credidit: unde et nauium stipendia illa aestate restaurare fecit, ne, si forte exercitus aduersariorum ciuitatem oppugnaret, ipse ab interioribus hostibus exterioribus traditus interiret. Quod cauens rursus ad tempus ut prudens cessit, et ascensis ratibus ac ciuitate relicta insulam Scepei dictam cum suis petiit"; *Encomium*, 22–5.

No other source mentions this episode, and the Anglo-Saxon Chronicle and John of Worcester agreed that the Danish army could not overcome the city's defences after the 1016 funeral and election.[56] It may be that this sole account of Cnut's enthronement was exaggerated or invented twenty-five years after the fact by an author committed to establishing his royal legitimacy in retrospect. Enthronement was a standard element of royal inaugurations, and the ritual *ordo* used in English coronations from the mid-tenth century confirmed the king's authority upon his installation *in hoc regni solio*, "on the throne of the kingdom," a phrase closely echoed by the Encomiast.[57] Nevertheless, the author's measured praise of Cnut's hasty exit – it was a savvy tactical move by a wise leader, not a retreat from imminent danger – could be an attempt to salvage a botched ritual that his audience still remembered in the 1040s.[58] If, as the *Encomium* implied, Cnut was not coming to London to subdue the citizens by force, his desire to enter an enemy stronghold despite his distrust of its residents indicates that he believed that there was some advantage in a London enthronement.[59] Why not have himself enthroned in the north, where he enjoyed considerable political support, or in Winchester, where he had subdued the surrounding population? Even if he was unable to secure control of London at this time, Cnut or his English partisans apparently recognized the city as the requisite staging point for such an important ceremonial event. The royal centre's association with lawful authority must have appealed to a foreign conqueror seeking legitimacy.

If Cnut's first visit to London was an attempt to assert his royal authority, the effort failed – perhaps even exacerbating hostilities and necessitating his quick withdrawal from the city. Circumstances changed after Edmund died in November 1016. Cnut returned to London to secure oaths of loyalty from the citizens and assembled magnates, and it was there that he executed a swathe of the Anglo-Saxon nobility.[60] His appropriation of the royal centre for these events would have confirmed his

56 ASC and John of Worcester each described Cnut's unsuccessful siege of the city soon after Æthelred died, and neither depicted Cnut entering London until after Edmund's death, when he held a council there: ASC CDEF 1016; JW 481–91.

57 Ward, "Anglo-Saxon Coronation Ceremony," 357; *Encomium*, 22–3. For enthronement, see Nelson, "Ritual and Reality," 334–5.

58 Compare Koziol, "Problem of Sacrality," 137–41; Buc, *Dangers of Ritual*, 8–10.

59 Cnut was coming to "peacefully receive the city" [ciuitatem pacifice susciperet]; *Encomium*, 22–3.

60 JW 494–5 and 504–5.

deposition of the West Saxon dynasty: some of the English nobility forswore the West Saxon kings in their own stronghold; others died where Æthelred and Edmund had organized their resistance against the Danes. Such displays would have left no doubt that London had been subjugated to the will of its new king, but they also served as a reminder that Cnut and his father had taken the realm by force, not by hereditary right.[61] To counter this impression, Cnut grounded his claims of legitimate authority upon his treaty with Edmund after the Battle of Assandun in October 1016: the two men had agreed to share the realm and become each other's heir. By this logic, Cnut's succession, the execution of rebellious nobles, and the disenfranchisement of Edmund's kin were all lawful and just.[62]

In order for this argument to provide a legal basis for Cnut's accession, it required that he recognize the legitimacy of Edmund's brief reign. At the end of 1016, this meant providing his rival with a fitting funeral. Edmund died in London on 30 November but he was entombed in Glastonbury, approximately one hundred miles away; afterwards, Cnut confirmed the allegiance of his new subjects in London.[63] The choice of Glastonbury as Edmund's burial place was an appropriately honourable one, as the monastery already housed the tombs of his grandfather and great-grandfather.[64] However, relegating the body to such a faraway foundation must have been a strategic decision.[65] As influential a monastery as Glastonbury was, it was well removed in this period from England's leading economic and administrative centres. Instead of being buried conveniently with his father at St Paul's or with his older brother at Winchester, Edmund was entrusted to a monastery located toward the political periphery of Cnut's new kingdom. It is also significant, in this context, that Cnut waited to convene his inaugural council in London until after Edmund was buried. Rather than securing his subjects' allegiance as soon as Edmund died or assembling the English magnates in Glastonbury immediately after the funeral, Cnut confirmed his rule after Edmund's remains were installed far away from London. Where Æthelred's funeral united London's citizens

61 Stafford, "Royal Promises," 282–3; Stafford, *Unification and Conquest*, 72–3.

62 ASC CDEF 1016; *Encomium*, 28–31; JW 492–5.

63 JW 492–5.

64 These were kings Edgar and Edmund: above, chapter 2.

65 Compare Brooks, "Career of Dunstan," 11.

around his successor, Edmund's ensured that his body exerted minimal influence over the political debate that followed and could not become a rallying point for a citizenry which had long resisted Danish rule.[66]

In addition to removing a problematic body from the kingdom's political centre, the hundred-mile trip to Glastonbury may have helped Cnut's transition into power. Edmund's remains could have been displayed en route, giving his subjects an opportunity to acknowledge and mourn their king's death and providing his reign ceremonial closure.[67] Although it is unclear to what extent Cnut participated in the funeral, it is possible that he accompanied Edmund's body on some stage of its journey or attended its burial. If this were the case, the visual impact of the two kings – one living, one dead – would have conveyed a dual message. On the one hand, Cnut's presence at the funeral could provide a sense of stability: the new king would be seen honouring his treaty with Edmund and assuming his place without a prolonged interregnum. On the other hand, the sight of a foreign invader consigning a West Saxon king to the grave would accentuate the fact that Cnut had overcome England's native dynasty.[68] Edmund's funeral provided a simultaneous demonstration of continuity and conquest, displaying Cnut's respect for the institution of English kingship but also his indisputable practical power.

A final episode provides an epilogue to this discussion of Edmund's burial. In the early 1030s, Cnut came to Glastonbury and renewed its privileges, as many of his Anglo-Saxon predecessors had done.[69] During the visit, he paid his respects at Edmund's tomb:

66 A similar strategy is evident in Cnut's translation of St Ælfheah's relics from London to Canterbury in 1023: below, chapter 6.

67 Compare with funeral processions of Ottonian kings and bishops, which often included stops on the way to the burial church: Thietmar, *Chronik*, 166–70; Bernhardt, "Henry II of Germany," 44–6; Warner, *Ottonian Germany*, 187–90; Warner, "Adventus," 264–5.

68 Cnut's presence would also have prevented any challengers from taking control of Edmund's body or using his funeral to make their own bid for the kingdom. Edmund's brother Eadwig, who was exiled as soon as Cnut came to power, may have been a particular threat: ASC CDE 1017; JW 494–7 and 502–5.

69 S 966, which confirmed the renewal of privileges, is preserved only by William of Malmesbury and may be spurious in its current form: Abrams, *Anglo-Saxon Glastonbury*, 15n31, 18–19, and 128–30; Lawson, *Cnut*, 239; Keynes, "Cnut's Earls," 52n51.

> When Cnut came there during a journey on the feast of St Andrew, honouring the fraternal remains with pious laments, he placed upon the sepulcher his cloak, which seemed to be interwoven with multicoloured peacock feathers.[70]

The fact that this occurred on St Andrew's day, the anniversary of Edmund's death, suggests that this was a carefully planned visit motivated by political concerns. Perhaps Cnut – seeking to ensure his sons' succession at a time when exiled West Saxon æthelings were coming of age – stressed his honorary kinship with Edmund in order to remind his English subjects that his accession had been legitimate.[71] The Glastonbury charter claimed that Cnut renewed the community's privileges for "the remission of my sins and for the soul of my brother King Edmund," and post-Conquest chroniclers maintained that Cnut referred to Edmund as his brother from the outset of his reign.[72] While this fraternal rhetoric must be approached cautiously, given its preservation in later sources, it seems that Cnut did in fact recognize the long-term political value of cultivating Edmund's memory and treating his body with respect.

Although he became king by military conquest, Cnut's use of English royal ritual allowed him to cultivate a narrative of legitimate hereditary succession. By allowing Edmund a prestigious royal burial, Cnut could portray himself as his lawful heir by treaty, not a pretender scrambling for power. The appropriation of London, where Æthelred had been buried and Edmund elected, as a staging point for his accession provided a sense of administrative continuity with the previous regimes but also recalled and reinforced his displacement of the West Saxon dynasty. His 1017 marriage to Æthelred's widow, Emma, must have conveyed a similar message. Yet there is no indication that Cnut sought a consecration at Kingston, as earlier Anglo-Saxon kings had. Edmund had been acclaimed in London, after his father's funeral, and Cnut followed his example. As a foreign conqueror, Cnut sought legitimacy from the memory of his immediate, West Saxon predecessor.

---

70 "Quo cum Cnuto uie occasione in festo sancti Andree uenisset, pia querela fraternos manes honorans, super sepulcrum eius pallium misit, uersicoloribus pennis pauonum, ut uidetur, intextum"; *De Antiquitate*, 132–3. The episode is also related in William of Malmesbury, *GR* ii.184.2.

71 Lawson, *Cnut*, 138–9; and below, chapter 6.

72 "Peccaminum meorum remissionem et animam fratris mei regis Edmundi"; William of Malmesbury, *GR* ii.184.2, and see also ii.181.2.

Harold Harefoot, Harthacnut, and Edward the Confessor: 1035–1043

Cnut died at Shaftesbury in November 1035 and was interred in Winchester's Old Minster, a location which posthumously confirmed his legitimacy: his burial in the cathedral of Wessex's pre-eminent royal centre reinforced his family's patronage of the city and placed his remains on par with those of earlier West Saxon kings.[73] According to the *Encomium*, he intended the realm to pass directly to Harthacnut, his son by Emma, who was ruling Cnut's Danish kingdom at the time.[74] In Harthacnut's absence, Harold Harefoot, Cnut's son by a previous union with Ælfgifu of Northampton, pushed his own claim.[75] Despite Harold's apparent lack of popularity among his father's West Saxon subjects, he won enough support among the northern nobility in late 1035 to gain control over part of the kingdom, and he was recognized as full king of England in 1037. Just three years later, in 1040, he died at Oxford and was buried at the reformed monastery at Westminster.

Contemporary narrative sources for Harold's tenure were one-sided and unflattering. The most extensive account of his reign was provided in

73 For Cnut's burial and the later treatment of his remains, see Crook, "Movement of Cnut's Bones," 169–76. For a possible controversy surrounding his burial at Winchester, see: Keynes, "Introduction to the Reprint," xliv; Keynes and Love, "Earl Godwine's Ship," 194.

74 Emma, known in England as Ælfgifu, was the daughter of Duke Richard I of Normandy and the sister of Richard II. In 1002, she married Æthelred, with whom she had two sons: Edward (later "the Confessor") and Alfred (killed during the reign of Harold Harefoot). In 1017, she married Cnut, with whom she had Harthacnut. She left England in 1037 but returned in 1040 when Harthacnut became king. As an anointed queen, she was an influential figure at the courts of Æthelred, Cnut, and Harthacnut, but enjoyed less favour under Edward. She died in 1052 and was buried beside Cnut in Old Minster. On Emma's life and influence, see: Stafford, *Emma and Edith*, 209–54; Stafford, "Powers of the Queen"; Stafford, "King's Wife in Wessex"; Campbell, "Introduction," xl–l [cxxii–cxxxii]; Keynes, "Introduction to the Reprint," xiii–xxxviii and lxxi–lxxx.

75 Before he married Emma, Cnut's wife (or possibly his concubine) was Ælfgifu of Northampton, the daughter of a noble family of Scandinavian descent. Her brothers Ulfgeat and Wulfheah were blinded under Æthelred in 1006, and her father, Ælfhelm, was allegedly murdered by Eadric Streona during Æthelred's reign. Cnut had two sons with Ælfgifu: Swein, who would later rule Norway with his mother as regent; and Harold Harefoot, who would claim the English throne at Cnut's death. See ASC CDEF 1006; Campbell, "Emma and Ælfgifu," especially 68–70; Stafford, *Emma and Edith*, 24–5 and 233–4; Stafford, "King's Wife in Wessex," 14–15; Keynes, "Introduction to the Reprint," xxxii–xxxiii; Lawson, *Cnut*, 131–2; Stevenson, "Alleged Son of Harold Harefoot," 115–16; John, *Reassessing*, 157. On Ælfgifu's extended family, see: Sawyer, *Charters of Burton*, xxxviii–xliii; Baxter, *Earls of Mercia*, 301.

the *Encomium Emmae*, which vilified him at every opportunity.[76] The Anglo-Saxon Chronicle and John of Worcester, though less extravagant in their censure than the Encomiast, were also unsympathetic, questioning Harold's parentage and elaborating on his misdeeds. All three texts agreed that Harold's accession was contested; that he oppressed Emma, seized her treasure, and drove her into exile; and that in 1036, he ordered the lethal mutilation of her son by Æthelred, the ætheling Alfred.[77] In addition, all three accounts were vague in their assessment of Harold's royal status and implied that he came to power only because Harthacnut was not present to claim the realm in person. The Anglo-Saxon Chronicle and the *Encomium* stated that Harold had won enough popular support at a council in Oxford in 1035 – specifically from London's fleet and northern thegns – to assume practical control of the realm in spite of the objections of the West Saxon magnates.[78] Manuscript E of the Chronicle reported that the assembly "chose Harold to hold all of England," but he was not called king (*cyng*) until the end of the annal, suggesting that some time had passed before this status was confirmed.[79] This phrasing – marked especially by the absence of the formula *feng to rice*, which was typically used in the Chronicle to describe royal accessions – implies that an election had occurred but that Harold was chosen to hold the kingdom as regent, presumably until Harthacnut returned.[80] He shared this regency with Emma, who stayed in Winchester surrounded by "the housecarls of her son [Harthacnut], the king, and held all Wessex in hand for him."[81] By 1037, with Harthacnut

76 For Emma's efforts to defame Harold, see Stafford, "Powers of the Queen," 6.

77 *Encomium*, 38–50; ASC CD 1035–40, EF 1036–9 (*recte* 1035–40); JW 520–5.

78 ASC E 1036; an abbreviated account was included in ASC F 1036. By this time, London housed a considerable Scandinavian population as well as a Danish garrison: Nightingale, "Origin of the Court of Husting," 559–69; Kelly, *Charters of St Paul's*, 40–2; Lawson, *Cnut*, 206.

79 "Gecuron Harold to healdes ealles Englalandes"; ASC EF 1036.

80 ASC D 1035 was the only version that said that Harold *feng to rice*; yet two years later in its annal for 1037, it reported that "here Harold was chosen as king over all" [her man geceas Harold ofer eall to kyninge], suggesting that his accession progressed in two distinct phases. On *feng to rice*, see Stafford, "Royal Promises, 182.

81 "Þæs cynges huscarlum hyra suna, 7 heoldan ealle Westseaxan him to handa"; ASC E 1036. John of Worcester maintained that after Cnut's death, the northern part of the kingdom was granted to Harold and the southern part to Harthacnut, but since Harthacnut did not return from Denmark, Harold won control of the entire kingdom: JW 520–5. For Harold and Emma's regencies, see: Stafford, *Emma and Edith*, 236–46; Keynes, "Introduction to the Reprint," xxix–xxx; Barlow, *Edward the Confessor*, 43–4.

still abroad, Emma's position was untenable. She was driven into exile, according to the Anglo-Saxon Chronicle, and Harold was finally made "full king over all England."[82]

Even after he had secured practical power as regent, Harold's royal legitimacy remained suspect; questions about his parentage were noted in all the English sources for his reign. The Chronicle asserted bluntly that Harold's claim to be Cnut's son "was not true," while more elaborate accounts maintained that he was the child of a servant or cobbler but that his mother, Ælfgifu, had passed him off as Cnut's.[83] Scepticism about his paternity may have motivated Harold to stress his kinship with Cnut as he sought to establish himself as the dead king's legitimate heir.[84] The funeral would have offered a prime opportunity to advertise this relationship, but there is no indication that Harold used the occasion to press his claim. Instead, the Chronicle reported that the entire *witan* met "directly after Cnut's death" at Oxford, a location conspicuously outside the West Saxon heartland.[85] Despite the urgency implied in this language, there must have been some delay after the funeral to allow all the kingdom's magnates to make the fifty mile journey from Old Minster, and it is telling that the council was not simply held at Winchester. Given its location on the old border between Wessex and Mercia, it is possible that Oxford was chosen in recognition of the political clout of the northern magnates.[86] Moreover, Oxford seems to have been a favoured residence of Harold's; he died there just a few years later.[87]

82 "Full cyng ofer eall Englaland"; ASC EF 1036. The phrase *full cyng* was also used of Swein Forkbeard when he gained control over the entire realm: ASC E 1013; Campbell, "Introduction," liii and lxiiin3; John, *Reassessing*, 165; Stafford, "Royal Promises," 182.

83 "Hit na soð nære"; ASC CD 1035. ASC E 1036 (*recte* 1035) noted that Harold's paternity "seemed very unbelievable to many people" [þuhte swiðe ungeleaflic manegum mannum]. For more damning accounts of Harold's lineage see: *Encomium*, 40; JW 520–1. For the persistence of rumours of Harold's illegitimacy, see McNulty, "Lady Aelfgyva in the Bayeux Tapestry." By contrast, Scandinavian sources did not question that Ælfgifu's sons were Cnut's: Stafford, *Emma and Edith*, 74–5.

84 Harold's parentage was evidently a point of concern from the beginning of his reign: Keynes, "Introduction to the Reprint," xxix.

85 "Sona æfter his forsiðe wæs ealra witena gemot on Oxnaforda"; ASC E 1036. Oxford had been acquired by Edward the Elder along with London in 911: see above, n. 13.

86 For Oxford's status, situation, and accessibility, see: Blair, *Oxfordshire*, 106, 158–9, and 167–70; Barlow, *Edward the Confessor*, 43; Wormald, *Making of English Law*, 438; Innes, "Danelaw Identities," 73.

87 Oxford had also hosted councils under Æthelred and Cnut. ASC CDE 1015 and 1018; Cnut 1020 13; Wormald, *Making of English Law*, 131 and 346.

The broader implication, however, is that Harold assumed power at Oxford because he was unwilling or unable to do so at Winchester. The Anglo-Saxon Chronicle's description of the 1035 succession, though somewhat opaque, suggests that Cnut's funeral was part of the political debate. Manuscript C, composed ca 1044, offers the earliest witness:[88]

> In this year King Cnut died at Shaftesbury and he was carried from there to Winchester and buried there. And Ælfgifu [Emma], the queen, stayed inside there. And Harold, who said that he was the son of Cnut and the other Ælfgifu, although it was not true. He sent and had taken from her all the best treasure which King Cnut possessed – which she could not hold on to. And she remained there afterwards as long as she could.[89]

The ambiguous phrasing of this passage allows for two different interpretations. One is that both Emma and Harold attended Cnut's funeral and stayed in Winchester afterward. In this case, the passage might be rendered: "Emma stayed in Winchester, and so did Harold, who said that he was the son of Cnut and the other Ælfgifu – although that was not true." This reading would imply that Harold first asserted his claim to the kingdom at his father's funeral, only to be thwarted by concerns about his parentage.[90] If this were so, it would seem to have been Emma herself who posed the greatest obstacle to Harold's accession. The queen kept a residence at Winchester, where she remained with Harthacnut's retinue after Cnut died, and she was likely involved in organizing her husband's funeral.[91] As an anointed queen, her status – and her son's – trumped that of any other wife or children, and Emma may have used the funeral to

88 The following translation retains the ambiguous punctuation of the manuscript.

89 "Her forðferde cnut cing … æt sceftesbyrig . 7 hine man ferode þanon to winceastre 7 hine þær bebyrigde . 7 ælfgyfu seo hlæfdie sæt þa ðærbinnan . 7 harold þe sæde þæt he cnutes sunnu wære 7 þære oðre ælfgyfe þeh hit na soð nare . he sende to 7 let numan of hyre ealle þa betstan gærsuma ðe heo ofhealdan ne mihte þe cnut cing ahte . 7 heo sæt þeh forð þærbinnan ða hwile þe heo moste"; ASC C 1035. The text is transcribed from O'Brien O'Keeffe, *Anglo-Saxon Manuscripts in Microfiche Facsimile* 10, Cotton Tiberius B.i fols. 155v–156r.

90 This in contrast to Pauline Stafford's suggestion that concerns about Harold's paternity first surfaced at Oxford: *Emma and Edith*, 238. See also Keynes "Introduction to the Reprint," xxix; and above, n. 84.

91 ASC CD 1035, E 1036 (*recte* 1035); *Encomium* 38–9; and compare Nelson, "Carolingian Royal Funerals," 146–9.

proclaim the absent Harthacnut his father's designated successor.[92] Surrounded by her son's housecarls and supported by "Earl Godwine and the eldest men of Wessex," as well as by the Winchester clergy she patronized, Emma would have been a political force to be reckoned with.[93] Even though Harold had been a recognized member of his father's household, Cnut's queen was better situated to deploy his memory for political ends at the time of his death and burial.[94]

A different interpretation of this passage turns on the assertion that Harold sent his men to seize Emma's treasure. In this case, the passage might be rendered: "Emma stayed in Winchester. And Harold, who said that he was the son of Cnut and the other Ælfgifu (although it was not true) sent and had taken from her all the best treasure which King Cnut possessed – which she could not hold on to." This phrasing would suggest that Emma was in Winchester directly after Cnut's funeral and Harold was not. It is conceivable that Harold did not arrive in time to see his father buried – perhaps a deliberate calculation on Emma's part.[95] Alternatively, it is possible that she and her supporters forcibly prevented Harold's attendance: the passage stated twice that the queen *sæt ðærbinnan*, a phrase used elsewhere in the Chronicle to describe a military siege.[96] Harold threatened (and perhaps used) violence against the queen on at least two occasions, in 1035, when he seized her treasure, and again in 1037, when he drove her into exile. In light of these subsequent encounters, it would have been reasonable for Emma to pre-emptively fortify

92 The *Encomium* reported that Cnut promised Emma that only his children by her would succeed to the kingdom: *Encomium* 32–3; Barlow, *Edward the Confessor*, 31–2; Stafford, "King's Wife in Wessex," 18. For consecrated queens and their sons' throne-worthiness, see: Stafford, "King's Wife in Wessex," 16–18; Stafford, "Powers of the Queen," 13–16; Stafford, *Emma and Edith*, 162–4 and 174–83; Barlow, *Edward the Confessor*, 31–2; John, *Reassessing*, 165.

93 "Godwine eorl 7 ealle þa yldestan menn on Westseaxon"; ASC E 1036 (*recte* 1035). ASC F 1036 (*recte* 1035) rendered this "all the best men" [ealle ða betstan men]. Emma and Cnut's patronage of the Winchester minsters is discussed by Gerchow, "Prayers for Cnut"; Heslop, "*De Luxe* Manuscripts," 86–8.

94 For Harold and Ælfgifu's continued presence in the public eye after Cnut's marriage to Emma, see: Stafford, *Emma and Edith*, 233; Lawson, *Cnut*, 131–2.

95 Compare Nelson, "Carolingian Royal Funerals," 146–9.

96 ASC C 1035, D 1036 (*recte* 1035). *Sæt binnan* (literally "sat inside") also appears in ASC A 900, CD 901, and D 1043. William of Malmesbury understood Emma to be under attack in Winchester: "at length, outclassed in power and in numbers, she yielded to force" [tandem, ui et numero impar, cessit uiolentiae]; *GR* ii.188.1. For Emma's military ambitions, see: Stafford, "Powers of the Queen," 6; Barlow, *Edward the Confessor*, 44.

Winchester against her stepson if she anticipated a conflict. If Harold were absent, there would be less chance that Emma's promotion of her son would be challenged, especially if Harthacnut was expected to return promptly and claim the kingdom.

With either interpretation, it is clear that Harold did not gain control of the kingdom at Winchester after his father's funeral in 1035. However, he made two tactical moves which helped him establish himself as regent soon afterward. First, he seized the royal treasury, which was in Emma's possession.[97] This not only put Emma at a disadvantage, as her control of Cnut's treasure had surely enhanced her political influence during the interregnum, but also gave Harold more clout in cultivating his own support among the nobility. In addition to increasing his financial strength, the Chronicle's reference to "the best treasures which King Cnut possessed" suggests that Harold had claimed these items as his birthright, identifying himself explicitly as his father's heir.[98] The implications of this claim would have held even more significance if the treasury included a crown or other regalia.[99] Even though there is no record of a formal coronation or consecration at this time, Harold's possession of his father's treasure may have helped bolster his image as a legitimate contender for the kingdom.

His second strategic move was to abandon Winchester after Cnut's funeral. His conflict with the queen, the opposition of the Wessex nobility, and questions about his parentage may have exacerbated political factionalism during the interregnum, but it seems that Harold's political position was strengthened by holding the succession council in Oxford. If he had failed to use his father's funeral to his political advantage, removing the debate from his grave site would have been a logical step: just as Edmund Ironside's remains might have proved a dangerous distraction at Cnut's accession, Cnut's tomb might have reminded the assembled *witan* that Harold's paternity had been challenged and that his father had another throne-worthy son. At Oxford, an enclave of political strength for Harold,

97 Edward the Confessor also deprived Emma, his mother, of her treasure soon after his consecration: ASC CD 1043, EF 1042 (*recte* 1043); Stafford, *Emma and Edith*, 249–53; Keynes, "Introduction to the Reprint," lxxii–lxxiii.

98 "Þa betstan gærsuma … þe cnut cing ahte"; ASC C 1035.

99 Stafford, "Queens and Treasure," 65–6 and 72–9; Stafford, *Emma and Edith*, 237; Keynes, "Introduction to the Reprint," xiii; Campbell, "Emma and Ælfgifu," 77; Tyler, "Treasure and Artifice," 254–7; and compare the ideological importance of Edward the Confessor's regalia: *Vita Ædwardi*, 115–17. See further below, n. 101.

the political impact of Cnut's memory would have been subdued.[100] Although he failed to secure an election as king, he did establish himself as regent and gain de facto control of most of his father's kingdom.

Harold spent the next two years consolidating his power in England, directing military efforts against Emma and her family but also making diplomatic advances towards his influential opponents and attempting to stage legitimizing royal ritual. Notably, he seems to have sought a royal consecration early in his regency. In an episode recorded only in the *Encomium*, Harold approached Archbishop Æthelnoth of Canterbury shortly after his election:

> He commanded and prayed that he should be consecrated king, and that he should be given the royal crown and the scepter, which was committed to the archbishop's custody, and that he should be led by the archbishop to the high throne of the kingdom, since this could not be done by anyone else.[101]

The archbishop, exceedingly loyal to Cnut and Emma, refused to consecrate him and prohibited all other bishops from doing so – an outcome that so enraged Harold, according to the Encomiast, that he shunned Christianity for the rest of his life.[102] The vivid language of this passage served to vilify Harold, as did the claim of his apostasy, and these propagandistic details cast doubt upon the historicity of the exchange. However, behind the stylized account lies the real possibility that Harold approached Æthelnoth for support, hoping that his father's chief spiritual adviser might endorse his claim to be Cnut's legitimate heir.[103] The Encomiast took for granted that his audience knew that Harold had not been consecrated at this juncture, but the timing of his request, soon after the Oxford assembly, coincided with a documented effort by Harold and his mother

100 Oxford was near the estates of Harold's mother's family: Campbell, "Emma and Ælfgifu," 76; Barlow, *Edward the Confessor*, 43.

101 "Imperat ... et orat se benedici in regem, sibique tradi cum corona regale suae custodiae commissum sceptrum, et se duci ab eodem, quia ab alio non fas fuerat, in sublime regni solium"; *Encomium*, 40–1. The Encomiast situated this exchange soon after Harold's election in 1035, and the episode must have occurred before the archbishop's death in 1038: Stafford, *Emma and Edith*, 237.

102 *Encomium*, 40–1.

103 *Encomium*, 40–1; and see also William of Malmesbury, *GR* ii.184.1.

to draw influential figures away from Emma.[104] The most significant individual to change allegiance was Earl Godwine, who had withdrawn his support for the queen by 1036; episcopal appointments of the later 1030s indicate that Harold had likewise come to terms with a number of Cnut's clerical supporters.[105] A consecration certainly would have provided Harold the legitimacy he sought, but the endorsement of an archbishop who had been prominent at his father's court may have been just as valuable a prize. Although the Encomiast used this episode to illuminate how Cnut's true subjects remained loyal to Emma, Harold's solicitation of Æthelnoth was entirely consistent with his political efforts at the time.

The attempt to win over his father's allies accentuates the importance of continuity in Harold's campaign for the kingdom.[106] His efforts clearly fell short at the beginning of his regency, as Emma's appropriation and deployment of Cnut's memory at Winchester put her stepson at a political disadvantage. Yet her own son's prolonged absence proved the most important factor in Harold's ascent. In 1036, when Harthacnut still had not returned to England, Emma turned her attention to her two sons by her first marriage to Æthelred. The West Saxon æthelings Alfred and Edward (later the Confessor) had been exiled from England since Cnut came to power, and Emma now encouraged them to return and claim the kingdom – a move which caused many of the nobles who had kept faith with the queen to withdraw their support.[107] Emma's departure from (what she had insisted was) Cnut's intention for the succession marked a shift in the political climate: the king's memory no longer provided the influence she needed to resist Harold. The appeal to her older sons was a dramatic, even desperate change in strategy, motivated by the fact that Harold's practical power had increased to the point where his ambitions were no longer

104 For Ælfgifu of Northampton's efforts and the magnates' changing alliances, see: Stevenson, "Alleged Son of Harold Harefoot," 115–16; Stafford, *Emma and Edith*, 238; Keynes, "Introduction to the Reprint," xxix–xxxiii; Barlow, *The Godwins*, 37–46.

105 For Godwine's change of allegiance, see: Keynes, "Introduction to the Reprint," xxix–xxxi; Barlow, *The Godwins*, 37–46. The episcopal appointments were all made after Æthelnoth's death in 1038 but may reflect earlier changes of allegiance: Eadsige, Cnut's chaplain, succeeded to Canterbury; Stigand, another chaplain of Cnut and Emma's close ally, received the East Anglian see; and Lyfing, a close ally of Godwine, was appointed to Worcester. For episcopal appointments, see: ASC EF 1038; JW 526–7; Freeman, *Norman Conquest* I, 563–4.

106 A similar ecclesiastical continuity is evident upon Cnut's ascension: Stafford, "Royal Policy and Action," 24–6; but compare Fleming, *Kings and Lords*, 39–52.

107 See above, nn. 104 and 105.

hindered by Cnut's legacy. He could now move with impunity against Emma. In late 1036, he had the ætheling Alfred captured and blinded, and the next year, he exiled his stepmother and was made "full king over all England."[108] He was probably consecrated by Æthelnoth in 1037.[109]

Despite Harold's efforts to establish his legitimacy and continuity with Cnut's reign, the extant sources recorded these events unsympathetically, from the perspective of Emma's family. Although Harold had maintained consistent allegiance in the north since 1035 and had a valid claim to succeed his father as king, the Anglo-Saxon Chronicle asserted that "it was not right" that he had attracted popular support, while the *Encomium* attributed his ascent to a misguided sense of loyalty among the English: "because they had elected him to be their king, they were ashamed to reject him, and they thus established that he should be their king to the end."[110] That end came on 17 March 1040, when Harold died at Oxford.[111] Harthacnut, who had remained in Denmark for nearly all of his half-brother's reign, had joined Emma in Flanders earlier that year, and the two were planning an invasion of England when they received news of Harold's death.[112] They were not present at the king's funeral at Westminster monastery.[113] Mother and son returned to England at midsummer, and Harthacnut was welcomed by the population when he appeared with

108 "Full cyng ofer eall Englaland"; ASC EF 1036 (*recte* 1037). The ætheling Alfred was brought to Ely, where he soon died: ASC CD 1036; *Encomium*, 44–7; Stafford, *Emma and Edith*, 239–46; Keynes, "Introduction to the Reprint," lxii–lxv and lxx; Campbell, "Introduction," cxlvi–cxlix [lxiv–lxvii]; O'Brien O'Keeffe, "Body and Law," 212–15; Kries, "Mutilation of Alfred," 42–53. Alfred's mutilation is discussed at length below, chapter 4.

109 ASC E 1036; Keynes, "Introduction to the Reprint," lxiiin2; Campbell, "Introduction," lxiii–lxiv [cxlv–cxlvi]; Stafford, *Emma and Edith*, 237 and 239.

110 "Hit unriht wære"; ASC CD 1036. "Quia hunc sibi regem elegerant, hunc erubuerunt deicere, ideoque disposuerunt hunc sibi regem fine tenus esse"; *Encomium*, 40–1. See also ASC CD 1035, E 1036. Harold's support network is discussed by Baxter, *Earls of Mercia*, 34–7.

111 Harold's death and burial are described in ASC E 1039 (*recte* 1040). John of Worcester maintained that Harold died in London, not Oxford; but a record of a property dispute – in which Harold restored lands to Christ Church, Canterbury on his deathbed – seems to confirm that the king succumbed to his final illness in Oxford: S 1467; JW 528–9; and compare William of Malmesbury, *GR* ii.188.2. See also Wormald, "Handlist," no. 83 and 276.

112 *Encomium*, 48–51.

113 Westminster was a small reformed monastery in the early eleventh century: Mason, *Westminster and Its People*, 11–12; and above, chapter 1.

his fleet at Sandwich: "he was immediately received as king both by the English and by the Danes."[114]

By the time the Chronicle entries for his reign were written, however, Harthacnut was labelled a poor ruler who "never did anything kingly as long as he reigned."[115] The foremost complaint against him was his imposition of exorbitant taxes, but he was also reproached for his spectacular maltreatment of Harold's corpse: according to the Anglo-Saxon Chronicle, "he commanded that the dead Harold be dragged up and thrown into a fen."[116] This episode is treated at length in the next chapter and will not be discussed in depth here. Still, it is pertinent to note that Harthacnut, despite having missed his predecessor's funeral, headed to his grave very soon after returning to England. His engagement with his predecessor's corpse – though meant to damage Harold's legacy – suggests that some sort of posthumous interaction with the previous king would have been expected from a new ruler establishing his authority. Harthacnut's decision to desecrate rather than honour the body was a blatant departure from typical activity at royal tombs, and it seems that he intended to invert normative burial practices, rejecting Harold's legitimacy by denying him the honourable burial a true king merited.

The only thing Harthacnut did right during his short reign, according to most chroniclers, was to bring his half-brother Edward back to England. The *Encomium*, which attributed this move to "brotherly love," stated that Harthacnut wanted Edward to "hold the kingdom with him."[117] The Anglo-Saxon Chronicle annal for 1041 is more explicit about this role:

> Edward, the son of King Æthelred, Harthacnut's brother by his mother, came from beyond the sea; and he was previously exiled from his country for many years, and nevertheless, he was sworn as king, and he thus dwelt in his brother's household as long as Harthacnut lived.[118]

114 "He wæs sona underfangen ge fram Anglum ge from Denum"; ASC EF 1039 (*recte* 1040).

115 "Ne gefremede ec naht cynelices þa hwile ðe he ricxode"; ASC CD 1040.

116 "He let dragan up þæne deadan Harald 7 hine on fen sceotan"; ASC CD 1040. According to John of Worcester, this episode occurred "as soon as he began to rule" [mox ut regnare cepit]; JW 530–1.

117 "Fraterno ... amore"; "secum optineret regnum"; *Encomium*, 52–3.

118 "Com Eadward his broðor on medren fram begeondan sæ Æþelrædes sunu cinges, ðe wæs ær for fela gearon of his earde adrifen, 7 ðeh wæs to cinge gesworen, 7 he wunode þa swa on his broðor hirede þa hwile ðe he leofode"; ASC CD 1041, and compare also ASC EF 1040 (*recte* 1041).

It seems that Edward was installed as a sort of sub-king during Harthacnut's lifetime.[119] The promotion of a half-brother so early in his reign may indicate that the king did not anticipate a long life, perhaps on account of an illness which caused his sudden death in 1042.[120] With no children of his own, it may be that Harthacnut – or even Emma – sought to ensure a smooth transition of power to a close kinsman. Harthacnut died on 8 June, a few days after collapsing at a wedding feast in Lambeth, near Westminster.[121] Like his father, he was buried at Old Minster, Winchester.

Edward succeeded his brother, and his inauguration consisted of three distinct stages, according to the Anglo-Saxon Chronicle. In 1041, while Harthacnut was still alive, he was "sworn as king"; at his death the following year, "all the people elected Edward king"; and in 1043, he was finally "consecrated king" in an ecclesiastical ceremony.[122] This three-part accession finds no parallel in earlier annals, which only occasionally distinguished between a new king's election and consecration, and the textual focus on these events seems designed to emphasize Edward's legitimacy – suggesting that his succession was not a foregone conclusion, despite his brother's endorsement. In fact, Harthacnut's body and memory may have been unusually prominent as Edward's rule was being established. Another unprecedented notice in the Chronicle reported that he was elected in the brief window between his brother's death at Lambeth and the funeral at Winchester: "before he was buried, all the people elected Edward king in London."[123] The mention of the unburied body may indicate that such haste was rare, perhaps even indecorous.[124] Alternatively, this overlap could simply be the result of the king's unexpected death. Edward's election offered a quick resolution to a sudden political crisis, ensuring that there would be no interregnum while funeral arrangements were made

119 William of Malmesbury and John of Worcester did not mention this office, stating only that Edward was a guest at Harthacnut's court: *GR* ii.188.3; JW 532–3.

120 This is suggested by William of Poitiers, *GG*, 6–7. There is no reference to an illness in the English chronicles, however: Barlow, *Edward the Confessor*, 49; Campbell, "Introduction," lxviii [cl].

121 ASC CD 1042; JW 532–5.

122 "To cinge gesworen," ASC CD 1041; "eall folc gecease Eadward to cynge," ASC EF 1041 (*recte* 1042); "gehalgod to cinge," ASC ACD 1043, EF 1042 (*recte* 1043).

123 "Ear þan þe he bebyrged wære. eall folc geceas Eadward to cynge on Lundene"; ASC EF 1041 (*recte* 1042).

124 Harold Godwineson's consecration in 1066 on the same day as Edward's funeral was condemned by his critics as overly hasty; see below.

and the body carried seventy miles to Winchester. However, given Lambeth's proximity to Westminster, it is significant that Harthacnut was not interred at the monastery there, as Harold Harefoot had been, or at nearby St Paul's, where Æthelred lay. Emma may have been responsible for her son's burial beside his father; she kept her household at Winchester in her later years and would complete this family group with her own burial at Old Minster in 1052. Yet Edward was elected in London before Harthacnut's funeral took place, and it is not impossible that his half-brother's body was still close by – perhaps being kept or displayed in the city before its final move to Winchester. If his election was conflated with an early stage of Harthacnut's funeral journey, the event would have accentuated the continuity between the two regimes and reinforced Edward's status as his half-brother's designated heir.

In addition to emphasizing his kinship with Harthacnut, Edward's acclamation in London also evoked his West Saxon heritage. Even though his father's reign had come under scrutiny during the period of Danish and Anglo-Danish rule, Edward's descent from the West Saxon royal line proved valuable in 1042. The Anglo-Saxon Chronicle introduced Edward by explicitly mentioning his ancestry: both recensions labelled him "the son of King Æthelred," and Manuscript E specified that he was also "King Harthacnut's brother; they were both sons of Emma, who was the daughter of Duke Richard."[125] Edward's lineage was also reiterated in John of Worcester's account of his election:

> In London, mainly by the exertions of Earl Godwine and Bishop Lyfing of Worcester, Edward was raised to the kingdom, whose father was Æthelred, whose father was Edgar, whose father was Edmund, whose father was Edward the Elder, whose father was Alfred.[126]

The professed need for Godwine and Lyfing's influence implies that Edward's accession was no sure thing, and there were in fact other viable candidates. Swein Esthrithson, a nephew of both Cnut and Earl Godwine,

---

125 "Æðelredes sunu cinges ... se wæs Hardacnutes cynges broðor; hi wæron begen Ælfgiues suna, seo wæs Ricardes dohtor eorles"; ASC E 1040 (*recte* 1041). Compare also ASC CD 1041, quoted above, n. 118.

126 "Eduuardus, annitentibus maxime comite Goduuino et Wigornensi presule Liuingo, Lundonie leuatur in regem, cuius pater Agelredus, cuius pater Eadgarus, cuius pater Eadmundus, cuius pater Eaduuardus Senior, cuius pater Alfredus"; JW 534–5. Compare also William of Malmesbury, *GR* ii.196.6.

may have issued a competing claim to the throne; and later sources claimed that Emma backed a bid for the kingdom by King Magnus of Norway.[127] Even the laudatory *Vita Ædwardi* conceded that Godwine had to persuade the English magnates to acknowledge Edward's "natural right" to the throne.[128] While his West Saxon pedigree alone was insufficient to secure his election, the reiteration of his lineage in the early sources suggests that his partisans made a strong case for dynastic continuity. An election near Æthelred's grave, at St Paul's or the adjoining royal residence, would have offered a material reminder of his West Saxon heritage.[129] If Harthacnut's body was also present, Edward's connection with both legitimizing royal lines would have been readily apparent.

A comparable effect would have been achieved the following Easter, when Edward was anointed at Winchester's Old Minster, the site of Harthacnut's tomb. The description of the 1043 consecration is uncharacteristically detailed:

> In this year, Edward was consecrated king in Winchester on Easter Day with great honour; and Easter fell on 3 April that year. Archbishop Eadsige consecrated him, and before all the people he taught him well and admonished him well as to his own need and to the need of all the people.[130]

This was the first explicit reference to a king being anointed (*gehalgod*) since Æthelred's summarily noted consecration in 979, and the author's extended focus on the ceremonial nature of Edward's accession may

127 On Godwine and Lyfing's influence, see: *Vita Ædwardi*, 9; William of Malmesbury, *GR* ii.188.6 and ii.196–7.1; JW 530–1; Cooper, *Anglo-Saxon Archbishops of York*, 15. The long delay between Edward's election and consecration may reflect the initial uncertainty of the succession: Keynes, "Introduction to the Reprint," lxxii–lxxiii; Barlow, *Edward the Confessor*, 54–60; Stafford, *Emma and Edith*, 249 and 251; Howard, "Harold II," 44–7; Campbell, "Emma and Ælfgifu," 67–8. A delayed consecration did not necessarily indicate a succession dispute, however; Garnett, "Coronation and Propaganda," 92–3; Nelson, "Inauguration Rituals," 298.

128 "Nativi iuris sui"; *Vita Ædwardi*, 9.

129 This impression is strengthened by a revised version of the *Encomium* produced after Harthacnut's death, which names and glorifies Æthelred as Edward's a legitimate progenitor: Keynes and Love, "Earl Godwine's Ship," 196.

130 "Her wæs Æðward gehalgod to cyng on Winceastre on Æsterdæg mid mycclum wurðscipe, 7 þa wæron Eastron on .iii. nonas Aprilis. Eadsige arcebiscop hine halgode 7 toforan eallum folce hine well lærde, 7 to his agenre neode 7 ealles folces well monude"; ASC EF 1042 (*recte* 1043). See also ASC C 1043.

indicate an exceptional amount of spectacle.[131] For a king who had been exiled from his homeland for the previous thirty years, an extravagant coronation that drew attention to his dynastic lineage and endorsement by the Church would surely have helped solidify his authority among his new subjects. Just as Cnut and Harthacnut's legitimacy was confirmed by their burial in Wessex's premier royal necropolis, Edward's consecration at this site associated his accession with past generations of kings: he was anointed near the tombs of his half-brother, stepfather, and earlier ancestors, in a foundation that had been reformed, rebuilt, and adopted for royal ceremonial during the reigns of his father Æthelred and grandfather Edgar.[132] No other Anglo-Saxon consecrations are attested at Winchester, and the fact that Edward chose this site – rather than Kingston, where his father was consecrated, or London, where he was buried – suggests that the event was meant to illustrate his unification of the two royal dynasties which had ruled England in the eleventh century.[133] Because he was a virtual stranger to his new subjects, Edward's consecration at the heart of Wessex, in close proximity to the tombs of his distant West Saxon and immediate Danish predecessors, allowed him to negotiate hereditary claims from two dynastic lines and proclaim continuity with England's royal past.

Harold Godwineson and William the Conqueror: 1066

The death of Edward the Confessor in January 1066 was recognized by later chroniclers as the beginning of the end for Anglo-Saxon England.[134] After a twenty-two-year reign and twenty-one-year marriage to Edith,

131 ASC C 978, ACDE 979, ASC F 980 (all *recte* 979); and see below, chapter 5. The 1043 annal was also the first to note a key element of the Anglo-Saxon coronation *ordo*: the archbishop's admonition to the king, in which he listed the responsibilities of a Christian ruler before the assembled crowd. For the bishop's admonition, which would be followed by the king's coronation oath, see: Ward, "Anglo-Saxon Coronation Ceremony," 350–1; Stubbs, *Memorials of Dunstan*, 356–67; Nelson, "Ritual and Reality," 337–8; Stafford, "Royal Promises," 180–6.

132 For Old Minster in the reigns of Edgar and Æthelred, see: Biddle, "*Felix Urbs Winthonia*," 301–8; Quirk, "Winchester Cathedral"; Crook, "King Edgar's Reliquary," 197–202; Sheerin, "Dedication of Old Minster." For Winchester as a site of West Saxon continuity, see Barlow, *Edward the Confessor*, 62.

133 Although it is not impossible that Cnut and his sons had been anointed at Winchester, there is no extant record of this. In the twelfth century, Ralph de Diceto and Gervase of Canterbury cited London as the site of their consecrations: Stubbs, *Ralph de Diceto*, 169 and 186; Stubbs, *Gervase of Canterbury*, 55–7.

134 Otter, "1066," 565–8.

Earl Godwine's daughter, Edward died in his palace at Westminster without any sons to inherit the kingdom. He was succeeded by Edith's brother, Harold Godwineson, whose authority was soon threatened by another brother, Tostig, after the latter allied with the Norwegian Harald Hardrada to invade northern England. Harold Godwineson was also challenged by Duke William of Normandy, who maintained that Edward had bequeathed him the kingdom and that Harold had sworn to endorse his accession. Harold's army defeated Tostig and the Scandinavian forces but was overcome by William at Hastings, in a battle that Harold himself did not survive. On Christmas Day 1066, William was consecrated king at Westminster.

Writing retrospectively, Norman chroniclers foregrounded the story of Harold's broken oath and illicit seizure of the kingdom. William of Poitiers, the Conqueror's chaplain and apologist, asserted in his *Gesta Guillelmi* that Edward made William his heir soon after he became king, sending hostages to Normandy to seal the agreement; he later renewed this understanding by dispatching Harold Godwineson "to confirm the pledge with an oath."[135] These exchanges were never mentioned in the earliest English accounts of the succession, which stated simply that Edward willed the kingdom to Harold as he was dying.[136] This deathbed bequest was acknowledged by Norman chroniclers as well, but they unequivocally dismissed its validity: William's claim predated Harold's; his inheritance had been promised with oaths and hostages; he was Edward's kinsman by blood, not marriage; and, most significantly, Harold had reneged on his oath not to challenge William's accession – an act of treachery that undermined his throne-worthiness.[137] In addition, at least one bystander speculated that Edward

---

135 "Fidem sacramento confirmaturum"; William of Poitiers, *GG*, 68–9; see also xxvi–xix, 18–21, 70–1, and 120–1. Compare Orderic Vitalis, *Ecclesiastical History* II, 134–49; Van Houts, *Gesta Normannorum Ducum* II, 158–61.

136 William of Malmesbury noted these conflicting interpretations, maintaining that Harold "seized the crown, though the English say that it was granted to him by the king" [arripuit diadema, quanuis Angli dicant a rege concessum]; *GR* ii.228.7, and compare also William of Malmesbury, *Vita Wulfstani*, i.16.1–2. The ASC, *Vita Ædwardi*, and John of Worcester did not report that Edward designated William as his heir or that Harold swore not to challenge William's succession. For Edward's deathbed bequest to Harold, see especially *Vita Ædwardi*, 79; William of Poitiers, *GG*, 118–21 and 140–1. ASC CD 1065 (*recte* 1066), E 1066, and JW 600–1 maintained that Harold succeeded to the kingdom just as Edward had wanted. For deathbed bequests in general, see Hazeltine, "General Preface," viii–xiii; William of Poitiers, *GG*, 118n3.

137 William of Poitiers, *GG*, 70–1, 76–9, 100–1, 118–23, and 150–1. These objections to Harold's succession were adopted by later chroniclers, including Orderic Vitalis, who added that Harold deceived Edward on his deathbed by claiming that William had forfeited his right to England: Orderic Vitalis, *Ecclesiastical History* II, 136–7.

was not of sound mind in his final hours, a state which could have undermined the legitimacy of his final will.[138]

These objections, all raised retrospectively, did not prevent Harold from becoming king in the first place, for he was acclaimed and consecrated at Westminster on 6 January 1066, the same day as the Confessor's funeral.[139] Harold's accession was the only recorded instance in which a king's election and consecration occurred on the same day, and post-Conquest commentators condemned the haste with which he was inaugurated.[140] William of Poitiers concluded that Harold "could not endure to await the decision of a public election" but took possession of (*occupauit*) the royal throne while the population was still in mourning; William of Malmesbury stated that he seized (*arripuit*) the crown while "grief for the king's death was still fresh"; and Orderic Vitalis reported that Harold had himself "consecrated without the common consent" and "stole by stealth the glory of the crown" before Edward's funeral had even finished.[141] Yet Harold's quick ascension was facilitated by a number of factors beyond his own eagerness to assume royal power, for the timing and location of Edward's death would have permitted an immediate end to the ensuing interregnum. The proximity of the royal residence to the king's burial church at Westminster obviated the need for a long funeral procession, and the realm's leading magnates would have already been gathered in London for Edward's Christmas assembly and the consecration of Westminster on 28 December.[142] Furthermore, the

138 This opinion was reportedly voiced by Archbishop Stigand at the king's deathbed: *Vita Ædwardi*, 76–7; William of Malmesbury, *GR* ii.227; Barlow, *Edward the Confessor*, 248–9.

139 ASC E 1066, CD 1065 (*recte* 1066).

140 Although a quick coronation was not unprecedented, Harold's immediate consecration would surely have been recognized as unusual: Nelson, "Inauguration Rituals," 299; Barlow, *Edward the Confessor*, 254–5.

141 "Nec sustinuit ... quid electio publica statueret consulere"; William of Poitiers, *GG*, 100–1. "Recenti adhuc regalis funeris luctu"; William of Malmesbury, *GR* ii.228.7. "Sine communi consensu ... consecratus, furtim præripuit diadematis ... decus"; Orderic Vitalis, *Ecclesiastical History* II, 136–9. See also Van Houts, *Gesta Normannorum Ducum* II, 160–1.

142 Sulcard noted that multitudes came to attend the double festival: "they were assembled there from all of Britain; they were assembled, I say, just as at Christmas for a royal court or for consecrating a famous church to Christ" [conuenitur eo a tota Britannia, conuenitur, inquam, ut in natali domini sicut ad regis curiam vel ad celebrem Christo consecrandam ecclesiam]; Scholz, "Sulcard," 91. See also: *Vita Ædwardi*, 71–2; Garnett, "Coronation and Propaganda," 93. For a list of possible attendees, see Barlow, *Edward the Confessor*, 244–6.

king's death would have been expected at least since Christmas, when he withdrew from court too ill to make any further public appearances.[143] Funeral arrangements could have begun some ten days in advance of the event, if not earlier, so that there would have been no need to delay the burial; the fact that the body could have lasted some time in the winter weather before it began to decay suggests that the necessary preparations were in place for Edward's immediate interment. Harold's accession may likewise have been anticipated among those at Westminster, and preparations for his acclamation and coronation could have been made at this time by his supporters, including Archbishops Ealdred of York and Stigand of Canterbury, who presided over his consecration.[144]

Although the quick sequence of ritual events was permitted by these practical conditions, this conflated schedule also lent Harold a significant political advantage: he was the only potential successor present at Westminster upon the king's death. William was in Normandy, where he received an "unexpected report" that Edward had died and Harold had been crowned; and Tostig was in exile in Flanders, having been driven out of his earldom of Northumbria after an uprising in 1065.[145] The number of influential Normans at Edward's court might have tipped the balance toward William's claim, had their candidate been present, whereas Tostig might have drawn support away from Harold if he had had the opportunity to capitalize on his own status as the Confessor's brother-in-law.[146] A prompt consecration cemented Harold's royal standing before either of his rivals was able to assert a claim in person, and this advantage would have been further strengthened by his attentive proximity to Edward both before and after his death. Harold's presence at the king's deathbed was recorded in English and Norman accounts of the succession, and according to the *Vita Ædwardi*, Edward entrusted his brother-in-law with the

143 Edward fell ill on Christmas Eve, briefly attended court on Christmas Day, and took to his bed the following day; he died on 5 January, the eve of Epiphany: ASC CD 1065 (*recte* 1066), E 1066; *Vita Ædwardi*, 71–3; JW 598–601; William of Malmesbury, *GR* II.228.6; Scholz, "Sulcard," 91.

144 William of Poitiers, *GG*, 100n2; Nelson, "Rites of the Conqueror," 124 and 127–8. For Stigand, see below, n. 152. Ealdred's loyalty to the Godwinesons is implied in ASC D 1052.

145 "Rumor insperato"; William of Poitiers, *GG*, 100–1. See also ASC CD 1065, E 1064; *Vita Ædwardi*, 50–4; JW 598–9.

146 According to the *Vita Ædwardi*, Edward returned from his exile accompanied by a retinue of Normans, whom he kept as close advisers: *Vita Ædwardi*, 17, but compare William of Poitiers, *GG*, 18–19. See also Barlow, *Edward the Confessor*, 245.

protection of both his kingdom and his wife just before he died.[147] Although Harold was already the kingdom's most powerful magnate before the king's bequest, he was now able to present himself as the Confessor's designated heir – a position bolstered by his kinship with Edward's widowed queen.[148] His consecration at Westminster's high altar, shortly after the funeral mass and within feet of his predecessor's body, would have reinforced his close association with the dead king.[149] Harold's immediate accession, conceived in concert with Edward's dying wishes and approved by the leading English magnates, seems a calculated response to an imminent and potentially protracted succession crisis in which at least three contenders had sufficient wealth and military resources to make serious bids for the throne. Harold capitalized on his predecessor's memory while preventing other contenders from doing so, maintaining a constant presence around the dying king and, later, his corpse. The rapid sequence of funeral, election, and consecration allowed the entire process of royal succession to be compressed into one continuous event, dominated by Harold from start to finish.

When Harold himself died later that year, he became the first English king in generations to be killed on the battlefield. Unlike his predecessor, he received no public funeral or memorialization, and the lack of ceremonial closure must have amplified the uncertainty of the interregnum that followed.[150] Although some of Harold's erstwhile supporters attempted to designate the Confessor's nephew Edgar their new ruler, William's military strength ultimately compelled the English to abandon their candidate and submit to Norman rule.[151] However, William's identity as a lawful king – and not a foreign invader – hinged on an understanding of his immediate predecessor's reign as illegitimate and his own accession as a restoration of law and order. Accordingly, Norman authors emphasized Harold's alleged

147 *Vita Ædwardi*, 79; William of Poitiers, *GG*, 118–19; and above, n. 136.

148 William of Poitiers maintained that Edith supported William's candidacy, but this claim seems to rely on her later reconciliation with the Conqueror; the *Vita Ædwardi*, a tribute to Edith and her family, nowhere implied that the queen did not support her brother's bid for the throne. William of Poitiers, *GG*, 114–15; Stafford, *Emma and Edith*, 275.

149 For Edward's funeral mass and the location of the grave in relation to the high altar, see *Vita Ædwardi*, 81, quoted above in the Introduction. Compare also Rodwell, "Edward the Confessor's Abbey," 154–5.

150 Harold's death and burial are discussed at length below, chapter 7.

151 ASC D 1066; William of Poitiers, *GG*, 146–7; JW 604–7.

perjury and deemed his very consecration void.[152] The violence of the conquest was justified, as William of Poitiers put it, because "it is honourable, glorious, and a worthy service to kill a tyrant."[153] Harold's lack of a public funeral confirmed that his reign had been unrighteous.

By contrast, Edward's tomb and memory were central to William's attempts to present himself as the lawful heir to the kingdom. This identification with the Confessor began with his coronation at Westminster on 25 December 1066, some two months after the Norman victory at Hastings. William waited until the end of the year to have himself consecrated, even though the English had tried to acclaim him king on at least two earlier occasions. The Anglo-Saxon Chronicle stated that England's most influential magnates (including the ætheling Edgar) submitted to William and declared him their king soon after Hastings, and William of Poitiers added that when the Conqueror first approached London, "the bishops and other magnates prayed that he would assume the crown, saying that they were accustomed to serving a king and wished to have a king as their lord."[154] William postponed, reportedly citing a disinclination to rush into a royal consecration and his desire to have his wife anointed with him, but even after his retinue convinced him not to delay any longer, there was still a space of time between his arrival in London and his formal accession to the kingdom.[155] It may be that the organizers of the ritual wanted the consecration to coincide with the next major feast day, as a number of earlier

152 The consecration was inaccurately attributed in Norman sources to Archbishop Stigand of Canterbury, who was under papal anathema in January 1066 and deposed by papal legates in 1070; it was almost certainly Archbishop Ealdred of York who consecrated Harold. ASC C 1043; *Vita Ædwardi*, 76–7; William of Poitiers, *GG*, 100–1, 150–1, and 160–1; JW 600–7; Raine, *Historians of the Church of York* II, 348; Stafford, *Emma and Edith*, 112–13; Barlow, *Edward the Confessor*, 248–9; Garnett, *Conquered England*, 1–44; Garnett, "Coronation and Propaganda," 107–8; Nelson, "Rites of the Conqueror," 127–8; Stenton, *Anglo-Saxon England*, 464–6 and 659–61.

153 "Tyrannum occidere sit pulchrum, fama gloriosum, beneficio gratum"; William of Poitiers, *GG* 138–9, and see also 156–7.

154 "Orant post haec ut coronam sumat una pontifices atque caeteri summates, se quidem solitos esse regi seruire, regem dominum habere uelle"; William of Poitiers, *GG*, 146–9. ASC D 1066 reported: "They gave hostages and swore oaths to him, and he promised them that he would be a loyal lord to them, and in spite of this, they meanwhile harried everywhere they rode" [Gysledan 7 sworon him aðas, 7 he heom behet þæt he wolde heom hold hlaford beon, 7 þeah onmang þisan hi hergedan eall þæt hi oferforon]; ASC D 1066. See also: Garnett, "Coronation and Propaganda," 91–5; Nelson, "Rites of the Conqueror," 117–18.

155 William of Poitiers, *GG*, 148–9.

English coronations had.[156] However, by waiting until Christmas, William could be crowned at Westminster on the first anniversary of Edward's last public appearance.[157] Like Harold, he chose not to have himself consecrated at Winchester, the site of the Confessor's own accession, but "in the basilica of St Peter the apostle, which rejoiced in the tomb of King Edward."[158] Perhaps it was from this vantage point near the Confessor's grave that he pledged to hold the law of England as it had been held in Edward's day.[159] It is telling that William of Poitiers offered a precise explanation of the Conqueror's family ties with Edward in his account of the consecration: his genealogy may have been cited at the coronation to highlight the new king's connection with an established English dynasty, just as Edward's own royal pedigree had been evoked when he came to the throne after the period of Danish rule.[160] This blood kinship may have been emphasized in order to draw a contrast with Harold, who was related to the Confessor by marriage only, but its inclusion was surely intended to dispel any doubts about William's hereditary right to the kingdom.

156 As implied by John of Worcester: "As the Christmas festival was approaching, he came to London with his whole army, so that he might be raised to the kingdom there" [Appropinquante igitur dominice Natiuitatis festiuitate, cum omni exercitu Lundoniam, ut ibi in regem sullimaretur, adiit]; JW 606–7.

157 Edward made an appearance at his Christmas court but retired soon after; he was too ill to attend Westminster's consecration on 28 December: *Vita Ædwardi*, 72–3.

158 "In basilica sancti Petri apostoli, quae regis Edwardi sepulchro gaudebat"; William of Poitiers, *GG*, 150–1. Compare also William of Malmesbury: "So the custom was established among William's successors that, in memory of Edward's burial, kings should receive their crowns there" [Consuetudo igitur apud posteros eualuit ut propter Eduardi inibi sepulti memoriam regiam regnaturi accipiant coronam]; William of Malmesbury, *GP* ii.73.6.

159 Edward's law may have been cited as part of William's coronation oath, which included a promise to retain existing laws; a direct reference was made to Edward's law in a London writ issued soon after William's consecration: Bates, *Regesta*, 593; Liebermann, *Gesetze*, 486; Wormald, *Making of English Law*, 398–9; Garnett, *Conquered England*, 12–13; William of Poitiers, *GG*, 158–9. For the coronation oath, see: ASC D 1066; Stafford, "Royal Promises," 186–7.

160 "If anyone asks the reckoning of this blood kinship, it is well known that he was related to King Edward by close ties of blood, being the son of Duke Robert, whose aunt, Emma, the sister of Richard II and daughter of Richard I, was Edward's mother" [Si ratio sanguinis poscitur, pernotum est quam proxima consanguinitate regem Edwardum attigerit filius ducis Rodberti, cuius amita Ricardi secundi soror, filia primi, Emma, genitrix fuit Edwardi]; William of Poitiers, *GG*, 150–1. For the Confessor's genealogy in the ASC accounts of his election in 1043, see above, nn. 125 and 126.

Despite these efforts to portray William as Edward's true heir, Harold's consecration – a large-scale public event, witnessed and recognized as lawful by the kingdom's leading magnates – would have been widely remembered. Norman accounts of Harold's tyranny and usurpation, as well as the misidentification of the anathematized Archbishop Stigand of Canterbury as officiant, were cited as reasons to retroactively invalidate his anointing. However, in December 1066, when William needed a consecration of his own, it was Harold's that provided the exemplar. Both rituals took place at Westminster's high altar, both were officiated by Archbishop Ealdred of York, and both employed a new version of the English coronation *ordo* which was first used in January 1066.[161] Nevertheless, where Harold was consecrated at the Confessor's tomb in order to draw attention to his relationship with his predecessor, the body of William's immediate predecessor was conspicuously absent during his inauguration. Even as he appropriated the ceremonial elements of Harold's consecration, William was portrayed as Edward's successor – not Harold's.

As a ceremonial display, however, William's consecration fell short. According to William of Poitiers, the Norman soldiers outside Westminster mistook the acclamation inside the church for an uprising and immediately set fire to the surrounding buildings.[162] Orderic Vitalis elaborated on the chaos:

> Only the bishops and a few clergy and monks remained, terrified, before the altar, and with difficulty completed the consecration of the king who was trembling from head to foot. And almost all the rest made for the scene of the raging fire, some to fight the flames and many others hoping to find loot for themselves in the general confusion.[163]

Although the event was meant to reinforce the continuity between Anglo-Saxon and Norman rule, the consecration's symbolic impact would have been undermined by the riot that drew observers away from William's

161 Nelson, "Rites of the Conqueror," 121–8.

162 William of Poitiers, *GG*, 150–1.

163 "Soli præsules et pauci clerici cum monachis nimium trepidantes ante aram perstiterunt, et officium consecrationis super regem uehementer trementem uix peregerunt; aliique pene omnes ad ignem nimis furentem cucurrerunt, quidam ut uim foci uiriliter ocarent; et plures ut in tanta perturbatione sibi prædas diriperent"; Orderic Vitalis, *Ecclesiastical History* II, 184–5. See also: Nelson, "Rites of the Conqueror," 122–3, Koziol, "Problem of Sacrality," 137.

inauguration in Edward's church. Ceremonial allusions to the Confessor's regime met with greater success on later occasions, as the Conqueror's English itinerary in the early years of his reign often mirrored the movements of Edward's court. William spent at least four of his first six Easters as king at Winchester, where Edward had been crowned on Easter Day 1043, and this became the regular site of post-Conquest Easter celebrations.[164] The king's early Pentecost and Christmas gatherings also replicated the itinerary of the closing years of Edward's reign.[165] Yet William's association with Westminster, the site most integrally associated with the Confessor's memory, was uneven. It remained a regular stop on the royal itinerary throughout his reign, and his wife Matilda was crowned there in 1068.[166] Nevertheless, Westminster did not attract significant royal patronage under the Norman and Angevin kings of England.[167] William's ambivalence towards Edward's burial church just a few years into his reign places his initial activity at the site into sharper relief: his early use of Westminster for demonstrations of royal continuity seems a deliberate attempt to adopt the ritual geography of Edward's final years at a time when his own royal authority was insecure.

Conclusions

This chapter has explored various ways that aspiring kings used earlier monarchs' remains, funerals, and graves to cement their own royal status. In each of the case studies presented here, a dead ruler's body functioned as a metonymic representation of his reign and legacy, which could be manipulated by his survivors in their attempts to gain the kingdom. There was no uniform way to treat a royal corpse, but three general trends may be identified in the fifty years leading up to the Norman Conquest. First was a candidate's establishment of a close association with the body or tomb of his predecessor. This approach, epitomized a century earlier by Edward the Elder's celebration of Alfred's remains, was employed in the eleventh century by Edmund Ironside, Edward the Confessor, Harold

164 Biddle, "Seasonal Festivals," 54–5 and 64–72.

165 Ibid.

166 Matilda's coronation was performed by Ealdred at Pentecost: Douglas, *William the Conqueror*, 213; Biddle, "Seasonal Festivals," 64.

167 Mason, "Westminster and the Monarchy," 279–80. William's interest in Westminster is examined more fully below, chapter 7.

Godwineson, and William of Normandy.[168] These kings all buttressed their claims to the throne by forging visible connections with the remains of a legitimizing predecessor, often as part of a display of royal ceremonial. By linking themselves with an established ruler, these men presented themselves as the natural heirs to the kingdom: as prominent mourners, they would be in an ideal position to portray themselves as the dead kings' chosen successors, regardless of whether they had actually been so designated. In addition, identification with their predecessors' reigns signalled their desire for administrative continuity, an important consideration for candidates eager to secure the support of magnates whose wealth and status might be threatened by a change in regime. Just as importantly, candidates who sustained their high-profile proximity to royal remains could prevent other claimants from taking control of the king's body and the political cachet that accrued to it.

Although potential successors aimed to be publicly identified with legitimizing royal remains, such attempts were not always successful. For Harold Harefoot in particular, a failed attempt to forge an association with his father's corpse led him to distance himself from Cnut's grave and the city that housed it until after he had secured power. During this period of political vulnerability, in which his very kinship with Cnut was called into question, his predecessor's memory became a liability rather than an asset. Harold's actions represent a second way in which royal corpses might be handled by potential successors: though recognized as potent symbolic objects, these bodies were distanced from political deliberations so that they would not influence the outcome of succession debates. Whatever William did with Harold Godwineson's body, he certainly did not bury it with Edward's at Westminster, where it might draw attention from William's own consecration and dilute his narrative of legitimate succession. Cnut's burial of Edmund Ironside in Glastonbury likewise minimized the impact of his rival's remains. In addition to removing a problematic body from a rising political centre, this distance would surely have made it easier for Edmund's former allies to renounce their loyalty to his brothers and sons in London. Cnut, Harold Harefoot, and William each claimed England as their inheritance, but their hereditary links to previous kings were tenuous. Accordingly, their identification with a legitimizing predecessor had the potential to backfire; a volatile political body might endanger an already insecure claim to the kingdom.

168 It was also used by Emma, although she was unable to maintain the authority she gained as a result.

Despite any anxiety they may have harboured about the influence of these royal bodies, Cnut, Harold Harefoot, and William each recognized the importance of royal tombs, appreciating that deference to a predecessor's memory could serve a candidate well during an uncertain interregnum. Respectful treatment of a dead king's remains was not guaranteed, however, and the posthumous degradation of a royal corpse was a real, if relatively rare, possibility in eleventh-century England. Harthacnut openly desecrated the honourably buried body of his predecessor, removing it from its consecrated grave and exposing it to the elements. William, although he did not make a spectacle of Harold Godwineson's remains, deprived his rival of the funeral his royal status merited. In these two instances, the new rulers' objective was to deny the royal identity of their immediate predecessors by inverting the norms of kingly burial. Yet whereas William was cautious with this tactic, perhaps fearing that open desecration would undermine his authority, Harthacnut's public exhumation of his half-brother earned him condemnation from most chroniclers of his reign. Though a viable course of action, denying a rival an honourable royal grave was a considerable political risk.

All of the rulers discussed in this chapter recognized that burying and memorializing kings was a matter of public concern, and I would contend that in most of these cases, their interactions with their predecessors' bodies did in fact help them establish and secure their rule. This is not to say that the treatment of royal remains was the dominant factor in pre-Conquest succession politics. Although the savvy manipulation of a previous king's mortal remains and posthumous memory might help a candidate secure his place in an established royal dynasty, aspiring monarchs relied heavily on their military resources and political supporters to get them on the throne. Edward the Confessor's identification with his half-brother's corpse may have lent additional weight to his hereditary claim in the face of Scandinavian challengers, but his success should surely be attributed to the efforts of Earl Godwine and other English allies. Conversely, Harold Harefoot's early inability to harness the ideological power of his father's tomb did not prevent him from eventually becoming full king. Yet the fact that every ruler who came to power between 1016 and 1066 interacted in some way with the earthly remains of a predecessor suggests that the evocation of dynastic memory was an accepted and expected element of royal transitions. Six of the seven kings considered in this chapter – Edmund Ironside, Cnut, Harold Harefoot, Edward the Confessor, Harold Godwineson, and William – asserted their right to the kingdom at the site of a predecessor's remains. In 1042, it was acceptable (if noteworthy) for Edward to be elected with his predecessor's corpse yet unburied; by the time William ascended to the realm, it was deemed advantageous to be inaugurated beside the Confessor's tomb. While it is possible that royal mausolea had long been recognized as particularly apt places to claim the throne, the previous centuries had seen West Saxon kings crowned at Kingston, some distance from the remains of the previous king, and separate elections were rarely mentioned by chroniclers. Between the death of Æthelred and the Norman Conquest, however, royal accessions were increasingly linked to burial sites, and authors began taking note.[169]

It is difficult to ascertain for how long a king's tomb might effectively be evoked for political purposes. Some rulers enjoyed prolonged afterlives, with their tombs cultivated well into the post-Conquest period.[170] The most prominent eleventh-century royal corpse was Edward the Confessor's, whose tomb and incorrupt body eventually became the focus of a full-fledged saint's cult. After 1066, the Confessor was recognized as the royal link to the Anglo-Saxon past, and Norman and Angevin kings consistently claimed him as an ancestor. Nevertheless, although Westminster became the standard site of consecrations, the abbey did not attract an exceptional degree of patronage in the century following the Conquest, and if Edward's tomb was evoked in the coronation ritual or attracted royal attention in other ceremonial contexts, there is little evidence of it before the twelfth century.[171] It may be that after the accession of William I, Westminster was valued simply as a site of ritual continuity, as Kingston had been in the tenth century: it was its ceremonial history, not its royal tomb, that now imbued the abbey with ideological importance.

I would conclude that the same was true of the other eleventh-century royal mausolea discussed in this chapter. Even if kings' tombs continued to draw interest and respect, bringing prestige to the institutions that housed them, their impact was most significant during interregna and succession

169 See table 2.

170 Below, chapter 7.

171 Henry II was instrumental in securing Edward's canonization in 1161 and participated in his translation in 1163; during the reigns of Henry's successors, the Westminster palace became the kingdom's premier administrative centre. By 1220, the coronation regalia began to be identified as Edward's, and from 1308, the coronation oath specifically included a promise to uphold Edward's law. No kings were buried at Westminster between 1066 and 1272, when Henry III had himself buried near Edward's relics. Binski, *Westminster*, 1–7, 52–3, and 131–5; Mason, "Site of King-Making," 63–4; Mason, "Westminster and the Monarchy," 278–87.

debates. Given the emphasis on dynastic and administrative continuity, the political shelf life of a king's remains was necessarily short. In the midst of succession debates, the rulers discussed above never sought legitimizing corpses at more than one generation's remove, focusing their efforts on the remains of biological or surrogate fathers and brothers. Once a recent kinsman could be evoked in support of a candidate's succession, more distant ancestors fell by the wayside. Thus, interest in Æthelred's body as a legitimizing object may have been revived at his son's 1042 accession, but it seems not to have been sustained after Edward's reign. Despite Edmund Ironside's impeccable royal pedigree, no later West Saxon candidates are said to have used his tomb to support claims to the kingdom.[172] Although the Confessor's corpse would later be recast as a saintly body, it lost much of its cachet as a political object soon after Harold and William's accessions. Although these rulers' individual legacies endured in the legal and historical writings that helped shape contemporary perceptions of the royal office through the Norman Conquest, the memory of a king's reign was no longer tethered to his tomb.

172 A tentative exception may be found in the vision of Bishop Brihtwald at Glastonbury: above, chapter 2.

4 Royal Body as Executed Body: Physical Propaganda in the Reigns of Harold Harefoot and Harthacnut

So far, this study has investigated how rulers' bodies, tombs, and funerals were used to promote the idea of royal continuity – a persistent ideal, despite the fact that regular patrilineal succession was rare in pre-Conquest England. The fragility of royal claims, external threats to the kingdom, and an increasingly powerful class of elite nobility made legitimizing rituals especially appealing for those attempting to establish themselves as kings. Even when candidates had an impeccable West Saxon pedigree, like Edmund Ironside and Edward the Confessor, or had secured their authority with decisive military action, like Cnut and William, they still rendered respectful attention to the remains of a predecessor. The consistency of such interactions indicates that a ritual response to royal death was expected, in order to mark the close of one reign and mitigate the transition to the next. Even if a king had been challenged or opposed during his lifetime, honourable interment was the default response when he died, and digression from this standard would have represented a perceptible departure from the status quo.

It is against this backdrop of prestigious burial practices that I approach the handful of instances in which royal bodies were denied royal funeral rites. Where honourable, public burial perpetuated the ideal (or illusion) of dynastic continuity, the desecration or obliteration of royal bodies signalled a desire for discontinuity with the previous regime. In such cases, royal bodies were not identified as legitimizing predecessors but as criminals – tyrants or usurpers whose actions caused them to forfeit the posthumous respect that rightful rulers merited. Condemnations of tyranny were familiar elements of classical and medieval texts and were employed by English authors on occasion.[1] The immediate, visceral impact of an abused or neglected royal body complemented written accusations.

1 Baraz, "Violence or Cruelty," 166 and 181–2; and further below.

Two particularly dramatic examples occurred during the succession debates that followed Cnut's death in 1035. Alfred the Ætheling, son of King Æthelred II and Emma, and Harold Harefoot, son of Cnut and his first wife Ælfgifu of Northampton, were each subjected to physical punishments that would ordinarily have been reserved for the worst offenders in Christian society. In 1036, Alfred returned to England from his lifelong exile only to be captured by Harold; the ætheling was mutilated and died soon afterwards. In 1040, Alfred's half-brother, the newly crowned King Harthacnut, had Harold exhumed from his monastic tomb and thrown in a swamp. Unlike honourable royal burial, which drew visual parallels with saints' shrines, the treatment of these bodies evoked the penalties inflicted on the bodies of criminals and excommunicants. Where royal bodies were carried in funeral processions, criminal bodies were exhibited on gallows or spikes; where royal bodies were entombed in monasteries and offered intercessory prayer, criminal bodies were denied consecrated graves and burial *ad sanctos*; and where a king's burial would reinforce the glory of his dynastic line, a criminal's burial sullied his posthumous memory and brought shame on his kin.[2] By implication, if a royal body suffered the same fate as a criminal corpse, its owner must have violated earthly or divine law and deserved his posthumous ignominy – just like any ordinary offender.

In Alfred and Harold's cases, however, this interpretation was not offered by contemporary commentators. Even though the royal bodies were subjected to punishments familiar in eleventh-century England, early authors uniformly labelled this treatment inappropriate and excessive, the result of the reigning king's poor leadership or outright cruelty. This could indicate that contemporaries were unable to grasp the ideological motives behind Alfred's mutilation and Harold's exhumation, or that they were unable to recognize that these men's bodies were subjected to criminal punishments. I do not think this is the case. Instead, I propose that medieval authors' broad condemnations demonstrate how completely these acts of propaganda backfired on their instigators. Within about five years of Alfred's death, his grave had attracted popular reverence and his suffering was lamented in Latin and vernacular texts, which invariably portrayed

2 The systematic exclusion of offenders from consecrated or honourable burial appears in Old English law codes beginning in the tenth century; II Æthelstan 26 is the earliest example. For this and other criminal punishments, see: Reynolds, *Deviant Burial Customs*; Reynolds, "Definition and Ideology"; Effros, "Beyond Cemetery Walls"; Thompson, *Dying and Death*, 170–80; Gates and Marafioti, *Capital and Corporal Punishment*; and below.

Harold as the episode's villain; moreover, the ætheling's humiliation galvanized his mother and half-brother to strike back against his oppressor. Harold's early death saved him from military retaliation, but he was nevertheless remembered in contemporary sources as a brutal, even maniacal king. Harthacnut's reputation did not fare much better after his exhumation of Harold. The desecration was quickly cited as evidence of Harthacnut's poor rulership, and a number of his subjects directly defied their new king by retrieving the disinterred body and reburying it in an appropriate, consecrated grave.

In the end, neither ruler successfully replaced his enemy's royal identity with a new, criminal identity by manipulating his body. Yet both men apparently believed that such treatment would improve their own political standing, and this chapter will explore why. In the following pages, I investigate what Harold and Harthacnut were trying to accomplish when they denied their rivals the trappings of a royal death and why contemporaries were not persuaded by the dishonourable treatment of the royal bodies. Whereas medieval chroniclers offered little background for these two episodes, flatly condemning the kings' behaviour without discussing their motivations or objectives, the following analysis attempts to place Alfred's mutilation and Harold's exhumation in their proper context. Though widely regarded as shocking and exceptional, these incidents should not be dismissed as irrational or isolated acts. Rather, they each exploited contemporary attitudes towards royal bodies and Christian burial, conveying a deliberate propagandistic message which was understood – if ultimately rejected – by contemporaries and chroniclers.

The Mutilation of Alfred the Ætheling: 1036

The blinding of the ætheling Alfred was perhaps the most scandalous element of the succession dispute that followed Cnut's death in 1035.[3] The presumptive heir to the kingdom was Harthacnut, Cnut's son by Emma, but he was in Denmark when his father died and did not return to England to claim his inheritance. In Harthacnut's absence, his half-brother Harold Harefoot ruled as regent in the north until 1037, while Emma held Wessex in her son's name. Harold increasingly drew English supporters away from his brother's cause, prompting Alfred and his brother Edward, the children of Emma's first marriage to Æthelred II, to return from a lifetime

3 The 1035 succession is treated above, chapter 3.

in exile.[4] Harthacnut's extended stay in Denmark and Harold's increasing political cachet may have led Emma to send for her older sons; alternatively, the æthelings may have decided to take advantage of the political turbulence and stake their own claim to the kingdom; or, as one contemporary source claimed, Harold may have lured them from Normandy with the intention of eliminating them altogether.[5] In any case, early commentators agreed that Alfred returned to England toward the end of 1036, that he was waylaid and blinded by a force of Harold's men under Earl Godwine's command, and that he died soon afterwards and was buried at the monastery of Ely.[6]

The earliest extant sources for this episode are the *Encomium Emmae Reginae* and the Anglo-Saxon Chronicle. The *Encomium*, composed within five years of the ætheling's death, depicted the assassination as a martyrdom and portrayed Alfred as an innocent saint.[7] According to this account, Earl Godwine met Alfred when he arrived in England and provided him hospitality for the night, unaware that Harold had ordered his own men to take the ætheling and his party captive. Harold's retainers disarmed Alfred's retinue as they slept and bound them in chains; most of the prisoners were executed the next morning without a hearing, and a few were kept or sold as slaves. Alfred, however, was spared for the time being and taken to the island of Ely:

> And then the most contemptible people were chosen to judge the lamented youth in their madness. Once these men had been set as judges, they decreed that he should first have both eyes put out as a sign of contempt. And so he was held by the impious men, and once his eyes had been dug out, he was most wickedly slain. Once this killing was accomplished, they left the lifeless body, which the servants of Christ (namely the monks of that very island of Ely) stole and honorably buried.[8]

---

4 Their exile is discussed by Keynes, "Æthelings in Normandy."

5 Keynes, "Introduction to the Reprint," xxx–xxxi and xxxiii–xxxiv; Keynes, "Æthelings in Normandy," 195–6.

6 Edward also came to England with a fleet at this time, making it as far as Southampton before encountering English forces and retreating to Normandy: Keynes, "Æthelings in Normandy," 195.

7 The date, authorship, and objectives of the *Encomium* are examined above, chapter 3.

8 "Deinde contemptibiliores eliguntur, ut horum ab insania flendus iuuenis diiudicetur. Qui iudices constituti decreuerunt, illi debere oculi utrique ad contemptum primum erui … Namque est ab inpiis tentus, effossis etiam luminibus inpiissime est occisus. Qua nece perfecta reliquunt corpus exanime, quod fideles Christi, monachi scilicet eiusdem insulae Haeli, rapientes sepelierunt honorifice"; *Encomium*, 44–7.

The *Encomium*, commissioned by Emma, blamed the incident entirely on Harold, who was portrayed throughout as cruel and tyrannical. Not only did he treacherously kill the innocent prince and his followers, according to this account, but he also wronged his own earl by betraying Godwine's guest to his death. Furthermore, the Encomiast accused Harold of luring Alfred to England in the first place, claiming that he forged a letter from Emma urging her sons to return home. The unlikely story of the forged letter, in conjunction with the unequivocal condemnation of Harold for the killing, seems expressly designed to dispel rumours that the queen was in any way involved in her son's death.[9] In addition, the insistent assertion that Godwine had only good intentions towards Alfred suggests that the earl also had been implicated in the act; the author was evidently determined to clear the name of a powerful magnate who had reaffirmed his allegiance to Emma by the time the *Encomium* was composed.[10] Just as importantly, the Encomiast absolved Alfred himself of any wrongdoing by portraying him as a saint:

> There are many miracles at the site of his tomb, as certain people report, who say that they have seen them very often. And deservedly so: for he was martyred in innocence, and therefore it is fitting that the power of the innocent be exercised through him. Therefore, let Queen Emma rejoice in such an intercessor, since the one she once had as a son on earth she now has as a patron in heaven.[11]

By identifying Alfred as a martyr, the Encomiast retroactively demonstrated the ætheling's innocence, implying that such a saint could never have been corrupt during his time on earth. Alfred's alleged sanctity also underscored Harold's own transgression, for the king did not simply violate earthly law by killing an innocent man; he violated divine law by persecuting God's chosen saint.[12]

---

9 Stafford, *Emma and Edith*, 36; Keynes, "Introduction to the Reprint," lxiii; Keynes, "Æthelings in Normandy," 196.

10 Keynes, "Introduction to the Reprint," lxiii–lxv. Godwine was explicitly implicated in ASC C 1036; see below.

11 "In loco autem sepulcri eius multa fiunt miracula, ut quidam aiunt, qui etiam se haec uidisse saepissime dicunt. Et merito: innocenter enim fuit martyrizatus, ideoque dignum est ut per eum innocencium exerceatur uirtus. Gaudeat igitur Emma regina de tanto intercessore, quia quem quondam in terris habuit filium nunc habet in caelis patronum"; *Encomium*, 46–7.

12 This logic is articulated by Rollason, "Murdered Royal Saints," 16–20.

A briefer account of Alfred's mutilation and death was included in the Anglo-Saxon Chronicle, which, like the *Encomium*, was sympathetic to the ætheling's plight and condemned Harold's actions towards him. Written within a decade of the events described, the C-manuscript's annal for 1036 begins as a prose entry but then shifts into verse:

> In this year, the innocent ætheling Alfred, the son of King Æthelred, came hither and wanted to go to his mother, who was in Winchester; but Earl Godwine would not let him, nor would other men who wielded great power, because opinion was then moving very much in Harold's favour, although this was not right.
> But Godwine then stopped him and placed him in bonds,
> And divided up his companions and killed some in various ways.
> Some were sold for money, some were cruelly killed,
> Some were bound, some were blinded,
> Some were mutilated, some were scalped.
> There was no worse deed done in this country
> Since the Danes came and made peace here.
> Now we should trust in beloved God,
> That they are rejoicing happily with Christ –
> Those who were so wretchedly killed without being guilty.
> Then the ætheling was still alive. He was beset with every evil,
> Until it was decided that he should be led
> To Ely, thus bound.
> As soon as he came onto the ship he was blinded
> And thus blind he was brought to the monks,
> And he dwelt there as long as he lived.
> Afterwards, he was buried as was fitting to him,
> Completely honourably, as he deserved,
> At the west end near the steeple,
> In the south portico; his soul is with Christ.[13]

---

13 "Her com Ælfred se unsceððiga æþeling Æþelrædes sunu cinges hider inn 7 wolde to his meder þe on Wincestre sæt, ac hit him ne geþafode Godwine eorl ne ec oþre men þe mycel mihton wealdan, forðan hit hleoðrode þa swiðe toward Haraldes, þeh hit unriht wære. Ac Godwine hine þa gelette 7 hine on hæft sette / 7 his geferan he todraf 7 sume mislice ofsloh. / Sume hi man wið feo sealde, sume hreowlice acwealde. / Sume hi man bende, sume hi man blende, / sume hamelode, sume hættode. / Ne wearð dreorlicre dæd gedon on þison earde / syþþan Dene comon 7 her frið namon. / Nu is to gelyfenne to ðan leofan Gode / þæt he blission bliðe mid Criste / þe wæron butan scylde swa

There are a number of inconsistencies between this account and the *Encomium*'s: the Chronicle did not explicitly describe Alfred as saintly, it clearly implicated Godwine in the mutilation, and it provided a fuller list of punishments endured by the ætheling's retinue.[14] Yet the most significant discrepancies concern the mode of Alfred's death and the fate of his body. Where the *Encomium* asserted that he was blinded and then slain and that his corpse was abandoned by the killers, the Chronicle maintained that the ætheling survived his blinding and was still living when he was handed over to the monks of Ely.

Later accounts of the mutilation followed the Chronicle's chronology for this episode, maintaining that Alfred was blinded but very much alive when he was delivered to the monks, and an early Ely calendar which noted the ætheling's death on 5 February 1037 indicates that he lived for some time after his mutilation in late 1036.[15] The *Encomium* was the only source which stated that Alfred was killed outright (*occisus*) by his oppressors, claiming that the ætheling was already dead by the time the monks found him. This discrepancy is best explained by the text's propagandistic objectives, which motivated the author to emphasize or even exaggerate Harold's cruelty towards Alfred while minimizing any suggestion that the ætheling's sufferings were warranted. Yet the *Encomium*'s vigorous defence of Emma and thorough condemnation of Harold imply that this propagandistic message was deployed in the 1040s to counter existing notions that Emma, Godwine, or even Alfred ought to be blamed for the mutilation. It is even possible that the work was intended to quash residual sympathy for Harold at a time when Harthacnut's own popularity was

---

earmlice acwealde. / Se æþeling lyfode þa gyt; ælc yfel man him gehet, / oð þæt man gerædde þæt man hine lædde / to Eligbyrig swa gebundenne. / Sona swa he lende on scype man hine blende / 7 hine swa blindne brohte to ðam munecon, / 7 he þar wunode ða hwile þe he lyfode. / Syððan hine man byrigde swa him wel gebyrede, / ful wurðlice, swa he wyrðe wæs, / æt þam westende þam styple ful gehende, / on þam suðportice, seo saul is mid Criste"; ASC C 1036. Compare ASC D 1036, which adapted the poem to eliminate any reference to Godwine's involvement, disrupting the metre and rhyme of ASC C. The poem's metre, rhyme, and context are discussed by O'Brien O'Keeffe, *MS C*, lxix; O'Brien O'Keeffe, *Visible Song*, 135; Bredehoft, *Textual Histories*, 110–11, Bredehoft, *Early English Metre*, 92–3; Kries, "Mutilation of Alfred."

14 However, the *Encomium* did not describe the specific mutilations suffered by Alfred's men, as the ASC did: *Encomium*, 42–5.

15 For the dating, see Keynes, "Introduction to the Reprint," xxxi–xxxii. Compare also Blake, *Liber Eliensis*, xxiii–xxiv and 159; Fairweather, *Liber Eliensis*, 189–90 and n. 411; JW 522–5; William of Poitiers, *GG*, 4–5; William of Malmesbury *GR* ii.188.5.

faltering. The *Encomium*'s account may thus be read as a point-by-point response to critics who blamed Emma and her allies for Alfred's fate or who thought Harold's actions towards his rival were just.

The logistics of the event suggest that such rumours about Emma's involvement were not unfounded. Alfred's return from Normandy in 1036 coincided with Harold's attempts to consolidate his royal authority, and although he was not yet recognized as full king, he had by this time secured the allegiance of a number of powerful magnates, including Earl Godwine.[16] The ætheling's appearance in England at this moment could only have exacerbated the tension between Harold's supporters and Emma's, especially if he arrived with a military escort, as the sources indicate. The Encomiast initially maintained that the ætheling was travelling only with his companions and a small retinue from Boulogne (*Bononiensium paucos*), but he later stated that lodging was needed for scores of men once they reached England; he further declared that nine out of every ten were killed by Harold's agents, who "condemned the worthy bodies of so many soldiers."[17] John of Worcester, the earliest chronicler to cite the number of dead, reported that six hundred of Alfred's men were killed and that many others were mutilated, tortured, or sold into slavery.[18] Given that it took only thirty-five men to make an army, according to an Old English law disseminated just over a century earlier, Alfred's force was surely perceived as a credible military threat – particularly if the ætheling had declared an intent to claim the throne.[19] While Emma must have seen Alfred's arrival as an opportunity to cleanse the realm of a false king and restore her own status, Harold would have regarded the ætheling as a usurper who wanted to seize the power that he had so painstakingly acquired. From this perspective, Alfred and his men were traitors who posed a military threat to a legitimately elected regime.

---

16 Above, chapter 3.

17 "Tot militum honesta dampnauerunt corpora"; *Encomium* 42–3. In the same passage, the Encomiast claimed that Alfred had declined a large force offered by Count Baldwin of Flanders. See also Stafford, *Emma and Edith*, 240.

18 JW 522–3.

19 Ine 13.1, which was circulated with King Alfred's law code of the late ninth century. The *Vita Ædwardi* implied that the bid for the throne was an express purpose of the expedition, stating that Alfred "incautiously moved towards acquiring the paternal kingdom" [patrio regno adipiscendo cum ageret incautius]; *Vita Ædwardi*, 20. Compare William of Poitiers, *GG*, 2–5.

The spectacular dispatch of enemy fighters was not unprecedented at this time, and the punishments suffered by Alfred's men might well have been considered appropriate for members of a rebel army.[20] However, there is no record of a military encounter, and all the early sources agree that Alfred's retinue was captured rather than defeated in battle.[21] It is telling that the Chronicle's list of indignities were all attested judicial sentences under Anglo-Saxon law. The men who were executed shared a fate with criminals convicted of *bot*-less, or unforgivable offences; those who were blinded, mutilated, or scalped suffered punishments which were explicitly prescribed for repeat offenders in the laws of Cnut; and those who escaped immediate physical afflictions were sold into penal slavery, a viable alternative to corporal penalties in the tenth and eleventh centuries.[22] Alfred's mutilation was also consistent with contemporary practice: blinding had long been regarded as an apt punishment for rebels, and it had recently been employed against leaders of a domestic revolt during the reign of Æthelred.[23] Ordinarily, however, treason against the king or one's lord merited a death sentence.[24] In the late tenth century, Edgar legislated that anyone who betrayed his lord would forfeit his life, and in the 1020s, Cnut ruled that "betrayal of a lord cannot be compensated according to earthly law."[25]

---

20 For the purportedly just killings of rebels after Hastings, see Garnett, "Coronation and Propaganda," 95–9.

21 The *Encomium* was explicit on this point: Alfred's men were captured and killed "not by military violence but by their enemies' deceitful traps" [non miliciae uiolentia sed fraudium suarum insidiis]; *Encomium*, 44–5.

22 II Cnut 30.4–30.5 prescribed extensive mutilations for repeat offenders which mirrored the punishments inflicted on Alfred's men. Penal slavery (*witeðeow*) appears in Ine 24, 48, and 54.2; II Edward 6; Edward and Guthrum 7.1; in Æthelstan's ordinance on Alms 1; in four wills (S 1485, S 1491, S 1492, S 1539); and in a lease of land (S 1285). For the judicial nature of the mutilations in the account of Alfred's death, see O'Brien O'Keeffe, "Body and Law," 214–15.

23 ASC CDEF 1006; Keynes, *Diplomas*, 211–13; Boyle, "Anglo-Saxon Political Mutilation." For blinding as an appropriate punishment for traitors and high-level offenders, see: Bührer-Thierry, "Blinding in the Early Medieval West," 80–8; van Eickels, "Castration and Blinding," 592–3.

24 On treason and theft as violations of a requisite loyalty oath in Anglo-Saxon England, see Wormald, "Charters, Law," 307. See also: Barrow "Demonstrative Behaviour," 136; Gillingham, "1066 and the Introduction of Chivalry," 221.

25 "Hlafordswice æfter woroldlage is botleas"; II Cnut 64. Edgar's law against treason is III Edgar 7.3: "whatever [sanctuary] a proven thief should seek, or one who is discovered to be a lord-betrayer, he should never have his life spared" [7 gesece se æbæra þeof þæt þæt he gesece, oððe se þe on hlafordsearwe gemet sy, þæt hi næfre feorh ne gesecan]. Compare also Alfred 4.

The treatment that Alfred and his men received marked them as criminal upstarts rather than a legitimate military force. It is significant that their punishments conformed entirely to the conventions of existing English law; the penalties were not foreign or unfamiliar, and neither were they arbitrary or excessive. Despite the rhetoric of the Chronicle and *Encomium*, treason was normally classified a *bot*-less offence, which surely explains why so many of Alfred's men were executed. In the early eleventh century, however, English legislation increasingly prescribed non-lethal sentences for even the most serious offenders, and it appears that this principle too was applied in Alfred's case. The importance of merciful punishment was first legislated in V Æthelred, penned by Archbishop Wulfstan of York:

> It is the decree of our lord and his council that Christian men not be condemned to death for too little. But rather, let mild punishments be decreed, for the people's need. Do not destroy God's handiwork and his own purchase, which he dearly bought, on account of little things.[26]

"God's handiwork," namely an offender's life and soul, was not to be frivolously destroyed by human agents, according to this statute, and this law's primary concern was that all offenders should have the opportunity to repent of their sins and attain salvation – an opportunity that would be lost if they were summarily executed.[27] Even if deviants refused to make amends for their misdeeds, non-lethal sentences would allow contrite offenders to live long enough to atone for their wrongs and save their souls. In this context, Alfred's blinding and the non-lethal corporal penalties suffered by his men should be understood as acts of merciful justice, in which Harold waived the death sentence traitors deserved and allowed the offenders the opportunity to repent before they died.[28]

In Alfred's case, a non-lethal judicial punishment may also have been politically expedient, as killing a prince might be perceived as a political assassination instead of the righteous exercise of justice. To emphasize this

---

26 "Ures hlafordes gerædnes 7 his witena is, þæt man Cristene men for ealles to lytlum to deaðe ne fordeme. Ac elles geræde man friðlice steora folce to þearfe. Ne forspille for lytlum Godes handgeweorc 7 his agenne ceap, þe he deore gebohte"; V Æthelred 3–3.1.

27 For Wulfstan's approach to capital and corporal punishment, see: Marafioti, "Punishing Bodies"; Thompson, *Dying and Death*, 180–4; Whitelock, "Wulfstan *Cantor*," 85–6.

28 For judicial blinding as royal mercy, see: Bührer-Thierry, "Blinding in the Early Medieval West," 79–81; van Eickels, "Castration and Blinding," 590.

distinction and ensure that the mutilation was lawful, Harold evidently had Alfred tried and sentenced before his punishment was carried out. The only witness to the legal process that preceded Alfred's blinding is the *Encomium*, which depicted the ætheling's trial as an illegitimate farce: although judges were chosen to try and sentence the captive, the author was clear that these individuals were both contemptible and insane.[29] However, the fact that the Encomiast included this episode at all implies that some sort of trial had in fact taken place, and his insistence that the judgment was the act of madmen was probably designed to counter an existing impression that Alfred had been lawfully condemned. If the author was responding to contemporaries who regarded Alfred's trial as legitimate, the ætheling's comparatively mild sentence of blinding might have been understood in some quarters as evidence of Harold's mercy towards his enemies and his respect for the West Saxon royal dynasty – in spite of the fact that one of its members had attempted to depose him.[30] Harold's apologists surely justified his actions against Alfred as a necessary but relatively lenient exercise of justice against an individual who had wrongfully tried to subvert royal authority.

The *Encomium* sought to persuade its readers that the opposite was true, asserting that Harold was in no way a just or magnanimous ruler: Alfred had been tricked into coming to England by the power-hungry royal pretender; he refused to bring an army with him but arrived with a small group of companions; his only intention was to visit his mother, who was being oppressed by a ruler who had stolen her son's crown. Neither Emma nor Alfred was guilty of any wrongdoing that might have justified Harold's unlawful and inordinate abuse of royal power, according to the *Encomium*, and its depiction of the ætheling's execution and abandoned corpse confirmed this point. If Alfred had been both blinded and killed by Harold's men, there could be no claim that the ætheling had been treated leniently. Eleventh-century legal discourse designated mutilation a merciful punishment because it was an alternative to immediate death and damnation, but it was nevertheless intended to be painful and humiliating.[31] Such treatment was mild only insofar as it provided the opportunity for an

29 The judges were *contemptibiliores* who condemned Alfred *ab insania*, in madness: *Encomium*, 44–5; and above, n. 8.

30 Analogous Carolingian examples are discussed by de Jong, "Political Coercion and Honour," 296–7.

31 Gates and Marafioti, *Capital and Corporal Punishment*; O'Brien O'Keeffe, "Body and Law," 216–17.

offender's soul to be saved; the punishment was merciful according to spiritual, not earthly standards.[32] As portrayed in the *Encomium*, however, the blinding provided no spiritual benefit. Alfred was killed immediately after his eyes were put out, giving him no time to atone for his sins. Read in this light, Alfred's mutilation was not merciful – as Harold surely intended – but cruel.

Two competing narratives were thus promulgated to explain the significance of the ætheling's fate. One, articulated in the *Encomium*, made Alfred the victim of a tyrant who abused the process of law. The other, communicated with physical punishments, identified Alfred and his men as traitors who had paid appropriately for their crimes. A maimed body would permanently identify a convicted individual as a deviant, distinguishing him physically from law-abiding members of his community and, in some cases, proclaiming the very nature of his crime.[33] Gruesome mutilations illustrated the consequences for disrupting the peace and would discourage others from replicating criminal behaviour; they transformed a body into a signifying object on which an individual's transgressions could be read.[34] For Emma, this would have been among the most detrimental aspects of Alfred's blinding.[35] Not only would his new deformity prevent her son from becoming king, but his alleged offence would now be indelibly inscribed on his body, marking him as a deviant for the remainder of his life.[36] Although withdrawal to a monastery might limit the exposure of his signifying disfigurement, the symbolic impact of Alfred's mutilation would only be fully neutralized once his body was concealed in a grave.

Accordingly, the Encomiast did not linger over Alfred's disfigured form. Although he introduced his narrative by imagining how distressing his description of the mutilation and killing must be for his patroness, he provided a thorough account of the circumstances that brought Alfred to

32 Marafioti, "Punishing Bodies."

33 O'Brien O'Keeffe, "Body and Law," 226–8. Some penalties stopped people from repeating a particular transgression by removing the offending member: IV Æthelred 5.3; Alfred 25.1; Whitelock, "Wulfstan *Cantor*," 85.

34 O'Brien O'Keeffe, "Body and Law," 224–8; Foucault, *Discipline and Punish*, 3–69.

35 For the mutilated body as a text, see: O'Brien O'Keefe, "Body and Law," especially 228; Richards, "Body as Text," especially 105–6.

36 For Alfred's ineligibility for the throne after his blinding, see O'Brien O'Keefe, "Body and Law," 214. For the political and religious implications of blinding as a punishment, see: Bührer-Thierry, "Blinding in the Early Medieval West"; van Eickels, "Castration and Blinding," 591; Bernstein, "Blinding of Harold," 54–8.

England and a graphic description of his companions' deaths. By contrast, he offered only a brief summary of the ætheling's sufferings. After mentioning that Alfred was held down by four men as others prepared to blind him, the Encomiast shifted his gaze away from his subject:

> Why do I linger over this in sorrow? My pen trembles as I write, as I am horrified at what the most blessed youth suffered. Therefore, I would sooner avoid the misery of such a great calamity, and touch upon the conclusion of this martyrdom until its end.[37]

Following this digression, his return to Alfred's body was brief and anticlimactic: "he was held fast by the impious men, and after his eyes had been dug out was most wickedly slain."[38] The remainder of the episode was devoted to a description of how the monks of Ely recovered Alfred's corpse, how they gave him an honourable tomb, and how the innocent ætheling was now a martyr. By telescoping the narrative and conflating his subject's mutilation, death, and burial, the Encomiast ensured that only a fleeting image of Alfred's broken body appeared in his text. His audience was presented with an unblemished living prince and the entombed relics of a martyr, with just a brief glimpse of the act of blinding and killing. The living mutilated body, which would proclaim the ætheling's supposed crimes, was suppressed.[39]

Alfred's lifeless body (*corpus exanime*) did appear briefly in the *Encomium*, however: it was left by his captors at the site of his execution until it was retrieved by the monks of Ely. The abandonment of the corpse added further insult to the ætheling's considerable injury, from the Encomiast's perspective, for only the most incorrigible members of Christian society were denied burial in eleventh-century England. Although executed criminals were typically excluded from consecrated cemeteries, their bodies often received some crude form of interment.[40] Excommunicants, by contrast, were to be refused any kind of grave. Medieval anathema formulas instructed that

37 "Quid hoc in dolore detineor? Mihi ipsi scribenti tremit calamus, dum horreo quae iuuenis passus est beatissimus. Euadam ergo breuius tantae calamitatis miseriam, finemque huius martyrii fine tenus perstringam"; *Encomium*, 44–5.

38 "Namque est ab inpiis tentus, effossis etiam luminibus inpiissime est occisus"; *Encomium*, 44–7.

39 *Encomium*, 46–7.

40 Reynolds, "Definition and Ideology," 37; Hayman and Reynolds, "42–54 London Road, Staines," 237–8.

excommunicated bodies be deposited on dung heaps or left as food for birds and beasts; an Old English homiletic account clarified that "no one may bury an excommunicant within a consecrated minster, nor even bring him to a heathen burial pit; rather, drag him out without a coffin unless he repents."[41] For the Encomiast, however, the claim that Alfred's corpse was abandoned was not a statement about the ætheling's spiritual state, but his captors'. According to his interpretation, Harold's men wrongly equated the innocent Alfred with the worst Christian deviants – evidence of their own error and corruption. It is also possible that the Encomiast imagined the killers deliberately trying to prevent their victim's salvation by depriving him of last rites and a consecrated grave, which offered considerable spiritual advantages.[42] For an audience familiar with eleventh-century penal practice, the speedy completion of Alfred's sentence and his executioners' abandonment of the corpse implied that Harold was not simply eliminating a political threat; he was injuring his enemy's soul.

This attempt failed, by the Encomiast's reckoning, because the martyred ætheling went straight to heaven as a saint.[43] Yet as long as the body remained unburied, any observer (or reader) might assume that Alfred was an impious criminal with little hope of salvation. It was left to the community at Ely to remedy the situation, and the monks' provision of an honourable, consecrated grave restored Alfred's earthly reputation and ensured that his tomb reflected the actual status of his soul.[44] If the executioners had purposely denied their victim an appropriate burial, as the *Encomium* asserted, it would follow that the monks recovered the corpse in direct defiance of Harold: by providing the body a prestigious burial in hallowed ground, the monks would have undermined the killers' intentions to make a visual statement about the ætheling's criminal activity and

41 "Ne hi nan man ne burge binnan gehalgodan mynstre, ne furþum to hæþenum pytte ne bere, ac drage butan cyste butan hi geswicon"; Scragg, *Vercelli Homilies*, 161. Comparable prescriptions were included in the earliest collection of excommunication formulas, compiled by Regino of Prüm ca 906, and in the widely disseminated Romano-Germanic Pontifical, compiled ca 960: PL 132 col.362BC; Vogel and Elze, *Pontifical Romano-Germanique*, 316. See also: Little, *Benedictine Maledictions*, 36–9 and 257; Hamilton, "Penance and Excommunication," 93–4; Treharne, "Unique Old English Formula," 197–8; Thompson, *Dying and Death*, 171–2.

42 Marafioti, "Punishing Bodies."

43 Above, n. 11.

44 All the early sources agreed that the ætheling was brought to Ely around the time of his blinding and that he was buried in the monastery after his death, and all but the *Encomium* maintained that he lived with the monks during the interim; above, n. 15.

damage his spiritual well-being. Although the Encomiast did not explicitly remark on the monks' political loyalties, his account of this intervention suggests that the community at Ely, like Emma herself, opposed Harold's persecution of Alfred and willingly thwarted his plans to denigrate the ætheling's body and memory.

Yet in reality, the monks may have been acting in concert with Harold's wishes when they buried the remains. It is surely significant that Alfred was brought to Ely, whose monastery benefited from Emma and Cnut's patronage, rather than punished at the nearest serviceable locale.[45] This decision suggests that Harold or his agents intended to ensure Alfred humane treatment after his blinding. This scenario does not recall violent acts of royal martyrdom, as the *Encomium* would have it, as much as instances of problematic royalty being confined to monasteries by their political enemies.[46] When read in this context, it seems as though Alfred's captors expected him to survive his mutilation – at least for a time. Blinded, Alfred was no longer a threat to Harold's royal authority and could safely be left alive to atone for his sins, serving simultaneously as a demonstration of royal magnanimity and proof that Harold had the power to thoroughly dominate his enemies.[47]

Unfortunately for Harold, Alfred's mutilation was not interpreted by contemporary authors as commensurate justice issued by a good king. Emma's personal and political priorities guaranteed that there would be no reference to Harold's mercy or righteousness in the *Encomium*, and the text's claim that a martyr's cult emerged around Alfred's remains served to further vilify Harold as the persecutor of a Christian saint.[48] However, the *Encomium* was the only source to explicitly identify the ætheling as saintly, leading modern scholars to assume that his cult was short-lived, if it existed at all.[49] Nevertheless, I would contend that Alfred's tomb attracted

45 On Emma and Cnut's patronage of Ely, see: Stafford, *Emma and Edith*, 143, 157, and 244; Lawson, *Cnut*, 152–3; Heslop, "*De Luxe* Manuscripts," 185.

46 Ridyard, "Monk-Kings," 22–3; de Jong, "Political Coercion and Honour," 291–7; and compare Stancliffe, "Kings Who Opted Out"; Yorke, "Anglo-Saxon Royal Courts," 245–2.

47 De Jong, "Political Coercion and Honour," 297–8.

48 Rollason, "Murdered Royal Saints," 16–20; but compare below, n. 49.

49 For example, David Rollason dismisses the *Encomium*'s claim that the ætheling was a saint, concluding that "Alfred's cult seems never to have taken off" and excluding him from his list of murdered Anglo-Saxon saints; Susan Ridyard and Catherine Cubitt likewise omit him from their studies of royal saints: Rollason, *Saints and Relics*, 141; Rollason, "Murdered Royal Saints"; Ridyard, *Royal Saints*; Cubitt, "Murdered and Martyred Saints."

contemporary reverence, not necessarily because it was regarded a saint's shrine but because it was the burial place of a prince whose extraordinary mutilation and death sparked popular interest. The fact that a vernacular, rhyming poem about Alfred's ordeal was deemed worthy of inclusion in the Anglo-Saxon Chronicle suggests that the text's compiler considered the episode a pivotal moment in English history.[50] The concluding lines of the poem are particularly revealing: "he was buried as was fitting to him, completely honourably, as he deserved, at the west end near the steeple, in the south portico."[51] The chronicler made it clear that Alfred's tomb was no ordinary grave but was fully worthy of its royal inhabitant, reiterating three times how suitable and honourable the burial was. Even more remarkably for the Chronicle, the poem described the exact location of Alfred's remains within the church. The precision of this information recalls the Old English list of saints' resting places, which provided the geographical locations of dozens of saints' shrines in eleventh-century England.[52] It may be that the Chronicle poem functioned as something of a pilgrim's guide; it is telling that the grave was deemed worthy of notice when the entry was committed to writing in the early 1040s.

With its focus on Alfred's body and tomb, this annal is quite different from the Chronicle's other poetic laments for dead rulers and seems not to be modelled after contemporary praise poetry. Instead, its structure and content more closely recall hagiographical works. No other royal death in the Chronicle was detailed as fully as Alfred's, and the extensive focus on physical afflictions in these twenty lines distinguishes the poem from other metrical entries, which provided almost no information about the cause or circumstances of their subjects' deaths.[53] As well as evoking the list of saints' resting places, the poem's description of physical suffering and detailed interest in Alfred's tomb resembles entries of the Old English Martyrology, which summarized each saint's persecution and death and frequently concluded with information about the location of his or her

50 The full text is above, n. 13. For the ASC poems, see: Bredehoft, *Textual Histories*, 72–118; O'Brien O'Keeffe, *Visible Song*, 108–37; Thormann, "*Anglo-Saxon Chronicle* Poems."

51 "Syððan hine man byrigde swa him wel gebyrede, / ful wurðlice, swa he wyrðe wæs, / æt þam westende þam styple ful gehende, / on þam suðportice"; ASC C 1036.

52 The text known as the *Secgan be þam Godes sanctum, þe on Engla lande ærost reston* listed the shrines of eighty-nine saints, all but one of which were located in England: Liebermann, *Heiligen Englands*, 9–20; Rollason, "Lists of Saints' Resting-Places."

53 Bredehoft, *Textual Histories*, 73–7 and 192–3n4; O'Brien O'Keeffe, *Visible Song*, 108–9.

relics.[54] Moreover, by emphasizing the number and scope of corporal penalties, the poet contrasted the brutality of the retinue's earthly treatment with the spiritual glory they received after their death – a common hagiographical motif. It was this final point which forced the clearest comparison between Harold's victims and well-established martyrs, for while ordinary Christians would have to wait for the Last Judgment before gaining admittance to heaven, Alfred and his men were already "rejoicing happily with Christ" – a privilege reserved for saints.[55]

Nevertheless, the words "saint" and "martyr" seem to have been carefully avoided in the Chronicle entry, despite the poem's hagiographical tone.[56] Although the poet depicted Alfred's death as a crime against both human and divine authority, and although he may have been willing to see Harold and Godwine identified as persecutors of Christian innocents, he stopped short of crediting the ætheling (or his companions) with miraculous or intercessory powers. Similarly, while Alfred's grave seems to have become a site of pilgrimage and reverence, it does not automatically follow that he was recognized as saintly. Perhaps his tomb appealed to the population as did the royal mausolea constructed by Edward the Elder and Edward the Confessor, which also drew pilgrims and expressions of reverence without saintly foci.[57] Just as the two Edwards appropriated the symbolic vocabulary of saints' cults in their burial churches, the Chronicle poet drew upon familiar hagiographic motifs to accentuate the exceptional glory of his royal subject. Even though the chronicler did not adopt the Encomiast's claim of sanctity – a claim which was likely instigated by Emma herself – both sources attest that a mutilated royal body could be reinvented as a worthy object of reverence.

Despite his allusions to the universal Christian theme of sanctity, however, the Chronicle poet firmly situated this episode within the course of English history, stating unequivocally that "there was no worse deed done

54 Rauer, *Old English Martyrology*; Kotzor, *Altenglische Martyrologium*; Rollason, "Lists of Saints' Resting-Places," 74.

55 See for example Revelations 20:4–5; Augustine, *City of God*, XX.9. The ASC quotation is above, n. 13.

56 Compare the poetic account of the death of Edward the Martyr, in which the dead king was explicitly called a saint (*sanct*), and the corresponding prose entry which stated that he was martyred (*gemartyrad*): ASC E 979 (*recte* 978) and C 978; the sources for Edward's death are treated in chapter 5.

57 Above, chapter 1.

in this country since the Danes came and made peace here."[58] Similar rhetorical formulas appear elsewhere in Old English literature: the Chronicle's account of King Edward's martyrdom in 978 claimed that no worse deed had been done since the Anglo-Saxons came to Britain, and *Genesis B* maintained that no worse deed was known to mankind than Eve's temptation.[59] Yet while the Chronicle author singled out Edward's martyrdom from the entire scope of English history and the *Genesis* poet identified Eve's transgression as the worst moment of human existence, Alfred's poet limited his rhetoric to the very recent past – the time since the Danes made peace in England. His historical retrospective may have gone back as far as the ninth century, when Alfred the Great established peace with the Vikings, but the poet was more likely referring to events in living memory when he mentioned the Danes.[60] English descriptions of Viking brutality were rife around the turn of the millennium: the Chronicle was full of accounts of burning, pillaging, and extortion, while Archbishop Wulfstan lamented that churches were regularly plundered, Christians were sold to heathens, and pagan worship was becoming a danger. Furthermore, the martyrdom of Archbishop Ælfheah in 1012 and the deposition of Æthelred in 1013 confirmed that no one at any level of society was safe from Scandinavian aggression.[61] In theory, Cnut's accession to the English throne in 1016 stopped all such atrocities (whether real or imagined), and this policy ought to have extended to his sons' reigns as well. By alluding to the Danish peace, the Chronicle poet depicted Alfred's death as an egregious violation of this implicit truce, associating the ætheling's mutilation with earlier Viking violence by drawing explicit attention to Harold's Danish heritage.[62] Where

58 "Ne wearð dreorlicre dæd gedon on þison earde / syþþan Dene comon 7 her frið namon"; ASC C 1036.

59 ASC E 979 (*recte* 978); Krapp, *Junius Manuscript*, 21, ll.594–5. The conclusion of *The Battle of Brunanburh* includes a similar passage, which claimed that the island had never seen such a great slaughter "since the Angles and Saxons came hither from the east" [siþþan eastan hider / Engle 7 Seaxe up becoman]; ASC A 937. For a comparison of these exclamations, see: Kries, "Mutilation of Alfred," 47–8; Bredehoft, *Textual Histories*, 110.

60 Bredehoft, *Textual Histories*, 110–11.

61 ASC CDEF 981–1016. Wulfstan's concerns about the causes and results of the Danish incursions were articulated most forcefully in his *Sermo Lupi ad Anglos*: Bethurum, *Homilies of Wulfstan*, 255–75. Æthelred's deposition and Ælfheah's martyrdom are discussed in chapters 3 and 6.

62 Compare the rather different interpretations proposed by Kries, "Mutilation of Alfred," 48; Bredehoft, *Textual Histories*, 111. The importance of ethnic designations during times of political crisis is examined by Geary, "Ethnic Identity as a Situational Construct," 24–6.

Cnut was remembered as having promoted peaceful coexistence between Danish and English populations, the Chronicle implicitly identified Harold as a successor to heathen Viking raiders.[63]

Certainly, this was not the interpretation Harold had in mind when he sent his underlings to dispose of the ætheling. The king seems to have construed his actions against Alfred as a necessary exercise of justice against an individual who had intended to subvert royal power – thereby provoking the ætheling's survivors and supporters to refute this view. Accordingly, the Chronicle stressed the severity of the physical torments endured by Alfred and his men and implicitly linked Harold's actions with Viking atrocities and the persecution of Christian martyrs; the *Encomium* aimed to clear Emma's family of any wrongdoing and turn popular opinion against Harold by detailing the outrageous treatment of a royal innocent. By the time these two texts were committed to writing in the early 1040s, the claim that Alfred and his companions were groundlessly persecuted must have been credible. If the ætheling's grave attracted reverence and his blinding remained a source of scandal in the years following 1036, it appears that the mutilation did lasting damage to Harold's reputation and may even have generated sympathy for the disenfranchised Emma. Such a shift in public sentiment could help explain why the English magnates were so eager to acclaim Harthacnut in 1040, despite his neglect of the kingdom after his father's death. Yet the elimination of Alfred served Harold well in the short term and initially strengthened his political position: in 1037, Emma was driven into exile and Harold was finally acclaimed full king over the English.[64] It was not until later that his mistreatment of Alfred came back to haunt him. Luckily for Harold, he was already dead by the time it did.

---

63 A few decades later, the *Vita Ædwardi* explicitly associated Harold's accession with Danish power in a way that the ASC did not: "At the instigation of the Danes, who had a faction and power in the kingdom at that time, one of Cnut's sons, Harold – who, they say, was not born of his blood – succeeded to the kingdom, an arrogant man (it is said) and not of good character" [Agentibus Danis qui tunc temporis in regno potentes et factiosi habebantur, quidam filiorum eius Haroldus, obliquo ut aiunt sanguine ei natus, successisset in regnum, homo ut fertur insolens et non bonarum artium]; *Vita Ædwardi*, 20.

64 Above, chapter 3.

The Exhumation of Harold Harefoot: 1040

In 1039, Harthacnut reunited with Emma in Flanders, where the two began organizing an invasion of England. Harold died before the plan was implemented, however, and the English magnates invited Harthacnut to be their king. He arrived with his mother around midsummer in 1040, and his succession proceeded quickly. Nevertheless, a new kingdom was apparently not satisfaction enough for the wrongs Harold had committed against Emma's family. Soon after his accession, Harthacnut had his half-brother's corpse removed from its Westminster grave and thrown in a swamp. According to later sources, he commanded that the body be beheaded and dumped in the Thames, where it was recovered by a fisherman and reburied in London's Danish cemetery.

The exhumation and desecration of the king's body were unprecedented in pre-Conquest England. Like Alfred's mutilation, Harold's removal from his grave inverted normative practice and indicated that he was unworthy of royal honours. However, while Alfred's mutilated body elicited sympathy and allowed him to be re-identified as a martyr, exhumation did not have a similar effect on Harold's posthumous reputation. His resurfacing corpse seems to have inspired shock and disgust rather than spontaneous reverence. The fact that the cadaver had been in the ground for months must have contributed to this reaction. In Anglo-Saxon political discourse, royal bodies were extraordinary bodies: they were anointed agents of Christ, representations of the undying body politic, and physical manifestations of dynastic lines.[65] Although individual kings were unquestionably mortal, the office of kingship exalted the royal body and set it apart from those of other Christians. Yet when Harold's body was exhumed, in the middle of summer after spending four months in the grave, it would have contrasted sharply with the idealized image of a king. His remains were probably in an advanced state of decay, and the sight and smell of rotting flesh would have confirmed beyond doubt that this body was ordinary, mortal, and corrupt. The public memory of Harold's royal funeral, during which his remains were borne to their monastic resting place and buried amid ecclesiastical ritual, would now be replaced with the image of a stinking, disintegrating corpse.

The earliest record of Harold's exhumation appears in Manuscript C of the Anglo-Saxon Chronicle, in an entry that detailed the succession of 1040 and critiqued the first year of Harthacnut's reign:

---

65 For example, see: VIII Æthelred 2.1; Nelson, "Carolingian Royal Funerals," 136; Nelson, "Inauguration Rituals"; and compare Kantorowicz, *King's Two Bodies*, 42–8.

> In this year King Harold died. Then men sent to Bruges for Harthacnut – they thought that they did well – and then he came here with sixty ships before midsummer and established such a heavy tax that men came to it uneasily: that tax was eight marks for every oar [of Harthacnut's fleet], and all those who supported him before were then disloyal to him, and he never did anything kingly as long as he reigned. He ordered the dead Harold to be dragged up and to be thrown into a fen.[66]

It is significant that the exhumation merited an explicit mention in this terse annal. Although the report was phrased dispassionately, a condemnation is evident in its placement at the end of the Chronicler's list of grievances against the king; Harthacnut's treatment of Harold's remains contributed to the author's low opinion of him. A century later, fuller descriptions and interpretations of the event began to appear. According to John of Worcester:

> As soon as Harthacnut began to rule, not unmindful of the injuries which his predecessor King Harold, who was thought to be his brother, had perpetrated against either him or his mother, he sent Archbishop Ælfric of York, Earl Godwine, Stor the master of his household, Eadric his steward, Thrond his executioner, and other men of great rank to London, and he ordered them to dig up Harold's body and throw it into a marsh. When it had been thrown there, he commanded it to be pulled out and thrown into the River Thames. However, a short time later, it was retrieved by a certain fisherman and carried in haste to the Danes, and was honourably buried by them in the cemetery they had in London.[67]

---

66 "Her swealt Harald cing. Þa sende man æfter Harðacnute to Bricge – wende þæt man wel dyde – 7 he com ða hider mid .lx. scipum foran to middan sumera 7 astealde þa swiðe strang gyld þæt man hit uneaðe acom; þæt wæs .viii. marc æt hamelan. 7 him wæs þa unhold eall þæt his ær gyrnde, 7 he ne gefremede ec naht cynelices þa hwile ðe he ricxode. He let dragan up þæne deadan Harald 7 hine on fen sceotan"; ASC CD 1040. ASC AF 1040 and ASC E 1039 (*recte* 1040) mentioned Harthacnut's accession but not the exhumation. The entry in ASC C was composed ca 1045: O'Brien O'Keeffe, *MS C*, xxvi–xxxviii.

67 "Mox ut regnare cepit, iniuriarum quas uel sibi uel sue genitrici suus antecessor fecerat rex Haroldus, qui frater suus putabatur, non immemor, Alfricum Eboracensem archiepiscopum, Goduuinum comitem, Styr maiorem domus, Edricum dispensatorem, Thrond suum carnificem et alios magne dignitatis uiros Lundoniam misit, et ipsius Haroldi corpus effodere et in gronnam proicere iussit. Quod cum proiectum fuisset, id extrahere et in flumen Tamense mandauit proicere. Breui autem post tempore, a quodam captum est piscatore, et ad Danos allatum sub festinatione, in cimiterio, quod habuerunt Lundonie, sepultum est ab ipsis cum honore"; JW 530–1.

William of Malmesbury provided the following variation:

> Harthacnut, immature in other respects, ordered through the agency of Bishop Ælfric of York and others, whom I would rather not name, that Harold's corpse be exhumed and beheaded, and his head (a pitiable spectacle to men) thrown into the Thames. The head was pulled up by a fisherman in his net and buried in the Danish cemetery in London.[68]

John and William based their work closely on earlier accounts, but unlike the Anglo-Saxon Chronicler, they both situated the exhumation before Harthacnut's imposition of excessive taxes; John explicitly stated that the event took place as soon as the new king had secured his power (*mox ut regnare cepit*).[69] Both twelfth-century authors also described the exhumation as a high-profile event, enacted and witnessed by leading secular and ecclesiastical magnates. This detail was absent from the Anglo-Saxon Chronicle, but all three sources portrayed the episode as evidence of Harthacnut's poor rulership.

The differences between John's and William's accounts suggest that more than one version of the episode was circulating when they were writing; it seems that the story still commanded interest a century after the fact. Contemporary attitudes are more elusive. The author of the Anglo-Saxon Chronicle account was clearly not impressed with Harthacnut's decision to dig up his brother's corpse, notwithstanding the unflattering portrait of Harold in the preceding annals. John's and William's assertions that Harold's corpse (or head) was retrieved and reburied after the desecration implies that some segment of the population must have been willing to defy Harthacnut by restoring Harold's body to a consecrated grave. Discomfort with the exhumation is also implicit in the silence of the *Encomium*. Emma commissioned the text in 1041 or 1042, after Harthacnut became king, and the conspicuous absence of any mention of the event suggests that the deed was nothing for a mother to boast about.[70]

---

68 "Veruntamen immaturus in ceteris, per Elfricum Eboracensem episcopum et alios quos nominare piget Haroldi cadauere defosso caput truncari et miserando mortalibus exemplo in Tamensem proici iussit. Id a quodam piscatore exceptum sagena in cimiterio Danorum Lundoniae tumulatur"; William of Malmesbury, *GR* ii.188.4. For William's slightly different account in the *GP*, see below, n. 85.

69 John is quoted above, n. 67. For these authors' possible attempts to reconcile multiple accounts, see Freeman, *Norman Conquest* I, 788–90.

70 This silence is also characteristic of later sources sympathetic to Harthacnut, for example Henry of Huntingdon, *Historia Anglorum*, vi.20.

In light of the implicit disapproval of Harthacnut's actions, it is remarkable that so many high-ranking individuals reportedly participated in the event. In addition to the members of the royal household and various unnamed London dignitaries cited by John and William, the operation was evidently spearheaded by Ælfric, Archbishop of York, a figure whose ecclesiastical status would have bestowed credibility upon the exhumation. Also prominent was Earl Godwine, one of the most influential laymen in the kingdom. It is possible that the individuals who carried out the exhumation felt they had little choice but to comply with their new king's wishes; the distaste with which later commentators related the incident suggests that there was not much honour to be gained by unearthing Harold's corpse, no matter how prestigious a company did the digging. Still, the number of magnates involved suggests that disinterring the dead king seemed like a valid – even respectable – course of action at the time. Could Harthacnut and his supporters have anticipated that there would have been a negative response? If so, why did they follow through with their plan? If not, why did later commentators find this episode so problematic? The answer seems to be that this was a piece of spectacular propaganda which failed to persuade its audience. I propose that the exhumation was intended to reinforce the allegation that Harold was a usurper and a false king by denying him the signifying trappings of a royal death – a message consistent with contemporary attitudes towards royal bodies and Christian burial. Much as Harold had attempted to delegitimize Alfred's royal claims by subjecting him to criminal punishments, Harthacnut sought to re-identify his half-brother as a false king through a signifying display of his corpse.

This message would have been conveyed in part by the state of Harold's body when it was first brought to light. In itself, the exposure of a rotting corpse would not have been particularly shocking for eleventh-century witnesses. Relic translations, public executions, and high-status funerals regularly brought the living into contact with corpses in varying degrees of decay; moreover, care for the dead was generally undertaken by family members in Anglo-Saxon England, so encounters with human remains would have been familiar to most.[71] A king's body, however, was not typically seen in an advanced stage of decomposition, for the corpse would ideally have been buried by the time disintegration began in earnest. The occasional exceptions to this rule confirm the importance of physical

71 Hadley and Buckberry, "Caring for the Dead," 147.

integrity at royal funerals. The remains of the Carolingian king Charles the Bald, for instance, disintegrated so quickly that his custodians were overwhelmed by the smell, burying the stinking corpse en route instead of completing the journey to the royal necropolis at Saint-Denis.[72] Two centuries later, the funeral of William the Conqueror at Caen was completely disrupted by the stench of the king's body, which forced all but the most steadfast clergymen to evacuate the church.[73] These two Continental examples, described disparagingly by contemporary chroniclers, demonstrate how thoroughly a royal funeral could be undermined by inconveniently rotting flesh. The remains of Harold Harefoot may have elicited similar disgust among witnesses to his exhumation. His body had been in the ground long enough to have begun disintegrating, but it would not yet have been reduced to bone and dust.[74] In its partially decomposed state, brought into the open air in the middle of summer, the sight and smell of decay would have been unavoidable.

The spectacle of Harold's partially rotted corpse was compounded by another humiliation: his expulsion from consecrated ground. Intramural burial at Westminster distinguished Harold from the ranks of ordinary Christian dead and secured the attention of the monastic community entrusted with praying for his soul.[75] His exhumation deprived him of these extraordinary spiritual benefits. Yet Harthacnut did not simply deny his half-brother a royal tomb; he denied him Christian burial altogether by removing his body from hallowed ground. From at least the tenth century, consecrated burial was expected for individuals in good standing with the Church and was perceived as a step towards salvation.[76] By this reasoning,

72 Charles the Bald's funeral procession in 877 was described in the *Annals of St-Bertin*, translated and discussed by Nelson, "Carolingian Royal Funerals," 163–5; see also Buc, *Dangers of Ritual*, 85–7.

73 William the Conqueror's funeral in 1087 was related by Orderic Vitalis, *Ecclesiastical History* IV, 102–7; it is discussed by Koziol, "Problem of Sacrality," 137.

74 For the rate of bodily decay, see Iserson, "Rigor Mortis," 723.

75 For Harold's interest in a Westminster tomb, see Mason, *Westminster and Its People*, 11–12.

76 Gittos, "Anglo-Saxon Rites," 195–201; Zadora-Rio, "Making of Churchyards," 11–13; Rosenwein, *Negotiating Space*, 178–81; Hadley and Buckberry, "Caring for the Dead," 122–3 and 126–7; Morris, *Church in British Archaeology*, 64–5; Bullough, "Burial, Community and Belief," 183–4; Effros, "Monuments and Memory"; Effros, "Beyond Cemetery Walls," 5–6 and 20–1; Hadley, "Burial Practices in the Northern Danelaw"; Biddle, "Cult of Saints"; Freke and Thacker, "Southworth Hall Farm, Winwick"; Thompson, *Dying and Death*, 173; Marafioti, "Punishing Bodies"; and see also II Edgar 1–2 and VIII Æthelred 5.

burials outside of consecrated bounds were regarded as exceptional or deviant.[77] The deposition of Harold's remains in a swamp or river signalled that Harold was unworthy of a hallowed grave. Rather, he was equated with excommunicants and criminals, the only members of Christian society systematically denied consecrated burial.[78] By relegating Harold's remains to unconsecrated ground or water, Harthacnut indicated that his predecessor deserved the same fate. This was not an immature or vengeful act of aggression against a corpse, as twelfth-century chroniclers indicated, but a political commentary on the previous regime, achieved through a signifying inversion of normative Christian and royal burial practices.

The characterization of Harold as a criminal and excommunicant extended beyond the exhumation of his body, however. It also found voice in the *Encomium*, which offered a condemnation of Harold's reign as part of its propagandistic defence of Harthacnut and Emma, even without any mention of the exhumation. Writing shortly after Harold's body was removed from Westminster, the Encomiast levelled three major accusations against the dead king. The first was that he had come to the throne illegally, disregarding Cnut's declaration that Harthacnut should succeed him and allowing himself to be elected by traitorous Englishmen; moreover, he was not really Cnut's son but a low-born impostor.[79] The *Encomium* explicitly labelled Harold a tyrant (*tyrannus*) and a usurper (*inuasor*), and throughout the work, the unlawfulness of his accession was recognized by those who righteously remained loyal to Cnut.[80] Chief among these was Æthelnoth, Archbishop of Canterbury, who refused Harold's request to be consecrated and prohibited all other clergymen from anointing him.[81] This exchange provided the context for the Encomiast's second accusation against Harold: that he was a terrible Christian. When the archbishop refused to submit to pleas and threats, Harold rescinded his request for an episcopal blessing and "fled from the whole Christian religion."[82] If the

77 Reynolds, *Deviant Burial Customs*; Reynolds, "Definition and Ideology"; Reynolds, "Burials, Boundaries, and Charters"; Hadley and Buckberry, "Caring for the Dead," 127 and 130; Gittos, "Anglo-Saxon Rites," 202–4; Zadora-Rio, "Making of Churchyards," 12–13. For examples of delineated boundaries, see: Adams, "Addingham, West Yorkshire," 171; Stroud and Kemp, *St. Andrew, Fishergate*, 134; Boddington, *Raunds Furnells*, 11 and 14.

78 Above, nn. 2 and 41.

79 *Encomium*, 32–3 and 38–41.

80 Ibid., 42 and 48.

81 Ibid., 40–1; and above, chapter 3.

82 "Uniuersam fugeret Christianitatis religionem"; *Encomium*, 40–1.

archbishop's refusal to consecrate him was not enough to prove Harold's unworthiness, his apostasy demonstrated that he was unfit to rule a Christian nation. This point was confirmed by Harold's third major offence, the mutilation and execution of the ætheling Alfred, which the Encomiast portrayed as a martyrdom and an offence against God.

Though not necessarily fabricated, the *Encomium*'s accusations against Harold should be approached cautiously, given their propagandistic context. Taken at face value, however, they would have justified the posthumous characterization of Harold as a criminal, a usurping tyrant, and a man who rejected the Church – in short, a violator of secular and ecclesiastical law. Would such a person deserve to remain in an ordinary hallowed grave, much less a royal tomb in a prestigious monastery? If proven true, Harold's alleged offences against Harthacnut's family would have been enough to condemn him for treachery or even theft, either of which would have precluded his burial in consecrated ground. In this context, it is significant that John of Worcester stated that the king's executioner was present and William of Malmesbury asserted that the exhumed body was decapitated.[83] The twelfth-century chroniclers evidently recognized a judicial punishment being retroactively inflicted upon the corpse.

These authors also noted the involvement of Archbishop Ælfric of York, implying that the exhumation of a royal body had been deemed an acceptable course of action by one of England's leading prelates.[84] Ælfric headed the list of dignitaries provided by John of Worcester, and he was the only participant explicitly named in William of Malmesbury's *Gesta Regum*; by the time William composed the *Gesta Pontificum* just a few years later, he gave the archbishop credit for initiating the whole affair.[85] Whatever the exact nature of Ælfric's involvement, he apparently played some role in the proceedings. As archbishop, it was his prerogative to approve the exclusion of criminals from hallowed graves and issue excommunications. He would also have been acquainted with canons which mandated the removal of non-Christian corpses from consecrated churches: one decree required that the corpses of *infideles* should be ejected if they were discovered inside a consecrated church, while another stated bluntly that "dead gentiles should be thrown out of the places of the

83 Postmortem decapitation is discussed by Reynolds, *Deviant Burial Customs*, 77–8.

84 For Ælfric's career, see Cooper, *Anglo-Saxon Archbishops of York*, 14–18.

85 William of Malmesbury, *GP* iii.115.11.

saints."[86] Although these canons were composed in response to conversion-era questions about the purity of churches among a newly Christianized people, it is certainly possible that the pagan *infideles* of the early penitentials were reimagined in the eleventh century as the impious or excommunicated.[87]

Still, Ælfric's presence would have contributed more than a theological perspective on the spiritual implications of Harold's exhumation. Witnesses may have been reminded of royal or shire courts, where bishops worked alongside secular magnates to judge cases and issue sentences against offenders.[88] Ælfric's participation in the king's exhumation would also have evoked the most important ritualized interaction between archbishop and king: royal consecration. Despite the *Encomium*'s insistence that Archbishop Æthelnoth of Canterbury refused to anoint Harold when he came to power in 1035, Harold was probably consecrated in 1037, when the Anglo-Saxon Chronicle stated that he became full king.[89] To an observer, the exhumation may have represented not only the inversion of a royal funeral but the very reversal of Harold's royal anointing. Thirty-five years later, when Pope Gregory VII excommunicated Henry IV, the anointed king of Germany, he absolved Henry's supporters of their oath of loyalty to their ruler, threatening that they too would be excommunicated if they persisted in their fidelity to him.[90] It may be that Harthacnut's

86 "Gentiles mortui de locis sanctorum ejiciendi sunt." These canons were included in the seventh-century penitential attributed to Archbishop Theodore of Canterbury (r. 668–690); the earliest extant manuscripts date from the tenth century. The quotation cited above was an early addition to the text. Elsewhere, the text instructed that "it is not permitted to sanctify the altar in a church in which the bodies of dead infidels are buried" [in æcclesia in qua mortuorum cadavera infidelium sepeliuntur, sanctificare altare non licet] and added that if a pagan corpse should be discovered in a consecrated church, "it is better if the church is cleaned and the corpse thrown outside" [si vero paganus sit, mundari et jactari foras melius est]. Quotations from Haddan and Stubbs, *Councils and Ecclesiastical Documents*, 211 and 190–1. For the texts and their contexts, see: Frantzen, *Literature of Penance*, 62–9; Bullough, "Burial, Community and Belief," 189–90; Morris, *Church in British Archaeology*, 50; McNeill and Gamer, *Handbooks of Penance*, 199 and 216.

87 It is also possible that clauses concerning *infideles* or *gentiles* assumed a new significance with the influx of Scandinavian populations in England during the tenth and eleventh centuries.

88 For such collaboration, see: Giandrea, *Episcopal Culture*, 36–41 and 169–72; and III Edgar 5 and II Cnut 18.

89 Keynes, "Introduction to the Reprint," lxiiin2.

90 Vodola, *Excommunication in the Middle Ages*, 20–3.

supporters hoped to convey a similar message with their exhumation of Harold. If the dead king were effectively redefined as a criminal and excommunicant, those who continued to profess loyalty to him – or, significantly, to his heirs and partisans – could themselves be excluded from law-abiding, Christian society.[91]

Although there is no explicit mention in contemporary sources of a disputed succession in 1040, some of Harold's supporters may have preferred to install one of his living kinsmen or a Scandinavian candidate as king of England.[92] Others were in the awkward position of having abandoned their allegiance to Harthacnut during his prolonged absence in the 1030s. Pre-eminent among these was Earl Godwine, who had remained loyal to Emma immediately following Cnut's death but had allied with Harold by 1037, when he played a role in Alfred's mutilation. Given his betrayal of Emma and his involvement in the ætheling's blinding, Godwine made a particular effort to reconcile with his new king, giving him a magnificent ship and swearing publicly that "it had not been by his advice or at his wish that Harthacnut's brother was blinded, but that his lord King Harold had ordered him to do what he did."[93] Harold's exhumation, in this context, seems to have been another opportunity for Godwine to demonstrate his renewed fidelity to Harthacnut, for he was prominently named as the first layman in John of Worcester's list of participants in the event.[94] Together with other unnamed English dignitaries, Godwine evidently renounced his loyalty to his previous lord, not by simply forswearing his allegiance to him but by openly violating his grave and body.[95]

---

91 For contagious excommunication, see: Vodola, *Excommunication in the Middle Ages*, 8 and 20–4; Little, *Benedictine Maledictions*, 31; Treharne, "Unique Old English Formula," 195–7.

92 Keynes, "Introduction to the Reprint," lxix–lxx; Stevenson, "Alleged Son of Harold Harefoot."

93 "Non sui consilii nec sue uoluntatis fuisse quod frater eius cecatus fuisset, sed dominum suum regem Haroldum illum facere quod fecit iussisse"; JW 530–3. See also William of Malmesbury's account of Godwine's compensation and oath, *GR* ii.188.5–6. The political context is discussed by: Keynes and Love, "Earl Godwine's Ship"; Barrow, "Demonstrative Behaviour," 137.

94 John of Worcester maintained that Godwine gave his gift and oath to Harthacnut after the exhumation had taken place; he also noted that Archbishop Ælfric was instrumental in implicating Godwine in Alfred's death: JW 530–1; Cooper, *Anglo-Saxon Archbishops of York*, 15.

95 Compare the Anglo-Saxon nobility's repudiation of the West Saxon dynasty upon Cnut's accession in 1017: JW 294–5; and above, chapter 3.

Harold's removal from Westminster was not the act of a single power-hungry individual, as the Anglo-Saxon Chronicle intimated. The complex political, legal, and theological considerations that informed the event indicate that Harthacnut and his magnates fully understood the implications of the exhumation: the operation was motivated by ideological objectives that would have been readily understood by contemporaries. Though later dismissed as an immature and futile act of revenge against a dead enemy, the exhumation and desecration of Harold's corpse was not unprecedented, especially in the Norse world. Loose analogues can be found in Icelandic literature. Some sagas described corpses being exhumed and held hostage by enemies.[96] A closer parallel to Harold's exhumation may be found in examples of Vikings desecrating Christian graves. One instance of such behaviour in the British Isles occurred around the turn of the tenth century on the Isle of Man, where some sixteen Christian graves were obliterated in order to make room for a rich Norse ship burial.[97] While the reuse of desirable grave sites by future generations was by no means unusual at this time, in this instance, the existing graves were still fresh, and it appears that the appropriation of the site was part of a power struggle between an existing Christian community and a new Scandinavian population.[98] Comparable acts of desecration are attested in Norway and Denmark, where there is evidence of rich burials being vandalized soon after they were created: in these cases, grave goods were left behind but the tombs' inhabitants were exhumed and their remains scattered.[99] Such actions have been interpreted as a precaution against haunting, but I am more inclined to see this type of desecration as evidence of political competition, in which high-status tombs were understood to proclaim the authority of the deceased and his supporters.[100]

---

96 Miller, *Bloodtaking and Peacemaking*, 353n25.

97 The site is discussed by Bersu, *Three Viking Graves*, 1–44; Tarlow, "Violation and Desecration."

98 Bersu, *Three Viking Graves*, 13, but compare the critique of this interpretation at xiii–xiv.

99 Tarlow, "Violation and Desecration," 137–8; Christiansen, *Norsemen in the Viking Age*, 286.

100 The political significance of monumental burials is discussed by Carver, "Early Medieval Monumentality," 1–10; Williams, *Death and Memory*, 174. Haunting is proposed by Christiansen, *Norsemen in the Viking Age*, 286; and see for example Kunz, *Laxdæla saga*, 419; Pálsson and Edwards, *Eyrbyggja saga*, 95. There are no accounts of Harold Harefoot haunting Westminster, but compare William of Malmesbury's report that King Alfred's ghost was tormenting Winchester's clergy: above, chapter 1.

Harold's exhumation fits comfortably into this trend of political desecrations, and it may be that Harthacnut had witnessed similar activity during his years in Denmark. However, there was also precedent in England for disinterring corpses and relegating them to unconsecrated ground, and these actions could just as easily have provided a template for Harold's exhumation.[101] In either case, Harthacnut's political message proved ineffective in both the short and long term. The English magnates' dramatic renunciation of their loyalty to Harold was evidently not shared by the entire population, for his remains were soon retrieved and reinterred in a London churchyard.[102] The prompt, respectful reburial of Harold's body would have reaffirmed his status as a Christian, mitigated the insult of desecration, and allowed Harthacnut's detractors to contravene him. Perhaps the new grave attracted attention just as Alfred's tomb at Ely did; it is conceivable that the abuse of Harold's body inspired comparable sympathy and reverence.[103] At the very least, the retrieval and reburial of the corpse – whether motivated by loyalty to Harold, opposition to his successor, or disapproval of how the royal body was treated – would have proved that at least some of Harthacnut's subjects were willing to defy his wishes and continue to honour their dead ruler.

Such reactions to the exhumation may also reveal something about contemporary perceptions of kingship. The distaste evident in the early sources implies that Harold, however unpopular he had been during his lifetime, did not deserve posthumous humiliation. Physical desecration might have been an acceptable fate for offenders at other levels of society, but royalty should have been immune from such shameful treatment; any king merited an honourable royal grave. Harold himself appears to have adhered to this principle, as he allowed the ætheling Alfred to live at Ely after his blinding and be buried in an intramural monastic tomb. In fact, the *Encomium*'s claim that Harold's soldiers abandoned Alfred's corpse without burial is

---

101 For example, S 833 recorded a ruling by Æthelred II that a group of thieves' bodies did not have to be moved from consecrated to unconsecrated ground – implying that such movement would normally have taken place. See also III Æthelred 7.1, which provides conditions for removing a body from unconsecrated to consecrated ground. Another parallel in England is proposed below, chapter 6.

102 Ralph de Diceto, a twelfth-century canon of St Paul's, identified the cemetery as St Clemens, a Danish garrison church located just outside the city walls in an area of Scandinavian settlement: Stubbs, *Ralph de Diceto*, 186. On St Clemens, see: Brooke, "Central Middle Ages," 35–6; Blair, *Oxfordshire*, 170.

103 This is speculative in Harold's case, but compare Cubitt, "Murdered and Martyred Saints."

more reminiscent of Harthacnut's actions: it was Harthacnut – not Harold – who denied his rival a royal grave in consecrated ground. Nevertheless, Harthacnut evidently misjudged the political effect the exhumation would have. His subversion of normal royal burial practice did not make Harold any less of a king or obliterate the memory of his five-year reign. This may explain the Londoners' impulse to re-inter the corpse in an appropriate grave and the chroniclers' decision to record this restoration. The twelfth-century authors' apparent disgust with Harthacnut and their descriptions of the corpse's recovery suggest that such a blatant inversion of funerary custom could not simply be ignored or dismissed; it had to be addressed, condemned, and remedied. Although the exhumation was intended to cast aspersions on Harold's reign, it instead proved Harthacnut's inability to control his predecessor's posthumous legacy.

Harthacnut's attempt to re-identify his half-brother's corpse as a deviant body failed, according to all reports, and the exhumation may in fact have exacerbated dissatisfaction with the new king. Instead of providing evidence of Harold's impiety and criminality, the spectacular exposure of his decaying body was taken as evidence that Harthacnut was a poor leader who would not hesitate to violate graves of the Christian dead and wreak spectacular vengeance upon a defenceless corpse. For magnates like Godwine, whose political survival depended on their ability to stay in the king's good graces, the exhumation may have been a necessary evil; indeed, a blatant disregard for public disapproval could actually have improved their chances of convincing Harthacnut of their devotion. Those who were not directly invested in impressing the king, however, might have more openly expressed their outrage and disdain for such a flagrant inversion of royal burial practices. I would conclude that although the ideological implications of the 1040 exhumation were fully understood by Harthacnut's subjects, the abuse of the royal corpse was widely considered a dishonourable act – perhaps even by Harthacnut's partisans, if the silence of the *Encomium* may be taken as evidence. No matter how unpopular a king Harold had been or how badly he had wronged his successor, desecrating his body was an inappropriate course of action. In the end, Harthacnut's ideological message was lost: his exhumation of Harold was not remembered as a manifestation of divine will or an assertion of royal prerogative but as one of the various offences committed by a ruler who "never did anything kingly as long as he reigned."[104]

104 ASC C 1040; quotation above, n. 66.

Conclusions

Harold and Harthacnut were exceptional in their treatment of royal antagonists. Admittedly, violence against royal persons was not unusual during this period, especially at times of political crisis. The process of succession might be bloody, as it was for Edward the Elder in 899 and William of Normandy in 1066; it might inspire deadly political factionalism, as it did when half-brothers Æthelred II and Edward the Martyr competed for their father's throne in 975; or it might be characterized by suspicious deaths, as when Edmund of Wessex was stabbed to death in his own hall in 946, or when the ætheling Edward the Exile, next in line to Edward the Confessor's throne, died mysteriously within days of his arrival in London in 1057.[105] Yet none of these crises involved anything like the physical humiliation inflicted upon Alfred and Harold. Edward the Elder and William killed their royal rivals on the battlefield, publicly eliminating claimants to the throne by ostensibly legitimate military force. Edmund's stabbing was dismissed as an unforeseeable accident, and the death of Edward the Exile scarcely received any attention at all in extant texts; if these were assassinations, they were never explicitly recorded as premeditated political acts. Even Edward the Martyr's 978 regicide was accomplished secretly, and his body was hidden – not displayed or desecrated as the corpse of a conquered king.[106]

So why did Harold and Harthacnut do things so differently? One explanation might be their shared Danish background. The disfigurement of living enemies is attested in saga literature, the desecration of high-status burials is attested in Denmark and Norway, and the obliteration of Christian graves by Vikings was not unknown.[107] If mutilation and desecration were acceptable ways to defuse political or military threats in the Norse world, it is conceivable that these kings would have employed similar methods in their English realm. Certainly, ethnicity seems to have informed contemporary English commentary, for the Chronicle poet was acutely aware of Harold's Danish identity and used it to critique the king in his account of Alfred's mutilation. Yet there was no comparable ethnic reference point in the Chronicle annal which mentioned Harold's exhumation. This may be

105 All of these examples are discussed elsewhere in this book. For the suspicious deaths of tenth-century royalty, see: Stafford, *Emma and Edith*, 87; Keynes, "Crowland Psalter," 363–4.

106 Below, chapter 5.

107 Miller, *Bloodtaking and Peacemaking*, 196–7 and 352–3nn22–5; van Eickels, "Castration and Blinding," 594; and above, nn. 96–9.

explained by the structure and style of the two accounts: while the poetic lament on Alfred's death all but invited hyperbolic analysis, the laconic prose entry on Harold's exhumation employed straightforward rhetoric, offering clear but understated critiques of Harthacnut. In this context, a comment on the king's Danish ancestry would have been out of place. Moreover, Harold and Harthacnut's shared Scandinavian heritage made ethnicity a moot point in the 1040 annal. Whereas the earlier incident pitted the son of a Danish conqueror against an exiled West Saxon prince, the conflict between Harthacnut and Harold was not based on nationality: it was the legitimate and illegitimate sons of a single father fighting for the throne, not rival members of native and foreign dynasties. While the half-brothers' Scandinavian heritage did not prevent them from gaining legitimate royal authority, comparison with Vikings was a sort of rhetorical shorthand; it allowed the Chronicle poet to denounce Harold's abuses by associating him with a fraught ancestral past.

Still, Harold and Harthacnut's Danishness did not explain or justify their behaviour, for their father had treated the lives and bodies of his political enemies quite differently. When Cnut gained full control of England in 1017, he had little compunction about executing some of the kingdom's highest-ranking magnates. He refrained from taking similar action against the West Saxon æthelings, however, driving them into exile instead; and even as he required his new subjects to renounce their loyalty to the surviving members of the West Saxon dynasty, he allowed Edmund Ironside an honourable royal burial.[108] Neither Harold nor Harthacnut followed Cnut's example in their dealings with royal rivals. Where their father had mitigated tensions between English and Scandinavian populations through cautiously respectful interactions with royal remains, Harold and Harthacnut exacerbated political factionalism with their treatment of their rivals' bodies, firmly asserting their royal authority but ostracizing at least some of their subjects in the process.[109]

108 Cnut's relative lenience toward the West Saxon æthelings is discussed by Keynes, "Æthelings in Normandy," 174; but see: William of Malmesbury, *GR* ii.180.10; JW 402–5. For Cnut's execution and displacement of English magnates, see: ASC CDE 1017; Keynes, "Cnut's Earls," 79–80; Mack, "Cnut's Conquest," 378–80. Compare also Æthelred's own harsh treatment of his nobles in his later reign: Stafford, "Royal Policy and Action," 30–1. See also Gillingham, "1066 and the Introduction of Chivalry," 215–16.

109 For Cnut's assimilation into English legal and religious culture, see: Stafford, "Royal Promises"; Gerchow, "Prayers for Cnut"; and below, chapter 6.

Perhaps Cnut's sons lacked their father's political instincts, or perhaps they were simply not concerned that their actions might undermine their power. Harthacnut's initial support from the English magnates may have caused him to act recklessly from a political standpoint; if he believed that his royal authority was secure and unchallenged, he may have been more willing than Cnut to push the limits of acceptable practice. Nevertheless, there must have been objections to his exhumation of Harold. Even if his nobles and his archbishop egged him on, the community at Westminster surely resisted the exhumation, for a king's tomb would have brought prestige and financial support to a monastery which, in the 1040s, was still a modest foundation with limited means.[110] Although Harthacnut was not accused of encroaching on monastic property in the extant sources, the violation of consecrated space could have contributed to his poor reputation and may even have elicited negative comparisons with Cnut's reign: where Cnut patronized churches and gave them gifts of relics, Harthacnut destroyed monastic tombs and desecrated the bodies they contained.[111] Yet Cnut was an invading conqueror, while Harthacnut had been welcomed as a legitimate member of an established dynasty. His father's precarious political position had required him to emphasize even tenuous claims of continuity with the previous dynasty, but Harthacnut's pedigree was secure enough that he could risk denigrating a rival hereditary line through the humiliation of a corpse.[112] Aggravated monks may have seemed a small price to pay for the symbolic and sensory impact of such a display.

Harold, by contrast, struggled to establish his legitimacy and secure royal authority, exercising considerably more political savvy than Harthacnut during his reign. He successfully wrested his regency from Emma in 1035 and eventually won enough support to become full king; even his efforts to use Cnut's memory to his own advantage reveals an understanding of English succession politics. Harold probably considered his treatment of Alfred well within the scope of acceptable judicial practice, as the punishments inflicted upon the ætheling and his party were consistent with English legal prescriptions against treachery. However, Harold made two miscalculations. The first was the application of a standard corporal penalty to a prince who would not normally have been subjected to physical punishment. Given the frequency with which West Saxon æthelings were

110 Above, chapter 1.

111 Cnut's patronage of Westminster is discussed by Mason, *Westminster and Its People*, 10–12.

112 For the legitimacy of Cnut's dynasty in England, see Howard, "Harold II," 37.

exiled during Cnut's reign, there may well have been an implicit understanding that royal bodies ought to be immune from corporal sentences.[113] Harold's second mistake was to condemn so many of Alfred's men. Both the Chronicle and *Encomium* expressed outrage over the sheer number of lives and bodies destroyed, and while such casualties may have been acceptable on a battlefield, both sources implied that it was inappropriate to inflict such extensive punishments upon individuals captured in an ambush. Harold's treatment of Alfred and his men was inordinate, and it was the lack of royal restraint that inspired indignation, not the nature of the punishments themselves.[114]

Neither Harold nor Harthacnut was given a fair trial in the early sources. Chroniclers depicted Harold's mutilation of Alfred as an act of tyrannical cruelty against an innocent, and they attributed Harthacnut's exhumation of Harold to the king's poor leadership and his character flaws. Because of the political slant of the extant texts, we are provided in both cases with decontextualized condemnations that did not acknowledge the complex symbolic implications of these acts or the considerations that motivated them. A chronicler writing in support of Harold might have produced a damning account of Alfred's invasion and his righteous punishment at the hands of Cnut's eldest son; and an author less wary than the Encomiast might have described the desecration of Harold's corpse and deemed it too mild a punishment for such an impious and illegitimate ruler. Yet the *Encomium*'s silence concerning the exhumation suggests that its audience would not have been sympathetic to Harthacnut's abuse of his predecessor's remains: the author must have expected that he would damage his own case for Harthacnut's kingliness by mentioning that his hero had recently ordered his nobles to dig up a rotting corpse. Conversely, Harold must have been esteemed by a significant portion of the population, including those who helped him become king and those who restored his desecrated body to an honourable grave; textual condemnations of his reign provide only one side of the story. Although the scope and intentions of the extant sources severely limit our understanding of these episodes, it is clear that both Harold and Harthacnut – like their West Saxon predecessors – understood that royal bodies could be used as objects of political expression. They surely believed that they were advancing their political interests with their actions. However, they both pushed the limits

113 Above, n. 108.
114 For excessive royal violence, see Baraz, "Violence or Cruelty," 166.

of acceptable practice too far when they neglected to pay at least superficial respect to their predecessors' bodies. Harold and Harthacnut opened their reigns by advertising their discontinuity with deposed dynasties, and this apparent disrespect for the royal past – more than the acts of mutilation or desecration in themselves – confirmed their reputations as bad kings.

5 Body and Memory: The Missing Corpse of King Edward the Martyr

Some sixty years before the mutilation of the ætheling Alfred, the English endured another succession crisis accompanied by a scandalous royal death: the assassination of King Edward "the Martyr" by partisans of his younger half-brother, Æthelred. When their father Edgar died in 975, Edward was no more than eleven years old and Æthelred was about nine. Although Edward was Edgar's oldest son by his first wife, Æthelred was the child of Ælfthryth, his only wife to be consecrated queen – and therefore, according to his supporters, the more throne-worthy candidate.[1] Edward was elected and anointed in 975, but Æthelred's faction did not give up on their candidate.[2] On 18 March 978, as Edward was visiting his

1 Edgar was married two or three times: Edward was the product of his first marriage to Æthelflæd; his second union (possibly a marriage) with Wulfthryth produced a daughter, Edith, who became a nun at Wilton and was later revered as a saint; and his final marriage to Ælfthryth produced two sons, Edmund, who died in infancy in 971, and Æthelred. Ælfthryth had received a royal consecration while Æthelflæd had not, making the sons of Edgar's final marriage arguably more throne-worthy than those of his first. Later commentators postulated that Edgar had never actually married Æthelflæd, but this does not seem to have been cited as evidence for Edward's illegitimacy in the 970s. Keynes, *Diplomas*, 163–5; Stafford, *Emma and Edith*, 62–3; Stafford, "King's Wife in Wessex," 23–4; Nelson, "Inauguration Rituals," 300; Nelson, "Second English *Ordo*," 374; Dumville, "The Ætheling," 30–1; Ridyard, *Royal Saints*, 42–5; Yorke, "Women in Edgar's Life," 143–50. For Edward and Æthelred's ages at the time of Edgar's death, see Keynes, *Diplomas*, 164. For the polarized political situation in the years leading up to and following Edgar's death, see: Yorke, "Edward, King and Martyr," 102–7; Williams, "*Princeps Merciorum Gentis*," 160–70; Stafford, "Royal Policy and Action," 21–4; Stafford, *Unification and Conquest*, 57–9; Fisher, "Anti-Monastic Reaction," 261–70.

2 Edward's election is discussed above, chapter 2.

brother and stepmother at a royal residence, he was ambushed and killed by Æthelred's supporters. Nearly a year later, on 15 February 979, his body was retrieved and given an appropriate burial at Shaftesbury's nunnery. It would be another two decades before the remains would be recognized as saintly relics and translated into their own shrine. Meanwhile, shortly after his brother's death, the twelve-year-old Æthelred was elected king. He did not receive a royal consecration, however, until 14 May 979, three months after Edward's interment at Shaftesbury.[3]

The assassination of an anointed king was a shocking event, and by the end of the century, Edward's untimely death was widely recognized as a martyrdom. When set beside the reverential accounts of the ætheling Alfred's lethal mutilation, it would seem that veneration was a standard response to the unexpected, violent deaths of West Saxon royalty.[4] However, where the *Encomium Emmae* offered a prompt political narrative with only incidental references to Alfred's sanctity, nearly all the extant accounts of Edward's life and reign are hagiographical tributes composed a decade or more after his death. Accordingly, recent studies of Edward have focused extensively on his identity as a royal martyr and the political uses of his posthumous cult; discussions of his tenure as a living ruler have typically concentrated on the circumstances which led to his accession and eventual assassination.[5] These approaches have helped contextualize Edward's reign

3 The exact dating of these events is problematic, as the annal dates in the Anglo-Saxon Chronicle are confused. Simon Keynes dates the regicide to 978 and the translation and Æthelred's consecration to 979, based on the regnal years supplied in Æthelred's charters and the unlikelihood of a royal consecration taking place before a royal funeral; I follow his chronology throughout this chapter. David Dumville offers an alternative chronology, suggesting that the regicide and Æthelred's anointing occurred in 979 and the translation in 980, based on tenth- and eleventh-century claims that Edward reigned for three and a half years (i.e., from Edgar's death in 975 through 979). Keynes, *Diplomas*, 173–4 and 233n7; Keynes, "Shaftesbury Abbey," 48–9; Keynes, "Cult of King Edward," 117; Dumville, "Death of Edward the Martyr"; Dumville, "West Saxon Genealogical Regnal List," 27–8.

4 Rollason, "Murdered Royal Saints," 1–13.

5 For Edward's cult and its political uses, see: Ridyard, *Royal Saints*, 154–71; Rollason, "Murdered Royal Saints"; Rollason, *Saints and Relics*, 142–4; Fell, *Edward, King and Martyr*, xvii–xxv; Fell, "Anglo-Saxon Hagiographic Tradition"; Keynes, "Shaftesbury Abbey," 48–55; Dumville, "Death of Edward the Martyr"; Thacker, "Oswald and His Communities," 248–56; Cubitt, "Murdered and Martyred Saints," 67, 72–4, and 82–3. For discussions of Edward's accession, his assassination, and the political aftermath of the regicide, see: Keynes, *Diplomas*, 163–76; Stafford, "Royal Policy and Action," 21–4; Yorke, "Edward, King and Martyr"; Fisher, "Anti-Monastic Reaction"; Stenton, *Anglo-Saxon England*, 372–4.

and legacy, but they have also led scholars to distinguish firmly between the living king and the dead saint. This distinction is also evident in the tenth- and eleventh-century sources, which held that Edward's lot had improved with his transformation from earthly king to heavenly martyr.[6] Yet these two identities should not be regarded as mutually exclusive. Edward had not died defending Christianity, nor had he been considered saintly during his lifetime; it was his exceptional status as a king which allowed his murder to be understood as a martyrdom.[7] Nevertheless, Edward's new saintly identity seems not to have been immediately seized upon by contemporary observers, for it took at least a decade for his cult to gain recognition. In the aftermath of the regicide, he would have been regarded primarily as an earthly ruler.

Because Edward was a king, his reign ought to have ended with a public royal funeral. Yet by all accounts, there was no body to bury. His killers reportedly left the assassinated corpse in a makeshift grave, and the sequence of ceremonial events that would have normally followed the death of an anointed ruler never occurred. Instead of a ritualized funeral that would facilitate the transition between regimes, Edward's body was left unacknowledged near the site of his death for a full eleven months. Under these circumstances, it is impossible to know whether the corpse eventually interred at Shaftesbury was in fact the king's.[8] Regardless, a body identified as Edward's was retrieved and honourably interred despite the passage of time, indicating that a proper burial remained a matter of importance. The earliest hagiographical sources give the impression that Edward's subjects spent the year piously trying to locate the missing body, with descriptions of the assassination followed closely by accounts of the relics' recovery. It is more likely, however, that the long period between regicide and funeral exacerbated political tensions and prolonged the sense

6 This contrast is articulated most concisely in the ASC; see quotation below.

7 Rollason, "Murdered Royal Saints," 1–2; Ridyard, *Royal Saints*, 77; Nelson, "Royal Saints," 72.

8 It is possible that the recovered corpse was not actually Edward's. Bones found in a reliquary at Shaftesbury Abbey have been dated to the late tenth century, but they belonged to a man considerably older than the teenaged Edward and show evidence of post-mortem trauma; perhaps another body was substituted for Edward's at the time of the translation to Shaftesbury. For my present purposes, however, it is irrelevant whether the corpse in question was actually the king's, as long as contemporaries identified it as Edward's. For the body's identity and the bones recovered in the early twentieth century, see: Keynes, "Shaftesbury Abbey," 54–5; Yorke, "Edward, King and Martyr," 112.

of interregnum. Although later narratives would claim that the body was miraculously revealed, there must have been individuals – certainly the killers, possibly others – who knew where the corpse was hidden and could conceivably have helped recover it soon after the regicide.[9] The fact that it took nearly a year for the body to resurface suggests that there was disagreement about what should be done with Edward's corpse, for if there had been a consensus that the remains be moved, the translation could have been accomplished quickly. The eleven-month interval must have seen some debate over what to do with the body, with the case for honourable burial gaining traction over the course of the year.

The delayed funeral and consecration of Edward's successor would have had the additional effect of keeping the regicide fresh in the public consciousness. Without the ceremonial transfer of power from the dead king to his heir, the interregnum would continue indefinitely and the regicide would remain an unresolved scandal. This prolonged focus on the dead king was surely a key factor in the formation of his martyr's cult. Of the various Anglo-Saxon royals who had suffered violent or suspicious deaths in the preceding century, Edward was the only one to be regarded as saintly, and I suggest that the events of the year following his assassination caused him to be regarded as the victim of ideological persecution – a scenario which allowed his identification with Christian martyrs rather than with other casualties of mundane political struggles. Between March 978 and February 979, his death and body were left open to interpretation: those who concealed the corpse treated him as a false or disgraced king; those who sought to provide a royal funeral regarded him as a legitimate ruler; and there may have been some at this early date who already believed his remains to be saintly relics. Edward's body was integral to the construction of his posthumous identity, and his legacy – as king, saint, or something else entirely – was tied to the fate of his corpse.

This chapter argues that Edward's regicide sustained the factionalism that followed Edgar's death, with the king's absent body perpetuating political tension. Competing narratives emerged as Edward's subjects sought to make sense of the regicide, and the missing corpse became a signifying object in its own right. In the months between the regicide and translation to Shaftesbury, the question of how to remember Edward was up for debate; once his body was recovered and publicly entombed, his identity was securely established.

9 The earliest miraculous revelation appears in the *Passio Edwardi*; see below.

The Assassinated Body: Text and Law

Edward's death and its aftermath were treated in a handful of Latin and vernacular commentaries composed during Æthelred's reign. Among the earliest was the Anglo-Saxon Chronicle, which included a poetic account of the assassination composed before the end of the tenth century.[10] The entry for 978 reads in full:

> Here King Edward was slain in the evening at Corfesgeate on 18 March, and he was buried at Wareham without any kingly honour.
>
> There was no worse deed than this done among the English
> since they first sought the land of Britain.
> Men murdered him, but God glorified him.
> He was in life an earthly king;
> he is now after death a heavenly saint.
> His earthly kin did not wish to avenge him,
> but his heavenly father has avenged him greatly.
> Those earthly killers wanted to blot out his memory on earth,
> but the heavenly avenger has widely spread his memory in the heavens
> and on earth.
> Those who did not want to bow to his living body before,
> they now humbly bow on their knees to his dead bones.
> Now we can perceive that the wisdom of men
> and their intrigues and their counsels
> are nothing against God's intention.
>
> And here Æthelred acceded to the kingdom, and very soon after that, with great joy among the counselors of the English, he was consecrated king at Kingston.[11]

---

10 For the dating of this entry, see Keynes, *Diplomas*, 167; for its place in the ASC, see Bredehoft, *Textual Histories*, 79 and 106. The medieval accounts of Edward's death and translation are surveyed in: Ridyard, *Royal Saints*, 44–50; Keynes, *Diplomas*, 165–9; Fell, *Edward, King and Martyr*, xvi–xxi; Yorke, "Edward, King and Martyr," 99–102; Cubitt, "Murdered and Martyred Saints," 72–4; Rollason, "Murdered Royal Saints," 2.

11 "Her wæs Eadweard cyning ofslægen on æfentide æt Corfesgeate on .xv. kalendas Aprilis, 7 hine mon þa gebyrigde on Werhamme, butan ælcum cynelicum wurðscipe. Ne wearð Angelcynne nan wyrse dæd gedon, / þonne þeos wæs, syþþon hi ærest Britenland gesohton. / Menn hine ofmyrþredon, ac God hine mærsode. / He wæs on life eorðlic cyning; / he is nu æfter deaðe heofonlic sanct. / Hyne noldon his eorðlican magas wrecan, / ac hine hafað his heofonlic fæder swyðe gewrecen. / Þa eorþlican banan

The next year, the Chronicle reported, Ealdorman Ælfhere of Mercia "fetched the holy king's body from Wareham and bore it to Shaftesbury with much honour."[12]

Edward's assassination was next treated by Byrhtferth of Ramsey in his *Vita Oswaldi*, composed between 997 and 1002.[13] After detailing the succession crisis that followed Edgar's death and the severity of Edward's rule, Byrhtferth described how the king was ambushed during a visit to his brother and stepmother. When Edward arrived at the royal residence, the "zealous thegns of his brother" surrounded him as the Jews surrounded Christ; they assaulted and killed the king before he had even dismounted his horse.[14] Afterwards, the body was dishonourably buried:

> The martyr of God was lifted up by the thegns and brought to the house of a certain lowly person, where no Gregorian chant and no funeral lament was heard; rather, this illustrious king of the whole nation lay covered with a mean covering, waiting for the light of day.[15]

Although this treatment was unbefitting of a king, Byrhtferth asserted, God had not abandoned Edward as though he were "shameful and villainous"; rather, "he permitted him to be buried, not so worthily at that time as he

---

woldon his gemynd on eorðan adilgian, / ac se uplica wrecend hafað his gemynd on heofonum 7 on eorþan tobræd. / Þa ðe noldon ær to his libbendan lichaman onbugan, / þa nu eadmodlice on cneowum gebugað to his deada banum. / Nu we magan ongytan ðæt manna wisdom / 7 heora smeagunga 7 heore rædas / syndon nahtlice ongean Godes geðeaht. Her feng Æþelred to rice, 7 he wæs æfter þæm swyðe hrædlice mid micclum gefean Angelcynnes witan gehalgod to cyninge æt Cyngestun"; ASC DE 979 (*recte* 978), with all quotations in this chapter from D. This entry is not written as verse in either manuscript and may have been understood, as Thomas Bredehoft suggests, simply as "heightened prose." Nevertheless, I have followed Irvine's line breaks in her edition of ASC E. Bredehoft, *Textual Histories*, 86–8, quotation at 86; Irvine, *MS E*, 60 and n. 979.1; and compare the line breaks in Plummer, *Two Saxon Chronicles* I, 123. Shorter accounts of Edward's death and Æthelred's accession appear in ASC A 978, C 978–9, and F 979.

12 "Gefette þæs halgan cyninges lichaman æt Werhamme, 7 geferede hine mid micclum weorðscipe to Sceaftesbyrig"; ASC DE 980 (*recte* 979).

13 For Byrhtferth's authorship and the dating of the work, see: Lapidge, *Byrhtferth*, xxxvi–xxxviii and lxvii–lxviii; Lapidge, "Hermeneutic Style," 90–5. See also Whitelock, *EHD* I, 914–15 no. 236.

14 "Sui fratris zelantes … ministri"; Byrhtferth, *Vita Oswaldi*, 138–9.

15 "Sublatus est a ministris martir Dei, et ad domum cuiusdam impotentis perductus est, quo non Gregorianus concentus nec epichidion auditus est; sed tam inclitus rex totius patrie iacuit uili tegmine coopertus, exspectans lucem diei"; Byrhtferth, *Vita Oswaldi*, 140–1.

deigned to permit him to be later."[16] This later reburial was undertaken by Ealdorman Ælfhere, who unearthed the body, discovered it to be incorrupt, and translated it with full Christian honours.[17] Byrhtferth concluded his account by acknowledging the killers' lack of earthly punishment and their assumption that they had gotten away with their crime. Nevertheless, they would soon be punished by God, and indeed, one of the killers had already been struck blind in retribution for the regicide.[18]

This extensive hagiographical tribute is for the most part compatible with the Chronicle's account. However, Byrhtferth's claim that Edward's body was incorrupt was not corroborated by the Chronicle, and it was directly contradicted by a third early reference to the assassination: a brief mention by Archbishop Wulfstan of York in his 1014 *Sermo Lupi ad Anglos*.[19] In his catalogue of sins perpetrated by the English, which incurred God's wrath in the form of Viking raiders, Wulfstan stated:

> And there is also very great lord-betrayal in the world, so that a man betrays his lord's life or drives him living from the land, and both have happened in this country: Edward was betrayed and afterwards killed and after that completely burned.[20]

Writing more than three decades after the event, Wulfstan alluded only casually to Edward's death, presumably expecting that his audience would understand the context and implications of his statement without further elaboration. Although his reference to the burned corpse was unique, Wulfstan assumed it to be common knowledge that the king's body had been desecrated.[21] It is remarkable, however, that he did not refer to Edward

16 "Probosum et facinorosum"; "permisit eum sepelire, non tam digniter tunc sicut postea fieri concedere dignatus est"; Byrhtferth, *Vita Oswaldi*, 140–1.

17 Ibid., 140–3.

18 Ibid., 142–3.

19 Alan Thacker regards Byrhtferth's reference to incorruptibility as a reflection of local interest in incorrupt saints: "Oswald and His Communities," 250–1. Compare also Fell, *Edward, King and Martyr*, 9 and 13.

20 "And ful micel hlafordswice eac bið on worlde þæt man his hlaford of life forræde oððe of lande lifiende drife, 7 ægðer is geworden on ðisum earde: Eadweard man forrædde 7 siððan acwealde 7 æfter þam forbærnde"; Bethurum, *Homilies of Wulfstan*, 263. The passage goes on to cite Æthelred's exile in 1013 as a further example of treachery.

21 Dorothy Whitelock understands Wulfstan's comment to be representative of "general opinion," while ascribing Byrhtferth's claim of incorruptibility to hagiographic convention: Whitelock, *Sermo Lupi*, 56–7n78; and see also Cubitt, "Murdered and Martyred Saints," 82–3.

as a saint, even though he was already revered as a martyr at the time. Rather, it was Edward's role as a betrayed and assassinated king which gave this passage its rhetorical weight.

A final early description of the assassination appears in the anonymous Latin *Passio Sancti Eadwardi Regis et Martyris*. In its extant form, the *Passio* has been attributed to the hagiographer Goscelin, who likely composed the text between 1070 and 1080.[22] However, its opening section, which Goscelin claimed to have derived from an earlier written source, concluded with Edward's translation into a Shaftesbury shrine in 1001; the first recorded miracle occurred some fifty years later, implying that the *miracula* portion was produced at a considerably later date.[23] Despite some later interpolations, the *Passio*'s account of Edward's martyrdom was probably adapted from a text commissioned by the community at Shaftesbury in honour of the 1001 translation and should be tentatively included among the early sources for the assassination.[24] The *Passio*'s most striking feature is that it named Ælfthryth, Æthelred's mother, as the chief conspirator. According to this account, Edward was accidentally separated from his retinue while on the way to visit his younger brother. When he arrived alone at the royal residence, his stepmother had a drink brought to him, and as the king lifted the cup to his lips, the cupbearer, acting on the queen's orders, stabbed him to death with a knife. Fearing that this deed would be discovered, Ælfthryth commanded that the body

> be thrown into the house of a certain person which was nearby, so that what she had done should not be revealed. Obeying her order, her most impious ministers hastened there, dragged away the aforesaid holy body by the feet like a beast, and – as she had ordered – covered the body, which had been thrown into that rather contemptible house, with vile straw.[25]

Afterwards, to prevent the corpse from being discovered, the queen had it buried "in hidden and marshy places," but it was miraculously revealed to

---

22 The earliest extant manuscripts date from the twelfth century: Fell, *Edward, King and Martyr*, xx.

23 Ibid., xix.

24 Ibid., xix–xx.

25 "In domicilum quoddam quod iuxta erat proici, ne palam fieret quod fecerat. Cuius imperio ministri parentes nefandissimi ilico accurrunt, praedictum sacrum corpus more beluino per pedes abstrahunt, et in domicilium contemptibiliter ut iusserat proiectum uilibus stramentis cooperiunt"; ibid., 6.

the local people who retrieved it, brought it to Wareham, and buried it to the east of their church.[26] Ealdorman Ælfhere, distressed by the inappropriately humble burial Edward received at Wareham, translated the body to Shaftesbury soon after.[27]

All four of these early sources emphasized the mistreatment of Edward's body, with the lack of a royal funeral portrayed as a scandal in its own right. Yet it is significant that the three narrative accounts clearly indicate that the corpse was buried. In the Chronicle, Edward was denied kingly honours but was nevertheless interred at Wareham; in Byrhtferth's account, the corpse received no funeral rites but "lay covered with a mean covering"; and in the *Passio*, the queen's men dragged and dumped the body but took care to bury it afterwards.[28] Wulfstan's assertion that the body was completely burned (*forbærnde*) does not preclude the possibility that it was also buried, given the brevity of his reference to the regicide, but the claim is consistent with the other sources in that Edward's identity would have been obscured by the killers' action. Unlike Harold Harefoot's remains, which were publicly exposed to the elements, or the ætheling Alfred's dying body, which (according to the *Encomium*) was left unburied until it was recovered by the local monks, Edward's corpse was not made into a spectacle or left in the open to rot.[29] It is not impossible that this initial interment was intended as a show of respect for the dead ruler, so that his remains would not be reduced to carrion. However, it is more likely that the prompt burial of the assassinated body was intended to conceal evidence of the regicide. A king's disappearance could not have gone unnoticed for long, but a speedy burial in an unlikely location – perhaps compounded with posthumous disfigurement, as implied in Wulfstan's account – would have delayed the confirmation of Edward's death and thus protected the perpetrators from blame.

---

26 "In locis abditis et palustribus"; ibid., 7.

27 Another early source is a Latin poem commemorating Edward's translation from Wareham to Shaftesbury; it appears in a Canterbury manuscript of ca 1000 and may have been composed shortly after the recovery of Edward's body. The poet maintained that Edward was slain by his own people (*propria ... gente*) out of envy (*invidia*) but gave no specific details about the mode of his death or the treatment of his corpse before it was exhumed from the grave (*tumulo*) at Wareham and reinterred at Shaftesbury by Ealdorman Ælfhere. Because the poem provides few details on Edward's death or the fate of his body before its translation, it will not be treated at length here. The text is edited and translated by Dumville, "Death of Edward the Martyr," 280–1.

28 "Vili tegmine coopertus"; Byrhtferth, *Vita Oswaldi*, 140–1.

29 Above, chapter 4.

This strategy seems to have worked, for there is no indication that the killers were formally brought to justice. The Chronicle stated bluntly that Edward's family "did not wish to avenge him," and Byrhtferth expressed indignation that the assassins believed they had escaped unscathed, since they did not suffer "the punishments which mortals inflict on mortals."[30] Instead, Byrhtferth reported, God had struck one of the assassins blind and was reserving even greater punishments for the killers in the afterlife; the Chronicle simply noted that the regicides had already been afflicted by God's vengeance.[31] Wulfstan went a step further, indicating that the entire nation continued to suffer for the sin of regicide decades later.[32] Yet these authors' assurances of divine retribution draw attention to the lack of earthly consequences for the killing. Byrhtferth seems particularly hard pressed to justify why the killers were not punished sooner, concluding that God had allowed them time to repent – but that they wasted the opportunity by sinning further.[33] Wulfstan likewise implied that the assassins' supreme act of treachery had not been reconciled with God, while the Chronicler accused Edward's kin of negligence for refusing to exact blood vengeance. Even the typically hagiographical humiliation Ælfthryth suffers in the *Passio* – her horse miraculously refuses to carry her to Edward's translation, throwing her underfoot for her sins – reinforces that there was no justice for the assassins other than the supernatural.[34]

The lack of earthly retribution in these instances accentuates the expectation that the killers ought to have been subject to secular justice for such a serious offence. Wulfstan cited the regicide as an example of lord-betrayal (*hlafordswice*), which had been designated a *bot*-less, or unforgivable, offence by the late ninth century; the killers' treason against Edward could conceivably have been punished by death.[35] The Chronicle labelled the regicide *morð*, an unnatural or undeclared killing, another *bot*-less offence

30 "Hyne noldon his eorðlican magas wrecan"; ASC DE 979 (*recte* 978). "Penas quas mortales mortalibus ingerunt"; Byrhtferth, *Vita Oswaldi*, 142–3.
31 Byrhtferth, *Vita Oswaldi*, 142; and above, n. 11, for ASC.
32 Bethurum, *Homilies of Wulfstan*, 263; and quotation above, n. 20.
33 Byrhtferth, *Vita Oswaldi*, 142–3; Marafioti, "*Consolation of Philosophy*."
34 Fell, *Edward King and Martyr*, 10.
35 For instance: Alfred 4; II Æthelstan 4; III Edgar 7.3; II Cnut 57 and 64. Wulfstan's use of *hlafordswice* is quoted above, n. 20.

which merited death or outlawry.[36] Given that the law prescribed such severe responses for *hlafordswice* or *morð* against ordinary individuals, the consequences ought to have been proportionally greater for those who committed such offences against a king. With Edward's body missing, however, there would have been no material evidence for treason or *morð* after his disappearance. Although the most stringent measures of proof were needed to escape a death sentence for these crimes, the absence of a corpse may have stymied any attempt to bring the suspected assassins to justice.[37]

It is also possible that there was little genuine effort to find, try, and sentence the killers. As Edward's brother and successor, Æthelred would have been responsible for initiating action against the assassins: as a kinsman, he ought to have taken vengeance; as a king, he ought to have overseen the legal prosecution of the regicide.[38] Despite the emphasis Byrhtferth and the *Passio* placed upon the royal brothers' love for each other, Æthelred must have found himself in an awkward political position after Edward's death. He was only twelve years old when he came to the throne, and the supporters who had secured his accession were the likely perpetrators of the regicide.[39] The killers' political influence may also explain why they were not explicitly identified in the extant sources. The Anglo-Saxon Chronicle and Byrhtferth implied that Edward's killers were known, but neither source actually named them; and while the *Passio* stated that Edward's stepmother Ælfthryth was the author of the regicide, this claim has been regarded more as hagiographical convention than historical

36 ASC DE used the verb *ofmyrþredon*, a compound which incorporates the term *morð*. *Morð* is declared a *bot*-less offence in VI Æthelred 7; II Cnut 4–5 and 64; and the anonymous code *Be Blaserum*. See also: Wormald, *Making of English Law*, 363 and 367–8; O'Brien, "From *Morðor* to *Murdrum*," 335–7 and 343–7; Hyams, *Rancor and Reconciliation*, 106.

37 Mary Richards has argued that in Anglo-Saxon England, wounded bodies were exposed and examined in order to determine the appropriate compensation; it is not impossible that a similar procedure would be undertaken with victims of homicide, an attested practice in later Iceland. Richards, "Body as Text," 103–4; Dennis et al., *Grágás*, 146; and compare O'Brien, "From *Morðor* to *Murdrum*."

38 Compare II Cnut 56: "If a person is killed and it becomes an open killing, let the killer be given to the dead person's kin" [Gif open morð weorðe ðæt man amyrred sy, agyue man magum].

39 For Æthelred's conflicts of interest after Edward's death, see: Keynes, *Diplomas*, 173–5; Ridyard, *Royal Saints*, 166–7; Yorke, "Edward, King and Martyr," 108.

witness.[40] If the assassins continued to hold positions of power in the opening decades of Æthelred's reign, it may not have been expedient for contemporary chroniclers to accuse them outright. Nevertheless, the consistent claim that Edward was killed at Ælfthryth's estate could implicate her at least indirectly in the assassination.[41] Another suspect is Ealdorman Ælfhere of Mercia, the kingdom's most powerful magnate during the 970s.[42] As a close ally of Ælfthryth and a vocal supporter of Æthelred's candidacy in 975, he could certainly be characterized as one of Æthelred's "zealous thanes," and like the queen, Ælfhere would have had much to gain if his young protégé ascended to the kingdom.[43]

It is also possible, of course, that neither Ælfthryth nor Ælfhere instigated the regicide and that the perpetrators went unnamed in the extant texts.[44] Still, if the killers were high-ranking individuals, as seems probable, blood vengeance and judicial punishment may not have been practical possibilities for the young King Æthelred, even if the identities of the regicides were known. The Anglo-Saxon Chronicle and Byrhtferth agreed that the assassins had not suffered earthly penalties for their crime, and there is no indication that the suspected killers were brought to the ordeal, as the law required for accusations of *morð*.[45] The deepest consequences for regicide were evidently not put into effect, but perhaps Æthelred waived the most severe punishments in favour of comparatively mild sentences.[46] Monetary settlement may have been one solution. In the late tenth century, Alfred's laws took for granted that a king's wergild was common knowledge; a

40 On Ælfthryth, see: Fell, "Anglo-Saxon Hagiographic Tradition," 10–11; Keynes, *Diplomas*, 171–3; Yorke, "Edward, King and Martyr," 100–1; Yorke, "Women in Edgar's Life," 153–4; Ridyard, *Royal Saints*, 162–3; Cubitt, "Murdered and Martyred Saints," 74.

41 It may be significant that Edward's remains were not elevated from their Shaftesbury grave into the reliquary until after Ælfthryth's death in 1000 or 1001: Yorke, "Edward, King and Martyr," 112.

42 For Ælfhere's family and career, see: Williams, "*Princeps Merciorum Gentis*," with reference to Edward's death at 170; Fisher, "Anti-Monastic Reaction," 261–70; Yorke, "Edward, King and Martyr," 106–7; Keynes, *Diplomas*, 169 and 172–3.

43 "Zelantes ... ministri"; Byrhtferth, *Vita Oswaldi*, 138–9. Ælfhere's guilt is suggested by Thacker, "Oswald and His Communities," 246–9; Rollason, "Murdered Royal Saints," 18–19; Rollason, *Saints and Relics*, 143. For an opposing view, see Keynes, *Diplomas*, 172–3.

44 Keynes, *Diplomas*, 173.

45 Compare II Æthelstan 4; II Cnut 57; *Be Blaserum*.

46 For royal mercy: Hurnard, *King's Pardon for Homicide*, 1–5; Barrow, "Demonstrative Behaviour," 137.

hundred years later, Archbishop Wulfstan compiled a list of royal wergild values, suggesting that these sums were relevant around the turn of the millennium – maybe because such payments had recently been made, or maybe because they should have been but were not.[47] Although the cost of a king's life was enormous, according to the values provided in these documents, it is conceivable that Æthelred accepted some sort of payment from supporters whom he was unable or unwilling to bring to more violent justice.[48] Alternatively, Ealdorman Ælfhere's 979 removal of Edward's remains from Wareham to Shaftesbury may have served as atonement for the killing, for by the twelfth century, the translation was remembered as penitential compensation for his role in the assassination.[49] Given the ealdorman's early opposition to Edward's ascension and his vigorous support of Æthelred, his ceremonial, public, and undoubtedly expensive relocation of the corpse to a royal monastery may have constituted a recognizable act of contrition for his part in the regicide, allowing him, as so many Old English laws required, to compensate for his actions both "before God and before the world."[50]

If such a settlement was reached with Æthelred, it is conceivable that the killers were able to retain their wealth and position once compensation was rendered.[51] It is not impossible that the assassins expected this course

47 The king's wergild was referenced in Alfred 4.1. Royal wergild values were included in archaic Northumbrian and Mercian codes, which were recodified by Wulfstan: Bethurum, "Six Anonymous Codes," 457–9; Wormald, *Making of English Law*, 391–4; Whitelock, *EHD* I, 468–70 no. 51. The texts are edited by Liebermann as *Norðleoda Laga* and *Mircna Laga*.

48 *Norðleoda Laga* stipulated that a wergild of 15,000 *thrymsas* (a unit equal to three pennies) be paid to the kin and an additional 15,000 *thrymsas* of *cynebot* be paid to the kingdom; *Mircna Laga* required a wergild and a *cynebot* of 30,000 *sceattas* each. For Ælfhere's ability to pay these sums, see Williams, "*Princeps Merciorum Gentis*," 155–7.

49 William of Malmesbury, *GR* ii.162.4.

50 "For gode 7 for worulde"; see for instance: III Edgar 1.2; II Cnut 11.1 and 38.1. For earlier examples in which the endorsement of a royal cult functioned as penance for regicide, see: Rollason, "Murdered Royal Saints," 13–14 and 18–19; Rollason, *Saints and Relics*, 92–3; Scargill, "Oswiu and the Murder of King Oswine," 39–46; Yorke, "Edward, King and Martyr," 108; Williams, "*Princeps Merciorum Gentis*," 170. The Canterbury poem describing Edward's translation notes the presence of many nobles and clergy, indicating the importance of this event: Dumville, "Death of Edward the Martyr," 280–1; and above, n. 27.

51 Compare Earl Godwine's lavish attempts to reconcile with Edward the Confessor: Barrow, "Demonstrative Behaviour," 137; Keynes and Love, "Earl Godwine's Ship"; and above, chapter 4. For restrictions on the king's ability to act against his nobles, see Stafford, "Royal Policy and Action."

of events from the outset, which might explain why they had no apparent qualms about killing a lawfully elected and consecrated king. For Æthelred, however, his brother's missing body could have provided an excuse for his leniency toward the killers: without a corpse as evidence, the mild punishments might be attributed to insufficient proof of wrongdoing rather than the young king's inability to control or reprimand his nobles. For the Chronicler and Byrhtferth, then, the problem may not have been that no penalties had been exacted but that the relatively minor consequences were disproportionate to the magnitude of the offence. The destruction and concealment of an anointed royal body had not been appropriately punished, and this fact was interpreted by early commentators as a miscarriage of earthly justice. If the missing corpse indeed provided the perpetrators a legal loophole, it also made the absence of royal retribution all the more scandalous.

The Obliterated Body: Anonymous Burial as Political Ideology

Whatever legal considerations may have motivated the concealment of Edward's remains, the early chroniclers favoured an ideological rather than practical explanation for the missing corpse. The Anglo-Saxon Chronicle claimed that the king's killers "wanted to destroy his memory on earth," presenting the assassination as a sort of *damnatio memoriae*.[52] This possibility was made explicit in the *Passio*:

> The queen quickly ordered her men to secretly bear the body away into hidden and marshy places, where it would not seem to be buried in the earth, so that it could not be found by anyone else. With these orders having been fulfilled without delay, she issued an edict by which no one might speak any harsh thing or mourn for his killing, evidently believing that she had entirely erased his memory from the earth.[53]

Both accounts went on to clarify that these attempts at obliteration failed. The Chronicle couplet concluded with the assertion that "the heavenly

52 "Woldon his gemynd on eorðan adilgian"; ASC DE 979 (*recte* 978).

53 "Imperat itaque celeriter satellitibus clanculo illud efferri, et in locis abditis et palustribus ubi minus putaretur humo tegi, ne ab aliquo amplius inueniri potuisset. Quibus iussa sine mora complentibus, edictum quo nil inclementius proposuit, ne quis de interitu eius gemeret aut omnino loqueretur, se nimirum memoriam eius de terra omnino delere existimans"; Fell, *Edward, King and Martyr*, 7.

avenger has widely spread his memory in the heavens and on earth," while the *Passio* detailed the miraculous discovery and translation of Edward's body.[54] Nevertheless, the fact that the destruction of the king's memory (*memoria* or *gemynd*) featured so prominently in both sources suggests that obliteration was recognized as a particularly insidious component of the regicide. Without a corpse, Edward's survivors could not provide a public funeral; the king's reign would have had no ceremonial closure and his body no fitting memorial.[55] The Chronicle's observation that he was initially buried at Wareham "without any kingly honour" indicates that the lack of royal ceremony was a serious omission.[56] Yet in addition to the political consequences, there are implications that Edward had not received a Christian burial at all. The *Passio*'s "hidden and marshy places" were far removed from the hallowed ground in which Christians aspired to be buried, and Wulfstan's assertion that Edward's body was burned was incompatible with tenth-century funeral rites.[57] Byrhtferth remarked that the body was disposed of without appropriate ceremony, but he also emphasized that Edward was not a "shameful and villainous" individual, presumably to distinguish him from criminals and excommunicants who were deservedly denied consecrated graves – and to dispel any notion that such a description might apply to the king.[58] Whatever the killers had actually done with the body, attempted obliteration and denial of Christian burial soon became part of the tradition surrounding Edward's death.[59]

The authors of these accounts accentuated the killers' disrespect for a royal body and memory through biblical allusion. The Chronicle's statement that Edward's killers "wished to destroy his memory on earth" (*woldon his gemynd on eorðan adilgian*) closely echoes Psalm 33:17: "the face of the Lord is above evildoers so that he wipes their memory from the

54 "Se uplica wrecend hafað his gemynd on heofonum 7 on eorþan tobræd"; ASC DE 979 (*recte* 978).

55 Compare above, chapters 1 and 2.

56 "Butan ælcum cynelicum wurðscipe"; ASC DE 979 (*recte* 978).

57 "Locis abditis et palustribus"; Fell, *Edward, King and Martyr*, 7.

58 "Probosum et facinorosum"; Byrhtferth, *Vita Oswaldi*, 140–1. This is further clarified in Byrhtferth's description of Edward's reburial at Shaftesbury, where he was buried honourably amid rituals "for the redemption of his soul" [pro eiusdem anime redemptione]; 142–3. The association of royal bodies with criminal and excommunicated bodies is discussed above, chapter 4.

59 Compare for example William of Malmesbury, who explicitly stated that Edward's killers deprived him of consecrated burial: *GR* ii.162.2.

earth" (*adylige of eorðan hyra gemynd*).[60] The verbal parallels suggest that the assassins wrongfully appropriated divine prerogative by trying to suppress Edward's memory. Obliteration also featured in contemporary hagiography. Ælfric of Eynsham related that the bodies of St Vincent and St Sebastian were hidden so that their memories could not be perpetuated, while St Margaret's Old English *passio* claimed that her judge wanted to kill her and blot out her memory from the earth (*gemynd of eorðan adiligian*).[61] In this context, accounts of Edward's obliteration would have helped frame his death as a martyrdom and his recovered body as a miraculously revealed relic. Given that the king had not died like a typical martyr in defence of the Christian faith, this recognizable hagiographical motif could reinforce claims of his sanctity. In addition, the rhetoric of obliteration equated the assassins with early persecutors of Christians. The echoes of biblical and hagiographical obliteration imply that the killers had violated more than just earthly law when they slew their king and hid the body.

Nevertheless, the fact that obliteration was depicted as a genuine threat to an English king suggests that there was more at work than simply hagiographical convention. Rather, it appears that the audiences of these texts understood a lack of proper burial and the destruction of memory as horrific punishments in their own right. For a tenth-century Christian, the pious cultivation of remembrance was beneficial to the soul, and such remembrance often focused on the grave: the arrangement and adornment of the body provided a final, deliberate image of the deceased before the remains were covered over, while above-ground markers advertised the

60 The Vulgate of Psalm 33:17 reads: "Facies Domini super facientes mala ut perdat de terra memoriam eorum"; a parallel sentiment appears in Job 18:17. The Old English rendering appears in MS A of the *Capitula* of Theodulf: "Drihtenes ondwlita bið ofer þa yfeldondan men to þon þæt he hig forspille 7 adylige of eorðan hyra gemynd." Similar phrasing is used in MS B of the *Capitula* and the Paris Psalter: Sauer, *Theodulfi Capitula in England*, 347; O'Neill, *First Fifty Psalms*, 138. The phrase could also have evoked diplomatic sanction clauses which mentioned the destruction of memory: compare S 142, S 470, S 537, S 743, S 1259, S 1326, S 1370; see also Little, *Benedictine Maledictions*, 68–9.

61 Ælfric's examples are LS I 5.456–60 and LS II 37.255–8; the Latin source for St Sebastian is edited in Bollandus, *Acta Sanctorum* Ian. II, 278. For St Margaret, see Clayton and Magennis, *Margaret*, 118, with the Latin source at 200. Compare also the anonymous Old English legend of the Seven Sleepers, in which pagan persecutors strive to obliterate the memory of Christianity from the earth (*ælcne myne ofer eorðan adylgian*): Magennis, *Seven Sleepers*, 33.

identity and status of the grave's inhabitant.[62] A physical witness to its occupant's time on earth, the grave allowed the dead to escape oblivion. More importantly, religious memorialization could improve a Christian's fate in the afterlife. Burial in consecrated ground was considered a preliminary step towards salvation; interment on church or monastic property would secure the intercessory prayers of the ecclesiastical community and inclusion in their *liber vitae*; and provisions in wills for memorial masses and alms to be administered on the anniversary of one's death – literally, the memory-day (*gemynddæg*) – guaranteed that the soul would receive perpetual attention.[63] Thus, by contemporary standards, Edward was at a spiritual disadvantage. He was killed suddenly, before he had made provisions for his soul, and he was denied a grave that might serve as a focus for prayer and rememberance.

The consequences of such obliteration would have been all the more pronounced because of Edward's royal status. Kings were among the most remembered individuals in the Anglo-Saxon period, with their memories actively cultivated during and after their lifetimes. Their accomplishments were recorded in written (and no doubt unwritten) histories, their deaths were commemorated in chronicles and poetry, their tombs were contained safely and prominently inside churches, and their legacies were evoked by later generations of rulers. If the cultivation of memory was recognized as a defining aspect of royal identity, posthumous oblivion would have represented the antithesis of royal dignity.[64] If kings were not to be forgotten,

62 For the composition and impact of the grave, see: Williams, *Death and Memory*, 1–78; Williams, "Death Warmed Up," 263–7; Halsall, "Burial, Ritual, and Merovingian Society," 327–9; Härke, "Cemeteries as Places of Power," 12–13; Thompson, *Dying and Death*, 117–18. For stone memorials, see: Rodwell and Rodwell, "St Peter's Church, Barton-Upon-Humber," 300; Phillips, *Excavations at York Minster* I.1, 84; Gilmour and Stocker, *St Mark's Church*, 16 and 55–6; Biddle, "Fourth Interim Report," 325; Boddington, *Raunds Furnells*, 11–13; Jones, "Excavations at Lincoln," 98; Kjølbye-Biddle, "Disposal of the Winchester Dead," 227; Okasha, "Memorial Stones," 91–5. For wooden grave markers, see: Rodwell and Rodwell, "St Peter's Church, Barton Upon-Humber," 292 and 300; Gilmour and Stocker, *St Mark's Church*, 20–1; Hadley and Buckberry, "Caring for the Dead," 140–1.

63 For consecrated ground, see: Gittos, "Anglo-Saxon Rites"; Hadley and Buckberry, "Caring for the Dead," 126–7. On *libri vitae*, see: Little, *Benedictine Maledictions*, 195–6; Keynes, "*Liber Vitae*"; McKitterick, *History and Memory*, 174–85; Okasha, "Memorial Stones," 97–100. Death anniversaries are mentioned in S 385, S 1188, S 1289, S 1297, S 1510, S 1511, S 1513, S 1533. The term *gemynddæg* is also attested in the Old English Bede and in Alfred 43, where it refers to saints' feast days.

64 Flower, *Art of Forgetting*, 6–9.

how could a forgotten man have been king? By this logic, if Edward's remains were denied a royal funeral and consigned to an anonymous grave, his royal status, in hindsight, would have been suspect. Like the disgraced and unburied bodies of Harold Harefoot and the ætheling Alfred, some sixty years later, Edward's maltreated corpse conveyed an ideological message: this man was not a true king.

However, where Harold Harefoot's corpse was made into a spectacle and Alfred's body was publicly mutilated, Edward was killed in secret and his remains concealed. Unlike Harold and Alfred's damaged bodies, which were displayed in deliberate contrast to contemporary understandings of what a king should look like, Edward's corpse was removed entirely from the public gaze. Instead of attempting to recast Edward as an illegitimate king through a shaming exhibition of his remains, the killers minimized the importance of his reign altogether. Without a signifying display, no posthumous identity – of a king, a criminal, or even a Christian – would be inscribed on his body. Although it is improbable that there was an official prohibition against mourning Edward's death, as claimed in the *Passio*, the absence of a funeral and tomb would have impacted the king's legacy.[65] Royal graves served as repositories of dynastic memory, and for someone like Edward – a teenaged king who ruled for just three years – a tomb might have been the most lasting monument to his reign. Were it not for the exceptional nature of Edward's death, a *damnatio memoriae* would hardly have been necessary; he would have likely been remembered only as a minor figure in the history of the West Saxon dynasty.[66]

Accordingly, it was the indignity of the regicide and its aftermath – not the king's own accomplishments – that kept Edward so prominent in the public memory despite the lack of formal commemoration. Particularly scandalous was the fact that the king was assassinated despite having been elected and anointed, a process which should have guaranteed his safety.[67] Edward was consecrated just two years after Edgar's imperial-style coronation at Bath, and the quick sequence of these ceremonial events should have reinforced the idea of a divinely sanctioned, inviolate kingship.[68]

65 Compare Flower, *Art of Forgetting*, 1–13. The *Passio* is quoted above, n. 53.

66 Compare the deletion of individuals from royal genealogies, or the cursory treatment in the ASC of kings with similarly short reigns: Dumville, "Kingship, Genealogies and Regnal Lists," 81–3; Stafford, *Unification and Conquest*, 80–1.

67 This point was surely not lost on the twelve-year-old Æthelred: Ridyard, *Royal Saints*, 167; Rollason, "Murdered Royal Saints," 16–17.

68 For Edgar's imperial coronation, see Nelson, "Inauguration Rituals," 296–301.

According to tenth-century political thought, there should have been no further challenges to Edward's authority after he was anointed. Nonetheless, he was killed by individuals who ought to have sworn him allegiance at his accession. It would be nearly a century before another consecrated king of England would be slain by a challenger for the throne, and after William's army defeated and killed Harold Godwineson in 1066, the new Norman regime struggled to find a way to justify the violent deposition of an anointed ruler. Their eventual solution was to depict Harold as a tyrant and usurper, whose overthrow was an exercise of pious justice by a rightful king.[69] Edward's political opponents seem to have taken a similar approach, for even sources sympathetic to the king recount controversy concerning his royal credentials. His birth was one point of contention. Some commentators claimed that he was born out of wedlock, while others observed that his mother had never been consecrated queen.[70] In either case, the implication was that Æthelred, Edgar's youngest son by his only consecrated queen, was more throne-worthy than his elder half-brother. Another issue was the lack of consensus at Edward's accession. The 975 coronation had been orchestrated by Archbishop Dunstan and his allies, who reportedly disregarded the objections of Æthelred's partisans and held an election with only some of the *witan* present.[71] The Anglo-Saxon Chronicle's assertion that the killers "did not want to bow to his living body" could indicate that some English magnates refused to acknowledge Edward's status as king, despite his coronation.[72] Concerns about his birth and his election featured in the accounts composed after Edward's death; questions about the legitimacy of his succession persisted through the duration of his short reign.

A more enigmatic critique was offered by Byrhtferth, who contrasted Edward's style of ruling with Æthelred's. In the midst of his hagiographical tribute, Byrhtferth reported that Edward "struck not only fear but even terror into everyone; he hounded them not only with words but even with cruel beatings – and especially those who were members of his own

69 Garnett, *Conquered England*, 33–40.

70 For a review of these accounts, see: Keynes, *Diplomas*, 163–5; Nelson, "Inauguration Rituals," 300; Stafford, *Emma and Edith*, 62–3.

71 Above, chapter 2.

72 "Noldon … to his libbendan lichaman onbugan"; ASC DE 979 (*recte* 978). See also Byrhtferth, *Vita Oswaldi*, 136–9.

household."[73] Given Byrhtferth's otherwise unequivocal praise of Edward and clear condemnation of the regicide, this anomalous characterization may reflect contemporary perceptions of the young king's reign. Indeed, Byrhtferth's broader point that it was wrong to kill an anointed king under any circumstances could indicate that this principle was somehow in doubt in Edward's case. Read in this light, the Chronicle's assertion that there was "great joy among the English *witan*" when Æthelred became king may constitute an implicit critique of his brother's rule shortly after his death.[74] Whether or not Edward was generally understood to have abused his power, it is possible that Æthelred's supporters attempted to portray his predecessor as a tyrannical ruler who had come to the throne illicitly. If this were the case, the denial of a traditional royal funeral could have been perceived in some circles as confirmation of his illegitimacy.[75]

In spite of this characterization, however, Edward's remains were translated to a respectable grave at Shaftesbury within the year. There seems to have been an intermediate relocation of the body: the *Passio* reported that the men of Wareham found the corpse after a miraculous revelation and buried it outside their church; it was translated afterward to Shaftesbury, lest "such a precious pearl be hidden in such a vile place."[76] The early sources indicate that there was considerable interest at various levels of society in recovering Edward's body from its original burial place. The Chronicle credited Ealdorman Ælfhere with the translation, Byrhtferth had Ælfhere retrieve the remains with a "multitude of people," and the *Passio* mentioned both the ealdorman and the mourning population of Wareham.[77] Even if claims concerning Edward's tyranny and illegitimacy

---

73 "Non solum timorem sed etiam terrorem incussit cunctis; qui persecutus est eos non uerbis tantum, uerum etiam diris uerberibus, et maxime suos secum mansitantes"; Byrhtferth, *Vita Oswaldi*, 136–9. See Yorke, "Edward, King and Martyr," 102, for a discussion of this passage. The *Passio*, by contrast, portrays Edward as a good ruler during his lifetime: Ridyard, *Royal Saints*, 95.

74 "Micclum gefean Angelcynnes witan"; ASC DE 979 (*recte* 978). Byrhtferth also mentioned that "there was great joy at his consecration" [ad cuius consecrationem magna letitia erat]; Byrhtferth, *Vita Oswaldi*, 154–5.

75 Compare Garnett, *Conquered England*, 33–40.

76 "Tam pretiosam margaritam in tam uili loco obfuscari"; Fell, *Edward King and Martyr*, 8. Compare also: ASC DE 979 (*recte* 978); Byrhtferth, *Vita Oswaldi*, 140–3; Keynes, "Shaftesbury Abbey," 49; and compare below, n. 81.

77 "Multitudine populi"; Byrhtferth, *Vita Oswaldi*, 140–1. See also Fell, *Edward, King and Martyr*, 7–8. The Canterbury poem on Edward's translation likewise notes the presence of Ealdorman Ælfhere along with numerous nobles and priests: Dumville, "Death of Edward the Martyr," 280–1; and above, n. 27.

had been credible, the mistreatment of the royal body seems to have gone too far toward subverting the social order, inspiring enough indignation that the killers' intentions for the corpse – both practical and ideological – were thwarted. Whether Ælfhere acted on his own initiative, was encouraged or coerced by Æthelred, or sought to capitalize on popular sentiment, the translation of the body to Shaftesbury's consecrated cemetery brought Edward back into the public eye and unambiguously restored his status as Christian royalty.

Nevertheless, Edward's interment at the nunnery at Shaftesbury was not a typical king's burial. It is revealing that the body was not brought to an established royal necropolis but to a female community without an established mausoleum.[78] Although the monastery had been founded by Alfred the Great and maintained close connections with the West Saxon house, it lacked the dynastic significance of Winchester, where generations of earlier kings were entombed, or Glastonbury, where Edward's father and grandfather were buried.[79] While convenience may have been a consideration in choosing Shaftesbury, as it was quite close to Wareham, it was surely not the definitive factor, as Winchester and Glastonbury were also reasonably nearby.[80] Even Wareham itself could have served the purpose, as its monastery already housed the grave of King Beorhtric of Wessex (r. 786–802).[81] In this context, it was probably the nuns of Shaftesbury who lobbied for possession of the body: royal tombs were coveted by monastic communities under the best of circumstances, and the scandal surrounding Edward's death would have ensured Shaftesbury

78 All other tenth-century kings were buried in male communities, making Edward's burial at a nunnery exceptional (although Æthelred's older brother, who died in infancy, was buried at the royal nunnery at Romsey): Yorke, *Nunneries*, 116 and 171; and above, chapter 2. Before it acquired Edward's remains, Shaftesbury's only royal corpse belonged to Ælfgifu, the wife of King Edmund of Wessex: Foot, *Veiled Women* II, 165–6 and 169; Rollason, *Saints and Relics*, 137–8; Ridyard, *Royal Saints*, 170.

79 Foot, *Veiled Women* II, 165–77; Yorke, *Nunneries*, especially 76–7 and 171–4.

80 Shaftesbury was about twenty miles from Wareham; Winchester and Glastonbury were each approximately thirty miles away.

81 ASC A 783, DE 784 (all *recte* 786); Foot, *Veiled Women* II, 201–2; Yorke, *Nunneries*, 74; Yorke, *Wessex in the Early Middle Ages*, 199. The rejection of Wareham could reflect a reluctance at this stage to legitimize Edward by association with another West Saxon king. However, Beorhtric was a problematic ruler for Alfred's branch of the dynasty; he was denounced by Asser and omitted from West Saxon genealogical lists: Keynes and Lapidge, *Alfred the Great*, 71–2; Dumville, "West Saxon Genealogical Regnal List," 14.

even greater attention.[82] Still, while the 979 translation was remembered as a high-profile event and Edward's new grave was considered prestigious, it appears that the choice of Shaftesbury was something of a compromise.[83] Even as the obliteration of his body was reversed, Edward was segregated from the legitimizing remains of earlier kings and relegated to a female community.

Although it is possible that rumours of sanctity had begun circulating by the time he was translated to Shaftesbury, Edward was not yet formally recognized by royal and ecclesiastical leaders as a martyr. In fact, there appears to have been some residual doubt about his legitimacy as king. Yet I argue that the inaccessibility of the body allowed the creation of competing legacies. Without the ritual closure provided by a royal funeral, Edward's reign was unresolved and his death remained open to interpretation. Had he been given a prompt, honourable burial, the respectful treatment of his body might have helped minimize public interest in the scandal surrounding his death. Alternatively, had the body been displayed as the rightfully desecrated corpse of a deposed tyrant, perhaps the case against his legitimacy would have been more persuasive.[84] As things stood from March 978 through February 979, the missing corpse – and, by extension, the subversion of normative burial and succession rites – seems to have turned public sentiment against the killers, whether their identities were known or simply suspected. In this environment, even Æthelred may have been vulnerable: although no contemporary sources directly accused him of fratricide, he was the chief beneficiary of his brother's assassination and could conceivably have been implicated in the crime.[85] Accordingly, it was in the young king's best interest that Edward's corpse be respectfully buried and his posthumous identity finally settled. Once installed at Shaftesbury, there could be no doubt that the king was worthy of an honourable, consecrated grave. Edward's reputation was rehabilitated, and by the turn of the millennium, he was remembered not as an oppressor or usurper but as an "illustrious and elected king" and a "heavenly saint."[86]

---

82 Ridyard, *Royal Saints*, 169–71; Foot, *Veiled Women* II, 170; Yorke, *Nunneries*, 171–2; Yorke, "Edward, King and Martyr," 109–10. A parallel may be found in Dunstan's efforts to create a royal mausoleum at Glastonbury: Yorke, "Royal Burial," 42; Yorke, *Nunneries*, 114–15; and above, chapter 2.

83 Yorke, *Nunneries*, 171.

84 Compare above, chapter 4.

85 Keynes, "Declining Reputation," 237–8; Ridyard, *Royal Saints*, 158–62.

86 "Conspicuus atque electus rex"; Byrhtferth, *Vita Oswaldi*, 138–9. "Heofonlic sanct"; ASC DE 979 (*recte* 978).

The Saintly Body: Royal Martyrdom and Hagiography

Any ambiguity about Edward's status when he was brought to Shaftesbury in 979 was resolved in the following decades, and by the turn of the millennium, concerns about his royal credentials seem to have dissipated. In 1001, his remains were elevated to a reliquary, and a few months later, Æthelred issued a grant to the community in honour of "its saint, namely my brother Edward."[87] The anniversary of his death was listed in a number of pre-Conquest ecclesiastical calendars, and one of Æthelred's law codes required that his feast day be universally observed.[88] Byrhtferth's account of the assassination and the Anglo-Saxon Chronicle's poetic tribute to Edward, which each portrayed the regicide as a martyrdom, were likely circulating before the 1001 translation, and the earliest version of the unambiguously hagiographical *Passio* was arguably written in honour of that event.[89] Two decades after the fact, Edward's murder had been reclassified as a martyrdom.

This shift had two significant consequences. First, it kept the memory of the regicide active in the public imagination. From a political perspective, Edward's first burial at Shaftesbury should have marked a decline in his earthly influence, just as earlier royal funerals had signalled the ends of previous kings' reigns. The fact that Æthelred's own consecration was delayed for more than a year, until his brother was honourably buried, suggests that the political disruption caused by the regicide and missing body had finally come to a ceremonial close: Æthelred could fully assume his office while Edward could rest in peace.[90] Claims of Edward's sanctity undermined this sense of closure, however. Each anniversary of his death

87 "Sancto suo, germano scilicet meo Edwardo"; S 899, which later calls Edward "the blessed martyr" [beati martiris]. On the 1001 translation and charter, see: Fell, *Edward, King and Martyr*, xix and 12–13; Ridyard, *Royal Saints*, 156–7; Keynes, "Cult of King Edward," 121; Wormald, *Making of English Law*, 343–4n373. See also Thacker, "Oswald and His Communities," 248–9, for the distinct pre- and post-1001 phases of Edward's cult.

88 Edward's mass day was included in seventeen pre-1100 calendars, seven of which were produced before the Norman Conquest. Observance of Edward's feast day was decreed in V Æthelred 16, although it is debated whether this clause was original to the text or a later interpolation: Wormald, "Æthelred the Lawmaker," 53–4; Wormald, *Making of English Law*, 343–4; Fell, *Edward, King and Martyr*, xxi–xxii; Keynes, "Cult of King Edward," 123. Compare also Cnut 1018 14.6, I Cnut 17.1, and chapter 6 below.

89 Dating is discussed above nn. 22–4.

90 Keynes, *Diplomas*, 173–4 and 233n7; Keynes, "Cult of King Edward," 118; and further below.

and burial would have recalled the scandal of regicide, and indignation was still fresh enough for the story to be committed to parchment – with considerable hagiographical embellishment – some twenty years after his assassination. Second, the re-identification of Edward as a martyr transformed the mode of discourse used to describe his reign and death. Once he was recognized as a saint, the killers could in no way be regarded as righteous men cleansing the realm of an illegitimate or tyrannical pretender; the assassination had now become a cold-blooded assault on God's anointed. The conceptualization of the regicide as a martyrdom also forced a comparison between the way saintly relics should be honoured and the way that Edward's body was initially treated, making the denial of royal burial not merely an insult to the earthly ruler but an affront to a martyr whose relics deserved a worthy shrine. Edward's posthumous evolution into a saint made his killers into enemies of Christianity.

Although the rhetoric of sanctity was regularly applied to Edward by the end of the tenth century, it is unclear when exactly his death began to be recognized as a martyrdom. Given the fraught political situation in the late 970s, in which even an anointed king was vulnerable to attack, it is not surprising that it took some time for Edward's sanctity to be widely acknowledged; it was not until the 990s that miracles at his tomb began to be reported.[91] However, a hagiographical tribute to a different saint may help shed light on early responses to the regicide. In the mid-980s, while in residence at Ramsey, Abbo of Fleury composed the earliest Latin *vita* of King Edmund of East Anglia, who had been killed by Vikings in 869 and quickly became the focus of an extraordinarily popular martyr's cult.[92] Abbo wrote at the instigation of the monks of Ramsey, who would soon emerge as early and enthusiastic devotees of Edward's cult.[93] The text was dedicated to Archbishop Dunstan, Edward's political advocate, whose testimony was the source for much of Abbo's hagiographical material.[94] The promulgation

91 The chronology is provided by Byrhtferth, *Vita Oswaldi*, 144–5.

92 The text is dated between 985 and 987, the period in which Abbo was at Ramsey: Lapidge, *Byrhtferth*, xxii–xxv and xxviii; Mostert, "Edmund," 161. For Abbo's background and a discussion of the text, see Gransden, "Abbo's '*Passio Sancti Eadmundi*.'"

93 Royal martyrs' cults, including Edward's, flourished at Ramsey between 978 and 992 and presumably motivated the request for a *life* of Edmund: Thacker, "Oswald and His Communities," 245–51. For Byrhtferth's time at Ramsey, see Lapidge, *Byrhtferth*, xxviii–xxix.

94 Abbo, "Life of Edmund," 67–8; Keynes, *Diplomas*, 166. For Dunstan's support of Edward during the 975 succession debate, see above, n. 71, and chapter 2.

of Edmund's hagiography in the 980s coincided with a burgeoning interest in Edward's sanctity, and in this context, it is significant that Abbo's account of Edmund's death has striking parallels to the circumstances surrounding Edward's. In particular, the description of Edmund's abused corpse anticipated the accounts of Edward's obliterated remains that would emerge in the 990s. Abbo's narrative may well have reflected the concerns of an audience coping with the recent royal assassination.[95]

At first glance, the two regicides appear to be only superficially similar. Both kings were killed by a group of enemy attackers, but while Edward was ambushed by his countrymen, Edmund willingly sacrificed himself to the Viking invaders; and while Edward was killed quickly and secretly, Edmund was extensively ridiculed and tortured before being beheaded. Yet both royal bodies were concealed by the killers, recovered by the faithful, buried unworthily at first, and later translated to honourable shrines. In Edmund's case, Abbo reported that the Vikings abandoned the king's mutilated body but took his head into the woods, where they hid it in the undergrowth so that the English could not give him a decent burial. After a lengthy search, Edmund's subjects discovered the dismembered head when it miraculously called out to them. The people reunited the two pieces of the king's body and buried it, building a small church over the grave. Some years later, when the Vikings had gone, they translated the remains into an appropriately magnificent foundation.[96]

Abbo devoted a good deal of text to the Vikings' abuse of Edmund and the various indignities they inflicted upon the corpse. The king was beaten, whipped, and shot with arrows before being decapitated; afterwards, the trunk of his body was left unburied, and his head was hidden in the brush "to be devoured by birds and wild beasts."[97] For Abbo's English contemporaries, the treatment of Edmund's head and body would have recalled the punishments prescribed for criminals and excommunicants: offenders might be mutilated and left as carrion, and sometimes their heads were buried, displayed, or discarded some distance from the rest of their body.[98]

95 Cubitt, "Murdered and Martyred Saints," 67; Keynes, "Declining Reputation," 229–30.

96 Abbo, "Life of Edmund," 79–82.

97 "Aut auibus et feris deuorandum"; Abbo, "Life of Edmund," 80. Late Antique hagiographical sources for Edmund's torture are discussed by Frank, "Rite of the Blood-Eagle," 341–3.

98 Exposure of bodies to birds and beasts is discussed above, chapter 4. For execution by decapitation and the separate burial of heads and bodies, see: Reynolds, *Deviant Burial Customs*, 76–81; Reynolds, "Definition and Ideology," 35–7; Buckberry and Hadley,

These allusions surely would not have been lost on a tenth-century audience, and neither would Abbo's focus on the initial lack of a decent burial for the martyred king. In his account, the Danes' concealment of Edmund's head – which, Abbo noted, had been anointed with sacramental oil – was explicitly motivated by a desire to deny the king a royal tomb:

> They hid the head, throwing it as far as possible among the dense thickets of brambles, attempting to accomplish this with every cunning, so that the most holy body of the martyr should not be brought with its head to an honest sepulcher by the Christians for honourable burial.[99]

Abbo remarked again on the Vikings' motivation, just a few lines later:

> All [the English] who possessed true wisdom were confident that those worshippers of strange doctrine, out of envy for our faith, had carried away the head of the martyr, which they had probably hidden not very far away in the dense thicket, and had left concealed by the coarse undergrowth to be devoured by birds and wild beasts.[100]

In response to this insult, the English sought to restore the body and provide their king a respectful funeral,

> making a diligent search so that, once they discovered the head of their king and martyr, they might join it to the rest of the body and bury it with worthy honour, according to their ability.[101]

"Walkington Wold," 312–20; Hayman and Reynolds, "42–54 London Road, Staines," 234–9; Owen-Crocker, "Mutilation, Decapitation, and Unburied Dead," 93–9. For possible pagan origins, see Cubitt, "Murdered and Martyred Saints," 64.

99 "Inter densa ueprium frutecta longius proiectum occuluerunt, id omni sagacitate elaborantes ne a Christianis ... sacratissimum corpus martyris cum capite pro tumulantium modulo honestae traderetur sepulturae"; Abbo, "Life of Edmund," 80. Earlier in the same passage, Abbo wrote that the head "had not been anointed with the oil of sinners but with the sacramental oil of mystery" [non impinguauerat peccatoris oleum sed certi misterii sacramentum]; ibid., 79.

100 "Pro certo etenim omnibus uere sapientibus inerat quod alienae sectae cultores, inuidendo nostrae fidei, sustulissent caput martyris, quod non longius infra densitatem saltus abscondissent, aut uili cespite obrutum aut auibus et feris deuorandum"; Abbo, "Life of Edmund," 80. Earlier, the trunk of the body was described as having been "placed under the sky" [positum sub diuo]; ibid., 80.

101 "Diligenti inquisitione satagentes ut caput sui regis et martyris inuentum reliquo corpori unirent et iuxta suam facultatem condigno honore reconderent"; ibid., 80.

Although it is certainly conceivable that an invading army would have left the body of their enemy dismembered and exposed, Abbo suggested a precise ideological motive for the desecration in these passages: the Viking killers sought to mock the Christian religion by making it impossible for the king to receive an honourable funeral. As this interpretation reflects the sensibilities of his late tenth-century English audience more reliably than the professed goals of the ninth-century raiders, it provides a useful analogue for Edward's more recent missing body. Edward's killers, like Edmund's, denied his subjects the opportunity to provide their king with an honourable funeral, thereby demonstrating their disregard for the respectful disposal of the Christian dead. The implication is that Edward's English assassins were no better than Edmund's heathen Vikings.

Yet the Vikings, from Abbo's perspective, did not know any better. The bloodthirsty and barbaric invaders of his narrative were jealous of the Christian faith; it was only natural that they would assault churches and kings, targets which epitomized English civilization. Although they showed a special interest in Edmund's anointed head, they were concerned only with desecrating his body as an insult; they were not intentionally attacking the institution of kingship or debunking the efficacy of royal anointing.[102] Edward's killers, by contrast, were high-status English nobles and nominal Christians, who would have been expected to pledge their fidelity to him.[103] Byrhtferth's assertion that Edward, "instructed in divine law and strong and sturdy in body," sat calmly on his horse while the assassins surrounded him implies that he rightfully believed that he had nothing to fear from these men, for it would have been unthinkable for Christian magnates to ambush an anointed ruler and slay him in cold blood.[104] Unlike Edmund's attackers, Edward's killers should have understood that a royal consecration obliged them to protect their king from harm. However cruel Abbo imagined Edmund's Vikings to have been, they had professed no loyalty to the English king and were presumably unconcerned with the implications of royal anointing. Edward's killers

102 There is no evidence that the historical Edmund had been anointed, and while this textual silence does not necessarily mean that no consecration had occurred, Abbo's reference to the king's anointing surely reflected his understanding of kingship in the later tenth century. Moreover, it forced a clearer comparison with Edward. For anointing in Abbo's account, see Gransden, "Abbo's '*Passio Sancti Eadmundi*,'" 47–50.

103 Above, n. 72 and chapter 2.

104 "Doctus diuina lege ... et robustus erat corpore et durus"; Byrhtferth, *Vita Oswaldi*, 138–9.

could claim no such defence, making their actions all the more insidious and justifying the Latin authors' impulse to compare them to Judas, Pilate, and the Jews.[105]

Nevertheless, the hagiographical context of these works required that divine intervention thwart the assassins' attempts to suppress their victims' bodies and memories. Although the killers cut short Edward and Edmund's earthly lives, God gave them eternal life in heaven; and although the killers tried to stifle their memory by hiding their bodies (or body parts), God caused their remains and their sanctity to be revealed on earth. This theme was not unique to these two examples, as the recovery and subsequent veneration of kings' bodies had long been a feature of Anglo-Saxon royal saints' lives. In the seventh century, King Oswald's dismembered corpse was desecrated by his enemies before it was recovered and enshrined by his subjects; and King Edwin's remains had been buried after a battle in a makeshift grave, where they remained until their location was revealed through a miraculous vision.[106] Yet the desire to see rulers honourably interred was not limited to hagiographical discourse, and the determination of Harold Harefoot's supporters to retrieve their king's desecrated body and bury it respectfully – surely against the wishes of their new ruler – suggests that this impulse constituted more than a hagiographical trope.[107] In Abbo's account, it was the discovery of Edmund's head which finally permitted a restoration of the social order. Just as the royal body had been deprived of its head, the population had been deprived of its king; it was only after Edmund's corpse had been reunited and translated into a worthy intramural tomb that the status quo was re-established.[108] By analogy, the discovery and reburial of Edward's body was vital to reinstituting a social order which had been disrupted by his assassination and disappearance.[109] The importance of physical restoration

105 Byrhtferth, *Vita Oswaldi*, 138–41; Fell, *Edward King and Martyr*, 5.

106 Bede, *HE* III.12; Colgrave, *Life of Gregory*, 100–5. Oswald and Edwin were both killed in battle by Penda of Mercia and both kings' heads ended up in different places than their bodies: Yorke, *Nunneries*, 119; Cubitt, "Murdered and Martyred Saints," 60–6.

107 Above, chapter 4.

108 "Transtulit cum magna gloria," "sacrosanctum tumulum"; Abbo, "Life of Edmund," 82. In Abbo's account, there was no reference to the royal succession in relation to Edmund's violent death; the restoration of order was signalled by the expulsion of the Vikings and the provision of an appropriate burial for the saintly king.

109 For royal funerals as a restoration of order, see: Buc, *Dangers of Ritual*, 83; Binski, *Medieval Death*, 60–1; Kantorowicz, *King's Two Bodies*, 409–37.

is reflected in the textual focus on the successful recovery and appropriate burial of Edward's corpse, but it may also explain Æthelred's delayed consecration. Although the young king was elected immediately after his brother's death, he was not anointed until after the translation to Shaftesbury, and Edward's burial may have been the event which allowed plans for the consecration to finally proceed.[110] The hagiographical depiction of order being disrupted by a regicide and restored with a proper funeral closely reflects the political circumstances of 978 and 979.

Conclusions

Whether Archbishop Dunstan refused to consecrate a new ruler until the previous one was honourably buried, whether Edward's subjects were clamouring to pay their king the respect they believed he deserved, or whether Æthelred himself was determined to give his brother a proper royal funeral, the fact that there was an effort to recover Edward's body after so long an interval attests to the perceived value of royal remains. The killers certainly recognized the body as an important symbolic object which might undermine their ambitions, and their impulse to hide the royal corpse suggests that they were attempting to neutralize its impact on the ensuing political debate while protecting themselves from the consequences of their regicide. Had they displayed the vanquished body, they might have exacerbated simmering factionalism and irrevocably turned public sentiment against their cause; had they declared the homicide and brought the remains to be buried in the open, they could have been condemned for betraying and killing their lord. Concealing the corpse would surely have seemed the safest option for the perpetrators and for the new regime they would put in place.

Nevertheless, Edward's killers seem to have misjudged how the king's disappearance would be received by contemporaries. Even if they had anticipated that the hidden body would eventually be found and honoured, they must not have expected the outpouring of cultic reverence that followed the regicide, for although there was a long history of royal sanctity in pre-Conquest England, the development of a cult was by no means inevitable.[111] Given that Edward was the first West Saxon king to be deemed

110 Keynes, *Diplomas*, 173–4 and 233n7; but compare Dumville, "Death of Edward the Martyr."

111 For royal sanctity as an achieved rather than an ascribed status, see: Ridyard, *Royal Saints*, 76–7; Nelson, "Royal Saints," 72; and compare Chaney, *Cult of Kingship*.

a saint, the scale of his cult and the speed at which it developed were remarkable.[112] In the late tenth century, most Anglo-Saxon royal saints were either conversion-era rulers or monastic women; Edmund of East Anglia was an important exception, but he died resisting heathen aggressors – following the example of Edwin, Oswald, and other martyred kings.[113] Edward, ambushed and killed by his own Christian nobles, represented a new model of saintly kingship, and this novelty is vital to understanding contemporary reactions to the assassination.[114] The king's swift designation as a martyr was not an automatic response to regicide.[115] Rather, it reflected his subjects' need to rationalize a particularly scandalous royal murder and explain it in the context of a broader Christian cosmology.[116]

Still, whatever distress his assassination may have inspired among his loyal subjects, outrage alone would not have been sufficient cause for cultic reverence. Instead, I would conclude that claims of sanctity were an answer to the attempted denigration of the king's memory. Where the killers aimed to construct a negative legacy for Edward by destroying and obliterating his body, the king's supporters sought to re-establish his earthly status by retrieving, honouring, and memorializing the corpse. If interment at a royal nunnery was not enough to counter the accusations levelled against him, the declaration of his sanctity would have trumped any claims of irregular accession or improper rule. By this logic, if God saw fit to make Edward a saint, his reign must have been legitimate and

112 Before Edward, the most recent assassinated royal saint was Wigstan of Mercia (d. 849). Of the West Saxon royal saints who lived before Edward, most were monastic women. A possible exception was Edgar, whom William of Malmesbury described as saintly in the twelfth century, but there is no evidence that the king was revered as a saint before the mid-eleventh century: *De Antiquitate*, 134–5; William of Malmesbury, *GR* ii.160.2–3; Rollason, *Saints and Relics*, 140; and above, chapter 2.

113 The earliest account of Edmund's death reported that he died in battle: ASC A 870 (*recte* 869). On the model of royal sanctity adopted by Oswald and Edwin, see Klaniczay, *Holy Rulers*, 81–3, but compare the description of Edmund at 91.

114 Notably, interest in the regicide led not only to Edward's sanctification but to the revival of cults of other martyred royals: Thacker, "Oswald and His Communities," 247–53; Fell, "Anglo-Saxon Hagiographic Tradition"; Cubitt, "Murdered and Martyred Saints," 67.

115 As suggested by Rollason, "Murdered Royal Saints," 12; Keynes, "Cult of King Edward," 117.

116 Ridyard, *Royal Saints*, 167. For the implications of the scandalous assassination of an anointed king, see: Stafford, *Unification and Conquest*, 59; de Jong, "Power and Humility," 36–9.

just.[117] The martyr's cult thus appears to have grown out of the impulse to repair Edward's earthly reputation. It was not enough to simply restore his royal status; that status now needed to be enhanced with sanctity in order to rehabilitate the king's legacy.

Although it was not until the 990s that there is firm evidence of cultic activity at Shaftesbury, and although Edward's universal recognition as a martyr likely dates to the elevation of his relics in 1001, I would postulate that rumours of his saintliness had emerged by the time of the 979 translation, catalysed not by the murder itself but by the mistreatment of the royal body and memory.[118] Edward's supporters and opponents each manipulated the remains in order to construct a particular legacy for him: both factions appropriated recognizable, signifying modes of burial to make their case, with one side attempting to recast the king's body as a shamed corpse and the other trying to transform the disgraced remains into proof of royal legitimacy or, eventually, saintly relics. Although the body was central to the construction of Edward's posthumous identity, it was its absence which permitted the promotion of these competing characterizations. Once the remains were respectfully restored to the public gaze, the debate was closed. Although Edward might not have been universally loved or revered, there could no longer be any doubt that he was worthy of honourable, consecrated burial. Still, the humiliation of his body – an inversion of earthly and divine order so familiar in Christian history – was continually recalled and provided the impetus for hagiographical readings of the assassination in subsequent decades. His reign would now be reflected through a lens of sanctity, his body less a source of legitimizing dynastic memory than an instrument for communication with the divine. However, in the months immediately following his death, before his sanctity was widely acknowledged, Edward's body functioned primarily as a political object which had the power to restore an upset social hierarchy and determine how the king would be remembered by future generations. These were the considerations that inspired widespread interest in the royal remains and paved the way for the development of the king's enduring martyr's cult.

117 This is made explicit by Byrhtferth, *Vita Oswaldi*, 144.

118 Edward's feast day was entered and then erased from two early ecclesiastical calendars, suggesting that reverence for the king was initially controversial: Fell, *Edward, King and Martyr*, xxi–xxii.

6 Bodies of Conquest: Kings, Saints, and Conquerors in the Reign of Cnut

Half a century after Edward the Martyr's relics were translated from Wareham to Shaftesbury, another prominent English martyr was ceremonially brought home: St Ælfheah, the erstwhile archbishop of Canterbury, who had been killed by Vikings in 1012. Ælfheah had been seized by a Danish army and held captive in London, where he was executed when he refused to pay his captors tribute. According to the earliest account of the episode, recorded in the Anglo-Saxon Chronicle:

> They shamefully killed him there. They pelted him with bones and with ox-heads, and one of them struck him on the head with the back of an axe, so that he sank down from the blow, and his holy blood fell on the earth, and he sent his holy soul to God's kingdom. And in the morning his body was brought to London, and the bishops Eadnoth and Ælfhun and the citizens received it with all reverence and buried it in St Paul's minster. And God now shows there the might of the holy martyr.[1]

Ælfheah's death was shocking, like Edward's had been a generation earlier. Yet while Edward's assassination was an act of treason committed by individuals who had sworn loyalty to the king, Ælfheah was slain by outsiders

1 "Hine þær ða bysmorlice acwylmdon, oftorfedon mid banum 7 mid hryþera heafdum. 7 sloh hine ða an hiora mid anre æxe yre on þæt heafod, þæt mid þam dynte he nyþer asah, 7 his halige blod on þa eorðan feol, 7 his haligan sawle to Godes rice asende. 7 mon þone lichaman on mergen ferode to Lundene, 7 þa bisceopas Eadnoþ 7 Ælfun 7 seo buruhwaru hine underfengon mid ealre arwurðnysse 7 hine bebyrigdon on Sancte Paules mynstre, 7 þær nu God sutelað þæs halgan martires mihta"; ASC CDEF 1012. See also: Brooks, *Early History of Canterbury*, 283–5; Damon, "Advisors for Peace," 76–7.

who posed an external threat to English society. The Chronicle description of the archbishop's martyrdom juxtaposes Ælfheah's pious resistance with the Danes' greed and bloodlust, highlighting his killers' refusal to play by the rules. They went into a rage when Ælfheah denied them tribute, but refused to free him in exchange for payment; they did not give the archbishop a quick or honourable death after his week in captivity, but humiliated him instead, making him an object of sport and killing him with a blunt blow.[2] In refusing the Danes' demands, Ælfheah did more than resist an act of extortion – he rejected a way of life that readers would consider an assault on civilized Christian values, thereby earning his new status as a saint. Nevertheless, the archbishop's failed stand against his captors proved to contemporaries that no one, at any level of society, was safe from Viking violence. As foreign invaders who did not follow expected standards of conduct or respect the "head of the English people and of Christendom," these Danes were outsiders in England.[3]

After Cnut's accession as king in late 1016, this perception began to shift. The Danish conqueror promised to rule as well as his Anglo-Saxon predecessors, became a patron of churches and monasteries, advanced his subjects' interests on the Continent, and issued a magisterial body of Old English law. Yet even as Cnut met the expectations for a king of England, Ælfheah remained one of London's most popular saints and an unambiguous reminder of Viking atrocity in a city that had spent years under siege. Relations were uneasy between Cnut and the citizens in the opening years of his reign, as the king installed a Danish military garrison in the city and levied an exceptionally high tax on its inhabitants.[4] London suffered a further blow in 1023, when Cnut arranged for Ælfheah's relics to be removed from St Paul's and enshrined instead at Christ Church, Canterbury. The Anglo-Saxon Chronicle reported:

> In this year, in St Paul's minster in London, King Cnut gave full permission to Archbishop Æthelnoth [of Canterbury] and Bishop Brihtwine [of Wells]

---

2 ASC CDEF 1012. I follow Dorothy Whitelock's interpretation of *yr* as the blunt side of the weapon; *EHD* I, 245 no. 1.

3 "Heafod Angelkynnes 7 Cristendomes"; ASC CDEF 1011.

4 A Danish garrison was stationed in the city early in Cnut's reign: Nightingale, "Origin of the Court of Husting," 567–8; Kelly, *Charters of St Paul's*, 40–2. In 1018, Cnut levied a special tax of 15,000 pounds in London (the rest of the kingdom paid a total sum of 72,000 pounds): ASC CDE 1018; Lawson, "Danegeld," 721–6; Hill, "Urban Policy," 103–4.

> and to all God's servants who were with them to take up from the grave the archbishop St Ælfheah, and they did so on 8 June. And the glorious king and the archbishop and the bishops and the earls and very many clergy and also laity brought his holy body on a ship over the Thames to Southwark, and entrusted the holy martyr to the archbishop and his companions there. And then they brought him to Rochester, with a worthy troop and happy joy. Then on the third day, the lady Emma came with her royal child Harthacnut, and then they all brought the holy archbishop into Canterbury with great glory and joy and songs of praise, and so brought him worthily into Christ Church on 11 June.[5]

The bishops placed the body in its new shrine to the north of the altar eight days later. The annal concluded by entreating God to "have mercy on all Christian men, through the holy merits of St Ælfheah."[6]

The Chronicle construed the translation as a joyful event, which brought honour to Ælfheah and his home foundation in Canterbury, but it was also a political opportunity which allowed Cnut and his family to associate themselves with a prominent Anglo-Saxon saint. Certainly, it was not unusual for English kings to participate in relic translations. In recent generations, Æthelred had overseen elevations of his saintly siblings, Edward the Martyr and Edith of Wilton, and Edgar assumed a prominent role in the translation of Bishop Swithun's relics at Winchester.[7] Yet in 1023, more was at stake at Ælfheah's translation than an expression of royal piety, for by a certain logic, the new king of England was responsible for the martyrdom of London's most popular saint: Cnut and his father had led Scandinavian armies into England, and the perpetrators of the crime had

---

5 "Her Cnut kyning binnan Lundene on sancte Paules mynstre sealde fulle leaf Æðelnoðe arcebiscope 7 Bryhtwine biscope 7 eallon þam Godes þeowum þe heom mid wæron þæt hi moston nyman up of þam byrgene þone arcebiscop sancte Ælfheah, 7 hi þa swa dydon on .vi. idus Iunii. 7 se brema cyng 7 se arcebiscop 7 leodbiscopas 7 eorlas 7 swiðe manege hadode 7 eac læwede feredon on scype his þone halgan lichaman ofer Temese to Suðgeweorke, 7 þær þone halgan martyr þan arcebiscope 7 his geferum betæhton, 7 hi þa mid weorðlican weorode 7 wynsaman dreame hine to Hrofesceastre feredan. Ða on þam þryddan dæg com Imma seo hlæfdie mid hire cynelican bearne Hardacnute, 7 hi þa ealle mid mycclan þrymme 7 blisse 7 lofsange þonne halgan arcebiscop into Cantwarebyri feredon, 7 swa wurðlice into Cristes cyrcan brohton on .iii. idus Iunni"; ASC D 1023. On this passage, see Hayward, "Translation-Narratives," 70–1.

6 "God ælmihtig gemiltsie eallum Cristenum mannum þurh sanctę Ælfeges halgan gegearnunga"; ASC D 1023.

7 Ridyard, *Royal Saints*, 152–71; Keynes, *Diplomas*, 169–71; Crook, "King Edgar's Reliquary," 197–202.

been their subordinates.[8] Although neither king was directly implicated in the killing itself, Ælfheah's translation in effect reversed the damage their countrymen had inflicted and redeemed Cnut of any hint of complicity in the saint's death. In 1012, Danish invaders had ravaged Canterbury, seized the archbishop, and impoverished a harried population; in 1023, the Danish king gave Christ Church an invaluable gift of relics, restored the displaced archbishop to his proper place, and united the entire kingdom behind the effort.[9] Ælfheah's translation functioned as compensation for past wrongs and signalled a restoration of order by a Christian king of England – a Dane, but not a Viking.

Cnut's actions must have looked rather different from London than from Canterbury. While Ælfheah's translation was undoubtedly framed in reverential terms, the king publicly deprived St Paul's of a prestigious saint, whose relics had been cultivated by the cathedral clergy for more than a decade. Christ Church might have claimed Ælfheah as their pastor in life, but he had been martyred and buried in London; in death he belonged to St Paul's. The translation must have been seen by some as an insult to the community and city, and it is possible that the king had intended it as such.[10] Six years after Cnut's accession and eleven years after the saint's death, Ælfheah's body and cult remained an emblem of the suffering that the citizens had endured during the Scandinavian invasions.[11] By taking the relics from a problematic population and installing them in a foundation whose history with the new regime was less fraught, Cnut transformed Ælfheah from a reminder of past violence into a symbol of royal generosity, piety, and conciliation. The disenfranchisement of St Paul's was an acceptable price for firm allegiance in Canterbury, the kingdom's most venerable and influential ecclesiastical centre.[12]

If Ælfheah's translation reflects Cnut's concern with politically charged bodies, it also reveals his ability to defuse their impact. This was not the first time Cnut had removed a problematic corpse from a volatile area. Ælfheah's translation mirrors the relocation of Edmund Ironside's corpse

8 See further below.

9 Archbishops of Canterbury had been buried regularly at Christ Church since the eighth century: Brooks, *Early History of Canterbury*, 81; Potts, "Tombs of the Kings," 107–8.

10 Nightingale, "Origin of the Court of Husting," 567; Lawson, *Cnut*, 155; Hill, "Urban Policy," 103.

11 Above, chapter 3.

12 Cnut's relationship with Christ Church is surveyed by Brooks, *Early History of Canterbury*, 287–96, with Ælfheah's translation at 291–2.

from London to Glastonbury; evidently, the strategy was considered effective enough in 1016 to repeat in 1023.[13] Still, a funeral journey for a recently deceased rival was quite different from the translation of a long-dead saint. Where Edmund's funeral fulfilled an immediate need to dispose of a body, Ælfheah's translation was not an urgent priority. Moreover, while Edmund's interment at Glastonbury conformed to an existing geography of royal burial, Ælfheah's move to Canterbury altered the spiritual landscape.[14] Relocating an established saint required intent and planning, and it seems that Cnut's interaction with Ælfheah's relics was carefully choreographed. The translation thus raises broader questions about how a conqueror might cope with the bodily remnants of England's past. In the wake of a drawn-out and bloody invasion that deposed a four-hundred-year-old dynasty, how was a foreign ruler to treat the remains of prominent members of the native population? What would become of royal bodies that predated the conquest – the ancestors of the displaced West Saxon kings? Moreover, how should the conquerors themselves be memorialized?

The answer to this final question was seemingly straightforward by the time Cnut died in 1035: he was interred in Winchester's Old Minster, just like earlier generations of Anglo-Saxon rulers.[15] Although an erased passage concerning Cnut's burial in the *Encomium Emmae* may reflect some controversy surrounding the king's resting place, the grave remained secure enough that his son and widow would later be buried beside him in what remained one of the most prestigious royal mausolea in England.[16] In his nearly twenty years on the throne, Cnut reinvented himself as a legitimate Christian ruler of England, and the fact that he was buried in his adopted realm rather than in Denmark suggests that he and his survivors were intent on perpetuating his identity as a rightful king of England and legitimate heir to the West Saxon dynasty.[17]

During Cnut's lifetime, by contrast – and particularly in the decade after his father's death in 1014 – there was a pressing need to cope with corpses that could exacerbate the memory of raid and conquest. In late 1016, three

13 Above, chapter 3.

14 Glastonbury already housed the tombs of Kings Edmund and Edgar: above, chapter 2.

15 ASC CD 1035, EF 1036 (*recte* 1035); and above, chapter 3.

16 Harthacnut died in 1042 and Emma in 1052. For the erased passage in the *Encomium*, see: Keynes, "Introduction to the Reprint," xliv; Keynes and Love, "Earl Godwine's Ship," 194.

17 Cnut's identity as an English king is discussed by Treharne, *Living through Conquest*, 9–47. I am grateful to Dr Treharne for sharing her work in advance of publication.

such bodies were in London: those of Ælfheah and Æthelred, both buried in St Paul's, and that of Edmund Ironside, who died in the city in November amid a population that had rallied to his campaign against Cnut. Yet there were other problematic bodies, too. Wilton and Shaftesbury housed the relics of Æthelred's saintly siblings, Edith and Edward. As members of the deposed West Saxon dynasty, with cult centres at the heart of Wessex, these saints were inherently political and potentially dangerous to the Danish regime. The cult of King Edmund of East Anglia – a victim of ninth-century Viking attacks – likewise presented a challenge. Notwithstanding Edmund's early and steady reverence among England's Anglo-Scandinavian population, the saint's home foundation at Bury had been ravaged during the eleventh-century invasions and his relics displaced. Another difficult body belonged to Cnut's father, Swein Forkbeard, who was buried in York Minster in 1014 after a brief and tumultuous reign that cemented his legacy as a raider and conqueror. This prestigious interment proved only temporary, however, for within a year of his death, Swein's remains were exhumed from his grave and reburied in Denmark.

Cnut's contact with these bodies was, I propose, a response to the enduring memory of his family's conquest. Although each set of remains was treated with respect, their political significance was transformed, appropriated, or minimized under his regime. I have argued in an earlier chapter that the impact of Edmund Ironside's corpse was neutralized by his burial at the kingdom's political periphery, just as the more controversial aspects of Ælfheah's martyrdom would have been muted once his relics were entrusted to a sympathetic community. The present chapter contends that a similar modus operandi is evident in Cnut's interactions with other prominent bodies, which were treated with outward respect even as they were divested of their political influence. In light of Cnut's military victories and abrupt displacement of an established English dynasty, it is significant that he did not generally use the physical desecration of high-status bodies as propaganda, as his son Harthacnut would later attempt to do. Instead, corpses that could not be made instruments of the new regime were quietly removed from the public eye. Cnut evidently recognized the aftermath of conquest as a politically sensitive transitional moment: whatever violence he had committed – or continued to commit – against the English population as a whole, he understood that his (and his family's) political longevity relied on his ability to portray himself as a legitimate king and heir to the West Saxon dynasty. By containing and controlling the legacies of his predecessors, he aimed to prevent their bodies from becoming perpetual memorials to conquest.

Translating Swein Forkbeard

Early in the Danish regime, the most visceral relic of conquest may well have been the body of the conqueror himself: Swein Forkbeard, who died at Gainsborough on 3 February 1014 after a brief tenure as king of England; his remains were buried at York Minster.[18] Cnut was acclaimed king by the Danish fleet after his father's death, but Æthelred soon returned from exile and, with the endorsement of the *witan*, retook the realm.[19] With Æthelred's forces moving northward, Cnut was forced to flee to Denmark, abandoning the people of Lindsay who had pledged him their loyalty and mutilating his English hostages on his way out.[20] In early 1015, as Cnut was organizing his next offensive, Swein's body was exhumed from York and brought to Denmark, where it was buried a second time at Roskilde.[21]

The most extensive account of Swein's translation appears in the *Encomium Emmae Reginae*, which depicted the translation as a ceremonial event inspired by filial piety. The impetus for the move, in the Encomiast's account, was Swein's own deathbed request that Cnut

> should carry his father's body back with him and should not let him be buried a stranger in a foreign land; for he knew that because of the invasion of the kingdom, he was hateful to those people.[22]

---

18 Swein's death was recorded in ASC CDEF 1014; John of Worcester added that he died at Gainsborough. Also in the twelfth century, Geffrei Gaimar and Symeon of Durham cited York – about fifty miles from Gainsborough – as his burial place. JW 476–7; Gaimar, *Estoire des Engleis*, 132; Symeon of Durham, *Historia Regum*, 146; Demidoff, "Death of Svein Forkbeard," 40; Phillips, *Excavations at York Minster* II, 2. Some English and Norman sources indicated that Swein was originally buried in Denmark, a view also taken by later Icelandic authors: *De Miraculis Sancti Eadmundi*, 39; Van Houts, *Gesta Normannorum Ducum* II, 18–19; Orderic Vitalis, *Ecclesiastical History* I, 156; Demidoff, "Death of Svein Forkbeard," 43–5.

19 Cnut's election by the Danish fleet (*se flota*) is recorded in ASC CDE 1014. For Æthelred's return, see especially Stafford, "Royal Promises."

20 ASC CDE 1014.

21 Roskilde was dedicated to the Holy Trinity and cited as Swein's burial place in later Norse accounts; in the 1020s, one of its clergy attested a royal grant to Ely (S 958), suggesting a continued relationship with Swein's family: Campbell, "Introduction," lvii; Demidoff, "Death of Swein Forkbeard," 33–4.

22 "Corpus paternum reportaret secum, neue pateretur se aligenigenam in externis tumulari terris; nouerat enim, quia pro inuasione regni illis exosus erat populis"; *Encomium*, 14–15.

Shortly thereafter, while Cnut was in Denmark with his brother Harald, Swein's dying wish was carried out:

> A certain English matron had a ship prepared for her, and taking the body of King Swein, who had been buried in her country, and having embalmed it with aromatics and covered it with palls, she went to sea, and making a successful voyage, arrived at the ports of the Danes. Sending a messenger to the two brothers, she indicated that their father's body was there, so that they might hasten to receive it and place it in the tomb which he had prepared for himself. They came gladly and received the body with honour, and with yet more honour they placed it in the monastery which had been built by the same king in honour of the Holy Trinity, in the sepulcher which he had prepared for himself.[23]

The *Encomium* seems deliberately evasive in its details and contains a number of puzzling elements. First is the statement that Swein considered himself hateful (*exosus*) to his conquered subjects and a stranger in a foreign land (*aligenigenam in externis terris*), a sentiment at odds with the Encomiast's insistence just a few lines earlier that he was a glorious king concerned with the pious governence of England.[24] Second is the depiction of the translation as a ceremonial event, in which Swein's body was exhumed, embalmed, and moved from one major church to another amid the author's praise of the dead king's Christian devotion. Third is the role of the "certain English matron" (*quaedam matronarum Anglicarum*), an unnamed figure who seems to have had an extraordinary degree of access to the Danish royal family – living and dead – and who was portrayed as the primary actor in the translation. The most pressing question, however, is why Swein's body was moved at all. Given the military turmoil and political crisis of 1015, why was this considered an appropriate moment for a royal translation, and what was the move meant to accomplish?

23 "Quaedam matronarum Anglicarum nauim sibi fecit parari, et assumpto corpore Sueini regis sua in patria sepulti illoque aromatibus condito palliisque uelato, marc adiit, et prospero cursu appulsa ad portus Danorum peruenit. Mittens ergo utrisque fratribus nuntium mandat corpus adesse paternum, ut hoc maturent suscipere, tumuloque quod sibi parauerat locare. Illi hilares adsunt, honorifice corpus suscipiunt, honorificentiusque illud in monasterio in honore Sanctae Trinitatis ab eodem rege constructo, in sepulchro quod sibi parauerat, recondunt"; *Encomium*, 18–19.

24 *Encomium*, 14–15.

The starting point for this discussion is Swein's first interment in England. York Minster would have been a logical place to bury a Danish-born king whose English power was based in the Anglo-Scandinavian north.[25] An archiepiscopal see with conversion-era royal roots, York was effectively the capital of the Danelaw; from the invaders' perspective, it was friendly territory. The minster already housed the remains of five kings, ranging from its founder Edwin, whose decapitated head was claimed by the community in 632, to the Viking king Guthfrith, who died in 895.[26] Interment at York thus integrated Swein into England's royal past, associating him with early Anglo-Saxon rulers as well as the more recent Scandinavian kings of Northumbria. Located some fifty miles away from Gainsborough, where he died, York was not a convenient burial place but a site that was deliberately chosen for its political and religious prominence.

It is also significant that Swein's burial coincided with two other major ceremonial events. According to the Anglo-Saxon Chronicle, Swein died on 3 February; a new bishop of London, Ælfwig, was consecrated at York on 16 February, St Juliana's day; and on an unspecified date in the same period, the Danish fleet acclaimed Cnut king.[27] The episcopal consecration, which would have been planned before Swein died, meant that England's lay and ecclesiastical elite would have been present at York for the event, including Archbishop Wulfstan, who likely officiated.[28] The fact that a bishop of London was consecrated so far to the north confirms that York

25 Above, n. 18; and Hall, "York in the Early Tenth Century."

26 The others were Ælfwine (d. 678), Eadberht (d. 768), and Osbald (d. 799): Phillips, *Excavations at York Minster* II, 2; Hall, "York in the Early Tenth Century,"188–9. For Edwin's head, see also Bede, *HE* II.20.

27 "In this year Swein ended his days at Candlemas, on 3 February. And in the same year Ælfwig was consecrated bishop of London in York on St Juliana's massday. And the fleet all chose Cnut as king" [Her on þissum geare Swegen geendode his dagas to Candelmæssan .iii. Nonas Februarii. 7 þy ilcan geare man hadode ælfwig bisceop on Eoforwic to Lundenburuh on Sancta Iuliana mæssedæg. 7 se flota þa eall gecuron Cnut to cyninge]; ASC D 1014. Ælfwig was bishop of London 1014–35; he succeeded Ælfhun, who accompanied Æthelred and Emma's sons into exile in Normandy in late 1013. Cnut's relations with Ælfwig soured after 1014; he was bishop when the king stripped St Paul's of its estates and attested only three of Cnut's authentic charters: Whitelock, "Some Bishops of London," 31–2. York Minster was the probable site of the events of 1014: Norton, "York Minster," 233.

28 Howard, *Swein Forkbeard's Invasions*, 106 and 128; Whitelock, *Sermo Lupi ad Anglos*, 11; Norton, "York Minster," 233.

was functioning as a premier ecclesiastical centre at the time, making Swein's burial there all the more prestigious. Just as importantly, however, the timing of these events suggests that the funeral, the bishop's consecration, and Cnut's acclamation were all part of a single ceremonial gathering that began some two weeks after the king's death, allowing sufficient time for his body and the southern magnates to complete their journey to York. Despite its cursory treatment in the *Encomium* and the Anglo-Saxon Chronicle, Swein's funeral was apparently part of a series of ritual events that were choreographed to confirm his and Cnut's status as kings of England.

This was not an obscure burial, and the circumstances in no way indicate that it was meant to be temporary. Swein was the first king to be interred at York in over a century, and his placement there represented a clear departure from the southern mausolea favoured by the West Saxon dynasty. This regional shift could have been a political statement in its own right. Alternatively, the threat of military conflict may have discouraged Swein's followers from transporting his remains through hostile territory; indeed, this was the very logic that the Encomiast placed in the dying king's mouth.[29] Yet even though the *Encomium* did not refer directly to an attack on Swein's funeral or survivors and never specified that he had been buried at York, the considerable attention devoted to the translation suggests that the body's relocation needed explaining. In the early 1040s, the author and his audience would have been aware of the recent exhumation and desecration of Harold Harefoot's remains. In the context of that desecration, the *Encomium*'s pious rhetoric and hints of danger seem intended to dispel any suspicion that Swein's corpse had been threatened with comparable treatment in 1015 – indicating, perhaps, that it had.

A Continental account of the Danish conquest reinforces this impression. The earliest extant report of Swein's translation was composed before 1018 by Thietmar of Merseburg, who indicated that the king's body was in fact vulnerable at York. Thietmar reported that Swein, "impious among the faithful" (*inter pios impius*), died and was buried in England:

> When Æthelred, king of the English, who had been a fugitive for a long time, discovered this for certain, giving thanks to God he joyfully came back to his country; and assembling all his soldiers together, he attempted to destroy

29 The quotation is above, n. 22.

> (*exterminare*) the body of his enemy. But to prevent this, a certain matron who had been previously warned by her followers, raising the body from the ground – even though she was from that country – sent it by ship to its northern homeland.[30]

When the corpse arrived in Denmark, Thietmar continued, Cnut and his brother Harald

> tearfully received the body of their beloved father when it was brought, and buried it; and preparing their ships, they intended to avenge whatever disgrace the English had planned to inflict upon their father.[31]

This explicit threat of desecration is unique to Thietmar's account, and there was scant precedent for the dishonourable exhumation of royal remains in England in 1014 and 1015. However, it is not implausible that Æthelred or his supporters had designs against Swein's corpse. After the English renewed their loyalty to Æthelred, according to the Anglo-Saxon Chronicle, "they declared every Danish king an outlaw (*utlah*) from England forever" – a proclamation that had immediate implications for Cnut, who was driven out of the country, but may have been understood to apply to the dead Danish king as well.[32] Taken alongside the Old English *utlah*, Thietmar's *exterminare* could reflect an intention to expel the body from English soil, as much as a desire to destroy it. Even though Thietmar's details are occasionally confused, the fact that a contemporary chronicler believed that Æthelred had planned to abuse his usurper's corpse implies that his readers would regard desecration as a credible course of action.[33] Perhaps such concerns informed Cnut's unexplained complaint, in the

---

30 "Quod cum Aethelrad, rex Anglorum, multo tempore ab eodem fugatus, pro certo comperiret, gratias agens Deo patriam letus revisit et collectis in unum cunctis militibus suis corpus inimicum exterminare conatur. Et ut hoc non fieret, quaedam matrona prius per familiares suos ammonita servatum pignus a terra elevans, etsi indigena, tamen ad patrias navigio direxerat arctos, id est septemtrionalem plagam"; Thietmar, *Chronik*, 444, with translation adapted from Whitelock, *EHD* I, 348 no. 27.

31 "Dilecti genitoris corpus delatum flebiliter suscipiunt et tumulant et, quicquid dedecoris patri suimet ingeri ab Anglis propositum est, paratis navibus ulcisci studebant"; Thietmar, *Chronik*, 446, with translation adapted from Whitelock, *EHD* I, 348 no. 27.

32 "Æfre ælcne Deniscne cyng utlah of Englalande gecwædon"; ASC CDE 1014.

33 Notably, Thietmar confused the names of Æthelred's sons and mistook St Ælfheah for St Dunstan: Thietmar, *Chronik*, 447–8; Whitelock, *EHD* I, 348–9 no. 27.

Encomium, that he returned to Denmark "to avoid the unexpected audacity of barbarous madness."[34]

Whatever the situation in 1014 and 1015, by the time the Encomiast was writing in the early 1040s, the removal of Swein's corpse could be reimagined as a respectful translation, motivated by the king's dying wish to be buried at home rather than by any impending violation. Nevertheless, the episode had little impact on subsequent events in the *Encomium* and was not vital to the broader narrative: why did the author include it at all? The translation must have loomed large enough in the public memory that its absence would have been conspicuous, and the Encomiast's emphasis on its being a long-planned and honourable occasion suggests that the text's audience might have remembered it differently. If Swein's reburial had in fact been a response to a perceived threat, the move may have been understood by contemporaries as scandalous, shameful, or even ridiculous. In granting Swein agency over his body's fate and framing the translation in pious terms, it seems that the author was attempting to counteract any stigma still attached to the event twenty-five years later.

The evasiveness of the narrative extends to the English matron who took charge of the king's body. Although both Thietmar and the Encomiast were clear that she initiated the translation, neither named her explicitly. While this omission may be attributed to ignorance in Thietmar's case, since he was writing from a distance, it is more difficult to imagine that the Encomiast did not know who she was. She must have had considerable status if she was able to access the royal grave in York minster and leave with its contents, and it has been suggested that she was a concubine of Swein's.[35] I propose a different possibility: that she was Ælfgifu of Northampton, Cnut's Anglo-Scandinavian wife. When Cnut fled England in 1014, Æthelred began targeting Danish sympathizers, and by 1015, Ælfgifu's marriage could have put her in considerable danger, particularly if she was already the mother of Cnut's sons.[36] It is reasonable that she would have left the kingdom to seek her husband's protection, and if her father-in-law's body was thought to be in immediate danger, she seems a likely person to have brought it to safety in Scandinavia.

---

34 "Ut declinarem inprouisam temeritatem barbarici furoris"; *Encomium*, 16–17.

35 Freeman, *Norman Conquest* I, 403n4.

36 Cnut and Ælfgifu had at least one son by 1017: Stafford, *Emma and Edith*, 229; Howard, *Swein Forkbeard's Invasions*, 106 and 137. Æthelred's vengeance on the people of Lindsay for their loyalty to Cnut is noted in ASC CDE 1014.

This attribution may be supported by the fact that the Encomiast deliberately chose not to name the woman, a strategy applied to individuals with whom his patroness had difficult relationships. Just as the author referred to Emma's first husband Æthelred only as the English *princeps*, Ælfgifu was dismissed later in the text as an anonymous concubine (*cuiusdam … concubinae*).[37] If she were responsible for Swein's translation, the Encomiast would have faced a conflict: while he might have persuasively recast the king's exhumation as a pious undertaking by a devoted subject, his broader point about the religious and political legitimacy of Swein's descendants would have been undermined by the appearance of his patroness's rival in a positive context. By declining to identify the woman who translated Swein's remains, the Encomiast sidestepped the question of why this individual had such extensive access to Cnut's family. If she was in fact Ælfgifu, this tactic allowed the author to obscure the role of Emma's rival, even as he portrayed her actions as commendable.

As tempting as it is to equate Ælfgifu with the *Encomium*'s unnamed matron, her involvement is attested only by circumstantial evidence and her identification here must remain tentative. However, the individual one would expect to play a major role in this episode – Cnut himself – is remarkably passive throughout the translation narrative. It was the matron, not Cnut, who recovered and transported the remains, even though Swein entrusted the task to his son. Cnut and his brother Harald received the body with honour and committed it to the tomb, but the Encomiast reminded his readers that it was Swein, not his survivors, who had arranged the funeral in Denmark, commissioned an appropriate burial church, and prepared a sepulchre for himself – this final point so important that the Encomiast reiterated it twice.[38] Certainly, giving Swein agency over his own burial allowed the author to enhance the religious credentials of a king who was known as a persecutor of Christians in both England and Denmark.[39] Having built a burial church in his home territory, Swein could be imagined as an attentive Christian who was as concerned with his death, afterlife, and legacy as any English king. This transformation was vital to the Encomiast's narrative, for Swein proved a troublesome ancestor for

37 *Encomium*, 22 and 40. Compare the recently discovered "Edwardian Recension" of the *Encomium*, composed after Harthacnut's death and Edward the Confessor's accession, which includes an epilogue praising Æthelred by name: Keynes and Love, "Earl Godwine's Ship," 196.

38 *Encomium*, 14–15 and 18–19.

39 Lawson, *Cnut*, 129; Gerchow, "Prayers for Cnut," 222.

Cnut and Harthacnut. In the aftermath of the succession crisis of the 1030s, which threatened the primacy of the Danish dynasty and the royal claims of Emma's sons, a royal patriarch who had spent years ravaging England could easily have become a political liability for his descendants. Despite Cnut's successful rehabilitation of his own Viking past, Swein died too early in his reign to be remembered in most areas as anything but an unwelcome conqueror. Accordingly, in the 1040s, the Encomiast sanitized Swein's legacy and argued for his legitimacy but was nevertheless careful not to depict Cnut showing too much reverence for a father who had committed so much violence in England.

In 1015, by contrast, it seems unlikely that Cnut would have been overly concerned with his father's posthumous reputation among the English, had the body been left in peace. At York, where Swein's rule had been accepted early on, the king's remains probably would not have become a focal point for political opposition; over time, their prestigious burial in a major church could have helped mitigate the memory of his past offences. Furthermore, when Cnut was forced back to Denmark in 1014, he was more concerned with logistical than political problems, for he needed reinforcements and was compelled to ask his brother for help.[40] However, if Æthelred intended harm to Swein's body, Cnut's military and ideological interests would have intersected. If an exhumation or desecration were used to reinforce Æthelred's status as rightful king, the spectacle would have undermined the legitimacy Swein's funeral had provided and strained Cnut's claims in England. The *Encomium* noted that Cnut lacked sufficient manpower to keep the kingdom after his father died, and the defection of Swein's powerful ally Thorkell the Tall to Æthelred's camp may be emblematic of a more widespread desertion of the Danish cause.[41] The humiliation of Swein's corpse could have further exacerbated the situation.

If the king's body had become a liability for Cnut in England, it may have been an asset in Denmark. The *Encomium* reported that Harald, who gained the Danish throne after Swein's death, refused Cnut's proposal that they consolidate their patrimonies and reconquer England together.[42] Although the Encomiast portrayed the brothers' exchange as a civil conversation underpinned by fraternal love (*fraternus ... amor*), their disagreement over how to proceed in England likely represented a more substantial power

40 *Encomium*, 16–19.

41 Ibid., 14–17. For Thorkell's alliance with Æthelred in 1012 or 1013, see Keynes, "Cnut's Earls," 55.

42 *Encomium*, 16–19.

struggle.[43] If so, the timely appearance of Swein's corpse – and the need to avenge a perceived insult – might have goaded Harald into aiding his brother, as Thietmar indicated, and helped Cnut argue his case for invasion.[44] The body's arrival from York would have reminded witnesses of the dead king's dynastic ambitions in England, and this message would have been all the more poignant if the corpse were accompanied by Cnut's Anglo-Danish wife and young sons, one of whom was named for his paternal grandfather. Where Swein's first burial was followed by Cnut's acclamation as king of England, his second burial may have inspired those present to realize Swein's intentions abroad by supporting his son's cause.

Although Cnut could not have foreseen the outcome of his conquest or the success of his reign in early 1015, his father's translation may have inadvertently benefited the Danish rulers of England. In Denmark, Swein's grave could become a memorial to his reign and accomplishments. At York, by contrast, the body would have been a perpetual reminder of conquest, which could be evoked against Swein's son and grandsons at times of political conflict or contested succession. Whereas Cnut's stewardship of his adopted country justified his burial in the kingdom's premier mausoleum, Swein would be remembered in England as an invader; even in death he would remain, in the words of the Encomiast, "a stranger in a foreign land."[45] Yet Swein's translation also set a precedent for the way Cnut would cope with problematic bodies. Some eighteen months after his father's remains were moved to Roskilde, Cnut had Edmund Ironside's corpse interred at the periphery of Wessex; a few years after that, he moved Ælfheah's relics to Canterbury. The Encomiast, by depicting Swein's reburial as an intentional and honourable event, offered a translation account that was consistent with Cnut's subsequent history of respectfully but deliberately moving problematic bodies.

The Legacy of Conquest: Bury St Edmunds and Assandun Minster

One of Cnut's first acts as king of England was to kill a broad swathe of the Anglo-Saxon nobility, the political leaders who had led the military resistance against the Danes.[46] While there are no contemporary accounts

43 Ibid., 16; Lawson, *Cnut*, 89–91.
44 Thietmar, *Chronik*, 446.
45 *Encomium*, 14–15, quoted above, n. 22. See also Gerchow, "Prayers for Cnut," 220.
46 ASC 1017 CDEF.

of how exactly these individuals were dispatched, Hemming's cartulary of the later eleventh century described Eadric Streona, the most infamous of these casualties, suffering a humiliating death: "At the order of King Cnut, he was killed and shamefully thrown outside the walls of London; he was not even judged worthy of a sepulchre."[47] The fate of Eadric's corpse is consistent with the treatment of criminals' remains in the period, and it is likely that other victims of Cnut's purge in 1017 were formally condemned and executed as traitors.[48] Just a few years earlier, Cnut had mutilated a group of English hostages by cutting off their hands, ears, and noses – mutilations reserved for serious offenders under Anglo-Saxon law.[49] Whether Cnut was deliberately evoking the signifying punishments of English legislation or simply seeking to humiliate his opponents in life and death, these instances attest to the new king's willingness to be ruthless with the bodies of his enemies.

It is Cnut's history of mutilation and desecration that makes his comparatively respectful treatment of Anglo-Saxon royal bodies all the more remarkable. Edmund Ironside was given an honourable tomb in a prominent mausoleum, and it seems that Cnut regarded his rival's death as an opportunity to make an outward show of reconciliation with the displaced dynasty.[50] This approach was likewise applied to the remains of more distant Anglo-Saxon royalty, particularly the native saints whose achievements helped shape England's political and spiritual history. Cnut's best known act of patronage for a royal saint was his refoundation of the East Anglian abbey at Bury (or *Beodericisworth*), the cult centre of St Edmund. Like St Ælfheah, Edmund was quickly designated a martyr after his death at the hands of Vikings, and his cult was soon embraced by both the harried English population and newly settled Scandinavians.[51] Cnut was credited with refounding the community in 1020 and overseeing its reconsecration in 1032.[52]

47 "Jubente Cnut rege, occisus, atque extra murum Lundonie ignominiose projectus, nec etiam sepulture judicatus est dignus"; Hearne, *Hemingi Chartularium*, 281.

48 Gates, "Eadric *Streona*'s Execution"; Baxter, *Earls of Mercia*, 28–9.

49 ASC CDEF 1014. Compare II Cnut 30.4–30.5, which was drawn from earlier legislation: Whitelock, "Wulfstan *Cantor*," 84–7.

50 Cnut also attempted to reconcile with some of the families whose members were executed in 1017; see for example Baxter, *Earls of Mercia*, 164–5. Note that the executions of 1017 took place some time after Edmund's funeral.

51 Ridyard, *Royal Saints*, 211–18; Finlay, "Chronology, Genealogy, and Conversion," 50–7; and above, chapter 5.

52 The earliest reference to Cnut's involvement in the refoundation is a pair of short annals which probably originated at Bury; they record that Cnut ordered the refoundation of

Although his role in Bury's transformation may have been exaggerated by later authors, it is clear that Cnut was a benefactor who helped increase the foundation's wealth and prominence.[53] As with his patronage of Ælfheah's cult, Cnut's attention to Edmund's community counterbalanced the damage his family and countrymen had inflicted in the region. East Anglia had suffered during Swein's invasions, and Bury endured its share of ravaging and demands for tribute.[54] By the twelfth century, English chroniclers drew a direct correlation between Cnut's patronage and his father's offences against the community, with some authors even attributing Swein's sudden death to the long-dead Edmund. According to this tradition, the saint appeared to Swein in a vision as the king was meeting with his counsellors:

> He became frightened and began to yell very loudly: "Help," he said, "comrades, help! Look, St Edmund is coming to kill me!" And, while he was saying this, he was fiercely stabbed by the saint with a spear and fell from the horse on which he sat, and, tormented with great pain from that moment until evening, he finished his life with a miserable death.[55]

---

the monastery in 1020 and oversaw its consecration in 1032. These notices are preserved in two Bury manuscripts: Vatican Library, Reginensis Latini MS 12, produced in the second quarter of the eleventh century; and Oxford, Corpus Christi College 197, fol. 105r, where the annals are written in a hand of ca 1100. Dumville, *English Caroline Script*, 31–4; Gransden, "Cult of Mary," 632–3; Ker, *Catalogue*, 430. Narrative accounts of Cnut's refoundation and consecration of the monastery include *De Miraculis Sancti Eadmundi*, 47; William of Malmesbury, *GR* ii.181.4; JW 643–4 (an interpolation by a Bury chronicler). Compare also S 980, a possibly spurious grant of privileges by Cnut to St Edmund's.

53 Questions about Cnut's role in the refoundation are raised by Gransden, "Origins of Bury," 9–16, but see also Gransden, "Cult of Mary," 630n14 for a revised assessment based on the evidence of the Vatican manuscript; above, n. 52. Compare also Dumville, *English Caroline Script*, 33–4 and 38–43; Ridyard, *Royal Saints*, 225.

54 In 1004, Swein ravaged Norwich and Thetford, and neighbouring Bury must have been affected; he returned to East Anglia in 1013, and the population quickly submitted to his authority: ASC CDEF 1004 and 1013. Bury's dealings with Swein – particularly their refusal to pay tribute – are detailed in *De Miraculis Sancti Eadmundi*, 33–9.

55 "Expauit et nimio cum clamore uociferari cepit: 'Succurrite,' inquiens, 'commilitiones, succurrite, ecce sanctus Eadmundus me uenit occidere,' et, hec dicendo, acriter a sancto confossus cuspide de emissario cui insederat decidit, et usque ad noctis crepusculum magno cruciatus tormento… miserabili morte vitam finiuit"; JW 476–7. Versions of this story also appeared in *De Miraculis Sancti Eadmundi*, 32–7; William of Malmesbury, *GR* ii.179.1 and *GP* ii.74.28–9; Symeon of Durham, *Historia Regum*, 145–6; Orderic Vitalis, *Ecclesiastical History* I, 156; Snorri Sturluson, *Heimskringla*, 251–2. For an overview of these accounts, see Demidoff, "Death of Swein Forkbeard."

This account seems to have originated at Bury and may have emerged within a few years of Swein's death.[56] Even his son's patronage did not stop its promulgation, and by the 1120s, William of Malmesbury could assert that "Cnut knew this story, and therefore, there was nothing he did not do to placate the saint."[57] The community did in fact remember Cnut as a good ruler and generous patron, who restored to Bury its lands and rights along with other gifts – despite all expectations to the contrary.[58] However, it was his family's wartime actions in the region that made such acts of reconciliation necessary. According to the *De Miraculis Sancti Eadmundi*, the community blatantly refused to render tribute to Swein and enlisted their saint's aid against him.[59] Edmund and his community had endured generations' worth of Scandinavian aggression by the time Cnut came to power, and the saint's reputation as an enemy of Vikings meant that his cult might prove troublesome to the Danish regime. Like Ælfheah, Edmund needed to be made an ally, and Cnut's sponsorship of the monastery's refoundation in 1020 functioned as a necessary act of reconciliation with the saint and his community.

Cnut made a second effort to this effect the same year, also in East Anglia, when he founded Assandun Minster on the site of his 1016 victory against Edmund Ironside. The Anglo-Saxon Chronicle reported simply:

> In this year the king and Earl Thorkell went to Assandun, and Archbishop Wulfstan, and other bishops, and also abbots and many monks, and they consecrated the minster at Assandun.[60]

56 The earliest account was preserved in Bury's *De Miraculis Sancti Eadmundi*; the text was compiled in the early 1090s, but the chapters that contain this episode seem to be adapted from a work composed during Æthelred's lifetime: Gransden, "Composition and Authorship," 26–8; and Lawson, *Cnut*, 143 for a possible early date for this legend

57 "Sciebat haec Cnuto, ideoque nichil non effecit ut Sancto blandiretur"; *GP* ii.74.29. See also: *GR* ii.181.4–5; Ridyard, *Royal Saints*, 216–17; Rollason, *Saints and Relics*, 157, Lawson, *Cnut*, 143.

58 *De Miraculis Sancti Eadmundi*, 46–7.

59 This initiated the chain of events that led to Swein's supernatural death; *De Miraculis Sancti Eadmundi*, 33–9.

60 "On þisan geare for se cyng 7 Þurkyl eorl to Assandune, 7 Wulfstan arcebiscop, 7 oðre biscopas, 7 eac abbodas 7 manege munecas, 7 gehalgodan þæt mynster æt Assandune"; ASC D 1020, with abbreviated versions in ASC CE 1020.

The twelfth-century F-manuscript offered a bit more information:

> In this year Cnut went to Assandun and had a minster built there of stone and mortar, for the souls of the men who had been slain there, and gave it to a priest of his who was called Stigand.[61]

The exact location of Assandun has not been definitively identified, but there is little reason to doubt that a stone-and-mortar church existed on the site at the time Manuscript F was written.[62] Despite the cursory attention the event received in the Chronicle, the 1020 gathering at Assandun seems to have been a major event, with the kingdom's ecclesiastical elite in attendance.[63] The prominence of the English Archbishop Wulfstan and the Danish Earl Thorkell in the annal gives the impression that the kingdom's two populations had reconciled at the formerly divisive site, where they could now come together in prayer. William of Malmesbury claimed that both English and Danish nobles granted gifts on the occasion, specifying that the king installed clergy who "would pray to God for the souls of those who had fallen there."[64] Although the eleventh-century texts were not explicit about the pious motives that twelfth-century chroniclers attributed to Cnut, the descriptions of Assandun's foundation mirror the unifying rhetoric of Cnut's 1020 letter to his English subjects, in which he pledged to be a "loyal lord" so that "we might all together – through God's mercy – come to the joy of the heavenly kingdom."[65] At Assandun, as at

61 "On þisum geare he ferde to Assandune 7 let timbrian ðar an mynster of stane 7 lime far ðare manna sawle ðe ðar ofslagene wæran 7 gief hit his anum preoste þas nama was Stigand. Hoc anno perrexit ad Assandune et fecit ibi edificare ęcclesiam de lapidibus et cemento pro animabus omnium ibi occisorum"; ASC F 1020. ASC F claimed that Cnut built (*timbrian*, *edificare*) the minster in 1020, whereas ASC CD reported that it was consecrated (*gehalgodan*) in that year; it is unclear whether the visit marked the beginning or a final stage of the building project. Stigand's association with Assandun Minster is discussed by Hart, *Danelaw*, 563–4.

62 The most viable locations for the site are Ashingdon and Ashdon: both are in Essex, which fell within the earldom of East Anglia from 1017. For the debate, see: Rodwell, "*Assandun* and Its Memorial Church"; Hart, *The Danelaw*, 138 and 553–65; Townend, "*Assandūn* and *Assatún*."

63 Rodwell, "*Assandun* and Its Memorial Church," 142–3.

64 "Deo suplicarent pro animabus ibi occisorum"; *GR* ii.181.4.

65 "Hold hlaford"; "þæt we magan 7 moton ealle samod þurh þæs ecean Godes mildheortnesse 7 his halgena þingrædene to heofena rices myrhðe becuman"; Cnut 1020 2 and 20. See also Treharne, *Living through Conquest*, 22–7; Sheppard, *Families of the King*, 113–16.

Bury and in his 1020 proclamation, Cnut could shape a new identity for himself: rather than being immortalized as a Viking invader, he could now be remembered as a Christian king who sought to make pious amends for a bloody invasion.

Nevertheless, there were three major differences between Assandun and Bury. First, Assandun was an entirely new foundation, whereas Bury was well established. While Cnut had to negotiate his place in the history of St Edmund's, he could design Assandun from the outset to serve the interests of the new regime.[66] Second, Cnut was credited with lavish patronage at Bury and with the establishment of its new Benedictine community, but Assandun seems to have been a more modest foundation with a smaller endowment, entrusted to a priest of the royal household rather than a community of reformed monks.[67] Despite its status as a royal minster, Assandun evidently lacked the means and autonomy to exert much political influence. Third, there was no central relic or grave to serve as a focal point for the minster, as there was at Bury. Although the English nobility was decimated at Assandun, Edmund Ironside survived the fight and lived to make a treaty with Cnut; accordingly, even if the battlefield became a place of pilgrimage or housed impromptu memorials for the dead, there was no emblematic body for the conquered population to rally behind.[68] At Cnut's minster, reverence for the battle's dead could remain abstract. Together, these factors seem to have kept Assandun a minor foundation, notable primarily for its association with its royal founder.[69] As he did elsewhere, Cnut took charge of this potentially dangerous site, treated it with pious respect, and minimized its influence in the political landscape.

This is not to suggest that Cnut played down his 1016 victory at Assandun. On the contrary, the battle was central to constructing his legitimacy. In addition to demonstrating his military dominance over his English rival, Assandun catalysed the treaty that split England between Cnut and Edmund Ironside – and, by implication, established Cnut as Edmund's

66 It is not impossible that Cnut's minster appropriated an existing structure, but this seems unlikely: Rodwell, "*Assandun* and Its Memorial Church," 148.

67 The modest size of Assandun was noted by William of Malmesbury, *GR* ii.181.4; and see also Rodwell, "*Assandun* and Its Memorial Church," 147 and 155. For the comparative prestige of Benedictine monks, see Cubitt, "Images of St Peter."

68 See *Encomium* 28–9, for bodies buried on the Assandun battlefield after the battle; and below, chapter 7.

69 It is possible that the minster did not survive long after Cnut's reign: Rodwell, "*Assandun* and Its Memorial Church," 155; Hart, *Danelaw*, 564.

legal heir.[70] Even if Cnut sought to minimize or compensate for the blood spilled in the battle, its political outcome had to be remembered. Establishing the minster in 1020 was an initial step. Twelve years later, two additional events recalled the battle and its aftermath. One was his visit to Edmund Ironside's tomb at Glastonbury on St Andrew's Day, 30 November 1032, the sixteenth anniversary of his death. In emphasizing his purported kinship with his erstwhile rival and granting gifts and privileges to the foundation that housed his remains, Cnut evidently used this visit to emphasize his lawful, hereditary accession.[71] The other event was the consecration of Bury, which was not held on St Edmund's mass day, as might be expected, but on 18 October 1032, the sixteenth anniversary of the Battle of Assandun.[72] By linking the refoundation of Bury with his decisive battle for England, Cnut used the occasion to recall two Edmunds, each defeated by Scandinavian armies, nearly a century and a half apart. Thus, in the course of six weeks, Cnut engaged in two acts of ecclesiastical patronage that commemorated his victory at Assandun, honoured English kings who resisted Scandinavian incursions, and made amends for past offences against St Edmund, his community, and the casualties of conquest.

The overall message at Assandun and Bury seems to have been one of reconciliation, not dominance. Although they could conceivably have been transformed into monuments to conquest, it appears that Cnut's intent at both locations was to foster unity among his new subjects. By 1032, this may have been done with an eye towards the future of his dynasty.[73] Yet even as early as 1020, it seems that these acts of patronage were designed to buttress Cnut's claims to legitimate Christian authority and prevent potentially dangerous sites from becoming political liabilities. The Assandun battlefield, now commemorated with a royal minster entrusted to a royal chaplain, could hardly be evoked as evidence of Danish cruelty or heathenism. The relics of St Edmund, housed in a new foundation and tended by monks placed there by the king, could not easily become a mascot for opponents of the new regime. At Bury and Assandun, Cnut was no longer just the victor of a bloody conquest or a persecutor of St Edmund, but a pious patron and Christian king devoted to righting past wrongs.

---

70 Above, chapter 3.
71 Above, chapter 3.
72 Dumville, *English Caroline Script*, 41; Lawson, *Cnut*, 143.
73 This point is considered further below.

Cnut and the West Saxon Royal Past

Edmund was not the only royal saint with whom Cnut was concerned. The generation before the Danish conquest saw two English saints rise to prominence: Edward the Martyr and Edith of Wilton, Æthelred's saintly half-siblings. As individuals who had died in the recent past, their histories had not been lost to legend, as St Edmund's had, and as members of the West Saxon dynasty, their memories were inherently political. To date, Æthelred himself had been the most prominent patron of both cults, evoking his kinship ties to win support – earthly and divine – for his increasingly harried regime.[74] Once Cnut became king, however, the saints' relics would have become reminders of the legitimate spiritual authority of their deposed dynasty and, like the bodies of other English saints, had the potential to become rallying points for resistance.[75] In a post-conquest environment, it would have been risky for Cnut to ignore the political potential of Edward and Edith's cults or to leave their monastic custodians to their own devices. At the same time, any perceived offence against these West Saxon saints on Cnut's part would have recalled his family's tumultuous relations with the displaced native dynasty. Accordingly, rather than trying to extinguish their cults or disenfranchise their communities, the king harnessed the saints' political and spiritual potential. Cnut claimed to be the rightful heir to the West Saxon dynasty by virtue of his treaty with Edmund Ironside, and by identifying himself as Edmund's adoptive brother, he also became the honorary kinsmen of these royal saints.[76]

The challenge Cnut faced was to exploit the saints' authority without diluting his own claim to royal legitimacy. In Edward's case, this may have been accomplished in part by recalling his martyrdom as part of a broader narrative of conquest.[77] In 1018, Cnut's laws decreed that by the agreement of the *witan*, "St Edward's mass-day must be celebrated throughout England on 18 March," the anniversary of his death.[78] While it is debated

74 Ridyard, *Royal Saints*, 152–71.

75 The relics of some prominent Anglo-Saxon saints filled a comparable role after the Norman Conquest: Ridyard, "Post-Conquest Attitudes," 182.

76 Cnut's fraternal claims are discussed above, chapter 3; and see also: William of Malmesbury, *GR* ii. ii.181.2 and 184.2; *De Antiquitate*, 132–3; Rollason, "Murdered Royal Saints," 16.

77 Rollason, "Murdered Royal Saints," 17–18; Stafford, "Royal Promises," 181–2.

78 "And sancte eadwardes mæssedæg. witan habbað gecoran þæt man freolsian sceal. ofer eall englaland. on. xv. kalendas. Aprilis"; Cnut 1018 14.6, edited by Kennedy, "Cnut's Law Code of 1018." The decree was repeated a few years later in I Cnut 17.1.

whether this mandate originated during Cnut's reign, it is significant that the king included Edward in an early law code which mentioned no other English saint by name.[79] Celebration of this particular martyrdom drew attention to the succession dispute of the 970s and Æthelred's role in his brother's death: he may have been remembered as complicit, if not for the regicide itself then for his inaction after the fact.[80] If Æthelred could be construed in Cnut's reign as an enemy of the saint and the beneficiary of his martyrdom, then his eventual deposition by Danish kings could be portrayed as just. By this logic, Cnut's accession restored royal dignity to a kingdom whose previous ruler was contemptuous of human and divine law.

Edward's cult was not used exclusively to tarnish Æthelred's reputation, however. The saint's relics also assumed a new ideological message under the Danish regime, as Cnut sought to honour the remains while defusing any political threat they may have posed. This objective seems to have been achieved through the division and dissemination of Edward's body, for several foundations began claiming portions of the saint's relics after the Danish conquest. Cnut was specifically credited as a grantor of the saint's relics in two later monastic registers: that of Abingdon, where Edward's relics were brought in as part of a wondrous (*mirifice*) translation during Cnut's reign; and of Westminster, where a catalogue of Cnut's gifts lists Edward's relics among a substantial cache of saintly bones (which also included St Ælfheah's finger).[81] At Leominster, there appears to have been particular interest in Edward in the decades immediately following Æthelred's death, conceivably because his relics were acquired during that period; his cult, which flourished there in the twelfth century, may have

79 Patrick Wormald argues that this decree originated with Cnut and that its appearance in V Æthelred 16 is a later interpolation: "Æthelred the Lawmaker," 53–4; *Making of English Law*, 334–5 and 343–4. Others scholars are sceptical of Wormald's interpretation, notably Simon Keynes and Susan Ridyard: Keynes, *Diplomas*, 171; Ridyard, *Royal Saints*, 157. See also Rollason, "Murdered Royal Saints," 18. Unlike Cnut 18, the decree in I Cnut 17.1 required St Dunstan's feast to be celebrated as well.

80 Above, chapter 5.

81 For Abingdon's twelfth-century accounts of Cnut's patronage, see: Hudson, *History of the Church of Abingdon*, 182–3 and 358–9; Stevenson, *Chronicon Monasterii de Abingdon*, 442–3; Kelly, *Charters of Abingdon* I, xlii–xliii. Westminster's relic list was compiled in the fifteenth century by John Flete, *History of Westminster*, 70. Ailred of Rievaulx's account of the servant who confused Edward the Martyr and Edward the Confessor may indicate that the cult of the former was already well established at Westminster in the twelfth century; above, chapter 1.

been established by a formal translation or gift during Cnut's reign.[82] Edward was also the latest saint included in Exeter's eleventh-century relic list, and additional bits of the martyr would later be claimed by Durham, York, and St Albans.[83] By the early twelfth century, William of Malmesbury reported that Edward's relics were housed at Abingdon and Leominster, with only one body part left at Shaftesbury in his own day: the saint's miraculously animated lung.[84]

While much of the evidence for Cnut's division of Edward's remains is circumstantial or based on later sources, there are compelling reasons for attributing this dissemination to royal initiative. First, the nuns of Shaftesbury had lobbied to acquire the saint's body, and his cult brought the community prestige and prosperity.[85] There is little precedent for medieval monasteries simply giving away bodily relics on such a scale, and the removal of such valuable spiritual commodities therefore suggests that an influential outsider was involved.[86] Second, while the relics of foreign saints often circulated as fragments in Anglo-Saxon England, native saints were almost invariably enshrined with their remains intact. Unlike their Continental counterparts,

---

82 Edward received particular attention in a prayer book produced at Leominster between 1016 and 1047, with computational materials for the period 1029 through 1047 (now in two parts, BL Cotton Nero A.ii and BL Cotton Galba A.xiv). Edward is listed in the prayerbook's calendar and litany, and a prayer to the saint is included in the collection: Muir, *Pre-Conquest Prayer Book*; Hillaby, "Early Christian Leominster," 628–41; Dumville, "Late Anglo-Saxon Liturgical Manuscripts," 46–7. Edward's relic cult at Leominster is discussed by Hillaby and Hillaby, *Leominster Minster*, 25–7; and the relics' later transmission from Leominster to Reading is addressed by Bethell, "Twelfth-Century Relic Collection," 65–6.

83 An overview of the dating and manuscript tradition of the earliest Exeter relic lists is provided by Conner, *Anglo-Saxon Exeter*, 171–4, with a discussion of Edward's connection to the foundation during his lifetime at 29–31. Edward is the first English saint listed in Durham's twelfth-century relic list, and its fourteenth-century list specifically claims a piece of his rib; a fragment of his bone is listed in the thirteenth-century relic list in the York Gospels; and he was included in the fourteenth-century relic list from St Albans. Battiscombe, *Relics of Cuthbert*, 113; Fowler, *Abbey of Durham*, 428–9; Raine, *Fabric Rolls*, 151; Stevenson, "Yorkshire Surveys," 2; Riley, *Gesta Abbatum*, 543; Keynes, *Diplomas*, 167n53, Keynes, "Shaftesbury Abbey," 54.

84 William of Malmesbury, *GP* ii.86.6.

85 Ridyard, *Royal Saints*, 169–71.

86 Edward's cult at Shaftesbury survived the Norman Conquest, as attested by the Latin *passio* produced ca 1100, and the monastery itself continued to flourish despite the apparent loss of relics: Fell, *Edward, King and Martyr*, xx; Ridyard, *Royal Saints*, 171–5; Foot, *Veiled Women* II, 175–7; but also compare Hayward, "Translation-Narratives," 87–9.

English foundations were invested in preserving the integrity of saintly bodies and there were relatively few exceptions to this trend.[87] Saints who had been dismembered at their death, like the seventh-century kings Oswald and Edwin, might have their relics housed in two different foundations, but there is no indication that Edward's body had been decapitated or otherwise mutilated when it was recovered after the regicide.[88] A more compelling parallel dates to the reign of Edgar, when the king reportedly divided St Botulf's relics among three disputing foundations.[89] It is not impossible that Edward was the subject of a comparable division under Cnut's supervision, in which distribution of relics was presented as a way to spread the saint's influence more widely across the kingdom.

However, if such a dissemination occurred, its logistics more closely recall the translations of Edmund Ironside and Ælfheah. Edward's relics were brought to foundations that were unlikely to become centres of opposition to the Danish regime. Still, the body was treated with enough respect that Edward's memory and sanctity would have continued to be celebrated, even once he was removed in pieces from his original cult centre. The communities with the most substantial claims to have acquired Edward's relics during Cnut's lifetime – Abingdon, Exeter, Leominster, and Westminster – were all favoured foundations, and none possessed the bodies of any other West Saxon king at the time. Exeter and Leominster each had long histories of royal patronage but were located towards the kingdom's periphery, where they would be unlikely to become sites of political insurgence. Abingdon, though more central, was a considerable distance from Shaftesbury and was best known for its cult of St Vincent, of which Cnut was a lavish patron.[90] Westminster's royal residence rose to

87 Rollason, "Lists of Saints' Resting-Places," 80–2.

88 Yorke, *Nunneries*, 119. After the battlefield deaths of Edwin (d. 632) and Oswald (d. 642), Edwin's head was kept at York and his body buried at Whitby; while Oswald's head was brought to Lindisfarne, his arms to Bamburgh, and the rest of his body to Bardney: Bede, *HE* II.20, III.11–12, and III.24. The three sites that housed Oswald's head, arm, and remaining body parts were cited in the list of saints' resting places: Liebermann, *Heiligen Englands*, 9.

89 Rollason, "Lists of Saints' Resting-Places," 80–2. An account of Edgar's division of Botulf's relics was recorded in the late eleventh or early twelfth century in British Library, MS Harley 3097, edited in Birch, *Liber Vitae*, 286–90 at 288. There is also a possibility that Edgar divided St Vincent's relics between Abingdon and Glastonbury: Irvine, "Bones of Contention," 127.

90 For St Vincent's cult at Abingdon, see: Liebermann, *Heiligen Englands*, 15; Irvine, "Bones of Contention," 126–9. For Cnut's involvement, see: Hudson, *History of the Church of Abingdon*, 182–3 and 358–9; Stevenson, *Chronicon Monasterii de Abingdon*, 443.

prominence under Cnut, serving as an alternative to the West Saxon palace complex beside St Paul's; the record of his relic donations suggests that Cnut was a welcome patron for the small monastic community there.[91]

Finally, a few tentative observations about date. The Abingdon Chronicle placed the account of Edward's translation around the year 1034; Cnut's only authentic charters issued at Exeter date to 1031; and the references to Edward at Leominster can be dated after ca 1029.[92] Westminster was prominent enough to house Harold Harefoot's tomb in the 1040s, and it is likely that it had become London's preferred royal residence by the time Cnut died.[93] It would seem that Cnut's interactions with these foundations were concentrated toward the end of his reign, the same period in which he visited Edmund Ironside's tomb at Glastonbury and oversaw the consecration of St Edmund's new abbey at Bury.[94] This flurry of patronage coincided with an increased interest in imperial iconography, as exemplified by Cnut's portrait in the frontispiece of New Minster's *Liber Vitae*, produced in the early 1030s.[95]

One explanation for this timing is that Cnut sought to reinforce the legitimate authority of his dynasty just as his and Æthelred's sons were coming of age, to remind his subjects of his brotherly treaty with Edmund. If the king was distributing Edward's relics in this period, the ideological implications would be even more pronounced.[96] On the one hand, Cnut

91 Mason, *Westminster and Its People*, 11–12. The early history of Westminster is outlined above, chapter 1.

92 The Abingdon Chronicle included the account after two charters of Cnut, S 973 and S 964; the former is dated 1034: Hudson, *History of Abingdon*, 178–83 and 356–9; Keynes, "Cnut's Earls," 51; but compare Irvine, "Bones of Contention," 128. Cnut is credited with two other grants to Abingdon, but their authenticity is less certain: these are S 964, dated 1032; and S 967 dated 1033. The Exeter charters are S 963 and S 971; their authenticity is discussed by Keynes, "Cnut's Earls," 50. The Leominster prayerbook may have been produced in the late 1020s or early 1030s, based on the computational materials; above, n. 82.

93 Mason, *Westminster and Its People*, 10–12; and also Harvey, *Westminster and Its Estates*, 22–4, for the foundation's increasing prosperity between ca 959 and 1042.

94 The visit to Glastonbury and consecration of Bury are discussed above. There were also claims that Cnut reconfirmed the privileges of St Paul's, London, sometime between 1033 and 1035, although the confirmation is preserved in a writ of dubious authenticity: S 992; Harmer, *Writs*, 239–42; Lawson, *Cnut*, 66 and 155. It is not impossible, however, that Cnut sought to extend an olive branch to St Paul's in the 1030s in anticipation of a future succession dispute.

95 For imperial iconography and allusions, see: Gerchow, "Prayers for Cnut," 226–8; Karkov, *Ruler Portraits*, 136–8; Tyler, "Treasure and Artifice," 250–2; Treharne, *Living through Conquest*, 29–43.

96 Ridyard, *Royal Saints*, 168–9.

could portray himself as the patron and protector of a West Saxon royal saint, spreading the cult to increase Edward's glory, signal his respect for his Anglo-Saxon predecessors, and confirm his own credentials as a Christian ruler. On the other, by disseminating pieces of the saint's body to communities across the kingdom, he ensured that West Saxon sympathizers could not find a convincing focal point for their cause at Shaftesbury; the foundation's status as a royal cult centre would surely have been diminished by the fragmentation and dissemination of their saint.[97] Furthermore, by bringing Edward's relics back into the public eye and making them more widely accessible, attention would have been drawn once again to the treacherous circumstances of the saint's martyrdom and Æthelred's succession.[98] Perhaps Cnut considered it prudent to promote the saint again as the question of succession was becoming increasingly topical.

Cnut's interactions with Edward reflect the perceived value and danger of a prominent royal corpse and offer another example in which Cnut respectfully minimized a problematic body. This strategy likewise characterized his treatment of Edward's sister, Edith of Wilton, although his approach to her relics was quite different. Edith's cult, like Edward's, had been heavily promoted by Æthelred, and Cnut once again assumed his predecessor's role as royal patron. In the *Vita Edithe*, composed by the hagiographer Goscelin ca 1080 at the request of the Wilton nuns, Cnut was remembered as a regular visitor to the monastery who commissioned an intricate golden reliquary for the saint after she miraculously saved him from a shipwreck.[99] Despite his foreign origins, according to Goscelin's account, Cnut "was bound to her by so much love and affection, as if he himself were her brother Æthelred or nephew Edmund Ironside."[100]

Just a few decades later, however, William of Malmesbury would present the king's relationship with Edith in a rather different light. According to the *Gesta Pontificum*, Cnut publicly challenged Edith's sanctity during a visit to Wilton, saying that "he would never believe that the daughter of King Edgar was a saint, since Edgar was a vicious man, a great slave to lust, and more like a tyrant to his subjects."[101] To prove the point, Cnut ordered

97 Rollason, "Shrines of Saints," 32.

98 Compare above, n. 78.

99 Wilmart, "Édith," 278–81; Hollis, *Writing the Wilton Women*, 4.

100 "Tanto ei affecto et deuocione erat addictus acsi ipse uel frater Ethelredus uel nepos esset Edmundus"; Wilmart, "Édith," 278. See also: Ridyard, *Royal Saints*, 140–75; Yorke, "Women in Edgar's Life," 150–2.

101 "Numquam se crediturum filiam regis Edgari sanctam esse, qui uitiis detitus maximeque libidinis seruus in subiectos propior tiranno fuisset"; *GP* ii.87.7.

her tomb to be opened, only to have the saint rise out of her grave and attack him – an event made all the more horrifying by the fact that her body was not incorrupt.[102] The king promptly fell into a deathly faint, and when he recovered, he acknowledged Edith's sanctity and gave thanks that, "though severely punished, he had lived to repent."[103] This episode is jarring when set beside William's account of Cnut's pious patronage of English cults in the *Gesta Regum*. Given the author's focus on local communities in the *Gesta Pontificum*, it is conceivable that the story originated at Wilton itself, even though it did not appear in Edith's official hagiography.[104] William evidently did not feel the need to exercise restraint on this topic, as Goscelin may have, and perhaps he envisioned Cnut's lavish reliquary as penance for having insulted the saint.[105]

Notwithstanding Goscelin's insistence that Cnut had been a good ruler and patron to Wilton, William's account suggests an uneasy relationship between the Danish king and the West Saxon saint. The similarities between this episode and St Edmund's lethal attack on Swein are striking, even if miraculously punished sceptics and ill-advised openings of saints' tombs were commonplace in medieval *vitae*.[106] Maybe Cnut's family history informed the story of his early hostility to the community, for Swein had plundered and burned Wilton in 1003; it is possible that later authors conflated or confused father and son.[107] However, it is noteworthy that William of Malmesbury had Cnut identify Edgar as a tyrant and accuse him of scandalous impiety. Such characterizations were used with some frequency in the tenth and eleventh centuries to discredit deposed rulers: they were applied by Harthacnut to Harold Harefoot and by William of Normandy to Harold Godwineson; they may have been directed at Edward the Martyr by his assassins; and Cnut himself denounced Æthelred's behaviour in comparable

102 In the preceding passage, William recounted St Dunstan's dismay at finding Edith's body reduced to dust, except for her finger, which he had blessed during her lifetime, and her abdomen, which had always been free from lust: *GP* ii.87.6.

103 "Quanuis seuere castigatus, penitentiae reseruatus sit"; *GP* ii.87.9. See also Trelarne, *Living through Conquest*, 39–40.

104 Compare *GR* ii.181.4–5. William's familiarity with local traditions is discussed by Thompson and Winterbottom in William of Malmesbury, *GP* II, xl–xliv; Gransden, *Historical Writing*, 174–5.

105 As suggested by Lawson, *Cnut*, 157; Yorke, "Women in Edgar's Life," 154–5.

106 Compare for instance, Abbo, "Life of Edmund," 85.

107 ASC CDEF 1003, JW 454–5.

terms.[108] In the *Gesta Pontificum*, Cnut was portrayed as a conqueror who challenged the authority of the West Saxon house by publicly denouncing the dynasty's patriarch and violating the remains of his saintly daughter. The force with which Edith's tomb was unsealed – it was smashed (*effractus*), according to William – evokes the violence of conquest, with Cnut attempting to unseat yet another member of Æthelred's family.

The issue of royal legitimacy was a genuine concern during Cnut's reign, and it is surely significant that physical desecration figured into William's account of inter-dynastic tensions. Yet the literary purpose of this episode was to praise Cnut for repudiating his mistaken beliefs about Edith's sanctity and fully embracing her cult. Perhaps Goscelin's unwavering portrayal of the king's love and devotion was likewise intended to dispel rumours of early hostility toward the saint or her community. The reliquary Cnut provided certainly seems to have earned him respect at Wilton in the long run, and the gift was consistent with his efforts to ingratiate himself with other English foundations; he reportedly commissioned a comparable reliquary for St Vincent at Abingdon.[109] In both instances, the reliquary would have forged a link between Cnut and the saint, as supplicants would be inevitably reminded of the king's devotion as they approached the relics. At Abingdon, this connection was made explicit by an inscription which credited Cnut by name, and it is conceivable that Edith's shrine was similarly inscribed.[110] Yet at Wilton, Cnut's generosity had more weighty political implications, for the remains of the West Saxon princess were now contained and concealed in an object unambiguously associated with the Danish king. Edith's reliquary at once enhanced and obscured her remains, memorializing Cnut's piety while illustrating his power over a West Saxon royal body.

Certainly, not all of Cnut's encounters with saints in England were driven by the politics of conquest; his participation in these (and other) relic

108 These examples are all discussed elsewhere. For Cnut's insinuations about Æthelred, see Stafford, "Royal Promises," 181–2; and further below.

109 For Edith's reliquary, see: Wilmart, "Édith," 280–1; Hollis, *Writing the Wilton Women*, 78–9; Foot, *Veiled Women* II, 224; Heslop, "*De Luxe* Manuscripts," 186. For Vincent's, see: Hudson, *History of the Church of Abingdon*, 176–9; Stevenson, *Chronicon Monasterii de Abingdon*, 443.

110 The inscription began: "King Cnut and also Queen Ælfgifu [i.e., Emma] ordered the casting of this reliquary" [Rex Cnut hanc thecam necnon Ælfgiua regina / Cudere iusserunt], with an addendum that this was done under Æthelwine, who was abbot from 1016 through 1030: Hudson, *History of the Church of Abingdon*, 176–9.

translations was surely motivated by a variety of factors.[111] However, the hagiographical motif of violent interaction with a West Saxon royal saint seems an apt metaphor for conquest.[112] Perhaps early twelfth-century interest in Cnut's encounters with royal bodies reflects the concerns of a kingdom adjusting to Norman rule, with antagonistic encounters of the previous century standing in for later political tensions. Yet if Cnut was responsible for the division of Edward's body, as I have suggested, legends about his attack on Edith's shrine may have been rooted in genuine concerns about the saint's safety and integrity. If he had distributed her relics as he did Edward's or translated them as he did Ælfheah's, the effect on her community could have been devastating. Significantly, though, Edith and Edward survived the Danish regime, despite their high-profile West Saxon identities.[113] Under Cnut's supervision, they could be portrayed as emblems of unity; like Sts Edmund and Ælfheah, their relics offered opportunities for reconciliation and allegiance between the foreign king and his English subjects. It is telling that Cnut died at Edward's home foundation of Shaftesbury in 1035. Still, even as he nurtured their cults, the king appropriated these saints' influence for his own ends. His patronage allowed him a degree of control over Edward and Edith's legacies, and his dealings with their relics reinforced the thoroughness of Danish authority. In the institutional memories of the cults' later custodians, as in Cnut's own day, these royal remains became part of the narrative of conquest.

Conclusions

Many of the sources considered in this chapter were written well after Cnut's death and can offer only a limited view of how his conquest and reign were perceived by contemporaries. For authors writing in the Norman era, the Danish invasion might serve as a commentary on the more topical conquest of 1066 and its aftermath.[114] Accounts of pre-Norman royal

111 Cnut was reportedly involved with the translations of Sts Botulf, Iurmin, Felix, Mildrid, and Wystan: Lawson, *Cnut*, 139, 146, 152, and 155; Biddle, "Cult of Saints," 18; Dumville, *English Caroline Script*, 41–3; Rollason, *Saints and Relics*, 157–8; Rollason, *Mildrith Legend*, 57–8; Stafford, "Royal Promises," 183; Hayward, "Translation-Narratives," 85.

112 For a similar phenomenon after the Norman Conquest, see: Ridyard, "Post-Conquest Attitudes"; Abou-el-Haj, "Post-Conquest Appropriation," 179–81.

113 For the longevity of these cults, see Ridyard, *Royal Saints*, 171.

114 Townsend, "Anglo-Latin Hagiography," 412; Gates, "Eadric *Streona*'s Execution."

benefactors might bolster campaigns for ecclesiastical patronage or lend a monastic community more clout, while Cnut and Swein – as foreign conquerors themselves – could serve as unthreatening literary types, through which later authors might voice opinions about Norman kings.[115] However, Anglo-Norman depictions of the transition from West Saxon to Danish rule echoed very real concerns of the early eleventh century. The hagiographical accounts of conflict with Anglo-Saxon saints recall the extended violence that preceded Swein and Cnut's conquest, in which kings, bishops, and saints were rendered vulnerable. Conversely, later authors' praise for Cnut's piety was rooted in the king's substantial patronage of English religious houses and their resident saints, cementing his enduring reputation as a Christian benefactor.[116] As early as the 1040s, the *Encomium* sought to sanitize the Danish invasions by portraying Swein and Cnut as ideal Christian kings, but it was Cnut's own accomplishments – through collaboration with English magnates, a wide-ranging legislative program, a strategic marriage – that made the Encomiast's portrait credible. Cnut's ability to effectively navigate the politics of conquest meant that later accounts of the Danish invasions were not simply concerned with conflict; they could also offer a convincing narrative of reconciliation, recovery, and continuity.

During Cnut's lifetime, by contrast, the success of his reign was less certain than it would become in hindsight, and his interactions with royal and saintly bodies had more urgent contexts. Above all, the encounters detailed in this chapter sought to neutralize challenges to the king's power. Swein's 1015 translation prevented his corpse from becoming a tool for Æthelred or other opponents of Danish rule, but Cnut continued to be wary of the political dangers of bodies even after Æthelred and his sons were safely out of the way. A particular threat was posed at the beginning of his reign by Thorkell the Tall, a Danish noble who had fought variously for Swein, Æthelred, and Cnut in the early eleventh century. Cnut made him earl of East Anglia in 1017, but Thorkell's wealth, military strength, and political influence led to an uneasy relationship with the king: he was exiled from England in 1021, made terms with Cnut in 1023, and then disappeared from the historical record.[117] In 1020, however, he was credited

115 Ridyard, "Post-Conquest Attitudes"; Ridyard, *Royal Saints*, 251–2; Rollason, *Saints and Relics*, 196–214; Hayward, "Translation-Narratives"; Southern, "European Tradition of Historical Writing."

116 See for instance William of Malmesbury, *GR* ii.181.4.

117 Keynes, "Cnut's Earls," 54–7 and 82–4; Lawson, *Cnut*, 94–5; Townend, "Contextualizing the *Knútsdrápur*," 163–4.

along with Cnut with the foundation of Assandun and refoundation of Bury.[118] The nature of this collaboration is not clear. At Assandun, Cnut was consistently identified as the minster's founder, with Thorkell depicted as a secondary figure, but it is significant that this act of royal patronage was staged in the earl's East Anglian territory. Cnut's interest there, and at Bury, may have been part of a strategy to establish a network of patronage in a region controlled by a dangerously powerful subordinate.[119] While Thorkell's presence was surely expected at royal gatherings in his earldom, it is possible that events at both foundations were designed in part to emphasize his subordination to royal power. However, Thorkell's role at Bury seems to have been more substantial than at Assandun, based on his prominence in the textual accounts, and it is possible that he, not Cnut, was the community's chief benefactor. Perhaps, in recompense for having harried the region repeatedly, Thorkell sought to make peace with his new earldom of East Anglia through this generous act of piety.[120] In this scenario, Cnut's involvement might have been comparatively minor.

In either case, Thorkell's earlier offences against St Edmund would have been recalled, at least implicitly.[121] Had Thorkell been Bury's only patron in 1020, his demonstrative act of piety could have helped reinforce the legitimacy of his authority. With Cnut there, however, Thorkell's political impact would have been diluted, with Edmund's identity as a royal saint drawing attention to the extraordinary, superior status of the king. Cnut may have made a similar point just a few years later, when he translated St Ælfheah in June 1023. Earlier that year, the king had made a truce with Thorkell, who had been amassing power in Denmark since his exile in 1021; it is not impossible that he intended to re-establish himself in England despite his agreement with Cnut.[122] As early as 1018, Thorkell had been implicated in Ælfheah's martyrdom, and the decision to draw attention to the saint's relics just as Thorkell was again becoming relevant

118 Thorkell was also the only individual addressed by name in Cnut's proclamation of 1020.

119 Such strategies among the nobility are discussed by Baxter, *Earls of Mercia*, 152–203.

120 For the impact of Thorkell's army in England from 1009 through 1012, see: Keynes, *Diplomas*, 219–26; Keynes, "Cnut's Earls," 55.

121 Thorkell's raid on Ipswich in 1009 led the community to send Edmund's relics to London for safe keeping; above, chapter 3. For Cnut's manipulation of martyrs' cults to incriminate political enemies, see: Rollason, "Murdered Royal Saints," 18; Rollason, *Mildrith Legend*, 55–6; Cubitt, "Murdered and Martyred Saints," 54–5; Stafford, "Royal Promises," 183.

122 Lawson, *Cnut*, 94–5.

in English politics could have been intended to recall the scandal of the archbishop's death.[123] By returning Ælfheah to Canterbury, Cnut was at once remedying the harm that Thorkell had done in the region and reminding the population of the earl's supposed role in the martyrdom. In addition to enhancing his own credentials as a Christian king, Cnut's interactions in the early 1020s with Sts Ælfheah and Edmund, both victims of recent Viking violence, evoked Thorkell's past actions as a persecutor of English saints.

In the later part of his reign, Cnut's approach was somewhat different. Rather than contending with a Danish political rival, he seems to have been looking towards the next generation, when his sons might be challenged by West Saxon æthelings. In the autumn of 1032, he oversaw the consecration of the completed abbey at Bury on the anniversary of the Battle of Assandun and undertook a reverential visit to Edmund Ironside's tomb on the anniversary of his death, events which would have recalled the treaty of 1016 and emphasized Cnut's purported kinship with Edmund – a reminder of his claims to be the legitimate, legal heir to the kingdom. Like his interactions with Edward the Martyr's relics, this renewed attention to West Saxon royal remains would have reminded his subjects that his accession had been a result of both treaty and conquest, thereby buttressing his family's claims to legitimate rule. At a moment when his own sons had come of age and the exiled West Saxon æthelings were poised to become a threat, Cnut's efforts seem designed to facilitate a smooth succession that would not be challenged by accusations of unlawful accession. His interactions with Anglo-Saxon royal bodies in the early 1030s seem a pre-emptive defence against Æthelred's sons.

In this context, it is remarkable that Cnut's method of coping with problematic royal corpses did not extend to Æthelred himself. There was no reverential visit to his tomb at St Paul's, as there was for Edmund Ironside; there was no annual memorialization of his death, as there was for Edward the Martyr; and his body was not translated into the care of a community friendly to the Danish regime, as was Ælfheah's. While it is possible that some attention was drawn to Æthelred's grave in 1017, when Cnut was acclaimed king in London, there is no indication that his body was moved or otherwise recognized from the time it was buried in 1016 until the fire of 1087, when it was transferred to a new tomb.[124] It may have

123 Thietmar, *Chronik*, 398; Whitelock, *EHD* I, 138; William of Malmesbury, *GR* ii.176 and ii.181.3.

124 Thacker, "Cult of the Saints," 113–16; Keynes, "Burial of King Æthelred," 144.

been practical circumstances that allowed Æthelred to rest in peace, for there was no pressing reason to draw attention to his remains. In the early years of the Danish regime, it might have been politically risky for Cnut to thrust the dead king back into the public eye by disturbing his grave for any reason, respectful or otherwise. The image of the Danish conqueror unearthing the English ruler who had borne the brunt of Viking attacks might well have done more damage to Cnut's reputation than to Æthelred's.

Nevertheless, Æthelred's may have been the least dangerous West Saxon body that Cnut encountered. Whereas Edmund Ironside had led a surge of resistance against the new regime and his saintly kinsmen attracted popular reverence, Æthelred's thirty-eight-year reign had been dominated by Viking raids which culminated in conquest just months after he died. Although it is possible that he was regarded by some as a defender against Viking violence, particularly once Edmund had begun making headway against Cnut, enthusiasm for Æthelred's memory seems to have been short lived. The hopeless tone of the Anglo-Saxon Chronicle entries for his final years gives the impression that Æthelred was an ineffective war leader and a disappointing king. From the standpoint of the annals' author – writing in London, perhaps from St Paul's, in the early 1020s – there must have been little expectation that the king would be more useful dead than alive.[125] It is also possible that the cathedral community was reluctant to draw attention to the royal grave. Cnut had deprived St Paul's of a valuable estate early in his reign, possibly to punish its resistance to his rule; the community may have minimized Æthelred's tomb in order to prevent further losses.[126]

That is not to say that Æthelred himself disappeared from public memory or political discourse. Cnut's claim to legitimacy relied on his ability to justify his status as a successor to the West Saxon dynasty: in addition to his treaty with Edmund Ironside, Cnut based his claim on his family's defeat and expulsion of Æthelred. When Æthelred returned from exile after Swein's death, he publicly pledged to be a better ruler – an event which seems to have confirmed his lawful resumption of the throne. However, during the brief interregnum of 1014, the line of succession was unclear, with Cnut claiming

125 For the ASC annals from 983–1022, see Keynes, "Declining Reputation," 229–32.

126 Domesday Book recorded that Cnut confiscated the thirty-hide estate of Southminster, Essex, from St Paul's: Lawson, *Cnut*, 155; Kelly, *Charters of St Paul's*, 39–40; Taylor, "Foundation and Endowment," 15. Compare the minimization of Edward the Confessor's grave at Westminster after the Norman Conquest: Mason, "Site of King-Making," 63–4; and chapters 1 and 7.

the kingdom before Æthelred came back.[127] I have argued above that Swein's funeral at York doubled as Cnut's acclamation as king of England, at which time he had already gained the support of some of the kingdom's leading magnates; and by Æthelred's death in 1016, Cnut had won enough English loyalty to effectively challenge Edmund's hereditary claims.[128] Even in light of his military strength, his support among England's nobility must have been underpinned by an understanding that Æthelred had abdicated and Swein's accession had been legitimate.[129] Accordingly, it seems that Cnut promoted his own family's throne-worthiness through reference to his predecessor's perceived shortcomings. In 1017, his coronation oath included a promise not to exploit his royal authority as Æthelred had done.[130] In 1018, he mandated the celebration of Edward the Martyr's feast day, a move which may have cast aspersions on Æthelred, the chief beneficiary of his brother's assassination.[131] Mentions of Cnut's defeat of Æthelred in skaldic praise poetry suggest that the memory of Danish military superiority continued to be cultivated at the Anglo-Danish court.[132] In this context, it is conceivable that the legacy promulgated by the new regime helped shape the Anglo-Saxon Chronicle's emblematic portrait of Æthelred's decline. By the twelfth century, Æthelred was not simply remembered as incompetent: in some accounts he was portrayed as impotent and ridiculous; in others, as tyrannical; in others, as a fratricide who had violated earthly and divine law.[133] As with the Anglo-Norman accounts of Sts Edith and Edward, these later witnesses to Æthelred's reputation must be treated with caution. Nevertheless, any of these accusations – weakness, tyranny, lawlessness – might have been used by Cnut's supporters in the eleventh century to justify the deposition of the West Saxon dynasty. As in sources produced under the Danish regime, Cnut's accession was often portrayed after the Norman Conquest as a restoration of strong and legitimate rulership.

---

127 Edmund Ironside also made a bid for the throne in this period: ASC CDEF 1015; Stafford, "Royal Policy and Action," 36.

128 For support from English magnates, including Archbishop Wulfstan, see Howard, *Swein Forkbeard's Invasions*, 104–7.

129 Tyler, "Treasure and Artifice," 254–5; Sheppard, *Families of the King*, 109.

130 Stafford, "Royal Promises," especially 175–87.

131 Kennedy, "Cnut's Law Code of 1018," 70; Wormald, "Æthelred the Lawmaker," 53–4; Wormald, *Making of English Law*, 343–4; and above, n. 78. For Cnut's political use of the cult of Edward and other martyred innocents, see: Ridyard, *Royal Saints*, 168–9; Rollason, "Murdered Royal Saints," 18; Rollason, *Saints and Relics*, 144–5; Lawson, *Cnut*, 139.

132 Whitelock, *EHD* I, 334–41 nos. 14–19; Townend, "Contextualizing the *Knútsdrápur*"; Treharne, *Living through Conquest*, 43–7.

133 Keynes, "Declining Reputation."

Even if Æthelred's tomb was never disturbed under Cnut or his sons, the apparent disinterest in the king's remains – along with the reapportioning of the early eleventh-century political landscape – may have constituted a political commentary in itself. Whereas Æthelred and Edmund Ironside had based their administrative, military, and ritual activity in London during their final years in power, Cnut made Winchester the effective capital of his new realm.[134] While this allowed him to participate in a long-standing culture of royal patronage in a city closely associated with Alfred, Edgar, and even Æthelred, the shift may also have been perceived as a slight to the citizens of London, who had enjoyed increased political clout in the preceding decades.[135] Nevertheless, it was in London that Cnut executed the English nobles in 1017; the following year, he levied an exceptionally high geld of 10,500 pounds upon the citizens; and he stationed Danish forces in the city soon after he came to power.[136] The removal of Ælfheah's relics in 1023 suggests that Cnut's relations with London remained strained. This impression is reinforced by a Latin *translatio* composed by Osbern of Canterbury later in the eleventh century, in which Ælfheah's translation was accompanied by an undercurrent of violence.[137] Cnut sent soldiers to incite strife (*seditiones concitent*) as a distraction while his party seized the relics; he lined the streets with armed men to ensure their safe escape from the city; the presiding archbishop feared that he would be killed by irate Londoners; and Ælfheah's shrine needed to be smashed open – an operation that recalls the king's supposed violation of Edith's tomb at Wilton.[138] Hagiographical motifs of violent relic theft notwithstanding, Osbern imagined Cnut causing material damage to

134 Kelly, *Charters of St Paul's*, 39–40; Townend, "Contextualizing the *Knútsdrápur*," 168–74; Taylor, "Foundation and Endowment," 15.

135 Hill, "Urban Policy," 103–4. Cnut's interest in a new royal residence at Westminster may likewise have been a slight to St Paul's, which adjoined the palace complex favoured by earlier kings.

136 The tax on London is recorded in ASC CDE 1018, and its implications are discussed by: Lawson, "Danegeld," 721–6; Hill, "Urban Policy," 103–4. For Eadric's execution in London, see: ASC F 1017; JW 504–5. For the possibility of a new, sustained military presence in London under Cnut, see: Nightingale, "Origin of the Court of Husting," 566–8; Lawson, *Cnut*, 182. See also Townend, "Contextualizing the *Knútsdrápur*," 167–8.

137 Rumble and Morris, "*Translatio Sancti Ælfegi*," 283–5; Townsend, "Anglo-Latin Hagiography," 409–12.

138 Rumble and Morris, "*Translatio Sancti Ælfegi*," 302–7. The monks whom Cnut ordered to break into the shrine "ripped up an iron candelabra" (*arripiunt ferreum… candelabrum*) that was installed nearby and used it to create a fracture (*effractionem*) in the tomb, after which the rest of the tomb miraculously crumbled; ibid., 304. Violence was not noted in the Anglo-Saxon Chronicle's account of the translation.

St Paul's in the face of a rebellious citizenry who were expected to physically oppose their king's will.[139]

However accurately (or inaccurately) Osbern's account captured the threat of violence in Danish-ruled London, relations with the city seem to have mellowed by the end of Cnut's reign. In the early 1040s, the Encomiast took for granted that London was vital to the process of succession and an important site for royal ceremonial.[140] The city's growing Danish population surely contributed to this transformation.[141] A purported renewal of St Paul's privileges in the 1030s, though recorded in a spurious writ, may indicate that Cnut eventually came to terms with the cathedral community – or at least that the community later believed they might benefit from the memory of reconciliation with the king.[142] Nevertheless, in London and at other sensitive sites, Cnut sought to regulate the political potential of the local landscape and history. For all his activity at Glastonbury, Wilton, and Shaftesbury, there is no record that Cnut granted these foundations substantial lands or otherwise enhanced their endowments; none of these houses appears to have received donations comparable to those given to Bury, Canterbury, or Winchester.[143] Although he rendered West Saxon bodies cautious reverence, Cnut did not provide their custodians the means to significantly increase their wealth or influence.

Cnut's regulated generosity and calculated interactions with the remains of royal bodies helped mitigate the trauma of conquest while reinforcing his status as the rightful heir to kings of the Anglo-Saxon past.[144] This strategy was surely shaped with the help of English advisers and allies, who could provide guidance on how best to intertwine ecclesiastical patronage

---

139 For hagiographical motifs, see ibid., 286–8.

140 Hill, "Development of Towns," 217; Hill, "Urban Policy," 103; Brooke and Keir, *London*, 21–3; Nightingale, "Origin of the Court of Husting," 560 and 566; Keynes, "Burial of King Æthelred."

141 Nightingale, "Origin of the Court of Husting," 559–69; Kelly, *Charters of St Paul's*, 40–2; Lawson, *Cnut*, 206.

142 S 992 (and compare also S 978); and above, n. 94.

143 For the lack of grants to Glastonbury, Wilton, and Shaftesbury, see: Lawson, *Cnut*, 155–6; Abrams, *Anglo-Saxon Glastonbury*, 347–9; Foot *Veiled Women* II, 175; Yorke, *Nunneries*, 89.

144 A similar motivation is ascribed to Cnut's earliest lawcode by Kennedy, "Cnut's Law Code of 1018," 70.

and politics.[145] Yet it was Cnut himself who was most often credited with acts of Christian generosity, with his reputation as a benefactor of religious houses enduring well beyond his lifetime.[146] During his reign, his interactions with monastic communities and their saintly patrons would have helped cement his status as a Christian king of England in spite of his history as a Viking raider.[147] A desire for legitimacy may explain why Cnut did not indulge in open violence against the remains and legacies of the West Saxon dynasty – a remarkable show of restraint, if Æthelred's designs against Swein's corpse were commonly known or suspected. In this instance, the Danish conqueror appeared more respectful towards dead royalty than his West Saxon predecessor had been. In his handling of royal bodies and burials, Cnut proved himself a worthy king of England.

145 Emma seems to have been particularly influential in this regard. On the couple's patronage, see: Heslop, "*De Luxe* Manuscripts," 157–8; Tyler, "Treasure and Artifice," 250–2. See also Baxter, *Earls of Mercia*, 152–203 for monastic patronage as a political strategy in vulnerable territory.

146 Heslop, "*De Luxe* Manuscripts," 158; Gerchow, "Prayers for Cnut," 221.

147 Gerchow, "Prayers for Cnut," especially 220 and 236; Heslop, "*De Luxe* Manuscripts," 179–80; Tyler, "Treasure and Artifice," 250–2.

7 Conclusions: William of Normandy and the Landscape of Anglo-Saxon Royal Burial

After his 1016 conquest of England, Cnut negotiated two political needs in his approach to royal remains: he established his legitimacy through continuity with the Anglo-Saxon royal past, and he asserted his superiority over a displaced dynasty whose members and supporters posed a continuous threat. William the Conqueror took a similar approach after his victory at Hastings, conveying distinct political messages with two royal bodies. His coronation beside Edward the Confessor's tomb linked his reign from the outset with the legacy of England's last West Saxon king; but William also sought to minimize the importance of Harold Godwineson, whose body disappeared from the Hastings battlefield.[1] By associating himself with the tomb of a legitimizing predecessor while effectively obliterating the corpse of his erstwhile rival, William used two royal bodies to punctuate his narrative of righteous accession. In 1066, the new king seems to have been as interested in royal remains as his pre-Conquest counterparts.

By ca 1070, William's priorities had shifted. As his rule became more secure, he installed Norman clergy and moved away from pre-Conquest forms of royal administration. At the same time, Norman authors began systematically referencing William's kinship ties with Edward and building a legal case against Harold, whom they identified as a usurper and perjurer whose very consecration was void.[2] Yet although William's claims to royal legitimacy still relied upon a narrative of royal continuity, the promulgation of this narrative was not accompanied by prominent interactions with either king's body. There is little indication that William's

1 Above, chapter 3.

2 Garnett, *Conquered England*, 1–44; Barlow, *Feudal Kingdom*, 93–4; Bates, *Regesta*, 49–50.

early ceremonial activity beside Edward's tomb was sustained throughout his reign, and it is telling that the Westminster community – rather than cultivating their patron's grave as a source of prestige – downplayed the significance of the royal burial in the generation after the Conquest.[3]

The post-Hastings handling of Harold Godwineson's body was similarly subdued. Despite being roundly condemned by Norman propagandists soon after the Conquest, there was no known desecration or display of his remains by the enemy army or the new king of England. The 1040 exposure of Harold Harefoot's decomposing corpse might have offered an apt exemplar in 1066, as both Harolds were portrayed by their successors' apologists as illegitimate rulers deserving of punishment. Instead, Harold Godwineson's body was treated with restraint. Rather than exhibiting the broken corpse as a trophy or evidence of divine will, it was disposed of quietly – recalling the concealment of Edward the Martyr's remains in 978. When considered alongside Edward's regicide and its aftermath, Harold's disappearance after Hastings seems to reflect a sense of discomfort or uncertainty about the impact his body would have on the political discourse to follow. In the unstable political climate of late 1066, it was evidently deemed prudent to obliterate rather than desecrate the royal remains. Even as Norman chroniclers discredited Harold's short reign and narrated the events that led to his death, none of the sources composed during William's lifetime provided definitive information about where his body was buried.

Whatever was done with Harold's corpse, then, William seems not to have exploited it for political gain. Unlike Cnut, who neutralized problematic bodies by bringing them into the public eye, William diverted attention from the remains of his rival. Whether this was a deliberate strategy or simply a result of shifting priorities, his actions set a precedent: royal bodies assumed a more muted role in political discourse after the initial transition to Norman rule. By way of conclusion, this chapter will consider the death of Harold Godwineson as a turning point in English royal burial practice. Harold was the only eleventh-century English king whose reign lacked the ceremonial closure provided by a royal funeral, and this fact would come to support the Norman narrative of conquest. Just as Norman authors deemed Harold's accession illegitimate because of an allegedly irregular consecration officiated by an allegedly excommunicated archbishop, the lack of a public funeral confirmed after the fact that he was

3 Mason, "Westminster and the Monarchy," 272; and further below.

not worthy of royal honours. In addition, the unkingly disposal of his body broke the pattern of converging funerals and coronations that had defined royal succession in eleventh-century England. However, in spite of its absence – or perhaps because of it – Harold's body remained a point of interest through the later Middle Ages. Without the closure provided by a royal funeral, the significance of his life, death, and burial remained open to debate.

The Life and Afterlife of Harold Godwineson

All early accounts of the Battle of Hastings agreed that Harold Godwineson died on the battlefield, with his despoiled corpse abandoned in the general carnage. According to William of Poitiers, the Conqueror's chaplain, Harold's remains were discovered among the dead "deprived of all ornament" and so badly mangled that his mistress had to identify him by "certain signs" on his body rather than by his face.[4] Other descriptions of Hastings reinforced the gruesome, unkingly nature of Harold's demise, and within a few decades of the battle, his death was attributed to a chance arrow to the head or eye – a manifestation of divine justice against a royal pretender, according to Norman apologists.[5] However, the sources did not agree on the fate of Harold's remains once they were identified. William of Malmesbury said that Harold's body was granted to his mother, while William of Poitiers asserted that her request for the corpse was denied; the community of Waltham Abbey claimed to have entombed Harold honourably soon after the battle, while Orderic Vitalis reported that he was buried on the seashore; the *Carmen de Hastingae Proelio* imagined his remains interred on a cliff, in a stone cairn; and the Anglo-Saxon Chronicle

4 "Carens omni decore"; "quibusdam signis, nequaquam facie, recognitus est"; William of Poitiers, *GG*, 140–1.

5 The earliest textual reference to the arrow appeared in the Montecassino chronicle of Amatus, composed between 1079 and 1081: Amatus, *History of the Normans*, 1–11 and 46; Barlow, *Carmen*, lxxxiv; William of Poitiers, *GG*, 136n3. William of Malmesbury reported that he was killed by an arrow to the head, shot from a distance; the Chronicle of Battle Abbey stated simply that Harold was killed by a chance blow (*fortuito ictu*); while the Bayeux Tapestry seems to depict Harold dying with an arrow to the eye, a tradition later followed by Henry of Huntingdon. William of Malmesbury, *GR* iii.242.3 and iii.243; Searle, *Chronicle of Battle*, 38–9; Wilson, *Bayeux Tapestry*, 71–2; Henry of Huntingdon, *Historia Anglorum*, vi.30; Bernstein, "Blinding of Harold," 49–64; but compare Foys, "Pulling the Arrow Out."

said nothing about his burial at all.[6] In addition to these conflicting accounts, there were persistent legends of Harold's survival and preternaturally long life, and by the later Middle Ages, at least two abbeys claimed to possess his body.[7]

The lack of consensus among so many sources indicates that there was no public funeral for Harold, at which his body could be viewed and his burial witnessed. He was certainly not entombed at Westminster or any established royal mausoleum. The most logical explanation is that Harold was buried secretly or anonymously after the battle – a fate that Norman chroniclers considered just, since "countless men remained unburied because of his excessive greed."[8] Whether or not Harold deserved such posthumous ignominy, it is unclear whether the treatment of his body was ideologically driven at the time of its disposal or even if his remains had been accurately identified. On the one hand, the disappearance of his body may have been a matter of convenience at a chaotic moment. It is conceivable that he was interred in a mass grave with other casualties of Hastings, either because his corpse was too badly damaged to be moved or because there was a desire to dispose of his remains as soon as possible.[9] In the aftermath of a battle which had been decisively won but had not settled the question of succession, concealing the remains of the deposed king would have offered a quick fix for a complicated problem.

On the other hand, there may have been a more deliberate effort to remove and conceal the body in order to neutralize its political effect. This was a strategy that William had used before, as he had secretly buried the bodies of drowned soldiers during the passage to England in order to keep up his troops' morale.[10] A similar tactic may have been employed after Hastings. Making Harold invisible, rather than honouring him with a royal

6 William of Malmesbury, *GR* iii.247.1; William of Poitiers, *GG*, 140–1; Watkiss and Chibnall, *Waltham Chronicle*, 50–7; Orderic Vitalis, *Ecclesiastical History* II, 178–9; Barlow, *Carmen*, 34–5.

7 Below, nn. 12 and 13.

8 "Cuius ob nimiam cupiditatem insepulti remanerent innumerabiles"; William of Poitiers, *GG*, 140–1. This logic was also followed by Orderic Vitalis, *Ecclesiastical History* II, 178–81.

9 For the tentative identification of a mass grave created quickly after the battle, see Searle, *Chronicle of Battle*, 15–16.

10 "Indeed, meeting adversity with counsel, he concealed the death of those who had drowned as much as he could by burying them secretly" [Quin et consilio aduersitatibus obuius, submersorum interitus quantum poterat occultauit, latentius tumulando]; William of Poitiers, *GG*, 108–9.

funeral or displaying his broken body as a trophy, would have diverted attention from the violent death of an anointed king and denied the English any opportunity to rally behind their fallen leader. The effect of such action would have been compounded if the body was relegated to unconsecrated ground, as seems likely.[11] Whatever the consequences for his soul, an unhallowed grave would have equated Harold in death with the criminal dead – an identity consistent with Norman claims that he had usurped William's place. If Harold's burial was underpinned by such political considerations, his dishonourable grave may have been something of an open secret.

While a quiet burial may have been the most practical course of action after Hastings, it also meant that Harold's life and reign lacked ceremonial closure; without a public funeral, his legacy remained open to interpretation. Accordingly, despite the arguments against Harold's royal legitimacy disseminated by William's partisans, two alternatives to the Norman narrative emerged soon after the battle. One was the survival legend. By the twelfth century, there were claims that Harold had survived Hastings, embarked on a religious life, and died at Chester long after the Conquest.[12] This story was most fully developed in the thirteenth-century *Vita Haroldi* and corroborated in the fourteenth century with the exhumation in Chester of a corpse supposed to be Harold's, complete with royal regalia.[13] Yet given the circumstances surrounding his death and burial, it is conceivable that this legend had Conquest-era roots. The battlefield identification of an unrecognizably mangled corpse as Harold's body may have seemed suspect after the fact, while the uncertain grave site and lack of a public funeral could have inspired rumours that he had not been buried at all. In its earliest manifestations, Harold's survival myth may have been a response to so much ambiguity.

A second alternative to the narrative promulgated by Norman authors was the suggestion that Harold was a saint. Claims of sanctity were particularly pronounced at Harold's foundation at Waltham, where, by the early twelfth century, the community maintained that they had been

---

11 Burial on the (presumably unconsecrated) seashore was reported by William of Poitiers, *GG*, 140–1; Orderic Vitalis, *Ecclesiastical History* II, 178–9; and see also Thacker, "Harold at Chester," 155.

12 Watkiss and Chibnall, *Waltham Chronicle*, xlvi–xlviii; Thacker, "Harold at Chester," 155–8; Cohen, "Survival Legends," 148–51; Fellows-Jensen, "Harold II's Survival"; Ashdown, "Survival of Harold Godwinson."

13 Thacker, "Harold at Chester," 156–9 and 163–4. The Waltham Chronicler forcefully denied stories of Harold's survival and later burial at Chester: Watkiss and Chibnall, *Waltham Chronicle*, 50–7. See also Ashe, "Harold Godwineson," 73–80.

granted their patron's body directly after Hastings.[14] While this assertion seems dubious, given the lack of corroboration in any of the earliest accounts, Waltham cultivated a grave they identified as Harold's: their chronicler reported that the body had been translated three times by the 1120s "because the brothers were revering the body, out of devotion."[15] By the early thirteenth century, another Waltham author stated that Harold was "now numbered among the saints," a sentiment echoed by the overtly hagiographical *Vita Haroldi.*[16] As with the survival legend, there are no explicit references to Harold's saintliness until a generation after the Conquest. However, two models of Anglo-Saxon royal sanctity could have applied to Harold in the 1060s. According to one model, claims of sanctity might emerge as a spontaneous response to the sudden or violent death of a king.[17] For Harold, the first English monarch to be killed in battle in more than a century, a designation of martyrdom could have helped his subjects make sense of his untimely death and cope with the trauma of foreign conquest. According to a second model, saints' cults could serve as political weapons against a king's killer: if a ruler was identified as a martyr, his slayer could be identified as an enemy of God.[18] In Harold's case, such an allegation could have been used to cast doubt upon William's claim to be the legitimate heir to the English throne. Even without an explicit religious conflict, the circumstances of Harold's death were consistent with those of earlier royal martyrs, making him a likely enough saint.

There is no indication of substantial cultic activity in the generation after the Conquest, however, and intentionally or not, Harold's hidden burial stopped his body from being identified as saintly relics after Hastings. Nevertheless, physical mementos of Harold could still have proved dangerous for the new regime, and in the 1060s, the Hastings battlefield itself may have attracted reverence. There was certainly precedent

---

14 S 1036; Watkiss and Chibnall, *Waltham Chronicle*, xxxviii–xliii, 24–39, and 50–7; Thacker, "Harold at Chester," 159–60.

15 "Deuotio fratrum reuerentiam corpori exibentium"; Watkiss and Chibnall, *Waltham Chronicle*, 56–7. The editors of the Waltham Chronicle suggest that Harold's third translation was meant to discourage reverence and avoid any political repercussions, but this reading is not borne out by the text: ibid., xiv. William of Malmesbury had already recorded Waltham's claim to the body in the 1120s: *GR* iii.247.1.

16 "Iam sanctis connumeratus"; quoted in Thacker, "Harold at Chester," 159 and 172n29 from London, British Library Harley MS 3776 fols. 31r–v. See also Watkiss and Chibnall, *Waltham Chronicle*, l–lii.

17 Cubitt, "Murdered and Martyred Saints."

18 Rollason, "Murdered Royal Saints."

for popular veneration at English battlefields: the cult of the saint-king Oswald of Northumbria manifested at sites of his pivotal battles, and the church that marked the spot where he was killed in 642 was still extant in the Norman era.[19] The Hastings battlefield may have likewise attracted attention as a place for mourning and reverence, given the magnitude of the battle and the number of dead – some of whom were likely buried on site.[20] If impromptu memorials had emerged there for Harold and other casualties, the battlefield could have become a focus for veneration and, potentially, for opposition to the new regime.

It is telling, in this context, that William's only English ecclesiastical foundation was situated precisely on this spot. Battle Abbey was established in 1067, according to its twelfth-century chronicler, in fulfilment of an oath that William made the moment he stepped onto the battlefield:

> I vow that on this very spot, for the salvation of all – and especially those who will die here – I shall found a monastery for the honour of God and his saints, with fitting liberties.[21]

William's pre-emptive promise was likely a twelfth-century creation, but the pious motivation cited by the Battle Chronicler echoed earlier sources.[22] A set of royal writs noted that William founded the abbey in exchange for "the victory which God granted me there," while the *Brevis Relatio de Origine Willelmi Conquestoris* claimed that the abbey was built both "for the memory of his victory and for absolution of the sins of all of those who

19 Oswald was killed in battle at Maserfelth, which was evidently the site of continuous cultic activity through the twelfth century, with a church attested there in 1086: Stancliffe, "Where Was Oswald Killed," especially 86–91. Reverence for Oswald also flourished at Heavenfield, which became an annual pilgrimage site: Bede, *HE* III.2; Thacker, "*Membra Disjecta*," 100–1 and 107–8; Cubitt, "Murdered and Martyred Saints," 60–3; Cubitt, "Universal and Local Saints," 425–6 and 430–5.

20 Above, n. 9.

21 "Uotum facio me in hoc certaminis loco, pro salute cunctorum et hic nominatim occumbencium, ad honorem Dei et sanctorum eius ... congruum cum digna libertate fundaturum monasterium"; Searle, *Chronicle of Battle*, 36–7. The text was produced in the 1180s.

22 While it is not impossible Battle's construction may have fulfilled a vow William made, it is unlikely that this vow was made as early as the Battle Chronicle indicates: Bates, *Regesta*, 137–8; Searle, *Chronicle of Battle*, 17–18.

were killed there."[23] It is possible that the abbey was linked to the imposition of penance by papal legates upon those who fought at Hastings.[24] Even the Anglo-Saxon Chronicle acknowledged that the creation of Battle – situated "in the very place where God granted that William win England" – was an act of Christian generosity by an otherwise "harsh and cruel man."[25]

William's pious motives were complemented by another tradition associated with Battle: by the early twelfth century, the abbey was believed to mark the exact place where Harold Godwineson had died. William of Malmesbury stated in the *Gesta Regum* that Battle's principal church was situated "where it was remembered that Harold was found among dense piles of corpses," clarifying in the *Gesta Pontificum* that the high altar marked the precise spot where his body fell.[26] The chronicler of Battle Abbey claimed that the Conqueror refused to have the church built anywhere but "the very spot where his enemy had fallen," insisting on his chosen site despite the inconvenient landscape; the high altar was finally set "on the very place where Harold's standard was seen to have dropped."[27] In the twelfth-century texts, William was imagined to have drawn explicit attention to his rival's death and defeat, making the abbey seem as much a monument to Norman supremacy as an expression of piety. The very name "Battle" surely reinforced this impression.[28] Coinciding with a program of castle building which the Anglo-Saxon Chronicle portrayed as oppressive, William's battlefield monastery – built of Norman stone, modelled on Continental architecture, and eventually staffed by French monks – may likewise have been perceived as a symbol of colonization.[29]

---

23 The writs both include the phrase "ob victoriam quam mihi Deus ibidem contulit"; Bates, *Regesta*, 138 and 140. The *Brevis Relatio* was composed at Battle shortly before 1120: "Ob memoriam huius uictorie et absolutionem peccatorum omnium illorum qui ibi interfecti sunt"; Van Houts, *Brevis Relatio*, 33, with a discussion of dating and provenance at 12–15.

24 This possibility has been debated: Searle, *Chronicle of Battle*, 20–1; Hallam, "War Memorials," 52. For the penance, see Morton, "Pope Alexander II," 376–8 and 381–2.

25 "On ðam ilcan steode þe God him geuðe þæt he moste Engleland gegan"; "stearc man 7 ræðe"; ASC E 1086 (*recte* 1087).

26 "Ubi inter confertos cadauerum aceruos Haroldus inuentus fuisse memoratur"; *GR* iii.267.3. Compare *GP* ii.97; and also John of Worcester, who echoes William's language in the *GP*: JW, *Chronicle* III, 154–5.

27 "In eodem loco quo hoste prostrato sibi cesserat"; "in eodem loco quo regis Haraldi signum, quod standard uocant, corruisse uisum est"; Searle, *Chronicle of Battle*, 44–5.

28 Hallam, "War Memorials," 54; Searle, *Chronicle of Battle*, 20–1.

29 ASC E 1066 and 1067; Hare, *Battle Abbey*, 20 and 66; Hare, "Buildings of Battle," 82–4; Searle, *Chronicle of Battle*, 44–7; Knowles, *Monastic Order*, 128.

While there is no reason to doubt that the community's mission was indeed to pray "for the dead of both sides," the appropriation of such a divisive site was no doubt motivated by mundane as well as spiritual interests.[30] Like Cnut's minster on the Assandun battlefield, Battle allowed a foreign conqueror to take control of a highly symbolic site at a moment of political volatility. It is certainly possible that the foundation was built on the reputed place of Harold's death, as later authors claimed: the inconvenient topography of the building site, at the top of a narrow hill, indicates that the location was not chosen for practical considerations.[31] If the spot where Harold's body or standard had been recovered had been marked in some way, it is logical that William would take control of the site. The pious foundation of a religious house would be a praiseworthy move, unlikely to inspire political backlash.

Still, given the significance and potential value of the site, Battle's growth was slow. It was nearly a decade after Hastings that a community was established there, with a small contingent of monks from Marmoutier moving into the abbey in 1076; and it was not until 1094, during the reign of William Rufus, that the foundation was finally consecrated.[32] Had Battle been an expression of Norman triumphalism or a victory monument intended to proclaim and perpetuate the message of conquest, its completion would surely have been a more urgent priority.[33] Rather, William's foundation signalled a gentler transition: the abbey offered a message of Christian reconciliation while preventing a volatile landscape from becoming a political liability. Even if Battle's Continental aesthetic was regarded by some as intrusive, Norman-style architecture had already been introduced at Edward the Confessor's Westminster.[34] As an ecclesiastical patron, William could appropriate an enduring emblem of conquest and transform it to serve his regime – even as he enhanced his royal credentials by replicating the pious generosity of English kings like Edgar, Cnut, and Edward the Confessor. Battle Abbey transformed a memento of Norman aggression and bloodshed into an expression of piety, reconciliation, and royal legitimacy.

---

30 "Pro interfectius utrius"; Van Houts, *Gesta Normannorum Ducum* II, 172–3.

31 Hare, *Battle Abbey*, 11 and 18; Hare, "Buildings of Battle," 80–2.

32 Searle, *Chronicle of Battle*, 96–7.

33 For interpretations of Battle as a monument to Norman triumph, see for example: Searle, *Chronicle of Battle*, 20–1; Hallam, "War Memorials"; Douglas, *William the Conqueror*, 328; Knowles, *Monastic Order*, 128. The delay before construction began and monks were installed is noted by Searle, *Chronicle of Battle*, 20.

34 Fernie, "Edward the Confessor's Westminster," 141–2.

It is impossible to know whether Harold was referenced at Battle's eventual consecration in 1094, or how consistently his memory was recalled by the community. However, around the same time that William's battlefield monastery was being consecrated, the monks of Waltham were translating a body they claimed was Harold's and cultivating his supposed tomb as "a perpetual memorial for our descendants."[35] Waltham's insistence that Harold was buried in their foundation – and their chronicler's sharp refutation of survival myths – reflects the perceived value of a royal body, even one that belonged to a conquered king.[36] His grave, inscribed with an epitaph that lauded him as "father of the country" and "glorious king of the English people," allowed Waltham to shape its own history, establishing links of patronage with the last Anglo-Saxon king but also with his first Norman successor: Harold gave the abbey its start, and William gave the abbey Harold.[37] As dubious as this latter claim was, it cast both kings in an honourable light, with Harold receiving the burial his royal status merited and William treating his enemy with Christian mercy. The Waltham Chronicle did not depict Harold's body as divisive or controversial, but as a prestigious link to the Anglo-Saxon past and an affirmation of Norman authority. Such patriotic memorialization of Harold – "killed for love of his country," as William of Malmesbury put it – was surely not what the Conqueror had in mind for his rival after Hastings.[38] Decades into the Norman regime, Harold's legacy remained open to interpretation.

Conquest and Continuity in Eleventh-Century England

William's treatment of his two predecessors' bodies was consistent with the textual interpretations of recent English regnal history: Harold Godwineson was to be remembered as a perjurer and usurper, not to be honoured in death, while Edward the Confessor was a legitimate ancestor whose memory was to be respected. It seems that William's regime easily negotiated two approaches to royal burial current in eleventh-century England, celebrating a legitimizing predecessor while denigrating a dynastic challenger

35 "Posteris nostris ... perpetuum sit monimentum"; Watkiss and Chibnall, *Waltham Chronicle*, 52–3.

36 Above, n. 13.

37 "Pater patrie"; "Anglorum gentis rex inclitus"; Watkiss and Chibnall, *Waltham Chronicle*, 90–1.

38 "Pro patriae caritate occisi"; William of Malmesbury, *GP* ii.97. See also JW, *Chronicle* III, 154–5.

– much as Cnut's had, fifty years earlier. Moreover, the commemorative abbey at Battle appears strikingly similar to Cnut's church at Assandun. Both foundations ostensibly promoted Christian unity and reconciliation with the conquered populace, even as they appropriated particularly volatile landscapes into the control of new foreign kings. The ideological similarities reflect a degree of continuity with pre-Norman English politics, and a tentative link between the two foundations may be identified in the person of Stigand, Archbishop of Canterbury. Stigand was entrusted with the care of Assandun in 1020, when he was a priest in Cnut's household, and he remained in favour with William until he was deposed from his see in 1070.[39] In the years between the Conquest and his deposition, Stigand may well have advocated policies of reconciliation that would smooth the political transition, much as Archbishop Wulfstan had under Cnut. As the original custodian of Cnut's minster at Assandun, Stigand would have been in a prime position to recommend a comparable gesture to another foreign king seeking to secure his rule.

Yet where Cnut sustained his conciliatory tone for the duration of his reign, William's emphasis on continuity was less consistent. He took a harder approach to his conquered subjects after the revolts of the later 1060s, focusing more on Norman strength than peaceful reconciliation. He purged high-ranking Anglo-Saxon clergy in 1070, and within a few years of the Conquest, his supporters began crafting legal arguments to demonstrate that Harold had never been a legitimate king.[40] The foundation of Battle Abbey was more consistent with his political strategies before ca 1070 than after. William's activity at Westminster seems to follow a similar trajectory. In the early part of his reign, he visited regularly. He spent Christmas there in 1066 and 1067, the first and second anniversary of the abbey's consecration and Edward the Confessor's last public appearance; and his wife Matilda was crowned queen there on Pentecost 1068, an event which would have recalled William's own coronation less than two years earlier.[41] After that, there is no record of William at

39 For Stigand as the original custodian of Assandun Minster, see: ASC F 1020 and above, chapter 6. For his initial favour under William and his deposition in 1070, see: Douglas, *William the Conqueror*, 324; Morton, "Pope Alexander II," 364–5.

40 Garnett, *Conquered England*, 1–44; Baxter, *Earls of Mercia*, 275–7; Douglas, *William the Conqueror*, 323–9.

41 ASC D 1067 (*recte* 1068); Bates, *Regesta*, 598; Biddle, "Seasonal Festivals," 64. The officiation of Matilda's coronation by Archbishop Ealdred of York reinforced the connection with William's consecration, as well as with Harold's; above, chapter 3.

Westminster until 1075, when he celebrated Christmas there after burying Edith, Edward's widow, who had died the week before; his next attested visits were at Christmas 1081 and Pentecost 1084 and 1086.[42] Although we have only an incomplete picture of William's itinerary, his known appearances at Westminster were concentrated at the beginning and end of his reign; in the later 1060s and the 1070s, they seem to have tapered off or lacked the ceremonial importance of his earlier visits.[43] It is also noteworthy that Westminster was not a beneficiary of substantial royal donations under William: while a series of writs confirms that the king remained engaged in the community's administrative affairs, he did not endow the abbey with substantial estates beyond those it already possessed.[44] When set beside the subdued attention to Edward's tomb before ca 1100, it appears that William was reluctant to allow Westminster – a foundation so intimately connected with the last West Saxon regime – to accumulate too much new wealth and influence.[45]

In spite of this apparent stinginess, however, Westminster remained important to the narrative of Conquest that was promulgated throughout William's lifetime, and it seems that the abbey's interests soon aligned with the king's. Norman abbots were installed there by the early 1070s.[46] The building work begun under Edward was continued through the subsequent decades, using stone quarried in Normandy and following Norman

42 Biddle, "Seasonal Festivals," 64. Edith died at Winchester, and her burial beside Edward at Westminster evidently contravened her intention to be buried at Wilton. Her death is recorded in ASC D 1076 (*recte* 1075), E 1075.

43 For William's itinerary, see: Biddle, "Seasonal Festivals," 64; Bates, *Regesta*, 75–82. William's obit in ASC E 1086 (*recte* 1087) noted that he wore his crown three times each year, including during Pentecost at Westminster. However, he celebrated Pentecost at Windsor in 1070 and 1073 and was likely in Normandy for the holiday from 1073 through 1080; he is attested at Westminster only in 1068 (for Matilda's coronation), 1084, and 1086, and he may also have been in England for Pentecost in 1083 and 1085.

44 Mason, "Westminster and the Monarchy," 278–9; Mason, *Westminster and Its People*, 21 and 24, Harvey, *Westminster and Its Estates*, 27–8.

45 Mason, *Westminster and Its People*, 16–17. Cnut followed a similar strategy at other West Saxon mausolea; above, chapter 6. For the community's subdued interest in Edward's tomb, see: Mason, "Site of King-Making," 63–4; and above, chapter 1.

46 Edwin, the last English abbot, probably died in 1068; his Norman successor, Geoffry, was first attested in 1072. In 1075, Geoffry was deposed for unspecified misconduct and replaced by Vitalis, formerly abbot of Bernay, who kept the office from 1076 through 1085: ASC D 1077 (*recte* 1076); Flete, *History of Westminster*, 81–5; Mason, *Westminster and Its People*, 21–4; Mason, "Site of King-Making," 61–2.

architectural models.[47] The abbey neared completion under Abbot Vitalis, who was credited with overseeing construction on the ecclesiastical buildings and perhaps also the adjoining royal palace; the old Anglo-Saxon monastery was fully demolished in this period.[48] During the final decade of William's reign, the enormous complex at Westminster may well have been regarded, like Battle, as a symbol of Norman dominance.[49] In light of twelfth-century assertions that William was as lavish a patron as Edward had been, he might have been responsible for funding some or all of this construction.[50] Indeed, in a letter composed ca 1076, William explicitly connected Westminster's prestige with its Conquest-era history:

> There lies that man of blessed memory, my lord and kinsman King Edward. Queen Edith, his glorious wife, is also buried there. And in that same place, by God's providence and mercy, I received the scepter and crown of the entire English kingdom.[51]

Also around this time, the monk Sulcard was commissioned to write an account of Westminster's construction.[52] His work traced the history of the

---

47 Building was continued and completed in the Norman era: Fernie, "Edward the Confessor's Westminster." Romanesque architecture was first introduced in England at Westminster during Edward's reign: Fernie, "Reconstructing Edward's Abbey," 66; Mason, *Westminster and Its People*, 13–16; and above, chapter 1, for Westminster's similarity to the Norman abbey of Jumièges. The use of stone quarried from Caen after the Conquest is attested by Goscelin in his *Life* of St Augustine of Canterbury; under Edward the Confessor, Westminster's stone had been brought from Reigate, Surrey: Gem, "Cushion Capital," 89–91 and 95; Gem, "Craftsmen and Administrators," 171–2; Fernie, *Architecture*, 156–7.

48 Gem, "Resistance to Romanesque Architecture," 132–5; Gem, "Romanesque Rebuilding," 37–9; Scholz, "Sulcard," 60 and 80–1; Mason, *Westminster and Its People*, 23. For work on the palace during the reign of William I, see Brown et al., *King's Works*, 45–6 and 491. But see Gem, "Cushion Capital," for questions about the extent of Vitalis's involvement in the building works, especially on the palace.

49 For Norman stone and architecture at Battle, see: Searle, *Chronicle of Battle*, 44–5; Knowles, *Monastic Order*, 128; Brown et al., *King's Works*, 49; and n. 47 above.

50 According to William of Malmesbury: "King William did no less [than Edward the Confessor], indeed much more, to exalt the place, lavishing on it revenues from estates; for it was here that he was crowned" [Nec minus sed multo etiam maius rex Willelmus extulit locum magnis reditibus prediorum quod ibi regni susceperit insignia]; *GP* ii.73.6.

51 "Ibi enim iacet vir beate memorię dominus meus et cognatus rex Ethuuardus. Ibi etiam tumulata est regina Etgith uxor eius inclita. Ego etiam ibidem, Dei clementia providente, sceptrum et coronam totius regni anglici suscepi"; Bates, *Regesta*, 466. See also: Scholz, "Sulcard," 60–1; Mason, "Site of King-Making," 62.

52 The work was commissioned by Abbot Vitalis: Scholz, "Sulcard," 59–62; Mason, "Site of King-Making," 63–4; and above, n. 48.

abbey from its supposed Roman-era roots to the conversion period, and from its tenth-century refoundation by St Dunstan to its later renovation under Edward – establishing a clear connection between the Anglo-Norman community and Westminster's pre-Conquest past.[53] By the last decade of William's reign, it seems the abbey had embraced Norman notions of continuity.

Edward's physical remains may have been another matter, for William's evocation of the dead king seems to have been more literary than material. Just as Harold Godwineson's memory was cultivated by Norman apologists but his corpse obscured, it seems that Edward's role as a legitimizing predecessor was cited without much signifying attention to his body. With the exception of Edith's burial in 1075, there are no contemporary reports that William had any contact or interaction with Edward's grave. Later legend revised this position, as twelfth-century authors claimed that Edward's relics were encased in a gold and silver coffin commissioned by William after witnessing a miracle at his tomb.[54] Although the hagiographical context and late provenance of this story make it unlikely that William was actually responsible for this gift, it is revealing that Westminster's twelfth-century authors sought to establish a pattern of royal patronage that dated back to the very beginning of Norman rule.

In the first generation after the Conquest, by contrast, it seems that the Westminster community deliberately downplayed the importance of their patron's body.[55] By the turn of the twelfth century, the monks professed uncertainty about where exactly his grave was located.[56] The confusion could be explained by his mode of burial: if Edward (and later, Edith) had been interred beneath the floor of the church, rather than in an above-ground tomb, it is conceivable that the next generation was unsure of the

53 Scholz, "Sulcard," 80–91. Notably, however, Sulcard ends his account with Edward's death and burial, without reference to Harold and William's coronations or to the Conquest and Norman rule.

54 Bloch, "Vie de Édouard," 120; PL 195 col.781D; Mason, "Wulfstan's Staff"; Scholz, "Canonization of Edward," 38n3. William was also credited in the twelfth century with providing Edward's queen, Edith, with a gold and silver coffin: William of Malmesbury, *GR* iii.273.2.

55 Mason, "Westminster and the Monarchy," 272; Mason, "Site of King-Making," 63–4. This may not always have been the case: Edwin, the last English abbot, reportedly paid daily visits to Edward's grave until he died ca 1068. Flete, *Westminster*, 82–3; Mason, *Westminster and Its People*, 21–2; and above, n. 46.

56 *Vita Ædwardi*, 113–15; Barlow, *Edward the Confessor*, 263–9. Sulcard seems also to express some uncertainty about the exact site of Edward's tomb: "he was buried, it seems, before the very altar of the prince of the apostles" [sepultusque est, vt videtur, ante ipsum altare principis apostolorum]. Scholz, "Sulcard," 91.

precise spot – particularly if the abbey's community made an effort to discourage popular reverence for the body immediately after the Conquest.[57] Even though William's reign was framed by reference to the time of King Edward, his predecessor's body was hidden in its own mausoleum: the remains were present but not visible.[58]

Conclusions

Future generations of English kings built on William's ideological groundwork, and in the ensuing centuries, Edward was cultivated as a valued ancestor of Norman and Angevin rulers.[59] Interest eventually returned to his remains. Edward's body was exhumed and discovered to be incorrupt in 1102, and the following decades saw repeated requests for papal canonization, which was finally granted in 1161.[60] Two years later, Henry II translated Edward's relics into a more accessible shrine, reportedly lifting his predecessor's remains on his own shoulders.[61] In the thirteenth century, Henry III adopted Edward as his patron saint, translating him again in 1269 and commissioning a renovation of Westminster that all but replaced the eleventh-century Romanesque structure.[62] Edward's cult did not attract widespread popularity in the Middle Ages, but devotion was concentrated among a small population – royalty, political elites, and the Westminster community – whose reverence was grounded in the saint's identity as a royal predecessor and patron.[63] The twelfth- and thirteenth-century kings who professed

---

57 William Rufus was reportedly buried under an unmarked paving stone, as were earlier Frankish kings: Brown et al., *King's Works*, 477; Wright, "Royal Tomb Program," 229; Brown, "Burying and Unburying," 242; Nelson, "Carolingian Royal Funerals," 142. Edward's twelfth-century hagiographers reported that his relics were translated into a silver shrine after the 1102 tomb opening – implying perhaps that his original burial was not worthy of his status: Crook, *Architectural Setting*, 216; and above, n. 54. Of course, it is possible that the unknown location of Edward's grave might have been a hagiographical invention: Mortimer, "Edward the Confessor," 35.

58 The time of Edward the Confessor (TRE) in Norman accounts of William's reign is discussed by Garnett, *Conquered England*, 9–24.

59 Barlow, *Edward the Confessor*, 265–7.

60 *Vita Ædwardi*, 113–32; Scholz, "Canonization of Edward."

61 Barlow, *Edward the Confessor*, 283–4; Barlow, *Thomas Becket*, 85, 95, and 296n14; Scholz, "Canonization of Edward," 56–7; Mason, "Westminster and the Monarchy," 284; Crook, *Architectural Setting*, 216.

62 Binski, *Westminster*, 52–4, 91–3, and 100–1; Harvey, *Westminster and Its Estates*, 28–9.

63 Mason, *Westminster and Its People*, 264–6; Mason, "Westminster and the Monarchy," 272–8; Binski, *Westminster*, 53–4; Harvey, *Westminster and Its Estates*, 43–4.

kinship with Edward strengthened their claims to both political and spiritual authority, linking their reigns to Anglo-Saxon and Conquest-era history while associating themselves with an ideal Christian ruler. Edward's legendary virginity added another level of retrospective legitimacy to the Conquest, as his saintly abstention from procreating meant that an heir needed to be found from more distant kin. The king's pious chastity could be understood as an implicit endorsement of future Norman rule.

In the eleventh century, however, English saints might be less kind to their foreign kings. Hagiographical accounts of aggressive rulers – both Norman and Danish – being miraculously punished by native saints reveal persistent concerns about the preservation of English identity and the Anglo-Saxon past.[64] That such stories continued circulating so long after Cnut and William's respective conquests could indicate that these kings' claims of legitimate succession from the West Saxon dynasty were met with scepticism. Nevertheless, both kings' treatment of royal bodies indicates that they valued the semblance of continuity and that they regarded interaction with their predecessors' remains as integral to the transfer of royal authority. Surely, they were guided in their initial efforts to this effect by advisers familiar with English politics, individuals like Emma and Archbishop Wulfstan in Cnut's case, and Archbishops Ealdred and Stigand in William's. However, their willingness to accept such guidance reflects a genuine interest in appearing legitimate. Remarkably, Cnut and William were the only eleventh-century rulers to successfully engage two modes of burial discourse at once, glorifying the remains of select predecessors while minimizing the impact of others. Although their military ruthlessness may have discouraged their new subjects from challenging them, the conquerors' effective and concurrent manipulation of royal bodies reflects a desire to follow English royal custom rather than to assert authority exclusively by force. They were not simply replicating the actions of previous kings but adapting English custom to their immediate needs; they built on precedent to convey their own complex political ideas.

Cnut and William diverged, however, in their own burials. While Cnut was interred in the West Saxon necropolis at Old Minster, William was buried in Normandy, in the abbey he founded at Caen. In a certain light, this might be seen as a final imitation of Edward the Confessor: rather

64 By the twelfth century, it was reported that William demanded to inspect St Cuthbert's relics, only to be punished by the saint – an episode strikingly similar to Cnut's supposed encounter with St Edith at Wilton: Ridyard, "Post-Conquest Attitudes," 197; Abou-el-Haj, "Post-Conquest Appropriation," 179–80; and above, chapter 6.

than having himself interred in a well-established mausoleum, he followed Edward's example by arranging to be buried in a newly commissioned foundation. Nevertheless, William's rejection of Anglo-Saxon royal mausolea set the standard for English kings' burials for the next two centuries. Instead of reinforcing dynastic legitimacy by associating themselves in death with past rulers, most Norman and Angevin kings were laid to rest in Continental churches or new English foundations.[65] Henry I was buried at the monastery he founded at Reading and Stephen at his own foundation at Faversham. Henry II and Richard I were both entombed at Fontevraud Abbey, in Anjou. John may at one time have intended to be buried at his new foundation at Beaulieu, but he was entombed instead at Worcester, which possessed no earlier kings' graves.[66] The only exception to this pattern was William Rufus, who was buried at the newly built Winchester Cathedral, into which Old Minster's collection of pre-Conquest royal bodies had recently been transferred; but this choice of burial place is best attributed to convenience, given his unexpected death and the hasty succession of his brother.[67] It was only in 1272 that royal burial resumed at Westminster, when Henry III opted to be entombed in the Confessor's vacated grave.[68] Edward I, Edward III, Richard II, and Henry V would later be buried at Westminster as well.[69]

This shift in the landscape of royal burial did not mean that pre-Conquest rulers were left to oblivion. A flurry of Anglo-Saxon saints' translations at the turn of the twelfth century was accompanied by the relocation of pre-Conquest kings' bodies into new tombs and Norman churches.[70]

65 Hallam, "Royal Burial," 369–71; Mason, "Westminster and the Monarchy," 271; Binski, *Westminster*, 92–3.

66 Duffy, *Royal Tombs*, 51–3, 55–8, and 60–2; Brown et al., *King's Works*, 478.

67 Mason, "Westminster and the Monarchy," 285–6; Brooke, "Bishop Walkelin," 5; Duffy, *Royal Tombs*, 46.

68 Henry's body was moved to a new tomb in 1290: Binski, *Westminster*, 94; Crook, *Architectural Setting*, 16.

69 Duffy, *Royal Tombs*, 96–8, 146–51, 167–73, and 207–15. Matilda, wife of Henry I, was also buried there in 1118; and the purported remains of King Sæberht, Westminster's conversion-era founder, were elevated into a royal tomb in 1307. ASC E 1118; Mason, "Westminster and the Monarchy," 270; Binski, *Westminster*, 123–4.

70 For example: Sts Dunstan, Ælfheah, and various other Anglo-Saxon archbishops of Canterbury were translated into the new Norman cathedral ca 1077; St Earconwald was translated after a fire at St Paul's in 1087; St Augustine and the earliest archbishops of Canterbury were translated into the newly built St Augustine's Abbey in 1091; St Swithun was translated into the new Winchester Cathedral in 1093; St Cuthbert was translated at Durham in 1104; the royal women of Ely were translated in 1106; and the

Æthelred II and Sæbbi were re-entombed at St Paul's after a fire in 1087; the royal bodies at Old Minster were moved into the newly built Winchester Cathedral, probably in 1094; St Edmund was translated at Bury in 1095; Edward the Confessor was exhumed in 1102; Alfred and Edward the Elder accompanied New Minster's community to Hyde Abbey in 1110; and the supposed remains of Harold Godwineson had been translated three times at Waltham by the 1120s.[71] Even as contemporary kings sought new burial places, pre-Conquest rulers continued to be memorialized by Anglo-Norman communities as part of their institutional and national histories.

The effect of changing royal burial practices upon English succession politics after the Norman Conquest is outside the scope of this study. In concluding, however, it is worth noting that royal coronations were held at Westminster from 1066 onward.[72] This consistency marks a return to an earlier pattern, in which legitimacy was tied to a static, symbolic location: Kingston had served a similar purpose among West Saxon rulers before the eleventh century, though less consistently than Westminster would in the later Middle Ages. After the accessions of Harold Godwineson and William I, continuity was no longer expressed at the time of coronation through interactions with the body or tomb of a predecessor; and after the reign of Harthacnut, legitimacy was no longer expressed through burial in existing dynastic mausolea. Rather, royal authority was tied at the beginning of a king's reign to an established ceremonial site, while burial became an opportunity for individual kings to distinguish themselves from the past.

saints of Hexham were translated in 1113. Crook, *Architectural Setting*, 210–41; Ridyard, "Post-Conquest Attitudes," 183, 196–7, and 203; Sharpe, "Augustine's Translation."

71 For St Paul's: Thacker, "Cult of the Saints," 113–16; Keynes, "Burial of King Æthelred." For Old Minster: Crook, "Movement of Cnut's Bones," 176–82; Biddle, *Winchester*, 308 and 311–12. For New Minster and Hyde Abbey: Biddle, *Winchester*, 317–18; Keynes, *Liber Vitae*, 42–3; Luard, *Annales Monasterii de Wintonia*, 43. For Bury: Ridyard, "Post-Conquest Attitudes," 189; Yarrow, *Saints and Their Communities*, 24–8. For Westminster: *Vita Ædwardi*, 113–19. For Waltham: Watkiss and Chibnall, *Waltham Chronicle*, 56–7.

72 Mason, "Site of King-Making"; Harvey, *Westminster and Its Estates*, 25.

Epilogue

It is clear from the case studies treated in this book that royal burial in the later Anglo-Saxon period was a central component of the political process. In addition to providing official closure to his reign, a king's funeral offered a forum for consensus and frequently culminated in the designation of a new ruler. Yet perhaps it is in the occasional deviations from traditional royal burial practice that the importance of these burials can be seen most clearly. Although the absence of a normative royal funeral resulted from exceptional circumstances – conquest, usurpation, or regicide – departures from standard modes of royal burial should not be regarded as aberrations. Even the most drastic examples of posthumous denigration were part of a familiar discourse of burial practice. Various types of burial were current in late Anglo-Saxon England: saintly relics were enshrined in churches, lay and ecclesiastical magnates were given prestigious tombs, ordinary Christians were interred in consecrated cemeteries, executed bodies were mutilated or exposed. Each of these practices conveyed precise information about the life, death, and soul of the deceased. Rulers who desecrated or obliterated their rivals' bodies did not do so in a cultural vacuum, nor did they introduce entirely new customs or depart fully from established tradition. Rather, they substituted one mode of signifying burial for another, and the repeated use of these methods by pre-Conquest kings indicates that burial practice was recognized as a legitimate form of political expression. It was the pervasive understanding of how dead kings ought to be remembered and what royal burial ought to entail that made dishonourable variations so unpalatable for contemporaries. Even strained displays of reverence were apparently sufficient to ease difficult transitions: Cnut's posthumous respect for Edmund Ironside and William's cultivation of Edward the Confessor's memory offered an impression of continuity that helped counter the trauma of conquest. The legitimizing narratives that these foreign conquerors created are only the most extreme examples of how new kings constructed identities for their predecessors and for themselves by manipulating the remains of earlier rulers.

It is important to note that while this study has focused predominantly on the ways in which bodies and funerals were deployed in political debates and conflicts, royal burial was more than simply a tool for aspiring or insecure kings. Although the extent of ecclesiastical involvement in royal funerals is often uncertain, the disposal of bodies had been associated with care for the soul from the earliest days of Christianity in England; by the mid-tenth century, the spiritual importance of consecrated burial was becoming increasingly pronounced in religious and legal writings. Concern for a king's fate in the afterlife undoubtedly influenced the logistics of royal funerals and the subsequent commemoration of the deceased. Certainly, interring kings in monumental burial churches had political implications, but the patronization of religious communities offered lasting spiritual benefits as well. In the words of one poet, "it behooves every man to consider his soul's journey, how, when death comes, body and soul will be deeply divided" – an exhortation which would have applied to kings and their subjects alike.[1] Funeral arrangements, a choice of burial place, final bequests to religious communities, and instructions for memorialization could provide a ruler or his survivors a final chance to influence the fate of his soul.

Burial should likewise be understood within its broader ritual context. Funerals were part of a cycle of royal ceremonial – acclamation, anointing, crown wearing – which marked a king as exceptional throughout his reign. In the tenth and eleventh centuries, English rulers stayed in power until their deaths, with funerals marking the formal close of their reigns.[2] There is no compelling evidence that these last rites were less impressive than any other public royal ritual. However, unlike most other aspects of a king's life, his death was both inevitable and unpredictable. Funerals could rarely be used proactively in response to particular problems or conflicts; rather, they had to be adapted in light of each new set of political circumstances.

1 *Soul and Body I*: "Huru, ðæs behofað hæleða æghwylc / þæt he his sawle sið sylfa geþence, / hu þæt bið deoplic þonne se deað cymeð, / asyndreð … / lic ond sawle!" Krapp, *Vercelli Book*, 54, ll.1–5.

2 Æthelred's exile in 1013–14 was a temporary exception to this trend. A number of earlier Anglo-Saxon kings, by contrast, died in retirement or exile: Stancliffe, "Kings Who Opted Out"; Yorke, "Anglo-Saxon Royal Courts," 245–52.

Their logistics and tone must have varied significantly depending on whether a king had died early or late in his reign, with his rule secure or under threat, with a named heir or a debated line of succession. If royal funerals represented a "ritualized crisis" whose "ultimate function [was] the restoration of order," it was incumbent upon each potential successor to negotiate the ritual aspects of his predecessor's funeral so that he would be credited with resolving the crisis and restoring order.[3] Certainly, all of the royal deaths and funerals considered in this study were accompanied by immediate political practicalities. Yet they also helped reinforce the institution of kingship, affirming its endurance beyond any single mortal lifetime.[4] Ceremony signalled stability and authority; it is no small thing that conquerors and usurpers sought to forge ritualized connections with the Anglo-Saxon royal past.

It is also vital to remember, in light of the many political implications of royal death, that funerals were opportunities for mourning. The account of Edward the Confessor's burial which opened this study was explicit in its description of his subjects' grief: the body was "washed in the nation's tears" and interred with "infinite mourning."[5] Similar sentiments appear in other narrative sources. Although the royal obits in the Anglo-Saxon Chronicle do not allude to mourning, the Annals of St Neots noted that Alfred's death was accompanied by "great sorrow."[6] The *Passio Eadwardi* portrayed the people of Wareham lamenting Edward the Martyr as they carried his body to a temporary grave, and the *Encomium Emmae* explained how extensively the kingdom wept at the deaths of Edmund Ironside and Cnut.[7] Such rhetoric may be characterized as literary convention; indeed, even physical signs of lamentation, like crying, might have been deliberate political display.[8] Nevertheless, the fact that bereavement

3 Buc, *Dangers of Ritual*, 83.

4 Kantorowicz, *King's Two Bodies*.

5 "Patrię lacrimis lotum"; "infinito merore": *Vita Ædwardi*, 80–1.

6 "Magno ... dolore"; Dumville and Lapidge, *Annals of St Neots*, 99.

7 In the *Passio*'s description of Edward's first burial, the procession of his subjects was "lamenting with one voice" [uox una ululantium] and carried the body with "mourning voices" [gementium vocimus]; Fell, *Edward, King and Martyr*, 7–8. The Encomiast stated that Edmund Ironside "was wept long and greatly by the people of the kingdom" [defletus diu multumque a patriensi populo] but described the mourning for Cnut more extensively, detailing the grief of various segments of the population who "wept for what they had lost" [flebant hoc quod perdiderant]; *Encomium*, 30–1 and 38–9. Similar language was used for Harthacnut's death in a newly discovered "Edwardian" recension of the text: Keynes and Love, "Earl Godwine's Ship," 195.

8 Compare Huntington and Metcalf, *Celebrations of Death*, 24–8.

was considered the appropriate response to the death of a king suggests that royal funerals served a purpose beyond immediate practical interests. Accounts of the grief expressed by Æthelred for his brother Edward, Emma for her son Alfred, and Edith for her husband Edward seem natural reactions to the loss of a close family member.[9] Old English elegiac poetry articulated the sorrow that accompanied the death of one's lord, and it is probable that such sentiments were present among the retinues of tenth- and eleventh-century kings.[10] Moreover, while religious communities might cultivate a ruler's grave and memory in acknowledgment of his patronage (or his survivors'), a royal family's ecclesiastical friends and allies may have genuinely desired to help the king's soul through intercessory prayer.[11] Despite the near impossibility of identifying authentic emotional responses to death in this period, the obligations and expectations which fell upon survivors of kings – and those of other Christian dead – might help the living come to terms with grief and loss.[12]

It is a commonplace of mortuary scholarship that the dead did not bury themselves. At its most basic, the respectful interment of bodies was a final act of human kindness which could never be reciprocated. Conversely, the insult of desecration could never be avenged first-hand. Yet whether a corpse was honoured or desecrated, its treatment confirmed the deceased's ultimate lack of agency; the body was at the mercy of those who controlled it. In most of the examples considered in this book, it is unclear precisely who organized the logistics of royal burials, but I have argued that the disposal of kings' bodies was used to advance the interests of potential or actual successors. In cases in which a hereditary claim was at stake, it is logical that a candidate would benefit from a funeral that allowed him close contact with the dead king: the burials of ordinary lay

9 Æthelred "received no consolation from anyone" [consolationem a nemine recipere] and could suppress "neither mourning nor tears" [neque luctu neque lacrimis] over his brother's death; Fell, *Edward, King and Martyr*, 7. Emma "was inconsolably upset" [inconsolabiliter contundebatur] over Alfred's death; *Encomium*, 46–7. Edith was "incessantly grieving" [indesinenter lugentem] at Edward's deathbed but "was consoled" [consolabatur] by her dying husband; *Vita Ædwardi*, 80.

10 As Edward the Confessor lay dying, for instance, the retinue at his bedside "stood and wept bitterly" [starent et flerent amare]; *Vita Ædwardi*, 79. Compare also *The Wanderer* and *The Seafarer*, in Krapp and Dobbie, *Exeter Book*, 134–7 and 143–7.

11 For example, a request for intercession is explicit in Alfred's will: S 1507; Keynes and Lapidge, *Alfred the Great*, 177. See also Thompson, *Dying and Death*, 74–5.

12 For the difficulty of identifying grief, see: Thompson, *Dying and Death*, 9; Rosenwein, *Emotional Communities*, 57–9.

Christians were typically arranged by relatives in this period, and an individual's prominent participation in a royal funeral might therefore give the appearance of a close familial bond.[13] Still, it is unlikely that the practical organization of a major ceremonial event would be handled solely by an aspiring heir. Royal funerals must have been collaborative efforts, arranged by the dead king's survivors and supporters, allies of one (or more) of his potential successors, and ecclesiastical authorities who would identify with one (or more) of these groups. In the aftermath of foreign conquest, a comparable set of advisers must have helped arrange Cnut's honourable burial of Edmund Ironside in a West Saxon mausoleum and William's ritual activity at the tomb of Edward the Confessor. Similar – though possibly more limited – consultations surely accompanied the dishonourable treatment of royal bodies. The concealment of Edward the Martyr's corpse and the exhumation of Harold Harefoot's remains were reportedly undertaken by groups of high-ranking magnates associated with the royal family, and the mutilation of Alfred the Ætheling and his burial at Ely were overseen by agents of the acting king; in Harold and Alfred's cases, clergymen were directly involved, and it is not impossible that clergy were also consulted around the time of Edward's assassination. The convergence of political, religious, and personal considerations that accompanied each royal death meant that knowledgeable advisers were indispensible.

From the political perspective which has informed this study, the objective of any royal burial – honourable or dishonourable – was to construct a legacy for the dead that would endure beyond the grave and exert influence among the living. This entailed a process of "selective remembering and … active forgetting," in which aspects of the ruler's life advantageous to his successor's interests were memorialized at the expense of other elements of his reign.[14] Edward the Elder's portrayal of Alfred as the legitimizing patriarch of a unified Anglo-Saxon kingdom exaggerated a single aspect of the dead king's accomplishments; Cnut's fraternal care for the body of Edmund Ironside made their final peace treaty a defining feature of Edmund's short reign; and Harthacnut's exhumation of Harold Harefoot was intended to immortalize his crimes against the new king's family. Just as an author of narrative texts might offer a one-sided perspective on a ruler's accomplishments, the individuals who orchestrated a king's burial sought to construct a particular identity for the dead through

13 Burial as a familial obligation is discussed by Hadley and Buckberry, "Caring for the Dead," 147.

14 Williams, *Death and Memory*, 2.

the treatment of his body. For ordinary laymen, burial in consecrated ground signalled membership in the Christian community and deviant burial confirmed criminals as outsiders; for a king, the location of his grave, the appearance of his tomb, and the ritual processes that accompanied his burial determined how he ought to be remembered. Although efforts to shape rulers' posthumous identities met with varying degrees of success in later Anglo-Saxon England, it is clear that kings' bodies were systematically used to validate royal authority and shape dynastic histories. Despite the silence of the sources, royal burial was a rich, established, and effective mode of political discourse.

Bibliography

Primary

Abbo of Fleury. "Life of St. Edmund." *Three Lives of English Saints*. Ed. Michael Winterbottom. Toronto: Toronto Medieval Latin Texts, 1972. Pp. 65–87.

Ælfric of Eynsham. *Ælfric's Catholic Homilies. The First Series: Text*. Ed. Peter Clemoes. EETS Supplementary Series 17. Oxford: Oxford University Press, 1997.

Ælfric of Eynsham. *Ælfric's Lives of Saints: Being a Set of Sermons on Saints' Days Formerly Observed by the English Church*, 2 vols. Ed. Walter W. Skeat. EETS Original Series 76, 82, 94, 114. 1881–1900.

Amatus of Montecassino. *The History of the Normans*. Ed. Graham A. Loud. Trans. Prescott N. Dunbar. Woodbridge: Boydell, 2004.

Arnold, Thomas, ed. *Memorials of St. Edmund's Abbey*, vol. 1. Rolls Series 96. London: 1890.

Augustine of Hippo. *City of God*. Trans. John O'Meara. London: Penguin, 1984.

Baker, P.S., ed. *The Anglo-Saxon Chronicle: A Collaborative Edition*, vol. 8: *MS F*. Cambridge: D.S. Brewer, 2000.

Barlow, Frank, ed. and trans. *The Carmen de Hastingae Proelio of Guy, Bishop of Amiens*. Oxford: Clarendon, 1999.

Barlow, Frank, ed. and trans. *The Life of King Edward Who Rests at Westminster, Attributed to a Monk of St Bertin*. London: Thomas Nelson and Sons, 1962.

Bately, Janet M., ed. *The Anglo-Saxon Chronicle: A Collaborative Edition*, vol. 3: *MS A*. Cambridge: D.S. Brewer, 1986.

Bates, David, ed. *Regesta Regum Anglo-Normannorum: The Acta of William I (1066–1087)*. Oxford: Clarendon, 1998.

Bede. *Ecclesiastical History of the English People*. Ed. and trans. Bertram Colgrave and R.A.B. Mynors. Oxford: Clarendon, 1969.

Bethurum, Dorothy, ed. *The Homilies of Wulfstan*. Oxford: Clarendon, 1957.
Biddle, Martin, ed. *Winchester in the Early Middle Ages: An Edition and Discussion of the Winton Domesday*. Winchester Studies 1. Oxford: Clarendon, 1976.
Birch, Walter de Gray, ed. *Liber Vitae: Register and Martyrology of New Minster and Hyde Abbey, Winchester*. London: Simpkin, 1892.
Blake, E.O., ed. *Liber Eliensis*. Camden 3rd Series 92. London: Royal Historical Society, 1962.
Bloch, Marc, ed. "La Vie de Édouard le Confesseur par Osbert de Clare." *Analecta Bollandiana* 41 (1922): 5–131.
Bollandus, Ioannes, and Godefridus Henschenius, eds. *Acta Sanctorum*. Antwerp: Ioannes Meursius, 1643. *Acta Sanctorum Full-Text Database*, 1999. http://acta.chadwyck.com.
Campbell, A., ed. and trans. *The Chronicle of Æthelweard*. London: Thomas Nelson and Sons, 1962.
Campbell, Alistair, ed. and trans. *Encomium Emmae Reginae*. Supplementary introduction by Simon Keynes. Camden Classic Reprints 4. London: Cambridge University Press, 1949, reprinted 1998.
Clayton, Mary, and Hugh Magennis, eds. *The Old English Lives of St Margaret*. Cambridge Studies in Anglo-Saxon England 9. Cambridge: Cambridge University Press, 1994.
Colgrave, Bertram, ed. and trans. *The Earliest Life of Gregory the Great*. Cambridge: Cambridge University Press, 1968.
Cubbin, G.P., ed. *The Anglo-Saxon Chronicle: A Collaborative Edition*, vol. 6: *MS D*. Cambridge: D.S. Brewer, 1996.
Dennis, Andrew, Peter Foote, and Richard Perkins, eds. and trans. *Laws of Early Iceland. Grágás: The Codex Regius of Grágás, With Material from Other Manuscripts*, vol. 1. Winnipeg: Manitoba University Press, 1980.
Dumville, David, and Michael Lapidge, eds. *The Anglo-Saxon Chronicle: A Collaborative Edition*, vol. 17: *The Annals of St Neots with Vita Prima Sancti Neoti*. Cambridge: D.S. Brewer, 1984.
Eadmer of Canterbury. *Lives and Miracles of Saints Oda, Dunstan, and Oswald*. Ed. and trans. Andrew J. Turner and Bernard J. Muir. Oxford: Clarendon, 2006.
Edwards, Edward, ed. *Liber Monasterii de Hyda*. Rolls Series 45. London: 1866.
Fairweather, Janet, trans. *Liber Eliensis: A History of the Isle of Ely from the Seventh Century to the Twelfth*. Woodbridge: Boydell, 2005.
Fell, Christine E., ed. *Edward, King and Martyr*. Leeds Texts and Monographs, New Series 3: 1971.
Flete, John. *The History of Westminster Abbey*. Ed. J. Armitage Robinson. Cambridge: Cambridge University Press, 1909.

Fowler, Joseph Thomas, ed. *Extracts from the Account Rolls of the Abbey of Durham*, vol. 2. Durham: Surtees Society, 1899.

Fulk, R.D., Robert E. Bjork, and John D. Niles, eds. *Klaeber's Beowulf*, 4th ed. Toronto: University of Toronto Press, 2008.

Gaimar, Geffrei. *L'Estoire des Engleis*. Ed. Alexander Bell. Anglo-Norman Texts 14–16. Oxford: Blackwell, 1960.

Haddan, Arthur West, and William Stubbs, eds. *Councils and Ecclesiastical Documents Relating to Great Britain and Ireland*, vol. 3. Oxford: Clarendon, 1871.

Harmer, Florence E., ed. and trans. *Anglo-Saxon Writs*. Manchester: Manchester University Press, 1952.

Hearne, T., ed. *Hemingi Chartularium Ecclesiæ Wigorniensis*. Oxford: 1723.

Henry of Huntingdon. *Historia Anglorum: The History of the English People*. Ed. and trans. Diana Greenway. Oxford: Clarendon, 1996.

Hollis, Stephanie, et al., eds. and trans. *Writing the Wilton Women: Goscelin's Legend of Edith and Liber Confortatorius*. Turnhout: Brepols, 2004.

Hudson, John, ed. and trans. *The History of the Church of Abingdon*, vol. 1. Oxford: Clarendon, 2007.

Irvine, Susan, ed. *The Anglo-Saxon Chronicle: A Collaborative Edition*, vol. 7: *MS. E*. Cambridge: D.S. Brewer, 2004.

John of Worcester. *The Chronicle of John of Worcester*, 3 vols. Ed. R.R. Darlington and P. McGurk. Trans. Jennifer Bray and P. McGurk. Oxford: Clarendon, 1995.

Kelly, S.E., ed. *Charters of Abingdon Abbey*, vol. 1. Anglo-Saxon Charters 7. Oxford: Oxford University Press, 2000.

Kelly, S.E., ed. *Charters of Glastonbury Abbey*. Anglo-Saxon Charters 15. Oxford: Oxford University Press, 2012.

Kelly, S.E., ed. *Charters of Malmesbury Abbey*. Anglo-Saxon Charters 11. Oxford: Oxford University Press, 2005.

Kelly, S.E., ed. *Charters of St Paul's, London*. Anglo-Saxon Charters 10. Oxford: Oxford University Press, 2004.

Kennedy, A.G., ed. and trans. "Cnut's Law Code of 1018." *Anglo-Saxon England* 11 (1983): 57–81.

Keynes, Simon, ed. *The Liber Vitae of the New Minster and Hyde Abbey Winchester. British Library Stowe 944*. Early English Manuscripts in Facsimile 26. Copenhagen: Rosenkilde and Bagger, 1996.

Keynes, Simon, and Michael Lapidge, eds. and trans. *Alfred the Great: Asser's Life of King Alfred and Other Contemporary Sources*. London: Penguin, 1983.

Kotzor, G., ed. *Das Altenglische Martyrologium*, 2 vols. Abhandlungen der Bayerischen Akademie der Wissenschaften, phil.-hist. Kl., ns.88.1–2. Munich: 1981.

Krapp, George Philip, ed. *The Junius Manuscript.* Anglo-Saxon Poetic Records 1. New York: Columbia University Press, 1931.

Krapp, George Philip, ed. *The Vercelli Book.* Anglo-Saxon Poetic Records 2. New York: Columbia University Press, 1932.

Krapp, George Philip, and Elliott van Kirk Dobbie, eds. *The Exeter Book.* Anglo-Saxon Poetic Records 3. New York: Columbia University Press, 1936.

Kunz, Keneva, trans. "Laxdæla Saga." *The Sagas of Icelanders.* Ed. Örnólfur Thorsson. London: Penguin, 2001. Pp. 270–421.

Lapidge, Michael, ed. and trans. *Byrhtferth of Ramsey: The Lives of St Oswald and St Ecgwine.* Oxford: Clarendon, 2009.

Lapidge, Michael, ed. and trans. *The Cult of St Swithun.* Winchester Studies 4.ii: The Anglo-Saxon Minsters of Winchester. Oxford: Clarendon, 2003.

Liebermann, F., ed. *Die Gesetze der Angelsachsen*, 3 vols. Halle: Max Niemeyer, 1903.

Liebermann, F., ed. *Der Heiligen Englands: Angelsächsisch und Lateinisch.* Hannover: Hahn, 1889.

Luard, Henry Richards, ed. *Annales Monastici*, vol. 2: *Annales Monasterii de Wintonia (*a.d. *519–1277), Annales Monasterii de Waverleia (*A.D. *1–1291).* Rolls Series 36. London: 1865.

Magennis, Hugh, ed. and trans. *The Anonymous Old English Legend of the Seven Sleepers.* Durham Medieval Texts 7. Durham: 1994.

Mason, Emma, ed. *Westminster Abbey Charters, 1066–c. 1214.* London: London Record Society, 1988.

McNeill, John T., and Helena M. Gamer, trans. *Medieval Handbooks of Penance: A Translation of the Principal Libri Poenitentiales.* New York: Columbia University Press, 1938.

Migne, Jacques-Paul, ed. *Patrologia Latina.* Paris: Garnieri Fratres, 1844–55 and 1862–5.

Miller, Sean, ed. *Charters of the New Minster, Winchester.* Anglo-Saxon Charters 9. Oxford: Oxford University Press, 2001.

Muir, Bernard James, ed. *A Pre-Conquest English Prayer-Book: BL MSS Cotton Galba A.xiv and Nero Aii (ff.3–13).* Henry Bradshaw Society 103. Woodbridge: Boydell, 1988.

O'Brien O'Keeffe, Katherine, ed. *The Anglo-Saxon Chronicle: A Collaborative Edition*, vol. 5: *MS C.* Cambridge: D.S. Brewer, 2001.

O'Brien O'Keeffe, Katherine, ed. *Manuscripts Containing the Anglo-Saxon Chronicle, Works by Bede, and Other Texts.* Anglo-Saxon Manuscripts in

Microfiche Facsimile, vol. 10. Tempe: Arizona Center for Medieval and Renaissance Studies, 2003.
O'Neill, Patrick P., ed. *King Alfred's Old English Prose Translation of the First Fifty Psalms*. Medieval Academy Books 104. Cambridge, MA: 2001.
Orderic Vitalis. *The Ecclesiastical History*, 6 vols. Ed. and trans. Marjorie Chibnall. Oxford: Clarendon, 1969–78.
Pálsson, Hermann, and Paul Edwards, eds. and trans. *Eyrbyggja Saga*. London: Penguin, 1989.
Plummer, Charles, ed. *Two of the Saxon Chronicles Parallel*, 2 vols. Oxford: Clarendon, 1892 and 1899.
Raine, James, ed. *The Fabric Rolls of York Minster*. Durham: Surtees Society, 1859.
Raine, James, ed. *The Historians of the Church of York*, 3 vols. Rolls Series 71. London: 1886.
Rauer, Christine, ed. and trans. *The Old English Martyrology: Edition, Translation and Commentary*. Anglo-Saxon Texts 10. Cambridge: D.S. Brewer, 2013.
Riley, Henry Thomas, ed. *Gesta Abbatum Monasterii Sancti Albani a Thoma Walsingham*, vol. 3. London: Longmans, Green, Reader, and Dyer, 1869.
Rumble, Alexander R., ed. and trans. *Property and Piety in Early Medieval Winchester: Documents Relating to the Topography of the Anglo-Saxon and Norman City and Its Minsters*. Winchester Studies 4.iii: The Anglo-Saxon Minsters of Winchester. Oxford: Clarendon, 2002.
Rumble, Alexander R., and Rosemary Morris, eds. and trans. "Osbern's *Translatio Sancti Ælfegi Cantuariensis Archiepiscopi et Martyris*: An Annotated Edition and Translation." *The Reign of Cnut: King of England, Denmark, and Norway*. Ed. Alexander R. Rumble. London: Leicester University Press, 1994. Pp. 283–315.
Sauer, Hans, ed. *Theodulfi Capitula in England: Die Altenglische Übersetzung, Zusammen Mit Dem Lateinischen Text*. Munich: W. Fink, 1978.
Sawyer, P.H., ed. *Charters of Burton Abbey*. Anglo-Saxon Charters 2. Oxford: Oxford University Press, 1979.
Scholz, Bernhard W., ed. "Sulcard of Westminster: 'Prologus de Construccione Westmonasterii.'" *Traditio* 20 (1964): 59–91.
Schreiber, Carolin, ed. *King Alfred's Old English Translation of Pope Gregory the Great's Regula Pastoralis and Its Cultural Context*. Frankfurt: Peter Lang, 2003.
Scott, John, ed. and trans. *The Early History of Glastonbury: An Edition, Translation and Study of William of Malmesbury's De Antiquitate Glastonie Ecclesie*. Woodbridge: Boydell, 1981.
Scragg, D.G., ed. *The Vercelli Homilies and Related Texts*. EETS Original Series 300. Oxford: Oxford University Press, 1992.

Searle, Eleanor, ed. and trans. *The Chronicle of Battle Abbey*. Oxford: Clarendon, 1980.

Snorri Sturluson. *Heimskringla: History of the Kings of Norway*. Trans. Lee M. Hollander. Austin: Texas University Press, 1964.

Stevenson, Joseph, ed. *Chronicon Monasterii de Abingdon*, vol. 1. Rolls Series 2. London: 1858.

Stevenson, William Henry, ed. *Asser's Life of King Alfred*. Oxford: Clarendon, 1959.

Stubbs, William, ed. *The Historical Works of Gervase of Canterbury*, vol. 2: *The Minor Works*. Rolls Series 73. London: 1880.

Stubbs, William, ed. *The Historical Works of Master Ralph de Diceto*, vol. 1. Rolls Series 68. London: 1876.

Stubbs, William, ed. *Memorials of Saint Dunstan, Archbishop of Canterbury*. Rolls Series 63. London: 1874.

Swanton, Michael, trans. *The Anglo-Saxon Chronicles*. London: Phoenix Press, 2000.

Symeon of Durham. *Symeonis Monachi Opera Omnia*, vol. 2: *Historia Regum*. Ed. Thomas Arnold. Rolls Series 75. London: 1885.

Symons, Thomas, ed. and trans. *Regularis Concordia: The Monastic Agreement of the Monks and Nuns of the English Nation.* London: Thomas Nelson and Sons, 1953.

Taylor, Simon, ed. *The Anglo-Saxon Chronicle: A Collaborative Edition*, vol. 4: *MS B*. Cambridge: D.S. Brewer, 1983.

Thietmar von Merseburg. *Chronik*. Ed. Werner Trillmich. Ausgewählte Quellen zur Deutschen Geschichte des Mittelalters 9. Darmstadt: Wissenschaftliche Buchgesellschaft, 2002.

Van Houts, Elisabeth M.C., ed. "The *Brevis Relatio de Guillelmo Nobilissimo Comite Normannorum*, Written by a Monk of Battle Abbey." *Chronology, Conquest and Conflict in Medieval England*. Camden 5th Series 10. Cambridge: Cambridge University Press, 1997. Pp. 6–48.

Van Houts, Elisabeth M.C., ed. and trans. *The Gesta Normannorum Ducum of William of Jumièges, Orderic Vitalis, and Robert of Torigni*, 2 vols. Oxford: Clarendon, 1992 and 1995.

Vogel, Cyrille, and Reinhard Elze, eds. *Le Pontifical Romano-Germanique du Dixième Siècle*, vol. 1: *Le Texte*. Studi e Testi 226. Vatican City: Biblioteca Apostolica Vaticana,1963.

Ward, Paul L., ed. "An Early Version of the Anglo-Saxon Coronation Ceremony." *English Historical Review* 57.227 (1942): 345–61.

Warner, David A., trans. *Ottonian Germany: The Chronicon of Thietmar of Merseburg*. Manchester: Manchester University Press, 2001.

Watkiss, Leslie, and Marjorie Chibnall, eds. and trans. *The Waltham Chronicle*. Oxford: Clarendon, 1994.

Whitelock, Dorothy, ed. and trans. *Anglo-Saxon Wills*. Cambridge: Cambridge University Press, 1930.

Whitelock, Dorothy, ed. and trans. *English Historical Documents*, vol. 1: *c. 500–1042*, 2nd ed. London: Methuen, 1979.

Whitelock, Dorothy, ed. and trans. *Sermo Lupi ad Anglos*. Exeter: Exeter University Press, 1976.

William of Malmesbury. *Gesta Pontificum Anglorum: The History of the English Bishops*, 2 vols. Ed. and trans. M. Winterbottom and R.M. Thompson. Oxford: Clarendon, 2007.

William of Malmesbury. *Gesta Regum Anglorum: The History of the English Kings*, 2 vols. Ed. and trans. R.A.B. Mynors, R.M. Thompson, and M. Winterbottom. Oxford: Clarendon, 1998.

William of Malmesbury. *Saints' Lives: Lives of Ss. Wulfstan, Dunstan, Patrick, Benignus and Indract*. Ed. and trans. M. Winterbottom and R.M. Thompson. Oxford: Clarendon, 2002.

William of Poitiers. *The Gesta Guillelmi*. Ed. and trans. R.H.C. Davis and Marjorie Chibnall. Oxford: Clarendon, 1998.

Wilmart, André, ed. "La légende de Ste Édith en prose et vers par le moine Goscelin." *Analecta Bollandiana* 56 (1938): 265–307.

Wilson, David M. *The Bayeux Tapestry*. New York: Thames and Hudson, 1985.

Winterbottom, Michael, and Michael Lapidge, eds. and trans. *The Early Lives of St Dunstan*. Oxford: Clarendon, 2012.

Wulfstan of Winchester. *The Life of St Æthelwold*. Ed. and trans. Michael Lapidge and Michael Winterbottom. Oxford: Clarendon, 1991.

Secondary

Abou-el-Haj, Barbara. "Saint Cuthbert: The Post-Conquest Appropriation of an Anglo-Saxon Cult." *Holy Men and Holy Women: Old English Prose Saints' Lives and Their Contexts*. Ed. Paul Szarmach. Albany: SUNY Press, 1996. Pp. 177–206.

Abrams, Lesley. *Anglo-Saxon Glastonbury: Church and Endowment*. Woodbridge: Boydell, 1996.

Abrams, Lesley. "'Lucid Intervals': A Rediscovered Anglo-Saxon Royal Diploma from Glastonbury Abbey." *Journal of the Society of Archivists* 10.2 (1989): 43–56.

Abrams, Lesley. "A Single-Sheet Facsimile of a Diploma of King Ine for Glastonbury." *The Archaeology and History of Glastonbury Abbey: Essays in Honour of the Ninetieth Birthday of C.A. Ralegh Radford*. Ed. Lesley Abrams and James P. Carley. Woodbridge: Boydell, 1991. Pp. 97–133.

Adams, Max. "Excavation of a Pre-Conquest Cemetery at Addingham, West Yorkshire." *Medieval Archaeology* 40 (1996): 151–91.

Ashdown, Margaret. "An Icelandic Account of the Survival of Harold Godwinson." *The Anglo-Saxons: Studies Presented to Bruce Dickins*. Ed. P. Clemoes. London: Bowes and Bowes, 1959. Pp. 122–36.

Ashe, Laura. "Harold Godwineson." *Heroes and Anti-Heroes in Medieval Romance*. Ed. Neil Cartlidge. Woodbridge: Boydell, 2012. Pp. 59–80.

Baraz, Daniel. "Violence or Cruelty? An Intercultural Perspective." *"A Great Effusion of Blood"? Interpreting Medieval Violence.* Ed. Mark D. Meyerson, Daniel Thiery, and Oren Falk. Toronto: University of Toronto Press, 2004. Pp. 164–89.

Barlow, Frank. *Edward the Confessor*. Berkeley: University of California Press, 1970.

Barlow, Frank. *The Feudal Kingdom of England, 1042–1216*, 4th ed. London: Longman, 1988.

Barlow, Frank. *The Godwins*. London: Pearson, 2002.

Barlow, Frank. *Thomas Becket*. Berkeley: University of California Press, 1986.

Barrow, Julia. "Demonstrative Behaviour and Political Communication in Later Anglo-Saxon England." *Anglo-Saxon England* 36 (2007): 127–50.

Battiscombe, C.F. *The Relics of Saint Cuthbert*. Oxford: Oxford University Press, 1956.

Baxter, Stephen. *The Earls of Mercia: Lordship and Power in Late Anglo-Saxon England*. Oxford: Oxford University Press, 2007.

Bernhardt, J.W. "King Henry II of Germany: Royal Self-Representation and Historical Memory." *Medieval Concepts of the Past: Ritual, Memory, Historiography*. Ed. G. Althoff, J. Fried, and P.J. Geary. Washington, DC: German Historical Institute, 2002. Pp. 39–69.

Bernstein, David. "The Blinding of Harold and the Meaning of the Bayeux Tapestry." *Anglo-Norman Studies* 5 (1982): 40–64.

Bersu, Gerhard, and David M. Wilson. *Three Viking Graves in the Isle of Man*. Society for Medieval Archaeology Monograph Series 1. London: 1966.

Bethell, Denis. "The Making of a Twelfth-Century Relic Collection." *Studies in Church History* 8 (1971): 61–72.

Bethurum, Dorothy. "Six Anonymous Old English Codes." *JEGP* 49 (1950): 449–63.

Biddle, Martin. "Archaeology, Architecture, and the Cult of Saints in Anglo-Saxon England." *The Anglo-Saxon Church: Papers on History, Architecture, and*

Archaeology in Honour of Dr. H.M. Taylor. Ed. L.A.S. Butler and R.K. Morris. Council for British Archaeology, Research Reports 60. London: 1986. Pp. 1–31.

Biddle, Martin. "A City in Transition: 400–800." *The City of London from Prehistoric Times to c. 1520*. Ed. Mary D. Lobel. Oxford: Oxford University Press, 1989. Pp. 20–9.

Biddle, Martin. "Excavations at Winchester 1965, Fourth Interim Report." *Antiquaries Journal* 46 (1966): 308–32.

Biddle, Martin. "*Felix Urbs Winthonia*: Winchester in the Age of Monastic Reform." *Tenth-Century Studies*. Ed. David Parsons. Chichester: Phillimore, 1975. Reprinted in *Anglo-Saxon History: Basic Readings*. Ed. David A.E. Pelteret. New York: Garland, 2000. Pp. 289–316.

Biddle, Martin. "Seasonal Festivals and Residence: Winchester, Westminster and Gloucester in the Tenth to Twelfth Centuries." *Anglo-Norman Studies* 8 (1985): 51–72.

Biddle, Martin. "Winchester: The Development of an Early Capital." *Vor- und Frühformen der Europäischen Stadt im Mittelalter* 1. Ed. Herbert Jankuhn, Walter Schlesinger, and Heiko Steuer. Göttingen: Vandenhoeck and Ruprecht, 1973. Pp. 229–61.

Biddle, Martin, and R.N. Quirk. "Excavations Near Winchester Cathedral, 1961." *Archaeological Journal* 119 (1962): 150–94.

Binski, Paul. *Medieval Death: Ritual and Representation*. London: British Museum Press, 1996.

Binski, Paul. *Westminster Abbey and the Plantagenets: Kingship and the Representation of Power, 1200–1400*. New Haven: Yale University Press, 1995.

Blair, John. "Anglo-Saxon Minsters: A Topographical Review." *Pastoral Care Before the Parish*. Ed. John Blair and Richard Sharpe. Leicester: Leicester University Press, 1992. Pp. 226–66.

Blair, John. *Anglo-Saxon Oxfordshire*. Stroud: Alan Sutton, 1994.

Blair, John. *The Church in Anglo-Saxon Society*. Oxford: Oxford University Press, 2005.

Blair, John. "Minster Churches in the Landscape." *Anglo-Saxon Settlements*. Ed. Della Hooke. Oxford: Blackwell, 1988. Pp. 35–58.

Bloch, Marc. *The Royal Touch: Sacred Monarchy and Scrofula in England and France*. Trans. J.E. Anderson. London: Routledge and Kegan Paul, 1973.

Blows, Matthew. "A Glastonbury Obit-List." *The Archaeology and History of Glastonbury Abbey: Essays in Honour of the Ninetieth Birthday of C.A. Ralegh Radford*. Ed. Lesley Abrams and James P. Carley. Woodbridge: Boydell, 1991. Pp. 257–69.

Blows, Matthew J. "Studies in the Pre-Conquest History of Glastonbury Abbey." PhD diss., University of London, 1991.

Boddington, Andy. "Models of Burial, Settlement and Worship: The Final Phase Reviewed." *Anglo-Saxon Cemeteries: A Reappraisal. Proceedings of a Conference Held at Liverpool Museum 1986*. Stroud: Alan Sutton, 1990. Pp. 177–99.

Boddington, Andy, et al. *Raunds Furnells: The Anglo-Saxon Church and Churchyard*. English Heritage Archaeological Report 7. London: 1996.

Boyle, Elizabeth. "A Welsh Record of an Anglo-Saxon Political Mutilation." *Anglo-Saxon England* 35 (2006): 245–9.

Boynton, Mark, and Susan Reynolds. "The Author of the Fonthill Letter." *Anglo-Saxon England* 25 (1996): 91–5.

Bozoky, Edina. "The Sanctity and Canonisation of Edward the Confessor." *Edward the Confessor: The Man and the Legend*. Ed. Richard Mortimer. Woodbridge: Boydell, 2009. Pp. 173–86.

Bredehoft, Thomas A. *Early English Metre*. Toronto: University of Toronto Press, 2005.

Bredehoft, Thomas A. *Textual Histories: Readings in the Anglo-Saxon Chronicle*. Toronto: University of Toronto Press, 2001.

Brett, Martin. "John of Worcester and his Contemporaries." *The Writing of History in the Middle Ages: Essays Presented to Richard William Southern*. Ed. R.H.C. Davis and J.M. Wallace-Hadrill. Oxford: Clarendon, 1981. Pp. 101–26.

Brooke, Christopher. "Bishop Walkelin and His Inheritance." *Winchester Cathedral: Nine Hundred Years, 1093–1993*. Ed. John Crook. Chichester: Phillimore, 1993. Pp. 1–12.

Brooke, Christopher. "The Central Middle Ages: 800–1270." *The City of London From Prehistoric Times to c. 1520*. Ed. Mary D. Lobel. Oxford: Oxford University Press, 1989. Pp. 30–41.

Brooke, Christopher. "Princes and Kings as Patrons of Monasteries: Normandy and England." *Il Monachesimo e la Riforma Ecclesiastica (1049–1122)*. Miscellanea del Centro di Studi Medioevali 7. Milan: Editrice Vita e Pensiero, 1971. Pp. 125–44.

Brooke, Christopher. *The Saxon and Norman Kings*, 3rd ed. Oxford: Blackwell, 2001.

Brooke, C.N.L. "The Earliest Times to 1485." *A History of St Paul's Cathedral and the Men Associated with It*. Ed. W.R. Matthews and W.M. Atkins. London: Phoenix House, 1957. Pp. 1–99.

Brooke, Christopher N.L., and Gillian Keir. *London 816–1216: The Shaping of a City*. Berkeley: University of California Press, 1975.

Brooks, Nicholas. *The Early History of the Church of Canterbury: Christ Church from 597 to 1066*. London: Leicester University Press, 1984.

Brooks, Nicholas P. "The Fonthill Letter, Ealdorman Ordlaf, and Anglo-Saxon Law in Practice." *Early Medieval Studies in Memory of Patrick Wormald*. Ed. Stephen Baxter et al. Farnham: Ashgate, 2009. Pp. 301–17.

Brooks, N.P. "The Career of St Dunstan." *St Dunstan: His Life, Times and Cult*. Ed. Nigel Ramsay, Margaret Sparks, and Tim Tatton-Brown. Woodbridge: Boydell, 1992. Pp. 1–23.

Brown, Elizabeth A.R. "Burying and Unburying the Kings of France." *Persons in Groups: Social Behavior as Identity Formation in Medieval and Renaissance Europe*. Ed. Richard C. Trexler. Medieval and Renaissance Texts and Studies 36. Binghamton, 1985. Pp. 241–66.

Brown, Peter. *The Cult of the Saints: Its Rise and Function in Latin Christianity*. Chicago: University of Chicago Press, 1981.

Brown, R. Allen, H.M. Colvin, and A.J. Taylor. *The History of the King's Work*, vol. 1: *The Middle Ages*. London: Her Majesty's Stationery Office, 1963.

Buc, Philippe. *The Dangers of Ritual: Between Early Medieval Texts and Social Scientific Theory*. Princeton: Princeton University Press, 2001.

Buckberry, J.L., and D.M. Hadley. "An Anglo-Saxon Execution Cemetery at Walkington Wold, Yorkshire." *Oxford Journal of Archaeology* 26.3 (2007): 309–29.

Bührer-Thierry, Geneviève. "'Just Anger' or 'Vengeful Anger'? The Punishment of Blinding in the Early Medieval West." *Anger's Past: The Social Uses of an Emotion in the Middle Ages*. Ed. Barbara H. Rosenwein. Ithaca, NY: Cornell University Press, 1998. Pp. 75–91.

Bullough, Donald. "Burial, Community and Belief in the Early Medieval West." *Ideal and Reality in Frankish and Anglo-Saxon Society*. Ed. Patrick Wormald. Oxford: Blackwell, 1983. Pp. 177–201.

Butler, Lawrence. "The Churchyard in Eastern England, AD 900–1100: Some Lines of Development." *Anglo-Saxon Cemeteries 1979: The Fourth Anglo-Saxon Symposium at Oxford*. Ed. Philip Rahtz, Tania Dickinson, and Lorna Watts. BAR British Series 82. Oxford: 1980. Pp. 383–9.

Camp, Cynthia Turner. "The Incorruptibility of Cuthbert, or, What the Lindisfarne Monks Saw in 698." Unpublished conference paper. International Medieval Congress. Kalamazoo, MI: May 2004.

Campbell, Alistair. "Introduction." *Encomium Emmae Reginae*. Ed. Alistair Campbell, with a supplementary introduction by Simon Keynes. Camden Classic Reprints 4. London: Cambridge University Press, 1949, reprinted 1998. Pp. xciii–cli [xciii–lxix].

Campbell, Miles W. "Queen Emma and Ælfgifu of Northampton: Canute the Great's Women." *Mediaeval Scandinavia* 4 (1971): 66–79.

Carver, M.O.H. *Sutton Hoo: A Seventh-Century Princely Burial Ground and Its Context*. London: British Museum Press, 2005.

Carver, Martin. "Why That? Why There? Why Then? The Politics of Early Medieval Monumentality." *Image and Power in the Archaeology of Early Medieval Britain: Essays in Honour of Rosemary Cramp*. Ed. Helena Hamerow and Arthur MacGregor. Oxford: Oxbow Books, 2001. Pp. 1–22.

Chaney, William A. *The Cult of Kingship in Anglo-Saxon England*. Manchester: Manchester University Press, 1970.

Christiansen, Eric. *The Norsemen in the Viking Age*. Oxford: Blackwell, 2002.

Cohen, Marc. "From Throndheim to Waltham to Chester: Viking- and Post-Viking Age Attitudes in the Survival Legends of Óláfr Tryggvason and Harold Godwinson." *The Middle Ages in the North-West*. Ed. Tom Scott and Pat Starkey. Oxford: Leopard's Head Press, 1995. Pp. 143–53.

Conner, Patrick W. *Anglo-Saxon Exeter: A Tenth-Century Cultural History*. Studies in Anglo-Saxon History 4. Woodbridge: Boydell, 1993.

Cooper, Janet M. *The Last Four Anglo-Saxon Archbishops of York*. Borthwick Papers 38. York: St Anthony's Press, 1970.

Cragoe, Carol Davidson. "Fabric, Tombs and Precinct, 1087–1540." *St Paul's: The Cathedral Church of London, 604–2004*. Ed. Derek Keene, Arthur Burns, and Andrew Saint. New Haven, CT: Yale University Press, 2004. Pp. 127–42 and 473–4.

Crook, John. *The Architectural Setting of the Cult of Saints in the Early Christian West, c. 300–1200*. Oxford: Clarendon, 2000.

Crook, John. "King Edgar's Reliquary of St Swithun." *Anglo-Saxon England* 21 (1992): 177–202.

Crook, John. "'A Worthy Antiquity': The Movement of King Cnut's Bones in Winchester Cathedral." *The Reign of Cnut: King of England, Denmark, and Norway*. Ed. Alexander R. Rumble. London: Leicester University Press, 1994. Pp. 165–92.

Cubitt, Catherine. "Images of St Peter: The Clergy and the Religious Life in Anglo-Saxon England." *The Christian Tradition in Anglo-Saxon England: Approaches to Current Scholarship and Teaching*. Ed. Paul Cavill. Cambridge: D.S. Brewer, 2004. Pp. 41–54.

Cubitt, Catherine. "Sites and Sanctity: Revisiting the Cult of Murdered and Martyred Anglo-Saxon Royal Saints." *Early Medieval Europe* 9.1 (2000): 53–83.

Cubitt, Catherine. "Universal and Local Saints in Anglo-Saxon England." *Local Saints and Local Churches in the Early Medieval West*. Ed. Alan Thacker and Richard Sharpe. Oxford: Oxford University Press, 2002. Pp. 423–53.

Damon, John Edward. "Advisors for Peace in the Reign of Æthelred Unræd." *Peace and Negotiation: Strategies for Coexistence in the Middle Ages and the Renaissance*. Ed. D. Wolfthal. Arizona Studies in the Middle Ages and the Renaissance 4. Turnhout: Brepols, 2000. Pp. 57–78.

Darlington, R.R., and P. McGurk. "The 'Chronicon Ex Chronicis' of 'Florence' of Worcester and Its Use of Sources for English History before 1066." *Anglo-Norman Studies* 5 (1982): 185–96.

De Jong, Mayke. "Monastic Prisoners or Opting Out? Political Coercion and Honour in the Frankish Kingdoms." *Topographies of Power in the Early Middle Ages*. Ed. Mayke de Jong. Leiden: Brill, 2001. Pp. 291–328.

De Jong, Mayke. "Power and Humility in Carolingian Society: The Public Penance of Louis the Pious." *Early Medieval Europe* 1.1 (1992): 29–52.

Deliyannis, Deborah Mauskopf. "Church Burial in Anglo-Saxon England: The Prerogative of Kings." *Frühmittelalterliche Studien: Jahrbuch des Instituts für Frühmittelalterforschung der Universität Münster* 29 (1995): 98–119.

Demidoff, Lene. "The Death of Svein Forkbeard – In Reality and Later Tradition." *Mediaeval Scandinavia* 11 (1978–9): 30–47.

Dodwell, C.R. *Anglo-Saxon Art: A New Perspective*. Manchester: Manchester University Press, 1982.

Douglas, David C. *William the Conqueror: The Norman Impact upon England*. Berkeley: University of California Press, 1964.

Duffy, Mark. *Royal Tombs of Medieval England*. Stroud: Tempus, 2003.

Dumville, David N. "The Ætheling: A Study in Anglo-Saxon Constitutional History." *Anglo-Saxon England* 8 (1979): 1–33.

Dumville, David N. "The Death of King Edward the Martyr – 18 March, 979?" *Anglo-Saxon* 1 (2007): 269–83.

Dumville, David N. *English Caroline Script and Monastic History: Studies in Benedictinism, AD 950–1030*. Woodbridge: Boydell, 1993.

Dumville, David N. "Kingship, Genealogies and Regnal Lists." *Early Medieval Kingship*. Ed. P.H. Sawyer and I.N. Wood. Leeds: School of History, 1977. Pp. 72–104.

Dumville, David N. "On the Dating of Some Late Anglo-Saxon Liturgical Manuscripts." *Transactions of the Cambridge Bibliographical Society* 10.1 (1991): 40–57.

Dumville, David N. *Wessex and England from Alfred to Edgar*. Woodbridge: Boydell, 1992.

Dumville, David N. "The West Saxon Genealogical Regnal List: Manuscripts and Texts." *Anglia* 104 (1986): 1–32.

Effros, Bonnie. "Beyond Cemetery Walls: Early Medieval Funerary Topography and Christian Salvation." *Early Medieval Europe* 6.1 (1997): 1–23.

Effros, Bonnie. *Merovingian Mortuary Archaeology and the Making of the Early Middle Ages*. Berkeley: University of California Press, 2003.

Effros, Bonnie. "Monuments and Memory: Repossessing Ancient Remains in Early Medieval Gaul." *Topographies of Power in the Early Middle Ages*.

Ed. Mayke de Jong, Frans Theuws, and Carine Van Rhijn. Leiden: Brill, 2001. Pp. 93–118.

Farmer, Hugh. "William of Malmesbury's Life and Works." *Journal of Ecclesiastical History* 13.1 (1962): 39–54.

Fell, Christine. "Edward King and Martyr and the Anglo-Saxon Hagiographic Tradition." *Ethelred the Unready: Papers from the Millenary Conference*. Ed. David Hill. BAR British Series 59. Oxford: 1978. Pp. 1–13.

Fellows-Jensen, Gillian. "The Myth of Harold II's Survival in the Scandinavian Sources." *King Harold II and the Bayeux Tapestry*. Ed. Gale Owen-Crocker. Woodbridge: Boydell, 2005. Pp. 53–64.

Fernie, Eric. *The Architecture of the Anglo-Saxons*. London: B.T. Batsford, 1982.

Fernie, Eric. "Edward the Confessor's Westminster Abbey." *Edward the Confessor: The Man and the Legend*. Ed. Richard Mortimer. Woodbridge: Boydell, 2009. Pp. 139–50.

Fernie, Eric. "Reconstructing Edward's Abbey at Westminster." *Romanesque and Gothic: Essays For George Zarnecki*, vol. 1: *Text*. Ed. Neil Stratford. Woodbridge: Boydell, 1987. Pp. 63–7.

Finlay, Alison. "Chronology, Genealogy and Conversion: The Afterlife of St Edmund in the North." *St Edmund King and Martyr: Changing Images of a Medieval Saint*. Ed. Anthony Bale. York: York Medieval Press, 2009. Pp. 45–62.

Fisher, D.J.V. "The Anti-Monastic Reaction in the Reign of Edward the Martyr." *Cambridge Historical Journal* 10.3 (1952): 254–70.

Fleming, Robin. *Kings and Lords in Conquest England*. Cambridge: Cambridge University Press, 1991.

Flower, Harriet I. *The Art of Forgetting: Disgrace and Oblivion in Roman Political Culture*. Chapel Hill: University of North Carolina Press, 2006.

Foot, Sarah. *Æthelstan: The First King of England*. New Haven, CT: Yale University Press, 2011.

Foot, Sarah. "Glastonbury's Early Abbots." *The Archaeology and History of Glastonbury Abbey: Essays in Honour of the Ninetieth Birthday of C.A. Ralegh Radford*. Ed. Lesley Abrams and James P. Carley. Woodbridge: Boydell, 1991. Pp. 163–89.

Foot, Sarah. *Veiled Women: Female Religious Communities in England, 871–1066*, 2 vols. Aldershot: Ashgate, 2000.

Foucault, Michel. *Discipline and Punish: The Birth of the Prison*. Trans. Alan Sheridan. New York: Random House, 1977.

Foys, Martin K. "Pulling the Arrow Out: The Legend of Harold's Death and the Bayeux Tapestry." *The Bayeux Tapestry: New Interpretations*. Ed. Martin K. Foys, Eileen Overbey, and Dan Terkla. Woodbridge: Boydell, 2009. Pp. 158–75.

Frank, Roberta. "King Cnut in the Verse of His Skalds." *The Reign of Cnut: King of England, Denmark, and Norway*. Ed. Alexander R. Rumble. London: Leicester University Press, 1994. Pp. 106–24.

Frank, Roberta. "Viking Atrocity and Skaldic Verse: The Rite of the Blood-Eagle." *English Historical Review* 99.391 (1984): 332–43.

Frantzen, Allen J. *The Literature of Penance in Anglo-Saxon England*. New Brunswick, NJ: Rutgers University Press, 1983.

Freeman, Edward A. *The History of the Norman Conquest of England: Its Causes and Results*, 6 vols. Oxford: Clarendon, 1867–79.

Freke, D.J., and A.T. Thacker. "The Inhumation Cemetery at Southworth Hall Farm, Winwick." *Journal of the Chester Archaeological Society* 70 (1987–88): 31–8.

Garnett, George. *Conquered England: Kingship, Succession, and Tenure, 1066–1166*. Oxford: Oxford University Press, 2007.

Garnett, George. "Coronation and Propaganda: Some Implications of the Norman Claim to the Throne of England in 1066." *Transactions of the Royal Historical Society*, 5th series, 36 (1986): 91–116.

Gates, Jay Paul. "The 'Worcester' Historians and Eadric *Streona*'s Execution." *Capital and Corporal Punishment in Anglo-Saxon England*. Ed. Jay Paul Gates and Nicole Marafioti. Woodbridge: Boydell, 2014.

Gates, Jay Paul, and Nicole Marafioti, eds. *Capital and Corporal Punishment in Anglo-Saxon England*. Woodbridge: Boydell, 2014.

Geary, Patrick J. "Ethnic Identity as a Situational Construct in the Early Middle Ages." *Mitteilungen der Anthropologischen Gesellschaft in Wien* 113 (1983): 15–26.

Geary, Patrick J. *Furta Sacra: Thefts of Relics in the Central Middle Ages*. Princeton, NJ: Princeton University Press, 1990.

Gem, Richard. "Canterbury and the Cushion Capital: A Commentary on Passages from Goscelin's *De Miraculis Sancti Augustini*." *Romanesque and Gothic: Essays For George Zarnecki*, vol. 1: *Text*. Ed. Neil Stratford. Woodbridge: Boydell, 1987. Pp. 83–101.

Gem, Richard. "Craftsmen and Administrators in the Building of the Confessor's Abbey." *Edward the Confessor: The Man and the Legend*. Ed. Richard Mortimer. Woodbridge: Boydell, 2009. Pp. 169–72.

Gem, Richard. "England and the Resistance to Romanesque Architecture." *Studies in Medieval History Presented to R. Allen Brown*. Ed. Christopher Harper-Bill, Christopher J. Holdsworth, and Janet L. Nelson. Woodbridge: Boydell, 1989. Pp. 129–39.

Gem, Richard. "How Much Can Anglo-Saxon Buildings Tell Us about Liturgy?" *The Liturgy of the Late Anglo-Saxon Church*. Ed. H. Gittos and M.B. Bedingfield. Henry Bradshaw Subsidia Series 5. Woodbridge: Boydell, 2005. Pp. 271–89.

Gem, Richard. "The Romanesque Architecture of Old St Paul's Cathedral and Its Late Eleventh-Century Context." *Medieval Art, Architecture and Archaeology in London*. Ed. Lindy Grant. British Archaeological Association Conference Transactions 10. London: 1990. Pp. 47–63.

Gem, R.D.H. "The Romanesque Rebuilding of Westminster Abbey." *Anglo-Norman Studies* 3 (1980): 33–60.

Gerchow, Jan. "Prayers for King Cnut: The Liturgical Commemoration of a Conqueror." *England in the Eleventh Century*. Ed. Carola Hicks. Harlaxton Medieval Studies 2. Stamford: Paul Watkins, 1992. Pp. 219–38.

Giandrea, Mary Frances. *Episcopal Culture in Late Anglo-Saxon England*. Anglo-Saxon Studies 7. Woodbridge: Boydell, 2007.

Gillingham, John. "1066 and the Introduction of Chivalry into England." *The English in the Twelfth Century: Imperialism, National Identity, and Political Values*. Woodbridge: Boydell, 2000. Pp. 209–31.

Gilmour, B.J.J., and D.A. Stocker. *St Mark's Church and Cemetery*. The Archaeology of Lincoln 13.1. London: Council for British Archaeology, 1986.

Gittos, Helen. "Creating the Sacred: Anglo-Saxon Rites for Consecrating Cemeteries." *Burial in Early Medieval England and Wales*. Ed. Sam Lucy and Andrew Reynolds. Society for Medieval Archaeology Monograph 17. Leeds: 2002. Pp. 195–208.

Godden, Malcolm. "Ælfric and Anglo-Saxon Kingship." *English Historical Review* 102 (1987): 911–15.

Gransden, Antonia. "Abbo of Fleury's '*Passio Sancti Eadmundi*.'" *Revue Bénédictine* 105.1–2 (1995): 20–78.

Gransden, Antonia. "The Composition and Authorship of the *De Miraculis Sancti Eadmundi* Attributed to 'Hermann the Archdeacon.'" *Journal of Medieval Latin* 5 (1995): 1–52.

Gransden, Antonia. "The Cult of St Mary at *Beodericisworth* and then in Bury St Edmunds Abbey to c. 1150." *Journal of Ecclesiastical History* 55.4 (2004): 627–53.

Gransden, Antonia. *Historical Writing in England, c. 550–c. 1307*. London: Routledge, 1996.

Gransden, Antonia. "The Legends and Traditions Concerning the Origins of the Abbey of Bury St Edmunds." *English Historical Review* 100.394 (1985): 1–24.

Gretsch, Mechthild. "The Fonthill Letter: Language, Law and the Discourse of Disciplines." *Anglia* 123.4 (2005): 667–86.

Gretsch, Mechthild. "The Language of 'the Fonthill Letter.'" *Anglo-Saxon England* 23 (1994): 57–102.

Grierson, Philip. "Grimbald of St. Bertin's." *English Historical Review* 45 (1940): 529–61.

Hadley, D.M. "Burial Practices in the Northern Danelaw, c. 650–1100." *Northern History* 36.2 (2000): 199–216.

Hadley, D.M. "Burial Practices in Northern England in the Later Anglo-Saxon Period." *Burial in Early Medieval England and Wales*. Ed. Sam Lucy and Andrew Reynolds. Society for Medieval Archaeology Monograph Series 17. Leeds: 2002. Pp. 209–28.

Hadley, D.M. "Burying the Socially and Physically Distinctive in Late Anglo-Saxon England." *Burial in Later Anglo-Saxon England, c. 650–1100 A.D.* Ed. Jo Buckberry and Annia Cherryson. Oxford: Oxbow Books, 2010. Pp. 103–15.

Hadley, Dawn M. and Jo Buckberry. "Caring for the Dead in Late Anglo-Saxon England." *Pastoral Care in Late Anglo-Saxon England*. Ed. Francesca Tinti. Anglo-Saxon Studies 6. Woodbridge: Boydell, 2005. Pp. 121–47.

Hall, David. "The Sanctuary of St Cuthbert." *St Cuthbert, His Cult and His Community to AD 1200*. Ed. Gerald Bonner, David Rollason, and Clare Stancliffe. Woodbridge: Boydell, 1989. Pp. 425–36.

Hall, Richard. "A Kingdom Too Far: York in the Early Tenth Century." *Edward the Elder: 899–924*. Ed. N.J. Higham and D.H. Hill. London: Routledge, 2001. Pp. 188–99.

Hallam, Elizabeth M. "Monasteries as War Memorials: Battle Abbey and La Victoire." *The Church and War*. Ed. W.J. Sheils. Studies in Church History 20. Oxford: Blackwell, 1983. Pp. 47–57.

Hallam, Elizabeth M. "Royal Burial and the Cult of Kingship in France and England, 1060–1330." *Journal of Medieval History* 8 (1982): 359–80.

Halsall, Guy. "Burial, Ritual, and Merovingian Society." *The Community, The Family, and The Saint: Patterns of Power in Early Medieval Europe*. Ed. J. Hill and M. Swan. Turnhout: Brepols, 1998. Pp. 325–38.

Halsall, Guy. "Childeric's Grave, Clovis' Succession, and the Origins of the Merovingian Kingdom." *Society and Culture in Late Antique Gaul: Revisiting the Sources*. Ed. Ralph W. Mathisen and Danuta Shanzer. Aldershot: Ashgate, 2001. Pp. 116–33.

Halsall, Guy. "Social Change around A.D. 600: An Austrasian Perspective." *The Age of Sutton Hoo: The Seventh Century in North-Western Europe*. Ed. M.O.H. Carver. Woodbridge: Boydell, 1992. Pp. 265–78.

Hamilton, Sarah. "Remedies for 'Great Transgressions': Penance and Excommunication in Late Anglo-Saxon England." *Pastoral Care in Late Anglo-Saxon England*. Ed. Francesca Tinti. Anglo-Saxon Studies 6. Woodbridge: Boydell, 2005. Pp. 83–105.

Hare, J.N. *Battle Abbey: The Eastern Range and the Excavations of 1978–80*. Historic Buildings and Monuments Commission for England, Archaeological Report 2. London: 1985.

Hare, J.N. "The Buildings of Battle Abbey: A Preliminary Survey." *Anglo-Norman Studies* 3 (1980): 78–95.

Härke, Heinrich. "Cemeteries as Places of Power." *Topographies of Power in the Early Middle Ages*. Ed. Mayke de Jong, Frans Theuws, and Carine Van Rhijn. Leiden: Brill, 2001. Pp. 9–30.

Härke, Heinrich. "'Warrior Graves'? The Background of the Anglo-Saxon Weapon Burial Rite." *Past and Present* 126 (1990): 22–43.

Hart, Cyril. *The Danelaw*. London: Hambledon, 1992.

Harvey, Barbara. *Westminster Abbey and Its Estates in the Middle Ages*. Oxford: Clarendon, 1977.

Haslam, Jeremy. "The Towns of Wiltshire." *Anglo-Saxon Towns*. Ed. Jeremy Haslam. Chichester: Phillimore, 1984. Pp. 87–147.

Hayman, Graham, and Andrew Reynolds. "A Saxon and Saxo-Norman Execution Cemetery at 42–54 London Road, Staines." *Archaeological Journal* 162 (2005): 215–55.

Hayward, Paul. "Translation-Narratives in Post-Conquest Hagiography and English Resistance to the Norman Conquest." *Anglo-Norman Studies* 21 (1999): 67–93.

Hazeltine, H.D. "General Preface." *Anglo-Saxon Wills*. Ed. and trans. Dorothy Whitelock. Cambridge: Cambridge University Press, 1930. Pp. vii–xl.

Heighway, Carolyn. "Gloucester and the New Minster of St Oswald." *Edward the Elder: 899–924*. Ed. N.J. Higham and D.H. Hill. London: Routledge, 2001. Pp. 102–11.

Heighway, Carolyn, Richard Bryant, et al. *The Golden Minster: The Anglo-Saxon Minster and Later Medieval Priory of St Oswald at Gloucester*. Council for British Archaeology, Research Report 117. York: 1999.

Heslop, T.A. "The Production of *De Luxe* Manuscripts and the Patronage of King Cnut and Queen Emma." *Anglo-Saxon England* 19 (1990): 151–95.

Hill, David. *An Atlas of Anglo-Saxon England*. Toronto: University of Toronto Press, 1981.

Hill, David. "Trends in the Development of Towns during the Reign of Ethelred II." *Ethelred the Unready: Papers from the Millenary Conference*. Ed. D. Hill. BAR British Series 59. Oxford: 1978. Pp. 213–26.

Hill, David. "An Urban Policy for Cnut?" *The Reign of Cnut: King of England, Denmark, and Norway*. Ed. Alexander R. Rumble. London: Leicester University Press, 1994. Pp. 101–5.

Hillaby, Joe. "Early Christian and Pre-Conquest Leominster: An Exploration of the Sources." *Transactions of the Woolhope Naturalists' Field Club* 45.3 (1987): 557–685.

Hillaby, Joe and Caroline Hillaby. *Leominster Minster, Priory and Borough, c. 660–1539*. Herefordshire: Friends of Leominster Priory, 2006.

Howard, Ian. "Harold II: A Throne-Worthy King." *King Harold II and the Bayeux Tapestry*. Ed. Gale R. Owen-Crocker. Woodbridge: Boydell, 2005. Pp. 35–52.

Howard, Ian. *Swein Forkbeard's Invasions and the Danish Conquest of England, 991–1017*. Woodbridge: Boydell, 2003.

Huntington, Richard and Peter Metcalf. *Celebrations of Death: The Anthropology of Mortuary Ritual*. Cambridge: Cambridge University Press, 1979.

Hurnard, Naomi D. *The King's Pardon for Homicide before* A.D. *1307*. Oxford: Clarendon, 1969.

Hyams, Paul R. *Rancor and Reconciliation in Medieval England*. Ithaca, NY: Cornell University Press, 2003.

Innes, Matthew. "Danelaw Identities: Ethnicity, Regionalism, and Political Allegiance." *Cultures in Contact: Scandinavian Settlement in England in the Ninth and Tenth Centuries*. Ed. Dawn M. Hadley and Julian D. Richards. Studies in the Early Middle Ages 2. Turnhout: Brepols, 2000. Pp. 65–88.

Irvine, Susan E. "Bones of Contention: The Context of Ælfric's Homily on St Vincent." *Anglo-Saxon England* 19 (1990): 117–32.

Iserson, Kenneth V. "Rigor Mortis and Other Postmortem Changes." *MacMillan Encyclopedia of Death and Dying*, vol. 2. Ed. Robert Kastenbaum. New York: Thompson Gale, 2003. Pp. 721–3.

James, Edward. "Merovingian Cemetery Studies and Some Implication for Anglo-Saxon England." *Anglo-Saxon Cemeteries 1979: The Fourth Anglo-Saxon Symposium at Oxford*. Ed. Philip Rahtz, Tania Dickinson, and Lorna Watts. BAR British Series 82. Oxford: 1980. Pp. 35–55.

Jayakumar, Shashi. "Eadwig and Edgar: Politics, Propaganda, Faction." *Edgar: King of the English, 959–975*. Ed. Donald Scragg. Woodbridge: Boydell, 2008. Pp. 84–103.

John, Eric. *Reassessing Anglo-Saxon England*. Manchester: Manchester University Press, 1996.

Jones, Lynn. "From *Anglorum Basileus* to Norman Saint: The Transformation of Edward the Confessor." *Haskins Society Journal* 12 (2002): 99–120.

Jones, M.J., et al. "Excavations at Lincoln. Third Interim Report: Sites Outside the Walled City 1972–1977." *Antiquaries Journal* 61 (1981): 83–114.

Kantorowicz, Ernst H. *The King's Two Bodies: A Study in Mediaeval Political Theology*. Princeton, NJ: Princeton University Press, 1997.

Karkov, Catherine E. "The Frontispiece to the New Minster Charter and the King's Two Bodies." *Edgar: King of the English, 959–975*. Ed. Donald Scragg. Woodbridge: Boydell, 2008. Pp. 224–41.

Karkov, Catherine E. *The Ruler Portraits of Anglo-Saxon England.* Anglo-Saxon Studies 3. Woodbridge: Boydell, 2004.

Keene, Derek. "From Conquest to Capital: St Paul's c. 1100–1300." *St Paul's: The Cathedral Church of London, 604–2004.* Ed. Derek Keene, Arthur Burns, and Andrew Saint. New Haven, CT: Yale University Press, 2004. Pp. 17–32 and 466–7.

Ker, N.R. *Catalogue of Manuscripts Containing Anglo-Saxon.* Oxford: Clarendon, 1957.

Keynes, Simon. "The Æthelings in Normandy." *Anglo-Norman Studies* 13 (1990): 173–205.

Keynes, Simon. "The Burial of King Æthelred the Unready at St Paul's." *The English and Their Legacy, 900–1200: Essays in Honour of Ann Williams.* Ed. David Roffe. Woodbridge: Boydell, 2012. Pp. 129–48.

Keynes, Simon. "Cnut's Earls." *The Reign of Cnut: King of England, Denmark, and Norway.* Ed. Alexander R. Rumble. London: Leicester University Press, 1994. Pp. 43–88.

Keynes, Simon. "The Crowland Psalter and the Sons of King Edmund Ironside." *Bodleian Library Record* 11.6 (1985): 359–70.

Keynes, Simon. "The Cult of King Edward the Martyr during the Reign of King Æthelred the Unready." *Gender and Historiography: Studies in the Earlier Middle Ages in Honour of Pauline Stafford.* Ed. Janet L. Nelson, Susan Reynolds, and Susan M. Johns. London: Institute of Historical Research, 2012. Pp. 115–25.

Keynes, Simon. "The Declining Reputation of King Æthelred the Unready." *Ethelred the Unready: Papers from the Millenary Conference.* Ed. David Hill. BAR British Series 59. Oxford: 1978. Pp. 227–53.

Keynes, Simon. *The Diplomas of King Æthelred "The Unready": 978–1016.* Cambridge: Cambridge University Press, 1980.

Keynes, Simon. "The 'Dunstan B' Charters." *Anglo-Saxon England* 23 (1994): 165–93.

Keynes, Simon. "Edgar, *Rex Admirabilis.*" *Edgar, King of the English 959–975.* Ed. Donald Scragg. Woodbridge: Boydell, 2008. Pp. 3–58.

Keynes, Simon. "Edward, King of the Anglo-Saxons." *Edward the Elder: 899–924.* Ed. N.J. Higham and D.H. Hill. London: Routledge, 2001. Pp. 40–66.

Keynes, Simon. "The Fonthill Letter." *Words, Texts and Manuscripts: Studies in Anglo-Saxon Culture Presented to Helmut Gneuss on the Occasion of His Sixty-Fifth Birthday.* Ed. M. Korhammer. Cambridge: D.S. Brewer, 1992. Pp. 53–97.

Keynes, Simon. "Introduction to the 1998 Reprint: Queen Emma and the *Encomium Emmae Reginae.*" *Encomium Emmae Reginae.* Ed. Alistair Campbell, with a supplementary introduction by Simon Keynes. Camden Classic Reprints 4. London: Cambridge University Press, 1949, reprinted 1998. Pp. xiii–lxxxvii.

Keynes, Simon. "King Alfred the Great and Shaftesbury Abbey." *Studies in the Early History of Shaftesbury Abbey*. Ed. Laurence Keen. Dorset: Dorset City Council, 1999. Pp. 17–72.

Keynes, Simon. "King Athelstan's Books." *Learning and Literature in Anglo-Saxon England*. Ed. Michael Lapidge and Helmut Gneuss. Cambridge: Cambridge University Press, 1985. Pp. 143–201.

Keynes, Simon. "Kingston-Upon-Thames, Surrey." *The Blackwell Encyclopaedia of Anglo-Saxon England*. Ed. Michael Lapidge, John Blair, Simon Keynes, and Donald Scragg. Malden, MA: Blackwell, 1999. P. 272.

Keynes, Simon. "The *Liber Vitae* of the New Minster, Winchester." *The Durham Liber Vitae and Its Context*. Ed. David Rollason, A.J. Piper, Margaret Harvey, and Lynda Rollason. Regions and Regionalism in History 1. Woodbridge: Boydell, 2004. Pp. 149–63.

Keynes, Simon. "A Tale of Two Kings: Alfred the Great and Æthelred the Unready." *Transactions of the Royal Historical Society*, 5th series, 36 (1986): 195–217.

Keynes, Simon. "The West Saxon Charters of King Æthelwulf and His Sons." *English Historical Review* 109 (1994): 1109–49.

Keynes, Simon, and Rosalind Love. "Earl Godwine's Ship." *Anglo-Saxon England* 38 (2009): 185–223.

Kjølbye-Biddle, Birthe. "A Cathedral Cemetery: Problems in Excavation and Interpretation." *World Archaeology* 7.1 (1975): 78–108.

Kjølbye-Biddle, Birthe. "Dispersal or Concentration: the Disposal of the Winchester Dead over 2000 Years." *Death in Towns: Urban Responses to the Dying and the Dead, 100–1600*. Ed. Steven Bassett. Leicester: Leicester University Press, 1992. Pp. 210–47.

Kjølbye-Biddle, Birthe. "Old Minster, St Swithun's Day 1093." *Winchester Cathedral: Nine Hundred Years, 1093–1993*. Ed. John Crook. Chichester: Phillimore, 1993. Pp. 13–20.

Kjølbye-Biddle, Birthe. "The 7th Century Minster at Winchester Interpreted." *The Anglo-Saxon Church: Papers on History, Architecture, and Archaeology in Honour of Dr. H.M. Taylor.* Ed. L.A.S. Butler and R.K. Morris. Council for British Archaeology, Research Report 60. London: 1986. Pp. 196–209.

Klaniczay, Gábor. *Holy Rulers and Blessed Princes: Dynastic Cults in Medieval Central Europe*. Trans. Éva Pálmai. Cambridge: Cambridge University Press, 2002.

Kleinberg, Aviad M. *Prophets in Their Own Country: Living Saints and the Making of Sainthood in the Later Middle Ages*. Chicago: University of Chicago Press, 1992.

Knowles, David. *The Monastic Order in England*. Cambridge: Cambridge University Press, 1963.

Knowles, David, C.N.L. Brooke, and Vera C.M. London. *The Heads of Religious Houses: England and Wales, 940–1216*, 2nd ed. Cambridge: Cambridge University Press, 2004.

Koziol, Geoffrey. "England, France, and the Problem of Sacrality in Twelfth-Century Ritual." *Cultures of Power: Lordship, Status, and Process in Twelfth-Century Europe*. Ed. T.N. Bisson. Philadelphia: University of Pennsylvania Press, 1995. Pp. 124–48.

Kries, Susanne. "English-Danish Rivalry and the Mutilation of Alfred in the Eleventh-Century *Chronicle* Poem *The Death of Alfred*." *JEGP* 104.1 (2005): 31–53.

Lambert, T.B. "Spiritual Protection and Secular Power: The Evolution of Sanctuary and Legal Privilege in Ripon and Beverly, 900–1300." *Peace and Protection in the Middle Ages*. Ed. T.B. Lambert and D. Rollason. Durham Medieval and Renaissance Monographs and Essays 1. Toronto: Pontifical Institute of Mediaeval Studies, 2009. Pp. 121–40.

Lapidge, Michael. "Dunstan [St Dunstan] (*d.* 988)." *Oxford Dictionary of National Biography*. Oxford: Oxford University Press, 2004. http://www.oxforddnb.com/index/101008288/DunstanQ1.

Lapidge, Michael. "The Hermeneutic Style in Tenth-Century Anglo-Latin Literature." *Anglo-Saxon England* 4 (1975): 67–111.

Lapidge, Michael. "A Metrical *Vita S. Iudoci* from Tenth-Century Winchester." *Journal of Medieval Latin* 10 (2000): 255–306.

Lapidge, Michael. "Some Latin Poems as Evidence for the Reign of Athelstan." *Anglo-Saxon England* 9 (1981): 61–98.

Lawson, M.K. *Cnut: The Danes in England in the Early Eleventh Century*. London: Longman, 1993.

Lawson, M.K. "The Collection of Danegeld and Heregeld in the Reigns of Aethelred II and Cnut." *English Historical Review* 99.393 (1984): 721–38.

Lee, Christina. *Feasting the Dead: Food and Drink in Anglo-Saxon Burial Rituals*. Anglo-Saxon Studies 9. Woodbridge: Boydell, 2007.

Little, Lester K. *Benedictine Maledictions: Liturgical Cursing in Romanesque France*. Ithaca, NY: Cornell University Press, 1993.

Mack, Katharin. "Changing Thegns: Cnut's Conquest and the English Aristocracy." *Albion* 16.4 (1984): 375–87.

Magennis, Hugh. *Anglo-Saxon Appetites: Food and Drink and Their Consumption in Old English and Related Literature*. Dublin: Four Courts Press, 1999.

Marafioti, Nicole. "Punishing Bodies and Saving Souls: Capital and Corporal Punishment in Late Anglo-Saxon England." *Haskins Society Journal* 20 (2008): 39–57.

Marafioti, Nicole. "Seeking Alfred's Body: Royal Tomb as Political Object in the Reign of Edward the Elder." Forthcoming.

Marafioti, Nicole. "Spiritual Dangers and Earthly Consequences: Judging and Punishing in the Old English *Consolation of Philosophy*." *Capital and Corporal Punishment in Anglo-Saxon England*. Ed. Jay Paul Gates and Nicole Marafioti. Woodbridge: Boydell, 2014.

Mason, Emma. "St Wulfstan's Staff: A Legend and Its Uses." *Medium Ævum* 53 (1984): 157–79.

Mason, Emma. "'The Site of King-Making and Consecration': Westminster Abbey and the Crown in the Eleventh and Twelfth Centuries." *The Church and Sovereignty c. 590–1918: Essays in Honour of Michael Wilks*. Ed. Diana Wood. Studies in Church History 9. Oxford: Blackwell, 1991. Pp. 57–76.

Mason, Emma. *Westminster Abbey and Its People, c. 1050–c. 1216*. Studies in the History of Medieval Religion 9. Woodbridge: Boydell, 1996.

Mason, Emma. "Westminster Abbey and the Monarchy Between the Reigns of William I and John (1066–1216)." *Journal of Ecclesiastical History* 41 (1990). Reprinted in *Westminster Abbey and Its People, c. 1050–c. 1216*. Studies in the History of Medieval Religion 9. Woodbridge: Boydell, 1996. Pp. 269–87.

McKitterick, Rosamond. *History and Memory in the Carolingian World*. Cambridge: Cambridge University Press, 2004.

McNulty, J. Bard. "The Lady Aelfgyva in the Bayeux Tapestry." *Speculum* 55.4 (1980): 659–68.

Miller, William Ian. *Bloodtaking and Peacemaking: Feud, Law, and Society in Saga Iceland*. Chicago: University of Chicago Press, 1990.

Morris, Richard. *The Church in British Archaeology*. Council for British Archaeology, Research Report 47. London: 1983.

Mortimer, Richard. "Edward the Confessor: The Man and the Legend." *Edward the Confessor: The Man and the Legend*. Ed. Richard Mortimer. Woodbridge: Boydell, 2009. Pp. 1–40.

Morton, Catherine. "Pope Alexander II and the Norman Conquest." *Latomus* 34 (1975): 362–82.

Mostert, Marco. "Edmund, St, King of East Anglia." *Blackwell Encyclopaedia of Anglo-Saxon England*. Ed. Michael Lapidge, John Blair, Simon Keynes, and Donald Scragg. Malden, MA: Blackwell, 1999. Pp. 160–1.

Nelson, Janet L. "The Earliest Surviving Royal *Ordo*: Some Liturgical and Historical Aspects." *Authority and Power: Studies in Medieval Law and Government Presented to Walter Ullmann*. Ed. B. Tierney and P. Linehan. Cambridge: Cambridge University Press, 1980. Reprinted in *Politics and Ritual in Early Medieval Europe*. London: Hambledon, 1986. Pp. 341–60.

Nelson, Janet L. "The First Use of the Second Anglo-Saxon *Ordo*." *Myth, Rulership, Church and Charters: Essays in Honour of Nicholas Brooks*. Ed. Julia Barrow and Andrew Wareham. Aldershot: Ashgate, 2008. Pp. 117–26.

Nelson, Janet L. "Inauguration Rituals." *Early Medieval Kingship*. Ed. P.H. Sawyer and I.N. Wood. Leeds: School of History, 1977. Reprinted in *Politics and Ritual in Early Medieval Europe*. London: Hambledon, 1986. Pp. 283–307.

Nelson, Janet L. "National Synods, Kingship as Office, and Royal Anointing: An Early Medieval Syndrome." *Studies in Church History* 7 (1971). Reprinted in *Politics and Ritual in Early Medieval Europe*. London: Hambledon, 1986. Pp. 240–57.

Nelson, Janet L. "Reconstructing a Royal Family: Reflections on Alfred, From Asser, Chapter 2." *People and Places in Northern Europe, 500–1600: Essays in Honour of Peter Hayes Sawyer*. Ed. Ian Wood and Niels Lund. Woodbridge: Boydell, 1991. Pp. 47–66.

Nelson, Janet L. "The Rites of the Conqueror." *Anglo-Norman Studies* 4 (1982): 117–32.

Nelson, Janet L. "Ritual and Reality in the Early Medieval *Ordines*." *Studies in Church History* 11 (1975). Reprinted in *Politics and Ritual in Early Medieval Europe*. London: Hambledon, 1986. Pp. 329–39.

Nelson, Janet L. "Royal Saints and Early Medieval Kingship." *Studies in Church History* 10 (1973). Reprinted in *Politics and Ritual in Early Medieval Europe*. London: Hambledon, 1986. Pp. 69–74.

Nelson, Janet L. "The Second English *Ordo*." *Politics and Ritual in Early Medieval Europe*. London: Hambledon, 1986. Pp. 361–74.

Nelson, Janet L. "Symbols in Context: Rulers' Inauguration Rituals in Byzantium and the West in the Early Middle Ages." *Studies in Church History* 13 (1976). Reprinted in *Politics and Ritual in Early Medieval Europe*. London: Hambledon, 1986. Pp. 259–81.

Nelson, J.L. "Carolingian Royal Funerals." *Rituals of Power: From Late Antiquity to the Early Middle Ages*. Ed. F. Theuws and J.L. Nelson. Leiden: Brill, 2000. Pp. 131–84.

Nightingale, Pamela. "The Origin of the Court of Husting and Danish Influence on London's Development into a Capital City." *English Historical Review* 102.404 (1987): 559–78.

Norton, Christopher. "York Minster in the Time of Wulfstan." *Wulfstan, Archbishop of York: The Proceedings of the Second Alcuin Conference*. Ed. Matthew Townend. Turnhout: Brepols, 2004. Pp. 207–34.

O'Brien, Bruce R. "From *Morðor* to *Murdrum*: The Pre-Conquest Origin and Norman Revival of the Murder Fine." *Speculum* 71.2 (1996): 321–57.

O'Brien O'Keeffe, Katherine. "Body and Law in Late Anglo-Saxon England." *Anglo-Saxon England* 27 (1998): 209–32.

O'Brien O'Keeffe, Katherine. *Visible Song: Transitional Literacy in Old English Verse*. Cambridge: Cambridge University Press, 1990.

Okasha, Elizabeth. "Memorial Stones or Grave Stones?" *The Christian Tradition in Anglo-Saxon England: Approaches to Current Scholarship and Teaching*. Ed. Paul Cavill. Cambridge: D.S. Brewer, 2004. Pp. 91–101.

Orme, Nicholas. "Glastonbury Abbey and Education." *The Archaeology and History of Glastonbury Abbey: Essays in Honour of the Ninetieth Birthday of C.A. Ralegh Radford*. Ed. Lesley Abrams and James P. Carley. Woodbridge: Boydell, 1991. Pp. 285–99.

Otter, Monika. "1066: The Moment of Transition in Two Narratives of the Norman Conquest." *Speculum* 74.3 (1999): 565–86.

Owen-Crocker, Gale R. "Horror in *Beowulf*: Mutilation, Decapitation, and Unburied Dead." *Early Medieval English Texts and Interpretations: Studies Presented to Donald G. Scragg*. Ed. Elaine Treharne and Susan Rosser. Medieval and Renaissance Texts and Studies 252. Tempe: Arizona Center for Medieval and Renaissance Studies, 2002. Pp. 81–100.

Phillips, Derek. *Excavations at York Minster*, 2 vols. London: Her Majesty's Stationary Office, 1985 and 1995.

Pickles, Christopher. *Texts and Monuments: A Study of Ten Anglo-Saxon Churches of the Pre-Viking Period*. BAR British Series 277. Oxford: 1999.

Potts, R.U. "The Tombs of the Kings and Archbishops in St Austin's Abbey, Canterbury." *Archaeologia Cantiana* 38 (1926): 97–112.

Quirk, R.N. "Winchester Cathedral in the Tenth Century." *Archaeological Journal* 114 (1957): 29–68.

Quirk, R.N. "Winchester New Minster and Its Tenth-Century Tower." *Journal of the British Archaeological Association*, 3rd series, 24 (1961): 16–54.

Radford, C.A.R. "Glastonbury Abbey before 1184: Interim Report on the Excavations, 1908–64." *Medieval Art and Architecture at Wells and Glastonbury*. Ed. Nicole Coldstream and Peter Draper. British Archaeological Association Conference Transactions 4. Leeds: 1981. Pp. 110–34.

Reynolds, Andrew. *Anglo-Saxon Deviant Burial Customs*. Oxford: Oxford University Press, 2009.

Reynolds, Andrew. "Burials, Boundaries and Charters in Anglo-Saxon England: A Reassessment." *Burial in Early Medieval England and Wales*. Ed. Sam Lucy and Andrew Reynolds. Society for Medieval Archaeology Monograph Series 17 (2002). Pp. 171–94.

Reynolds, Andrew. "The Definition and Ideology of Anglo-Saxon Execution Sites and Cemeteries." *Death and Burial in Medieval Europe: Papers of the 'Medieval Europe Brugge 1997' Conference*, vol. 2. Ed. G. DeBoe and F. Verhaeghe. Zellik: Instituut voor het Archeologisch Patrimonium, 1997. Pp. 33–41.

Richards, Mary P. "Body as Text in Early Anglo-Saxon Law." *Naked before God: Uncovering the Body in Anglo-Saxon England*. Ed. Benjamin C. Withers and

Jonathan Wilcox. Morgantown: West Virginia University Press, 2003. Pp. 97–115.

Ridyard, Susan J. "*Condigna Veneratio*: Post-Conquest Attitudes to the Saints of the Anglo-Saxons." *Anglo-Norman Studies* 9 (1987): 179–206.

Ridyard, Susan J. "Monk-Kings and the Anglo-Saxon Hagiographic Tradition." *Haskins Society Journal* 6 (1994): 13–27.

Ridyard, Susan J. *The Royal Saints of Anglo-Saxon England: A Study of West Saxon and East Anglian Cults*. Cambridge: Cambridge University Press, 1988.

Roberts, Jane. "What Did Anglo-Saxon Seals Seal When?" *The Power of Words: Essays in Lexicography, Lexicology, and Semantics in Honour of Christian J. Kay*. Ed. Graham D. Caie, Carole Hough, and Irene Wotherspoon. Amsterdam: Rodopi, 2006. Pp. 131–57.

Robertson, Nicola. "Dunstan and Monastic Reform: Tenth-Century Fact or Twelfth-Century Fiction?" *Anglo-Norman Studies* 28 (2005): 153–67.

Rodwell, Warwick. "The Battle of *Assandun* and Its Memorial Church: A Reappraisal." *The Battle of Maldon: Fiction and Fact*. Ed. Janet Cooper. London: Hambledon, 1993. Pp. 127–58.

Rodwell, Warwick. "New Glimpses of Edward the Confessor's Abbey at Westminster." *Edward the Confessor: The Man and the Legend*. Ed. Richard Mortimer. Woodbridge: Boydell, 2009. Pp. 151–67.

Rodwell, Warwick, and Kirsty Rodwell. "St Peter's Church, Barton-Upon-Humber: Excavation and Structural Study, 1978-81." *Antiquaries Journal* 62.2 (1982): 283–315.

Rollason, David. *Saints and Relics in Anglo-Saxon England*. Oxford: Blackwell, 1989.

Rollason, David. "The Shrines of Saints in Later Anglo-Saxon England: Distribution and Significance." *The Anglo-Saxon Church: Papers on History, Architecture, and Archaeology in Honour of Dr. H.M. Taylor*. Ed. L.A.S. Butler and R.K. Morris. Council for British Archaeology, Research Report 60. London: 1986. Pp. 32–43.

Rollason, D.W. "The Cults of Murdered Royal Saints in Anglo-Saxon England." *Anglo-Saxon England* 11 (1983): 1–22.

Rollason, D.W. "Lists of Saints' Resting-Places in Anglo-Saxon England." *Anglo-Saxon England* 7 (1978): 61–93.

Rollason, D.W. *The Mildrith Legend: A Study in Early Medieval Hagiography in England*. Leicester: Leicester University Press, 1982.

Rollason, D.W. "Relic-Cults as an Instrument of Royal Policy c. 900–c. 1050." *Anglo-Saxon England* 15 (1986): 91–103.

Rosenwein, Barbara H. *Emotional Communities in the Early Middle Ages*. Ithaca, NY: Cornell University Press, 2006.

Rosenwein, Barbara H. *Negotiating Space: Power, Restraint, and Privileges of Immunity in Early Medieval Europe*. Ithaca, NY: Cornell University Press, 1999.

Rosser, Gervase. *Medieval Westminster: 1200–1540*. Oxford: Clarendon, 1989.

Rumble, Alexander R. "Edward the Elder and the Churches of Winchester and Wessex." *Edward the Elder, 899–924*. Ed. David Hill. London: Routledge, 2001. Pp. 230–47.

Sapin, Christian. "Architecture and Funerary Space in the Early Middle Ages." Trans. Bailey K. Young. *Spaces of the Living and the Dead: An Archaeological Dialogue*. Ed. Catherine E. Karkov, Kelley M. Wickham-Crowley, and Bailey K. Young. American Early Medieval Studies 3. Oxford: Oxbow, 1999. Pp. 39–60.

Sawyer, P.H. *Anglo-Saxon Charters: An Annotated List and Bibliography*. London: Royal Historical Society, 1968.

Scargill, Christopher M. "A Token of Repentance and Reconciliation: Oswiu and the Murder of King Oswine." *Retribution, Repentance, and Reconciliation*. Ed. Kate Cooper and Jeremy Gregory. Studies in Church History 40. Woodbridge: Boydell, 2004. Pp. 39–46.

Scholz, Bernhard W. "The Canonization of Edward the Confessor." *Speculum* 36.1 (1961): 38–60.

Sharpe, Richard. "The Setting of St Augustine's Translation, 1091." *Canterbury and the Norman Conquest: Churches, Saints, and Scholars, 1066–1109*. Ed. Richard Eales and Richard Sharpe. London: Hambledon, 1995. Pp. 1–13.

Sharpe, Sheila. "The West Saxon Tradition of Dynastic Marriage, With Special Reference to the Family of Edward the Elder." *Edward the Elder: 899–924*. Ed. N.J. Higham and D.H. Hill. London: Routledge, 2001. Pp. 79–88.

Sheerin, Daniel J. "The Dedication of the Old Minster, Winchester, in 980." *Revue Bénédictine* 88 (1978): 261–73.

Sheppard, Alice. *Families of the King: Writing Identity in the Anglo-Saxon Chronicle*. Toronto: University of Toronto Press, 2004.

Smith, Scott Thompson. *Land and Book: Literature and Land Tenure in Anglo-Saxon England*. Toronto: University of Toronto Press, 2012.

Smyth, Alfred P. *King Alfred the Great*. Oxford: Oxford University Press, 1995.

Southern, R.W. "Aspects of the European Tradition of Historical Writing 4: The Sense of the Past." *Transactions of the Royal Historical Society*, 5th series, 23 (1973): 243–63.

Spiegel, Gabrielle M. "The Cult of Saint Denis and Capetian Kingship." *Journal of Medieval History* 1.1 (1975): 43–69.

Stafford, Pauline. "'The Annals of Æthelflæd: Annals, History and Politics in Early Tenth-Century England." *Myth, Rulership, Church and Charters: Essays in Honour of Nicholas Brooks*. Ed. Julia Barrow and Andrew Wareham. Aldershot: Ashgate, 2008. Pp. 101–16.

Stafford, Pauline. "Emma: The Powers of the Queen in the Eleventh Century." *Queens and Queenship in Medieval Europe*. Ed. Anne Duggan. Woodbridge: Boydell and Brewer, 1997. Pp. 3–26.

Stafford, Pauline. "The King's Wife in Wessex 800–1066." *Past and Present* 91 (1981): 3–27.

Stafford, Pauline. "The Laws of Cnut and the History of Anglo-Saxon Royal Promises." *Anglo-Saxon England* 10 (1982): 173–90.

Stafford, Pauline. *Queen Emma and Queen Edith: Queenship and Women's Power in Eleventh-Century England*. Oxford: Blackwell, 1997.

Stafford, Pauline. "Queens and Treasure in the Early Middle Ages." *Treasure in the Medieval West*. Ed. Elizabeth M. Tyler. Woodbridge: York Medieval Press, 2000. Pp. 61–82.

Stafford, Pauline. *Unification and Conquest: A Political and Social History of England in the Tenth and Eleventh Centuries*. London: Edward Arnold, 1989.

Stafford, P.A. "The Reign of Æthelred II: A Study in the Limitations on Royal Policy and Action." *Ethelred the Unready: Papers from the Millenary Conference*. Ed. D. Hill. BAR British Series 59. Oxford: 1978. Pp. 15–46.

Stancliffe, Clare. "Kings Who Opted Out." *Ideal and Reality in Frankish and Anglo-Saxon Society*. Ed. Patrick Wormald. Oxford: Blackwell, 1983. Pp. 154–76.

Stancliffe, Clare. "Where Was Oswald Killed?" *Oswald: Northumbrian King to European Saint*. Ed. Clare Stancliffe and Eric Cambridge. Stamford: Paul Watkins, 1995. Pp. 84–96.

Stenton, Frank. *Anglo-Saxon England*, 3rd ed. Oxford: Oxford University Press, 1971.

Stenton, F.M. "The Road System of Medieval England." *Economic History Review* 7.1 (1936): 1–21.

Stephens, W.R.W. "Brihtwold (*d.* 1045)." Rev. Marios Costambeys. *Oxford Dictionary of National Biography*. Oxford: Oxford University Press, 2004. http://www.oxforddnb.com/index/101003431Q2.

Stevenson, W.H. "An Alleged Son of King Harold Harefoot." *English Historical Review* 28.109 (1913): 112–17.

Stevenson, W.H. "Yorkshire Surveys and Other Eleventh-Century Documents in the York Gospels." *English Historical Review* 27.105 (1912): 1–25.

Stroud, G., and R.L. Kemp. *Cemeteries of the Church and Priory of St Andrew, Fishergate*. The Archaeology of York 12.2. York: Council for British Archaeology, 1993.

Tarlow, Sarah. "The Dread of Something after Death: Violation and Desecration on the Isle of Man in the Tenth Century." *Material Harm: Archaeological Studies of War and Violence*. Ed. John Carman. Glasgow: Cruithne Press, 1997. Pp. 132–42.

Taylor, H.M., and Joan Taylor. *Anglo-Saxon Architecture*, 3 vols. Cambridge: Cambridge University Press, 1965.

Taylor, Pamela. "Foundation and Endowment: St Paul's and the English Kingdoms, 604–1087." *St Paul's: The Cathedral Church of London, 604–2004*. Ed. Derek Keene, Arthur Burns, and Andrew Saint. New Haven, CT: Yale University Press, 2004. Pp. 5–16 and 465–6.

Thacker, Alan. "Chester and Gloucester: Early Ecclesiastical Organization in Two Mercian Burhs." *Northern History* 28 (1982): 199–211.

Thacker, Alan. "The Cult of King Harold at Chester." *The Middle Ages in the North-West*. Ed. Tom Scott and Pat Starkey. Oxford: Leopard's Head Press, 1995. Pp. 155–76.

Thacker, Alan. "The Cult of the Saints and the Liturgy." *St Paul's: The Cathedral Church of London, 604–2004*. Ed. Derek Keene, Arthur Burns, and Andrew Saint. New Haven, CT: Yale University Press, 2004. Pp. 113–20 and 472–3.

Thacker, Alan. "Dynastic Monasteries and Family Cults: Edward the Elder's Sainted Kindred." *Edward the Elder, 899–924*. Ed. N.J. Higham and D.H. Hill. London: Routledge, 2001. Pp. 248–63.

Thacker, Alan. "Kings, Saints, and Monasteries in Pre-Viking Mercia." *Midland History* 10 (1985): 1–25.

Thacker, Alan. "The Making of a Local Saint." *Local Saints and Local Churches in the Early Medieval West*. Ed. Alan Thacker and Richard Sharpe. Oxford: Oxford University Press, 2002. Pp. 45–73.

Thacker, Alan. "*Membra Disjecta*: The Division of the Body and the Diffusion of the Cult." *Oswald: Northumbrian King to European Saint*. Ed. Claire Stancliffe and Eric Cambridge. Stamford: Paul Watkins, 1995. Pp. 97–127.

Thacker, Alan. "*Peculiaris Patronus Noster*: The Saint as Patron of the State in the Early Middle Ages." *The Medieval State: Essays Presented to James Campbell*. Ed. J.R. Maddicott and D.M. Palliser. London: Hambledon, 2000. Pp. 1–24.

Thacker, Alan. "Saint-Making and Relic Collecting by Oswald and His Communities." *St Oswald of Worcester: Life and Influence*. Ed. Nicholas Brooks and Catherine Cubitt. London: Leicester University Press, 1996. Pp. 244–68.

Thompson, Victoria. *Dying and Death in Later Anglo-Saxon England*. Anglo Saxon Studies 4. Woodbridge: Boydell, 2004.

Thormann, Janet. "The *Anglo-Saxon Chronicle* Poems and the Making of the English Nation." *Anglo-Saxonism and the Construction of Social Identity*. Ed.

Allen J. Frantzen and John D. Niles. Gainesville: Florida University Press, 1997. Pp. 60–85.

Toller, T. Northcote, ed. *An Anglo-Saxon Dictionary Based on the Manuscript Collections of the Late Joseph Bosworth*. Oxford: Oxford University Press, 1898.

Townend, Matthew. "*Assandūn* and *Assatún*: The Value of Skaldic Evidence for English Place-Name Studies." *Journal of the English Place-Name Society* 27 (1995): 21–9.

Townend, Matthew. "Contextualizing the *Knútsdrápur*: Skaldic Praise-Poetry at the Court of Cnut." *Anglo-Saxon England* 30 (2002): 145–79.

Townsend, David. "Anglo-Latin Hagiography and the Norman Transition." *Exemplaria* 3.2 (1991): 385–433.

Treharne, Elaine. *Living through Conquest: The Politics of Early English, 1020–1220*. Oxford: Oxford University Press, 2012.

Treharne, E.M. "A Unique Old English Formula for Excommunication from Cambridge, Corpus Christi College 303." *Anglo-Saxon England* 24 (1995): 185–211.

Tyler, Elizabeth M. "'The Eyes of the Beholders Were Dazzled': Treasure and Artifice in *Encomium Emmae Reginae*." *Early Medieval Europe* 8.2 (1999): 247–70.

Van Eickels, Klaus. "Gendered Violence: Castration and Blinding as Punishment for Treason in Normandy and Anglo-Norman England." *Gender and History* 16.3 (2004): 588–602.

Vodola, Elisabeth. *Excommunication in the Middle Ages*. Berkeley: University of California Press, 1986.

Wainwright, F.T. "The Chronology of the 'Mercian Register.'" *English Historical Review* 60.238 (1945): 385–92.

Warner, David A. "Ritual and Memory in the Ottonian Reich: The Ceremony of Adventus." *Speculum* 76.2 (2001): 255–83.

White, William J. *Skeletal Remains from the Cemetery of St Nicholas Shambles, City of London*. London and Middlesex Archaeological Society, Monograph 9. London: 1988.

Whitelock, Dorothy. "Some Anglo-Saxon Bishops of London." Chambers Memorial Lecture: University College, London, 1974. Reprinted in Dorothy Whitelock, *History, Law and Literature in 10th–11th Century England*. London: Variorum, 1981. Pp. 3–35.

Whitelock, Dorothy. "Wulfstan *Cantor* and Anglo-Saxon Law." *Nordica et Anglica. Studies in Honor of Stefan Einarsson*. Ed. A.H. Orrick. The Hague: Mouton, 1968. Reprinted in Dorothy Whitelock, *History, Law and Literature in 10th–11th Century England*. London: Variorum, 1981. Pp. 83–92.

Williams, A. "*Princeps Merciorum Gentis*: The Family, Career and Connections of Ælfhere, Ealdorman of Mercia, 956–83." *Anglo-Saxon England* 10 (1982): 143–72.

Williams, Howard. "Ancient Landscapes and the Dead: The Reuse of Prehistoric and Roman Monuments as Early Anglo-Saxon Burial Sites." *Medieval Archaeology* 41 (1997): 1–32.

Williams, Howard. "Cemeteries as Central Places: Place and Identity in Migration Period Eastern England." *Central Places in the Migration and the Merovingian Periods: Papers from the 52nd Sachsensymposium, Lund, August 2001*. Ed. Birgitta Hårdh and Lars Larsson. Acta Archaeologica Lundensia 8.39. Stockholm: 2002. Pp. 341–62.

Williams, Howard. *Death and Memory in Early Medieval Britain*. Cambridge: Cambridge University Press, 2006.

Williams, Howard. "Death Warmed Up: The Agency of Bodies and Bones in Early Anglo-Saxon Cremation Rites." *Journal of Material Culture* 9.3 (2004): 263–91.

Wilson, S.E. "King Athelstan and St John of Beverly." *Northern History* 40.1 (2003): 5–23.

Wilson, S.E. *The Life and After-Life of St John of Beverly*. Aldershot: Ashgate, 2006.

Wood, M. "The Making of King Aethelstan's Empire: An English Charlemagne?" *Ideal and Reality in Frankish and Anglo-Saxon Society*. Ed. Patrick Wormald. Oxford: Blackwell, 1983. Pp. 250–72.

Wormald, Patrick. "Æthelred the Lawmaker." *Ethelred the Unready: Papers from the Millenary Conference*. Ed. David Hill. BAR British Series 59. Oxford: 1978. Pp. 47–80.

Wormald, Patrick. "Bede, the *Bretwaldas* and the Origins of the *Gens Anglorum*." *Ideal and Reality in Frankish and Anglo-Saxon Society*. Ed. Patrick Wormald. Oxford: Blackwell, 1983. Pp. 99–129.

Wormald, Patrick. "A Handlist of Anglo-Saxon Lawsuits." *Anglo-Saxon England* 17 (1989): 247–81.

Wormald, Patrick. "*Lex Scripta* and *Verbum Regis*: Legislation and Germanic Kingship, from Euric to Cnut." *Early Medieval Kingship*. Ed. P.H. Sawyer and I.N. Wood. Leeds: School of History, 1977. Pp. 105–38.

Wormald, Patrick. *The Making of English Law: King Alfred to the Twelfth Century*, vol. 1: *Legislation and Its Limits*. Oxford: Blackwell, 1999.

Wormald, P. "Charters, Law and the Settlement of Disputes in Anglo-Saxon England." *The Settlement of Disputes in Early Medieval Europe*. Ed. Wendy Davies and Paul Fouracre. Cambridge: Cambridge University Press, 1986. Pp. 149–68.

Wright, Georgia Sommers. "A Royal Tomb Program in the Reign of St. Louis." *Art Bulletin* 56.2 (1974): 224–43.

Yarrow, Simon. *Saints and Their Communities: Miracle Stories in Twelfth-Century England*. Oxford: Clarendon, 2006.

Yorke, Barbara. "The Adaptation of the Anglo-Saxon Royal Courts to Christianity." *The Cross Goes North: Processes of Conversion in Northern Europe, AD 300–1300*. Ed. M.O.H. Carver. Woodbridge: York Medieval Press, 2003. Pp. 243–58.

Yorke, Barbara. "Ælfsige (*d.* 959)." *Oxford Dictionary of National Biography*. Oxford: Oxford University Press, 2004. http://www.oxforddnb.com/index/101000192/Q3.

Yorke, Barbara. "Æthelwold and the Politics of the Tenth Century." *Bishop Æthelwold: His Career and Influence*. Ed. B. Yorke. Woodbridge: Boydell, 1988. Pp. 65–88.

Yorke, Barbara. "Anglo-Saxon Royal Burial: The Documentary Evidence." *Medieval Europe 1992: Pre-Printed Papers*, vol. 4: *Death and Burial*. Ed. T. Dickinson and E. James. York: Conference on Medieval Archaeology in Europe, 1992. Pp. 41–6.

Yorke, Barbara. "Edward as Ætheling." *Edward the Elder: 899–924*. Ed. N.J. Higham and D.H. Hill. London: Routledge, 2001. Pp. 25–39.

Yorke, Barbara. "Edward, King and Martyr: A Saxon Murder Mystery." *Studies in the Early History of Shaftesbury Abbey*. Ed. L. Keen. Dorchester: Dorset City Council, 1999. Pp. 99–116.

Yorke, Barbara. *Nunneries and the Anglo-Saxon Royal Houses*. London: Continuum, 2003.

Yorke, Barbara. *Wessex in the Early Middle Ages*. London: Leicester University Press, 1995.

Yorke, Barbara. "The Women in Edgar's Life." *Edgar, King of the English 959–975*. Ed. Donald Scragg. Woodbridge: Boydell, 2008. Pp. 143–57.

Yorke, Barbara A.E. "The Bishops of Winchester, the Kings of Wessex, and the Development of Winchester in the Ninth and Early Tenth Centuries." *Proceedings of the Hampshire Field Club and Archaeological Society* 40 (1984). Reprinted in *Anglo-Saxon History: Basic Readings*. Ed. David A.E. Pelteret. New York: Garland, 2000. Pp. 107–20.

Yorke, B.A.E. "The Foundation of the Old Minster and the Status of Winchester in the Seventh and Eighth Centuries." *Proceedings of the Hampshire Field Club and Archaeological Society* 38 (1982): 75–83.

Zadora-Rio, Elisabeth. "The Making of Churchyards and Parish Territories in the Early-Medieval Landscape of France and England in the 7th–12th Centuries: A Reconsideration." *Medieval Archaeology* 47 (2003): 1–19.

Index

Toronto Anglo-Saxon Series

1 *Preaching the Converted: The Style and Rhetoric of the Vercelli Book Homilies,* Samantha Zacher

2 *Say What I Am Called: The Old English Riddles of the Exeter Book and the Anglo-Latin Riddle Tradition*, Dieter Bitterli

3 *The Aesthetics of Nostalgia: Historical Representation in Anglo-Saxon Verse*, Renée Trilling

4 *New Readings in the Vercelli Book*, edited by Samantha Zacher and Andy Orchard

5 *Authors, Audiences, and Old English Verse*, Thomas A. Bredehoft

6 *On Aesthetics in* Beowulf *and Other Old English Poems*, edited by John M. Hill

7 *Old English Metre: An Introduction*, Jun Terasawa

8 *Anglo-Saxon Psychologies in the Vernacular and Latin Traditions*, Leslie Lockett

9 *The Body Legal in Barbarian Law*, Lisi Oliver

10 *Old English Literature and the Old Testament*, edited by Michael Fox and Manish Sharma

11 *Stealing Obedience: Narratives of Agency and Identity in Later Anglo-Saxon England*, Katherine O'Brien O'Keeffe

12 *Traditional Subjectivities: The Old English Poetics of Mentality*, Britt Mize

13 *Land and Book: Literature and Land Tenure in Anglo-Saxon England,* Scott T. Smith

14 *Writing Women Saints in Anglo-Saxon England*, edited by Paul E. Szarmach

15 *Anglo-Saxon Manuscripts: A Bibliographical Handlist of Manuscripts Written or Owned in England up to 1100*, Helmut Gneuss and Michael Lapidge

16 *The King's Body: Burial and Succession in Late Anglo-Saxon England*, Nicole Marafioti